ChronoForms 1.3 for Joomla! Site Cookbook

80 recipes for building attractive and interactive Joomla! forms

Bob Janes

BIRMINGHAM - MUMBAI

Chronofroms 1.3 for Joomla! Site Cookbook

Copyright © 2010 Packt Publishing

All rights reserved. No part of this book may be reproduced, stored in a retrieval system, or transmitted in any form or by any means, without the prior written permission of the publisher, except in the case of brief quotations embedded in critical articles or reviews.

Every effort has been made in the preparation of this book to ensure the accuracy of the information presented. However, the information contained in this book is sold without warranty, either express or implied. Neither the author, nor Packt Publishing, and its dealers and distributors will be held liable for any damages caused or alleged to be caused directly or indirectly by this book.

Packt Publishing has endeavored to provide trademark information about all of the companies and products mentioned in this book by the appropriate use of capitals. However, Packt Publishing cannot guarantee the accuracy of this information.

First published: August 2010

Production Reference: 1130810

Published by Packt Publishing Ltd.
32 Lincoln Road
Olton
Birmingham, B27 6PA, UK.

ISBN 978-1-849510-62-2

www.packtpub.com

Cover Image by Vinayak Chittar (vinayak.chittar@gmail.com)

Credits

Author
Bob Janes

Reviewers
Laurelle Keashley
Norm Douglas

Acquisition Editor
Usha Iyer

Development Editor
Mehul Shetty

Technical Editors
Tariq Rakhange
Krutika V. Katelia

Indexer
Rekha Nair

Editorial Team Leader
Mithun Sehgal

Project Team Leader
Priya Mukherji

Project Coordinator
Zainab Bagasrawala

Proofreader
Aaron Nash

Graphics
Geetanjali Sawant

Production Coordinator
Arvindkumar Gupta

Cover Work
Arvindkumar Gupta

About the Author

Bob Janes started programming with punched cards a long time ago. As the Finance Director of a multi-national business, he kept his finger in the IT pie, much to the chagrin of those in corporate IT, and delivered innovative and successful systems projects ranging from foreign exchange to manufacturing.

More recently, he has been able to return to hands-on coding and learned the basics of CMS coding with E-Xoops before turning his hand to Joomla! and WordPress. Bob enjoys learning through answering questions and has made more than 14,000 posts in the ChronoForms forums over the last few years.

Bob divides his time between Brittany and London, and divides his work between coding and coaching—he has Bachelor's degrees in both Mathematics and Psychology and a Master's degree in Organisational Consulting.

> I'd like to thank Max who developed ChronoForms, and all the ChronoForms users whose questions made this book possible; my wife, Jane, who puts up with my hours in front of my keyboard; and my father who set me off on this path many years ago.

About the Reviewer

Laurelle Keashly graduated with a B.Sc in Computer Science from the University of Calgary. After graduating, Laurelle moved to the Vancouver, BC metropolitan area where she has done software programming, user interface design, and development team management for embedded communication and PC based accounting systems. Taking some time off to raise a family in the Burnaby, BC area, Laurelle got into website design, development, and support with local non-profit organizations. As her family has grown, her interest in web technologies grew to where she started Keashly.ca Consulting which provides the full spectrum of website development, support, and services with a specialty in Joomla! CMS-based sites. Laurelle is a moderator and an active member of the Joomla! forum and has created and released several Joomla! extensions. Laurelle continues to explore and provide up-to-date web-based services by actively keeping herself aware and supporting other CMS systems besides Joomla! such as Wordpress and Drupal.

Norm Douglas loves technology. He has always built websites from as early as 1997. While researching and trying to develop his own rudimentary CMS from PHP, Norm stumbled upon Mambo, the precursor of Joomla!.

Seeing the benefits not only to him as a developer but also to his clients, Norm immediately set about learning everything he could about PHP, MYSQL, CSS, CMS, and ultimately, Joomla!.

Norm's broad range of IT experience and skills come together to make him an excellent all-round tutor. Not happy with just "showing" you how to do "x" and "y", Norm will explain concepts to you. His goal is to help as many people as he can become better developers, webmasters, content managers, or just contributors as he is, so that the open source community may grow larger.

He also runs "TeachingJoomla.com", a subscription-based site for Joomla enthusiasts and those that manage their own site. Norm is also behind RedsourceMedia.com and is the lead developer at KeyVision.com.au.

Table of Contents

Preface	**1**
Chapter 1: Creating a Simple Form	**7**
Introduction	7
Downloading and installing ChronoForms	7
Creating a simple form with the Form Wizard	12
Sending the form results by e-mail	18
Showing a "Thank You" page	26
Editing your form with the Wizard Edit	29
Redirecting the user to another page	32
Backing up and restoring your forms	34
Chapter 2: E-mailing Form Results	**37**
Introduction	37
Replying to e-mails	38
Getting your e-mails delivered safely	41
Sending a "Thank you" e-mail to the form submitter	44
Choosing e-mail addresses from a list	47
Attaching uploaded files to the e-mail	57
Attaching a "standard" file to the e-mail	58
Creating a "dynamic" subject line using info	60
from the form	60
Chapter 3: Styling your Form	**63**
Introduction	63
Using ChronoForms default style	63
Switching styles with "Transform Form"	67
Adding your own CSS styling	68

Table of Contents

Putting several inputs in one line	75
Adding your own HTML	76

Chapter 4: Saving Form Data in the Database — 79

Introduction	79
Creating a table to save your results and linking your form to it	80
Viewing your saved form results	90
Updating and changing DB Connections	93
Exporting your results to Excel or a CSV file	97

Chapter 5: Form Validation and Security — 99

Introduction	99
Making "required" fields	100
Specifying the types of input that are allowed—text, numbers, dates, and so on	103
Customizing validation error messages	107
Adding extra security with "server-side" validation of submitted information	108
Getting the user to confirm their data before submission	117
Adding an ImageVerification captcha / anti-spam check	121
Adding a reCAPTCHA anti-spam check	126
Limiting form access to registered users	129

Chapter 6: Showing your Form in your Site — 133

Introduction	133
Including your form in an article using the ChronoForms plugin	134
Showing your form on selected pages using the ChronoForms module	138
Linking to your form from Joomla! menus	144
Using a form to create a Joomla! article	147
Redirecting users to other Joomla! pages after submission	151

Chapter 7: Adding Features to your Form — 155

Introduction	155
Adding a validated checkbox	156
Adding an "other" box to a drop-down	160
Sending an SMS message on submission	165
Signing up to a newsletter service	169
Adding a conversion tracking script	173
Showing a YouTube video	175
Adding a barcode to a form e-mail	178
Adding a character counter to a textarea	184
Creating a double drop-down	187

Chapter 8: Uploading Files from your Forms — 193
- Introduction — 193
- Adding a file upload field to your form and setting the allowed types and sizes — 194
- Saving files to different folders — 199
- Renaming files — 202
- Linking files to e-mails — 205
- Resizing and copying image files — 208
- Displaying images in e-mails and articles — 212
- Troubleshooting problems with files — 215

Chapter 9: Writing Form HTML — 221
- Introduction — 221
- Moving an existing form to ChronoForms — 222
- Moving a form with JavaScript — 225
- Moving a form with CSS — 231
- Creating a form with Wufoo — 235
- Creating a form in Dreamweaver — 248

Chapter 10: Creating Common Forms — 251
- Introduction — 251
- Creating a simple newsletter signup — 252
- Creating a form to link to Acajoom — 257
- Creating a form to publish a Joomla! article — 264
- Creating a "Contact us" form — 265
- Creating an image or document upload form — 272
- Creating a multi-page form — 275

Chapter 11: Using Form Plug-ins — 281
- Introduction — 281
- Controlling form access by user group, day, and/or time with the Watchman plug-in — 283
- Creating multi-lingual forms with the Multi-Language plug-in — 287
- Showing and editing saved information with the Profile plug-in — 297
- Registering users with the Joomla! Registration plug-in — 302
- Creating a PayPal purchase form with the ReDirect plug-in — 312

Chapter 12: Adding Advanced Features — 319
- Introduction — 319
- Using PHP to create "select" dropdowns — 319
- Using Ajax to look up e-mail addresses — 325
- Getting information from a DB table to include in your form — 330

Table of Contents

Show a form in a light-box	**334**
Tracking site information	**338**
Controlling e-mails from form inputs	**340**
Building a complex multi-page form	**342**
Troubleshooting problems with forms	**350**
Index	**355**

Preface

Joomla! is a fantastic way to create a dynamic CMS. Now, you want to go to the next step and interact with your users. Forms are the way you ask questions and get replies. ChronoForms is the extension that lets you do that and this book tells you how.

From building your first form to creating rich, form-based applications, we will cover the features that ChronoForms offers you in a clear hands-on way. Drawing on three years' daily experience of using ChronoForms and supporting users, there is valuable help for new users and experienced developers alike.

We will take you through form development step-by-step from creating your first form using ChronoForms' built-in drag-and-drop tool, validating user input, emailing the results, saving data in the database, showing the form in your Joomla! site, and much more. Each chapter addresses a topic like "validation" or "e-mail" and each of the recipes in the chapters address the questions of different users from the beginner's question such as "How do I set up an email?" to more advanced questions like using some PHP to create a custom e-mail Subject line. Over 12 chapters and 80 recipes we cover all of the "Frequently Asked Questions" that new users and developers have about using ChronoForms. The recipe structure allows you to pick and choose just the solution that you need.

This practical book, packed with easy-to-flow recipes, tips, and tricks, will help you add interactive forms to your sites with the ChronoForms.

What this book covers

Chapter 1, Creating a Simple Form: This chapter will teach you how to download and install ChronoForms, create your first form with the drag-and-drop Form Wizard, send the form results by e-mail, customize the e-mail, show a "thank-you" page to the user, edit your form with the Wizard Edit, re-direct the user after they submit the form, back up, and restore your forms.

Chapter 2, E-mailing Form Results: This chapter covers sending form result to an administrator, getting your e-mails delivered safely, sending a message to the form user, sending emails to different people depending on the form results, attaching uploaded files to an email, sending a file to the user, and creating an e-mail subject line from the form results.

Preface

Chapter 3, Styling your Form: The topics covered use the ChronoForms built-in styles, switching to another form template, adding your own CSS, using the Wizard Edit to put several form inputs in one line, and changing the layout by adding your own HTML.

Chapter 4, Saving Form Data in the Database: The topics covered are creating a database table and linking your form to it, updating and changing database connections, viewing the saved data, and exporting data to Excel or CSV.

Chapter 5, Form Validation and Security: This chapter covers making form fields required with ChronoForms built-in validation, specifying the type of input required, customizing validation messages, adding extra "server-side" validation, getting the user to confirm their results, adding a ChronoForms "captcha" check to your form, using a "ReCaptcha" check instead, and limiting form access to registered users.

Chapter 6, Showing your Form in your Site: This covers showing your form in an article, or on selected pages in a module, linking to your form from a menu, using a form to create an article, and redirecting users to other Joomla! pages.

Chapter 7, Adding Features to your Form: Here we take a look at some ways to use ChronoForms, such as adding a "terms and conditions" checkbox, linking an "other" box to a select drop-down, sending an SMS message when the form is submitted, signing up to an off-site newsletter service, adding a Google conversion tracking script, showing a YouTube video, adding a barcode to an e-mail, adding a character counter to a textarea input, and creating a "double drop-down" where the second changes depending on the first.

Chapter 8, Uploading Files from your Forms: This chapter covers setting up file uploads, choosing where to save files, changing file names, linking flies to emails, resizing and copying uploaded image files, showing uploaded images in articles and emails, and troubleshooting file uploads.

Chapter 9, Writing Form HTML: Moving existing forms to ChronoForms; moving a form that uses JavaScript; and CSS; creating forms in Dreamweaver.

Chapter 10, Creating Common Forms: In this chapter, we create forms for newsletter sign-ups, "Contact Us", link to a Joomla! component like Acajoom, publish an article, image or document upload, and a multi-page form.

Chapter 11, Using Form Plug-ins: This chapter covers using ChronoForms "plugins" for extra performance: manage for access by user group or date and time, create multi-lingual forms, show and edit a saved record, register Joomla! users, and create a PayPal payment form.

Chapter 12, Adding Advanced Features: This chapter covers using AJAX with a form, using PHP to create select drop-downs, getting information from the database to use in your form, showing a form in a light box, tracking the page that the form was submitted from, controlling e-mails from form data, building a complex multi-page form, and hints and tips for troubleshooting your forms.

What you need for this book

You will need administrator access to a Joomla! 1.5 installation. In order to run Joomla! 1.5, the minimum requirement is to use a server running PHP 4.3.10, MySQL 3.23, and Apache 1.3 IIS 6.

Some parts of ChronoForms use functionality only available in PHP 5 and we recommend that you use the Joomla! -recommended specifications which are currently: PHP 5.2 or higher; MySQL 4.1 or higher, and Apache 2 or IIS 7.

You will also need to download the the latest release of the ChronoForms extension for Joomla!. Instructions for this are provided in Chapter 1.

Note: ChronoForms makes extensive use of the MooTools JavaScript library. Mootools version 1.1.2 is installed with Joomla!. The latest Joomla! Rrelease includes an option to enable MooTools 1.2.4 -— ChronoForms 1.3 will not run correctly if this option is enabled,.

Who this book is for

This is a practical hands-on book for people who want to add forms to their Joomla! site. Whether you just want to add a simple newsletter sign-up form or a complex multi-page interactive form, you'll find helpful suggestions and recipes that will get your forms working.

Many recipes will work out of the box using ChronoForms built-in capabilities. Other more advanced recipes require some knowledge of Joomla!, HTML, CSS, PHP, MySQL, or JavaScript. There is a working code with each recipe that you can adapt to, to meet your specific needs.

Conventions

In this book, you will find a number of styles of text that distinguish between different kinds of information. Here are some examples of these styles, and an explanation of their meaning.

Code words in text are shown as follows: "Message 5 in Section 3 is the $_POST array."

A block of code is set as follows:

```
<?php
$form_id = $MyForm->formrow->id;
$MyUploads =& CFUploads::getInstance($form_id);
$MyUploads->attachments[] = 'images/newsletter.pdf';
?>
```

Preface

When we wish to draw your attention to a particular part of a code block, the relevant lines or items are set in bold:

```
<?php
if ( !$mainframe->isSite() ) {return;}
function createRangeSelect($label, $name, $start, $end) {
?>
<div class="form_item">
```

New terms and important words are shown in bold. Words that you see on the screen, in menus or dialog boxes for example, appear in the text like this: "Save the form and go to the **Admin | Extensions | Module Manager**."

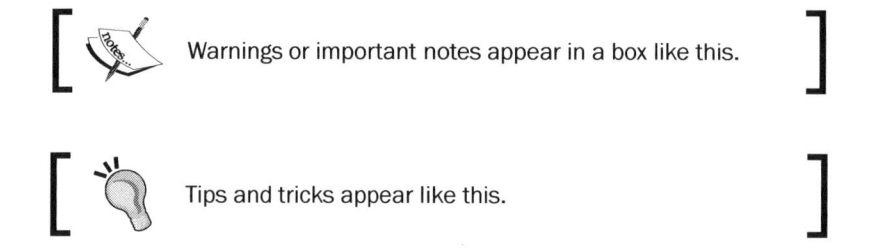

[Warnings or important notes appear in a box like this.]

[Tips and tricks appear like this.]

Reader feedback

Feedback from our readers is always welcome. Let us know what you think about this book—what you liked or may have disliked. Reader feedback is important for us to develop titles that you really get the most out of.

To send us general feedback, simply send an e-mail to `feedback@packtpub.com`, and mention the book title via the subject of your message.

If there is a book that you need and would like to see us publish, please send us a note in the **SUGGEST A TITLE** form on `www.packtpub.com` or e-mail `suggest@packtpub.com`.

If there is a topic that you have expertise in and you are interested in either writing or contributing to a book, see our author guide on `www.packtpub.com/authors`.

Customer support

Now that you are the proud owner of a Packt book, we have a number of things to help you to get the most from your purchase.

>
> **Downloading the example code for this book**
> You can download the example code files for all Packt books you have purchased from your account at `http://www.PacktPub.com`. If you purchased this book elsewhere, you can visit `http://www.PacktPub.com/support` and register to have the files e-mailed directly to you.

Errata

Although we have taken every care to ensure the accuracy of our content, mistakes do happen. If you find a mistake in one of our books—maybe a mistake in the text or the code—we would be grateful if you would report this to us. By doing so, you can save other readers from frustration and help us improve subsequent versions of this book. If you find any errata, please report them by visiting `http://www.packtpub.com/support`, selecting your book, clicking on the **errata submission form** link, and entering the details of your errata. Once your errata are verified, your submission will be accepted and the errata will be uploaded on our website, or added to any list of existing errata, under the Errata section of that title. Any existing errata can be viewed by selecting your title from `http://www.packtpub.com/support`.

Piracy

Piracy of copyright material on the Internet is an ongoing problem across all media. At Packt, we take the protection of our copyright and licenses very seriously. If you come across any illegal copies of our works, in any form, on the Internet, please provide us with the location address or website name immediately so that we can pursue a remedy.

Please contact us at `copyright@packtpub.com` with a link to the suspected pirated material.

We appreciate your help in protecting our authors, and our ability to bring you valuable content.

Questions

You can contact us at `questions@packtpub.com` if you are having a problem with any aspect of the book, and we will do our best to address it.

1
Creating a Simple Form

In this chapter, we will cover:

- ▶ Downloading and installing ChronoForms
- ▶ Creating a simple form with the Form Wizard
- ▶ Sending the form results by e-mail
- ▶ Formatting your e-mail
- ▶ Showing a "Thank You" page
- ▶ Editing your form with the Wizard Edit
- ▶ Redirecting the user to another page
- ▶ Backing up and restoring your forms

Introduction

Let's say that we want to add a very simple form to our Joomla! site. Probably the simplest is a newsletter sign-up. We will just collect the user's e-mail address and send the result to the site administrator. Later, in the book we'll be able to extend this form to do much more, but this simple version is a great place to start.

Downloading and installing ChronoForms

ChronoForms is a Joomla! extension that has been developed by Max (also known as ChronoMan) to allow you to add forms to a Joomla! site. Getting the extension and installing it is the first step.

Creating a Simple Form

Getting ready

You'll need a working Joomla! installation. We recommend that you use the latest version of Joomla! and keep your installation up to date with security releases. At the time of writing, the latest release is Joomla! 1.5.20.

 If you have an old Joomla! 1.0.x site, then there is an old version of ChronoForms that you can use; it has much less functionality than the current version described here. Both Joomla! .1.0.x and that old version of ChronoForms are deprecated, and little or no support is available. We strongly recommend that you upgrade to Joomla! 1.5.

How to do it...

1. Go to the **ChronoEngine** website (http://chronoengine.com/) and click the **Downloads** link. Follow the folder tree **ChronoForms | ChronoForms J1.5 Files | Component** and download the current release. Right now this is `ChronoForms_V3.1_RC5.5.zip`.

    Although this is an RC (Release Candidate) version, it is the latest and most stable ChronoForms release.

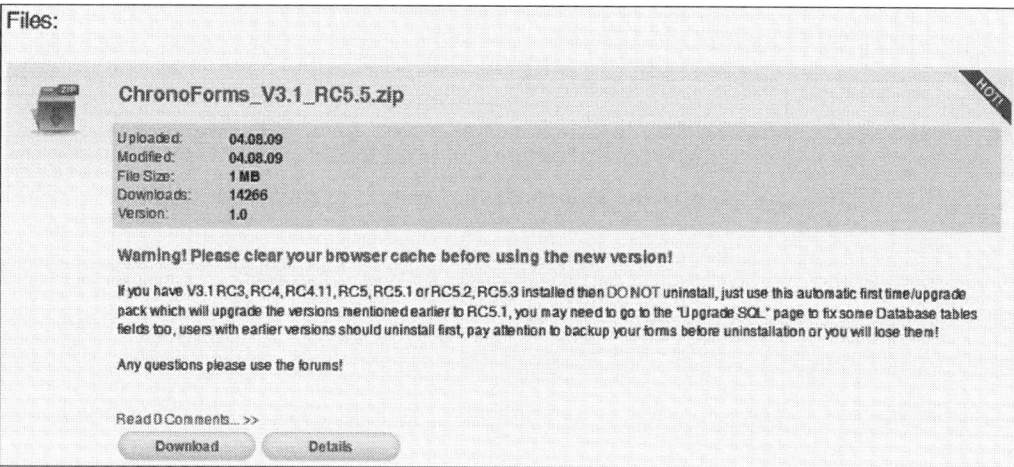

2. Download the file to your computer. Now open your browser and go to the administrator page for your Joomla! site, for example `http://www.example.com/administrator`, and log in.

Chapter 1

> **Caution**: Before installing any new extension it is sensible to back up your site and the site database. You should also check the Joomla! **Vulnerable Extensions List** at `http://docs.joomla.org/Vulnerable_Extensions_List` to make sure that there are no adverse reports about the extension.

3. Once the Administration page is open go to **Extensions | Install/Uninstall** and open the Joomla! **Extension Manager**.
4. Click the **Browse...** button and navigate to the downloaded ChronoForms ZIP file.
5. Click **Upload File & Install** and the installation process will begin. ChronoForms is quite a large extension and it may take a little while to upload.

> The standard Joomla! installation process usually works perfectly with ChronoForms. ChronoForms has been designed to work with this process, however occasionally it doesn't work as expected. If this happens then usually it is for one of these reasons:
>
> 1. The server settings are too restrictive and the installation "times out". Increasing the PHP `memory_limit` or `max_execution_time` settings may resolve this.
> 2. There are some permission restrictions on the site; speak to your ISP about these.
> 3. A previous installation attempt has left some files in place—you need to remove both the `administrator/components/com_chronocontact` and `components/com_chronocontact` folders and all the files in them.

> Often a "manual installation" will get you past these; see the **Joomla! Documentation** site at `http://docs.Joomla!.org/How_do_you_install_an_extension%3F` or a simple video here: `http://www.solarenergyhost.com/content/view/182/205/`.

[9]

Creating a Simple Form

6. Once the installation completes you will see the following screen:

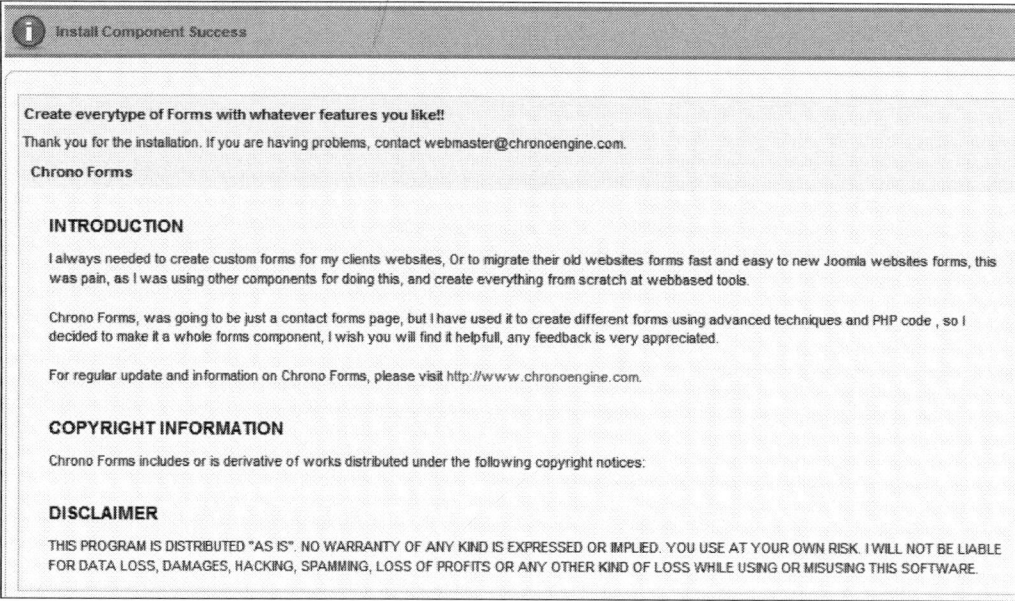

7. Congratulations, ChronoForms is successfully installed.

> You can install the **ChronoForms Plugin/Mambot** (used to show forms in Joomla! articles), and/or the **ChronoForms Module** (used to show forms in Joomla! template modules) at the same time, if you know you are going to need them. The process is exactly the same. We will meet these add-ons again in *Chapter 6, Showing your Form in your Site*.

8. While we are in the **Extension Manager** window, click on the **Components** link and look for the **Chrono Contact** entry. It tells you that this version—**3.1 RC5.5**—was created on **04 Aug 2009** by **Chronoman** (also known as Max). This version information is important when you want to upgrade ChronoForms in the future.

#	Component	Enabled	Version	Date	Author	Compatibility
1	Banners	✓	1.5.0	April 2006	Joomla! Project	✓
2	Chrono Contact	✓	3.1 RC5.5	04 Aug 2009	Chronoman	✓
3	Newsfeeds	✓	1.5.0	April 2006	Joomla! Project	✓
4	Polls	✓	1.5.0	July 2004	Joomla! Project	✓
5	Weblinks	✓	1.5.0	April 2006	Joomla! Project	✓
6	Content Page		1.5.0	April 2006	Joomla! Project	✓

9. Before we finish, click the **Components | ChronoForms | Forms Management** menu to go to the **Forms Manager**.

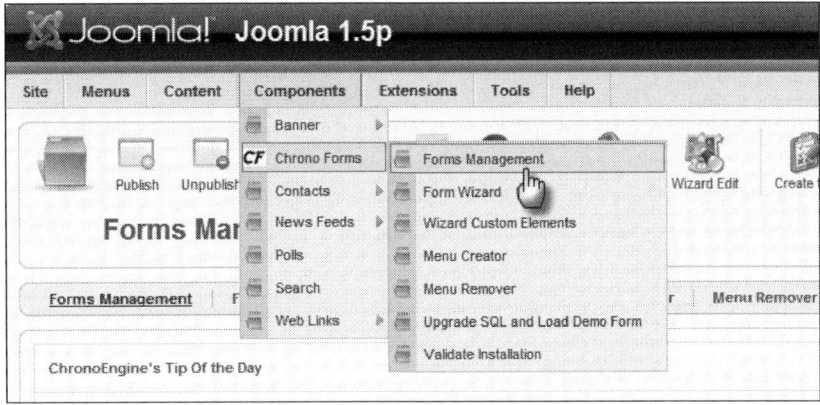

10. The **Forms Manager** is the "Control Panel" for ChronoForms and we'll be working with it more in other recipes later on.

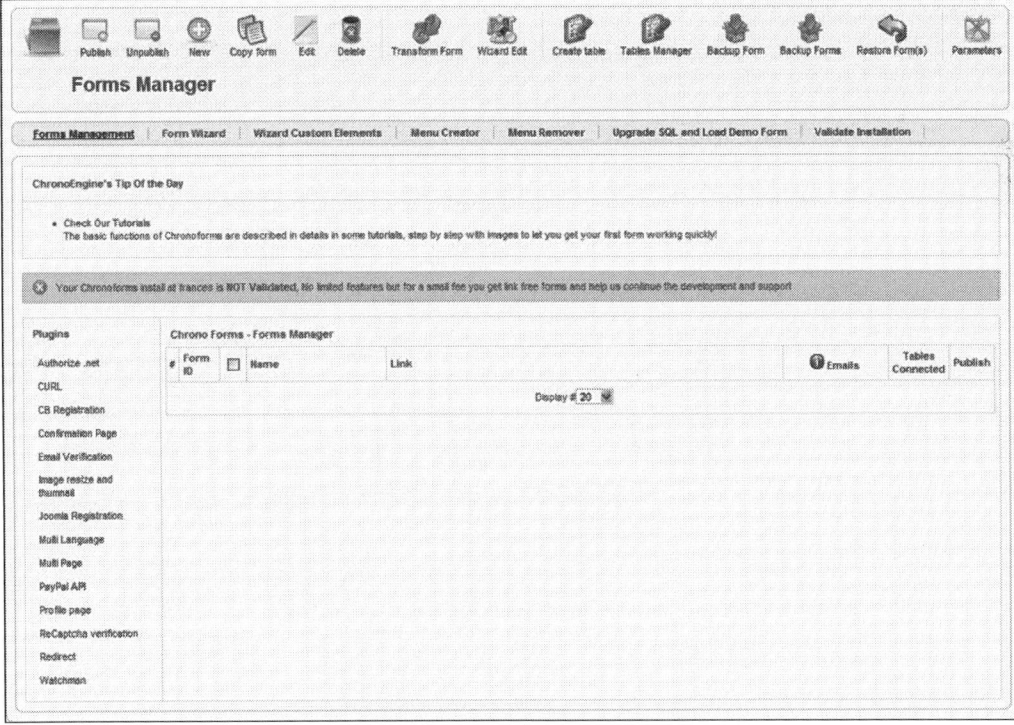

Creating a Simple Form

[The Forms Manager has a "Tip of the Day" feature. If you feel this gets in the way, you can turn it off by clicking the **Parameters** icon at the top right.

The pink validation bar can't be turned off, but it will turn green if you pay a small subscription to validate your copy of ChronoForms. The only difference between the validated and invalidated versions is this bar and a strap line, **Powered By ChronoForms - ChronoEngine.com**, which appears under all forms in the invalidated version. All the other features are identical.]

There's more...

Max is constantly reviewing ChronoForms, and a few times a year there is a new release. If your forms are working as you want them, there is no need to upgrade unless there is a security release. If there are new features that you want to use, you can upgrade by downloading the new release installation file and installing it as explained earlier in this recipe. You can install an upgrade over the existing version without uninstalling it.

To be safe, you should back up your database tables and all of your forms before you upgrade.

See also

- See the *Backing up and restoring your forms section*, later in this chapter for more information on how to do this.

Creating a simple form with the Form Wizard

ChronoForms is all about creating forms so this is where all the proper action starts.

Forms in Joomla! can do many things, from the very simple example that we will create here, to complex multi-page forms that change depending on the entries that are made, do calculations, send e-mails, and update databases. However, the basic building blocks are just the same.

In this recipe, we're going to create just about the simplest form possible. It's a newsletter signup with just one field for an e-mail address and a submit button:

12

Chapter 1

Getting ready

All you need is a Joomla! site with ChronoForms installed.

How to do it...

1. Go to the ChronoForms **Forms Manager** and click on **Form Wizard**, or choose **Components | ChronoForms | Form Wizard** from the Administrator Menus.

   The **Form Wizard** tab opens up looking like this:

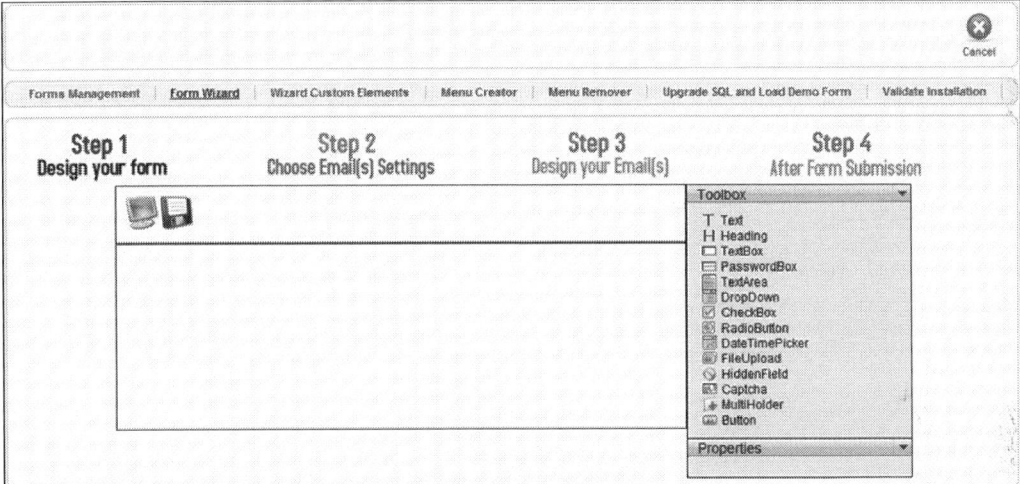

2. There are four steps that the Wizard can help with, though we're only going to use **Step 1 Design your form** here. There's an empty work area with **Preview** and **Save** icons to the top left and a **Toolbox** to the right with a **Properties box** below it that is currently empty. To the top right of the image is a **Cancel** button in case you change your mind.

 You can also click the other blue links above the "Steps"—**Forms Management**, **Wizard Custom Elements**, and so on—but if you do so without saving first, you will lose your work.

Creating a Simple Form

3. For our form we want a textbox for the e-mail address. Use your mouse to drag the **Textbox** entry from the **Toolbox** into the empty workspace.

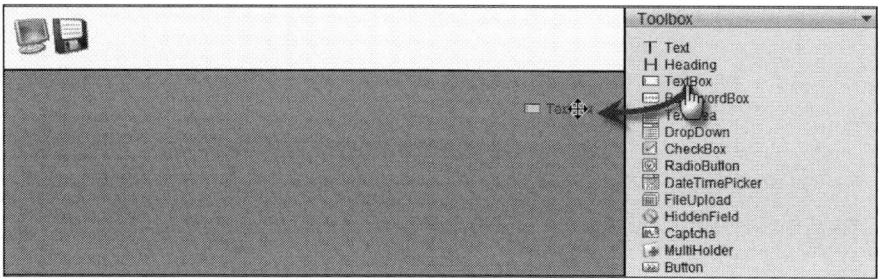

4. Once you drop the textbox into the workspace, you can see a new form element. When that is clicked, the **Properties** box for the form element opens up under the **Toolbox**.

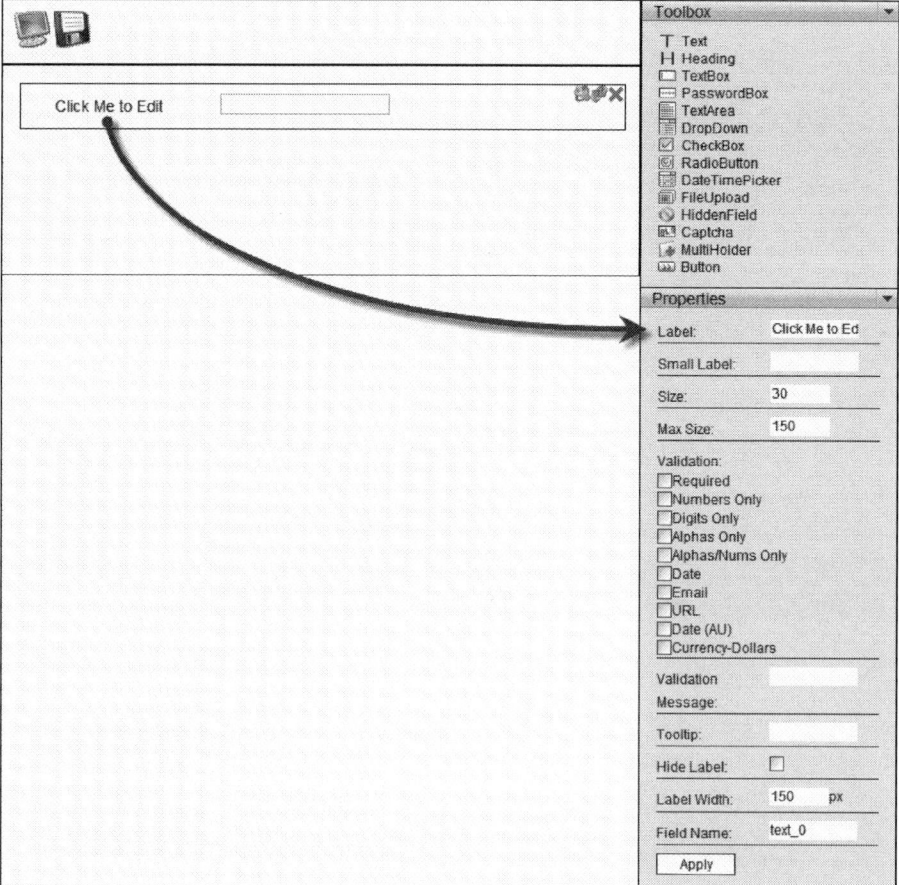

Chapter 1

This isn't the world's easiest screen layout but it will be fine once you get used to it.

5. There are a whole row of properties that you can set, but we're only going to change one right now. Click the form element so that the **Properties** box is open, then go to the input marked **Label** and delete the **Click Me to Edit** text; instead type `Email`. Then click **Apply** at the bottom of the **Properties** box.

   Although you can type into the input box in the workspace at the left, that has no effect. So, just leave it empty. You should only make changes in the **Property** box.

   Clicking **Apply** here records the properties. If you make a change then click on another element, or save the form without clicking **Apply** first, your changes will be lost. Note that **Apply** here does not save your form.

6. When you've relabeled the element, drag a **Button** into the workspace.

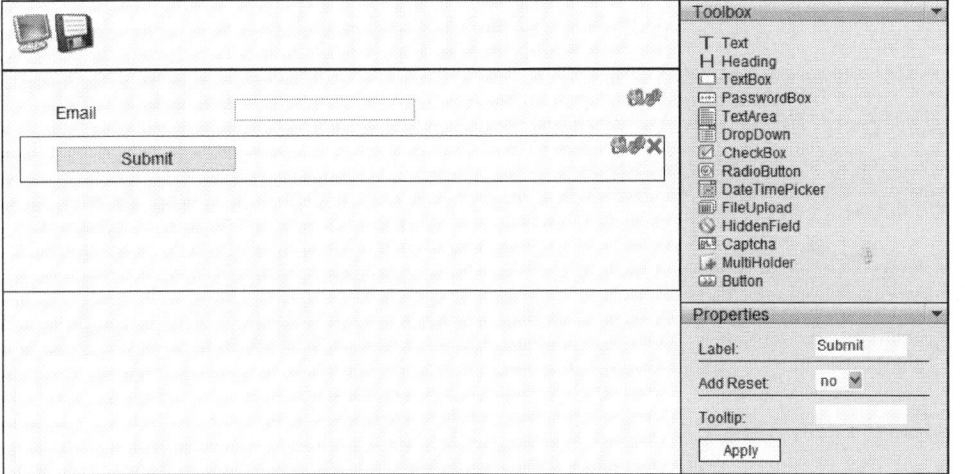

The button is automatically labelled as a **Submit** button. You can change this in the (much smaller) **Properties** box, but we'll leave it just as it is for now.

15

Creating a Simple Form

7. Now click the "blue screen" icon at the top left of the workspace to see a preview of our form.

   The preview opens in a "modal" window over the working area. While this is open you will not be able to access the administrator menus or tools. The preview is shown in the following screenshot:

   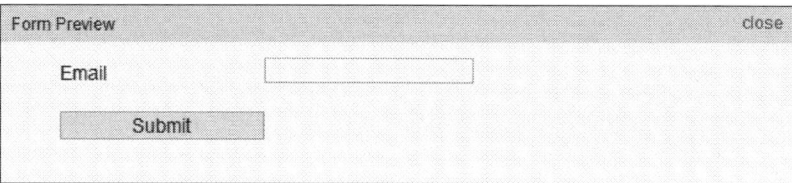

8. Perfect, now we just need to save it. Close the **Form Preview** window from the **close** link at the top right-hand corner, and then click the "floppy disk" icon to save the form.

   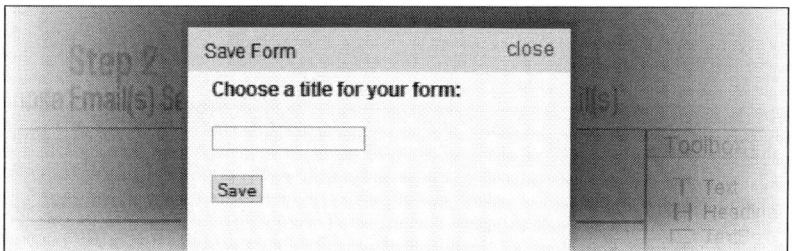

9. Type a name in the box. Let's use "newsletter_signup" and click **Save**.

Warning: The text box here will accept almost anything but some choices of name will cause problems later. The rule to follow is: Only use a-z 0-9 and underscore (no capital letters, no spaces, no dashes, or any other special or accented characters). We'll see these same rules applied later to names and IDs, and it's useful to be consistent here.

10. When you click **Save**, you'll be taken back to the **Forms Manager**, where there should now be a form in the list.

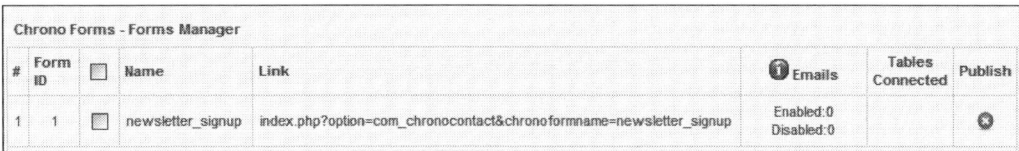

Reading across the form row, the entries are :

- **#** (form number): This is just the place in the list and may change
- **Form ID**: The unique ID of the form
- **Checkbox:** A check box is used for selecting the form when we want to work with some ChronoForms features
- **Name**: This is a link, if you click it the Form will open for editing
- **Link**: We'll come back to this in a minute
- **Emails** and **Tables Connected**: We'll save this for later
- **Publish**: The red icon shows the form is not available in the site front end and an error message will be displayed if the link is clicked

11. Click the publish icon now to make this form available and, after a moment, the icon should change to a green tick to show that the form is now published.

> You can also use the **Publish** and **Unpublish** icons in the Toolbar, which is useful if you want to change more than one form at a time.

12. Go back to the **Link** column and click on the form link there. This will open the form in a new browser window or tab showing the form as it will appear on your website.

13. And there we have it, our first fully-functioning ChronoForms form.

You can submit it, but nothing will happen yet. We have to set up a little more code to tell ChronoForms what to do when the submit button is pressed.

17

Creating a Simple Form

How it works...

There's been quite a lot going on behind the scenes here. The ChronoForms Form Wizard builds a set of Form HTML for your form. It also applies some CSS styling and sets up the framework for a lot more features and functionality that we will come to shortly.

Here's the Form HTML that's been generated for this form, copied from inside the **Form Editor**, as we'll see later:

```
<div class="form_item">
  <div class="form_element cf_textbox">
    <label class="cf_label" style="width: 150px;">
      Email</label>
    <input class="cf_inputbox" maxlength="150" size="30"
      title="" id="text_0" name="text_0" type="text" />
  </div>
  <div class="cfclear"> </div>
</div>

<div class="form_item">
  <div class="form_element cf_button">
    <input value="Submit" name="button_1" type="submit" />
  </div>
  <div class="cfclear"> </div>
</div>
```

Sending the form results by e-mail

We have a newsletter sign up form that works, but doesn't do anything. The simplest action to take when the form is submitted is to send an e-mail to the site administrator to say that a new form submission has been made.

Getting ready

You need the simple form that we created in the previous recipe, and to navigate to the ChronoForms **Forms Manager** view in the Site Administration area.

To actually send an e-mail successfully, your site must have access to a working mail server configured in **Site | Global Configuration | Server | Mail Settings** (see the Joomla! documentation at `http://docs.Joomla.org/Screen.config.15#Mail_Settings`).

How to do it...

1. We're going to use the **Wizard Edit** to add more to the existing form. Click the check box next to **newsletter_signup** in the **Forms Manager**, then click the **Wizard Edit** icon in the toolbar above:

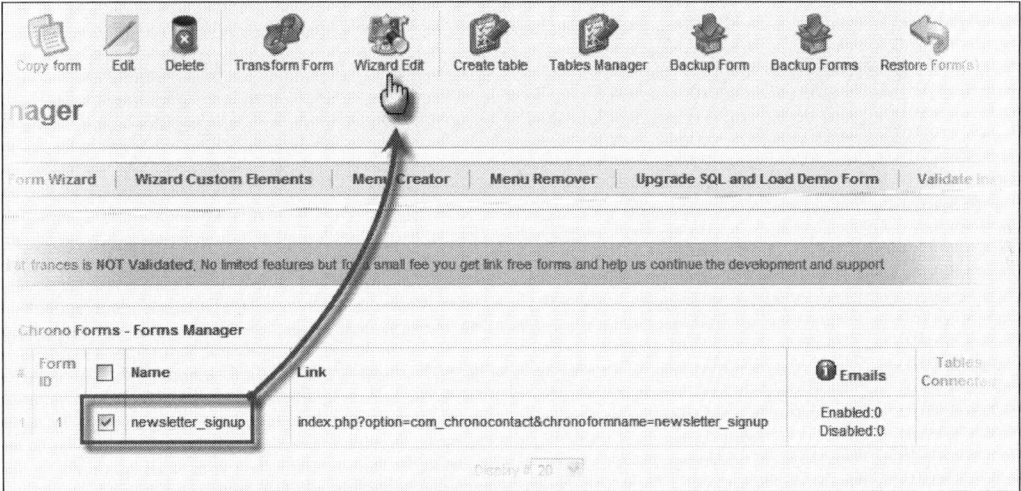

2. When you open your form with **Wizard Edit** there's a warning message that says, **Please note that any changes you made to the form HTML code in the Form edit page will be lost once you save new changes in the wizard!** We've made no changes to the Form HTML so we can click the **x** at the top right to close the warning window.

> ChronoForms saves the "source" code for the Wizard completely separately from the Form HTML that you will see in the **Form Editor**. And it isn't clever enough to re-interpret all the possible manual changes that could be made. One way to work is to use Wizard and Wizard edit to rough out a form, then add the finer details by manually editing the Form HTML, but then we can't use the Wizard on that form again.

Creating a Simple Form

3. Once the Wizard is open, click **Step2 Choose Email(s) Settings** and you will see a similar workspace, though with different entries in the **Toolbox**. There is also an "envelope" icon instead of the screen and an extra "garbage can" icon to delete an unwanted e-mail setup.

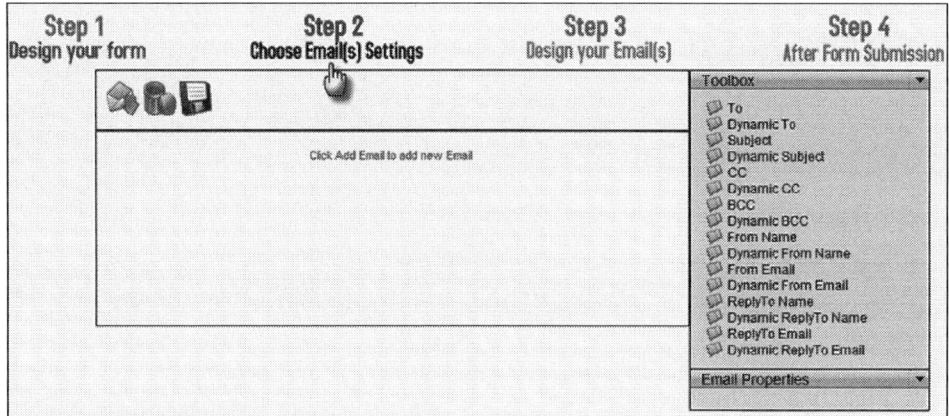

Notice that the **Toolbox** entries all relate to e-mail headers—**To**, **From Name**, **Subject**, **Reply to**, and so on. But at the moment we can't drag them into the workspace.

4. First, click the envelope icon to create a new e-mail setup. An **Email Setup** is a set of instructions to tell ChronoForms to send an e-mail using this particular set of headers.

 You can have more than one e-mail set up in this space by clicking the envelope icon again. So, for example, you could send one e-mail to the site admin and another, quite different one to the person who completed the form.

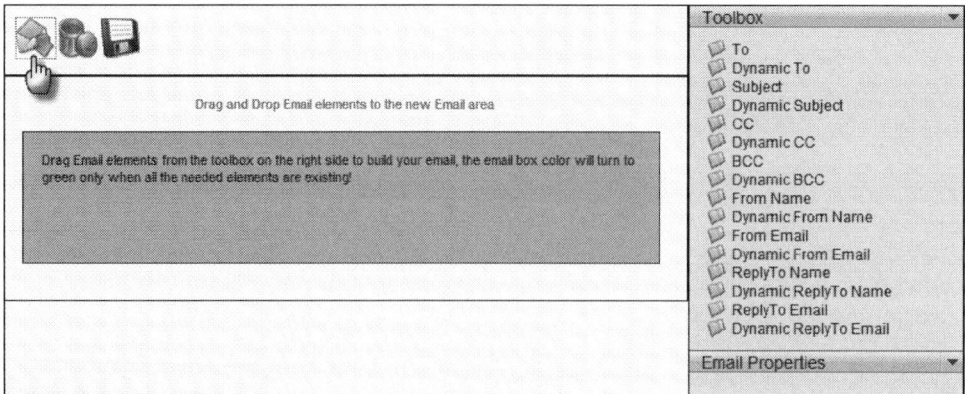

— 20 —

Chapter 1

Now we have an e-mail setup workspace coloured red.

5. Drag the following elements from the **Toolbox** into the red box in the workspace:
    - ❏ **To**
    - ❏ **Subject**
    - ❏ **From Name**
    - ❏ **From Email**

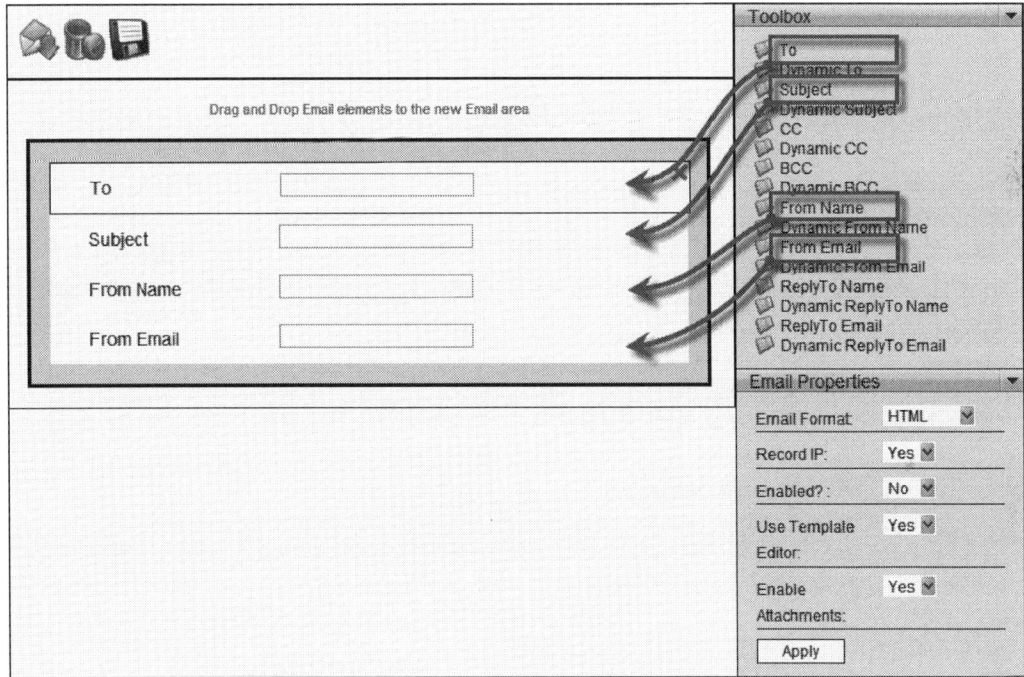

Two things have happened here. The Email Setup workspace box is no longer red, it's a yellow-green, and the **Email Properties** box now has some content.

 We've added the elements in the order **To**, **Subject**, and so on, but in practice the order doesn't matter. You can also use other elements but we'll come to them later.

If the workspace stays red, then you do not have the correct four elements in the workspace! Also notice that when the workspace is red the **Enabled?** option in the **Email Properties** box is greyed out.

21

Creating a Simple Form

6. We now need to add entries to each of these four boxes. Unlike the Form Design workspace where the boxes are left empty, in Email Setup they must be completed.

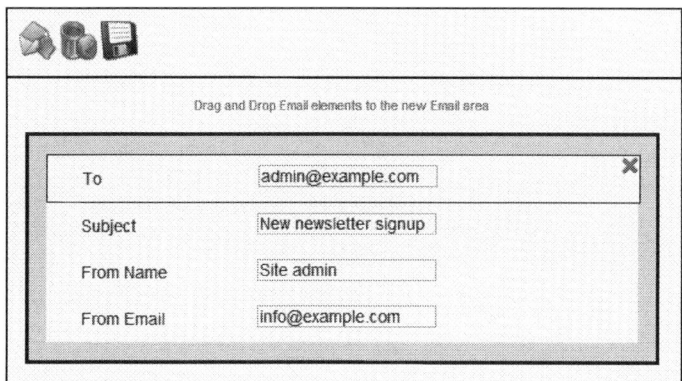

The preceding screenshot shows a completed Email Setup. Notice that the **To** and **From Email** boxes have valid e-mail addresses in them. If they are not valid the e-mail will fail—ChronoForms does not check these, it's up to you to get them right.

 We will use `example.com` as a generic domain throughout this book. You will need to replace this with the domain of your site as appropriate.

In the **Subject** and **From Name** boxes you can add any text string that you like, provided that it's not too long (the box will accept 150 characters, but a practical limit is around 50).

While you can put any valid e-mail address that you like in the **From Email** box, we strongly recommend that you use an address that has the same domain as your website. Many ISPs check e-mails being sent to make sure that the domains match. If they do not then the e-mail may be flagged as spam, or just dropped.

 We have used `admin@` in the **To** box and `info@` in the **From Email** box. It should be possible to use the same e-mail address in both boxes but we have seen a few cases where e-mails with identical **To** and **From Email** addresses have not been delivered.

7. To finalize the Email Setup there are a few more small things to do.

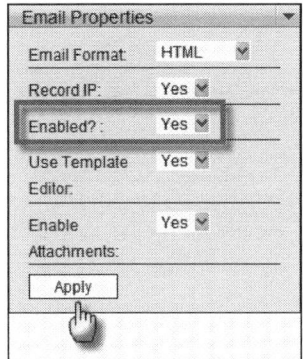

Set the **Enabled?** drop-down to **Yes**, and then click **Apply** to save the Email Setup.

Then click the "floppy disk" icon above the workspace to save the form again.

When you click the "save" icon you will be asked the name of the form that you want to save. This field defaults to the name of the form that you were currently editing, but if you wanted to save a new form, you could change the name of the form in the input box. We will just leave the form name that we are editing and update this form.

8. Back in the **Forms Manager** you can see that the **Emails** column has changed and now has an entry that says **Enabled:0 / Disabled:1**.

Creating a Simple Form

9. So we have our e-mail setup but it is still disabled. To enable e-mails we need to open the form for editing not in the Wizard Editor but in the standard ChronoForms Editor. To do this click the **newsletter_signup** link (over to the left in the image):

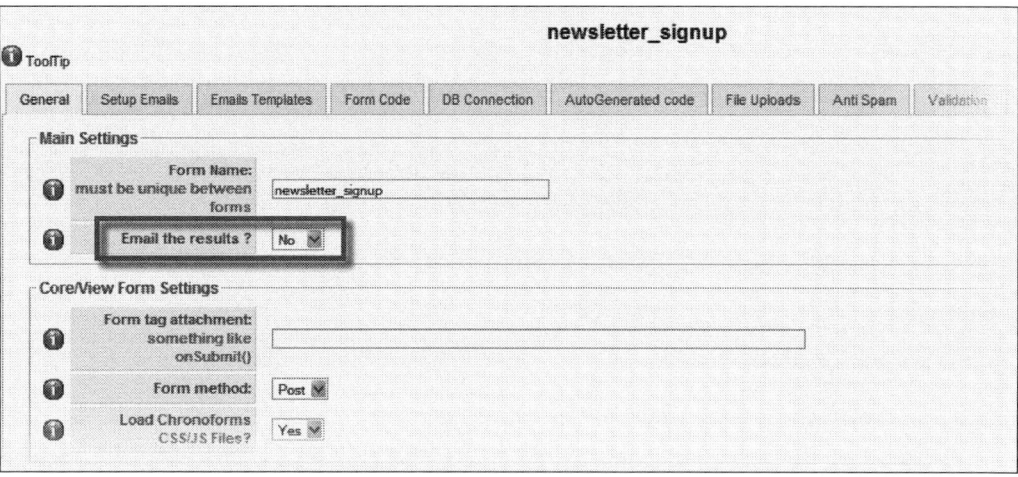

10. There are a lot of tabs here and many settings options, but we only need to change one. On the **General** tab find **Email the Results?** and change the setting to **Yes**.

11. Now click the **Save** icon (the floppy disk) to the top right of the screen to save the Forms configuration.

 This option turns "all" e-mails on or off, while the setting in the **Email Setup | Properties** box turns just that single Email Setup on or off. Of course, if you only have one Email Setup these are the same but it's useful with more complex forms.

Back in the Forms Manager view you can see that the **Emails** column now reads **Enabled:1 / Disabled:0**. Perfect!

12. We just need to test our form to check that the e-mail works correctly. Click the form "link" entry to open the form in a new browser window or tab; enter an e-mail address in the **Email** box and click **Submit**.

 If you still have the form open in your browser that's fine, but please click the **Re-Load** button in your browser to refresh the code before you test.

24

When you click **Submit** the form is submitted and you are left looking at an empty Joomla! page, that is unless you get an error message. We'll put a "Thank You" message on here in the next recipe.

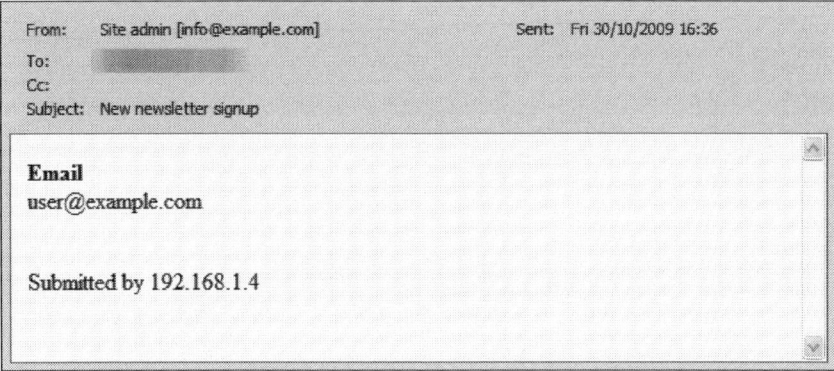

And here's the e-mail I received after submitting. Notice that ChronoForms has built the email using the information we put into the Email Setup (I've blanked out the real e-mail address I used to send it to).

And it has taken the information submitted from the form and included that in the e-mail body. That's clever!

There's also the **IP address** of the submitter; you can turn this off in the **Email Setup | Properties** if you don't want it.

13. Congratulations! Now you have a working form that carries out an action when it is submitted. My guess is that around half of all web forms work just like this, though maybe with a few more fields.

How it works...

ChronoForms has taken the information we input in the Email Setup and taken the form HTML to create a default body template for the e-mail, and combined all these together behind the scenes to create a rather basic but completely functional e-mail.

See also

- *Chapter 2, Emailing Form Results* for more advanced e-mail features and functionality. The *Getting your emails delivered safely* recipe has some useful hints for trouble-shooting problems with e-mails and Email Setups.
- *Chapter 8, Uploading Files from your Forms* has recipes on *Attaching files to e-mails* and *Displaying images in e-mails and articles*.

Creating a Simple Form

- Chapter 7, *Adding Features to your Form* includes the recipe *Adding a barcode to an e-mail*.
- Chapter 12, *Adding Advanced Features* has an advanced recipe on *Controlling e-mails from from inputs*.

Showing a "Thank You" page

When you submit a ChronoForms form, the default is to show you a blank page like the following screenshot:

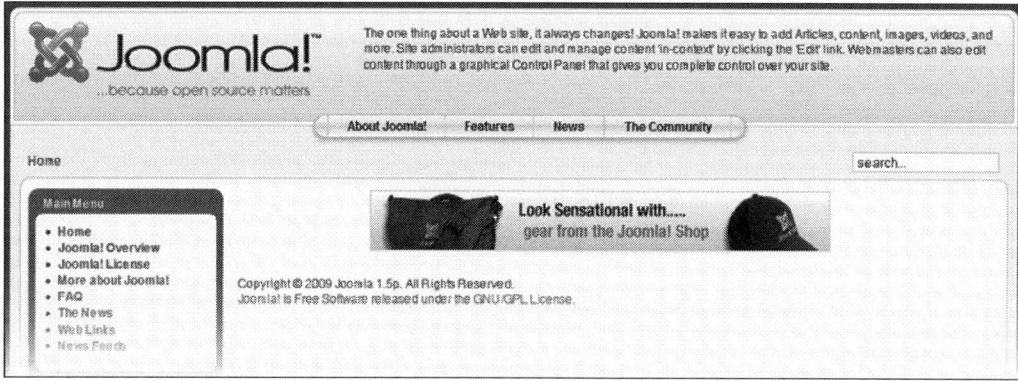

This isn't too friendly or helpful. There are a couple of ways of dealing with this—you can redirect the user to another page (see the *Redirect the user to another page* section a little further on) or you can show a "Thank You" message on this page. That's what we'll do here.

Getting ready

We'll be using the same form as the previous recipes.

How to do it...

1. From the ChronoForms **Forms Manager** select the **newsletter_signup** checkbox and click the Wizard Edit icon in the toolbar, close the warning message, and click **Step 4 After Form Submission**.

Chapter 1

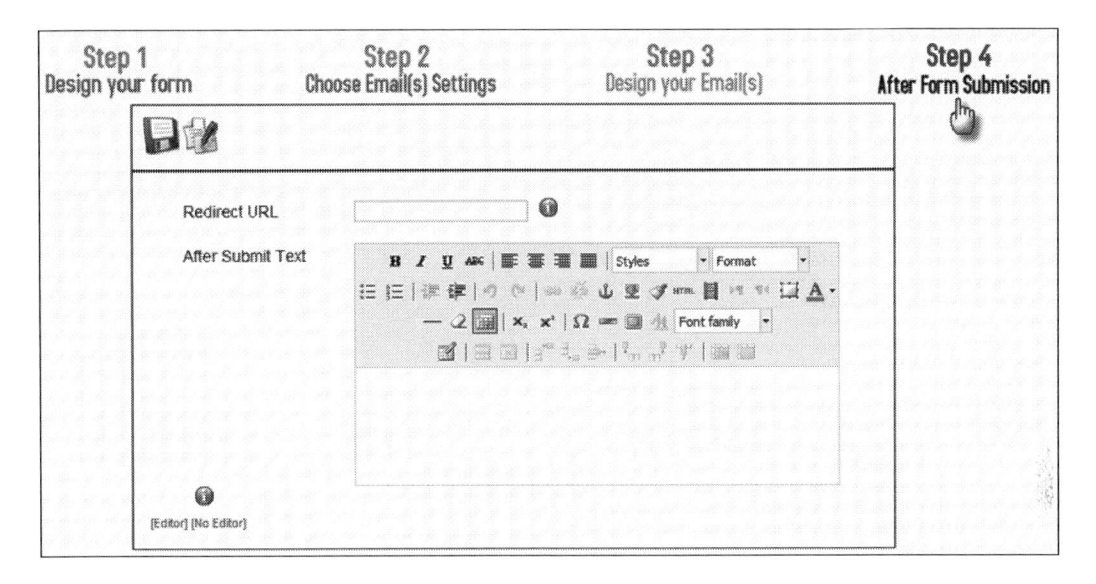

Again we have a different workspace. There's a new icon we'll come to later—a **ReDirect URL** box, a rich text editor and, down in the bottom left, some links to turn the editor on and off.

We are just going to enter a little thank you message in the rich text editor:

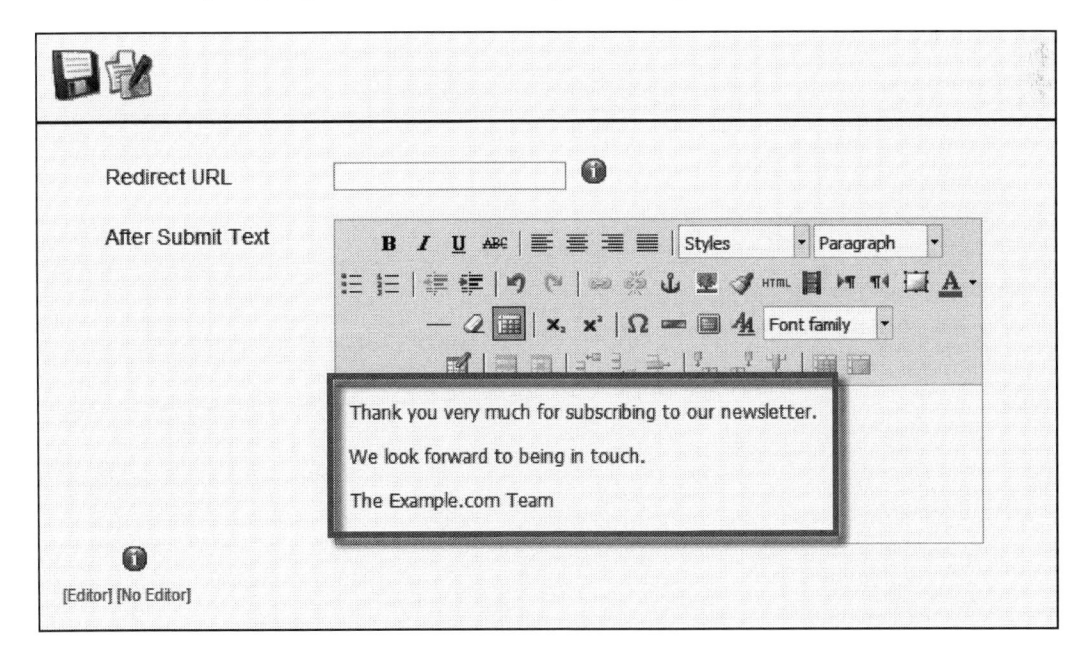

27

Creating a Simple Form

Put in what you like but here's the message I've used. You can also use the editor functions to make the message prettier if you like.

2. When you are done click the floppy disk icon to save the form again, then click **Save** on the modal window to save the form with the same name.

3. Back in the **Forms Manager**, click the form link to open it and submit the form. Here's what I see:

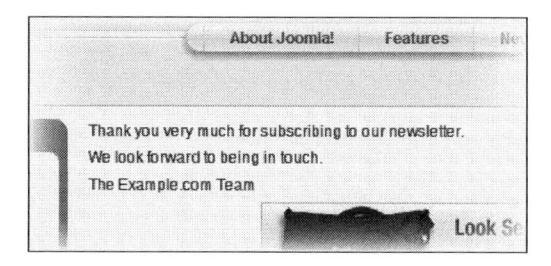

4. Mission accomplished!

How it works...

ChronoForms saves the text you enter and shows that as the content in the page it displayed after the form is submitted.

We just added some plain text here; in practice the text can be formatted and styled, you can show images, or links, and more, much more.

There's more...

Let's look at one more really useful feature here. ChronoForms can display the information entered in the form on the "Thank You" page. Let's show the e-mail address that they entered.

Go back to *Step 4* in the Wizard Edit and alter the first sentence to read **Thank you very much for subscribing to our newsletter with the email**. Leave your cursor right before the full-stop and click the new **Add field** icon (the pen and paper) to the right of the floppy disk icon.

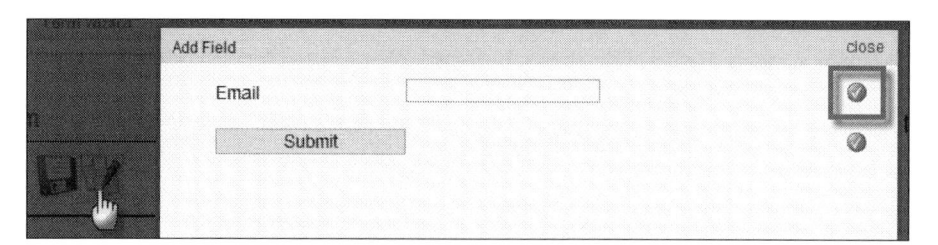

After you click the icon a window opens showing you a Form preview, except that this time there are some blue icons over to the right, one for each element. Click the top icon to select the **Email** element.

When you click the icon the window closes and there is a new text snippet in the editor where your cursor is. My first sentence now reads **Thank you very much for subscribing to our newsletter with the email** `{text_0}`. The new snippet `{text_0}` is the name of the element I chose inside curly brackets `{field_name}`.

Save the form again, open the Form window, submit the form, and you should then see something like this:

Where we had `{text_0}` in the template ChronoForms has placed the value `user@example.com`, which was entered into the form input.

Editing your form with the Wizard Edit

It's unusual for me (or my clients) to get form specifications right the first time. I often need to go back and add something that was forgotten.

In this case we decide that we want to collect the user's name as well as their e-mail address. For this we need to add a new text input.

Getting ready

We'll be using the same form as the previous recipes.

How to do it...

1. From the ChronoForms Forms Manager select the **newsletter_signup** checkbox and click the **Wizard Edit** icon in the toolbar, close the warning message, and click **Step 1 – Design your form**.
2. Drag a new **TextBox** element over from the **Toolbox** into the workspace and drop it near the top of the workspace. We want it before the e-mail element.

Creating a Simple Form

> If the box drops into the wrong place, you can drag the elements up and down inside the workspace with your mouse. In some browsers you can't grab the whole element—if so, then the right-hand, small icon on the element should work OK (if you look closely it's a pair of green arrows).

3. Click the element to open the **Properties** box and change the **Label** field to Name.
4. Apply the changes to the properties, save the form again, and open the form window.

   You should now see that we have two fields in the form:

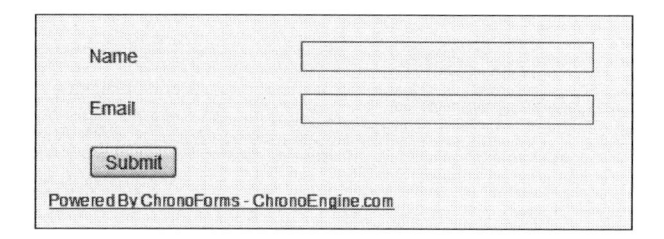

   Name

   Email

   [Submit]

   Powered By ChronoForms - ChronoEngine.com

   Just like that we've successfully added a second field to the form.

5. Unfortunately, when we submit it, the Email template has not been updated for us, it only shows the value of the e-mail input.

   We can update this easily enough though. By now the process is familiar. Use **Wizard Edit** and this time go to **Step 3: Design your Email(s)**.

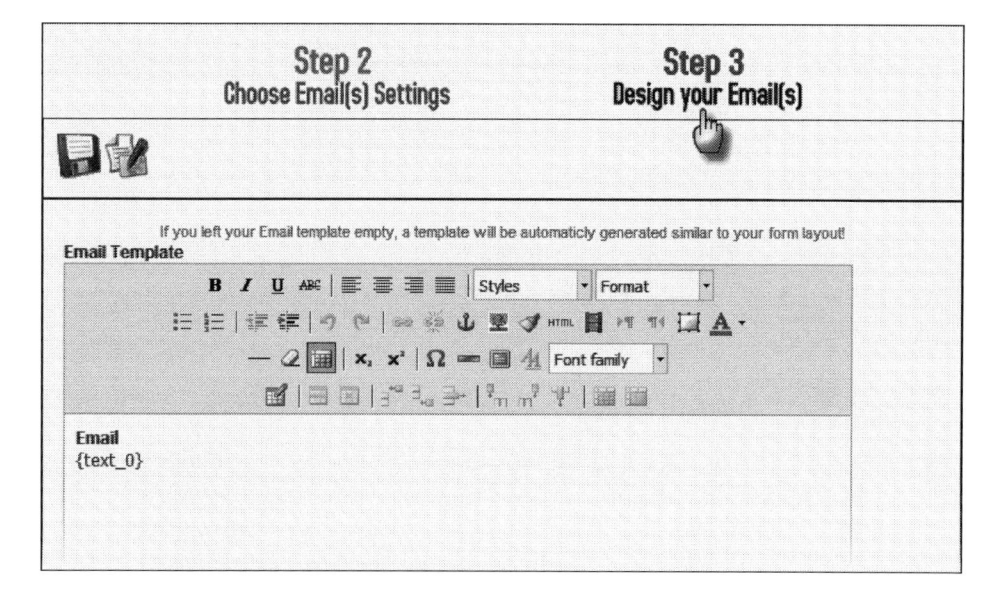

Step 2 Choose Email(s) Settings

Step 3 Design your Email(s)

If you left your Email template empty, a template will be automaticly generated similar to your form layout!

Email Template

Email
{text_0}

Here you can see the template that ChronoForms has created for your e-mail. It has similar syntax to the "Thank You" page with `{text_0}` as a place-holder for the input value.

We have the same **Add Field** icon too.

6. Put your cursor in the text editor field and use the **Add Field** icon to get the place-holder for the name field; it will probably be `{text_1}`.

> ChronoForms gives the input elements serial numbers by type. So, the next test input will be `text_2`, and the first 'select' input will be `'select_0'`. If you like, you can change these to something more user-friendly either in the element Properties box, or manually in the Form HTML, as we shall see later.

Let's make this e-mail a bit more meaningful though and enter the following text:

Dear Admin,

Just to let you know that `{text_1}` **whose email address is** `{text_0}` **has subscribed to the newsletter.**

Regards
The Example.com Website team

7. Save the Form again, submit it, and check the e-mail that is sent. Here's what I received:

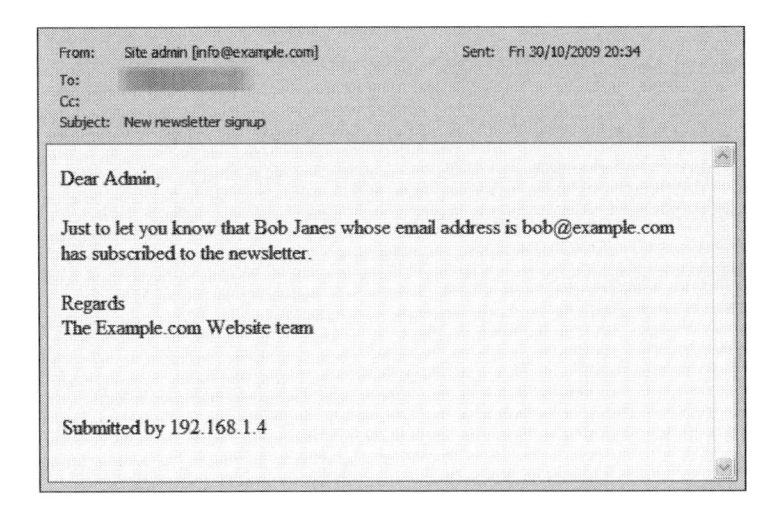

> From: Site admin [info@example.com] Sent: Fri 30/10/2009 20:34
> To:
> Cc:
> Subject: New newsletter signup
>
> Dear Admin,
>
> Just to let you know that Bob Janes whose email address is bob@example.com has subscribed to the newsletter.
>
> Regards
> The Example.com Website team
>
> Submitted by 192.168.1.4

Beyond this the world is your oyster; you can construct a fully customized e-mail with as much HTML as you like.

Creating a Simple Form

> There's a note in red on the e-mail template workspace that says **If you left your Email template empty, a template will be automaticly generated similar to your form layout!** [sic]. To make this work you need to delete everything from the Email template including any HTML that does not display, such as `<p> </p>`. Click the **HTML** button in the editor toolbar to see the underlying source code and delete everything that is there.

How it works...

ChronoForms keeps a special copy of the form layout in a Joomla! database table. When you use Wizard Edit it fetches this copy and recreates the form workspace for you to edit. Completely separately it also keeps the Form HTML created when you save. Any later changes you make in the Form HTML will be lost if you use Wizard Edit again. Hence the warning message when you start Wizard Edit.

For the Email Template, ChronoForms stores the HTML and before it uses it, it searches for values like `{field_name}` and substitutes the field values for these placeholders.

> You can also include PHP code in there to give even more flexibility but you cannot add this with the Rich Text editor in the Wizard Edit; you have to use the **Form Editor** instead.

Redirecting the user to another page

In an earlier recipe we created a "Thank You" page to display after the form is submitted. Sometimes though you may want to take the user to some other page on your site. We can do this too.

In this example we'll redirect to the site home page for simplicity. You can do exactly the same using any other URL on the site.

Getting ready

We'll be using that same form again.

How to do it...

1. From the ChronoForms Forms Manager select the **newsletter_signup** checkbox and click the **Wizard Edit** icon in the toolbar, then close the warning message. This time go to **Step 4 –After form Submission**.

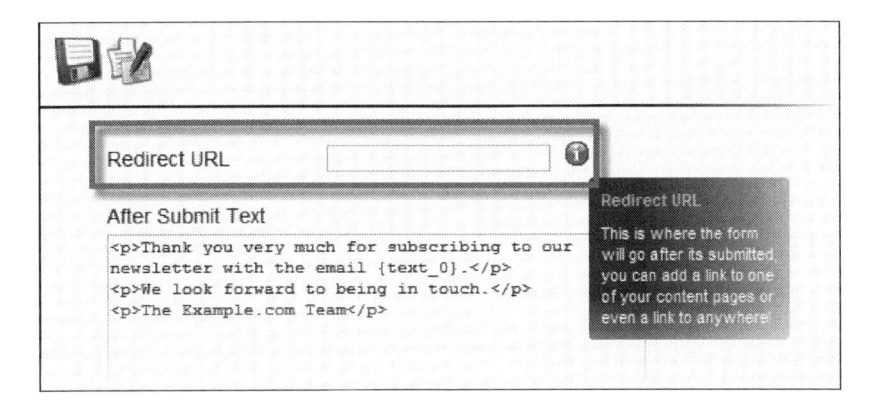

   [screenshot of Redirect URL field and After Submit Text with tooltip: "Redirect URL — This is where the form will go after its submitted, you can add a link to one of your content pages or even a link to anywhere"]

2. In the **Redirect URL** box, just type `index.php` or, if you prefer, `http://example.com/index.php` (but using your domain name in place of `example.com`).

3. Save the Form here, go back to view the form in the browser, and submit it. Now, instead of the "Thank You" page we are redirected to the site home page. You could choose to write a "Thank You" page as an article on your site, or take the user to some other page that you think might be relevant or interesting to them.

> Notice that in the preceding screenshot there's a help bubble; you can see these throughout ChronoForms by hovering your mouse over the blue tooltip (**i**) icons. Some of these are more helpful than others but it's always worth taking a look if you are uncertain of how something works.

There's more...

There is nothing to stop you from using any URL in there; you can redirect your user to any other page on the internet. And, as we shall see later, you can create redirect URLs dynamically to send the user to different pages depending on the information they submit in their form.

Creating a Simple Form

See also

- ▶ Chapter 6 has a recipe *Redirecting users to other Joomla! pages after submission* that looks at other ways to redirect
- ▶ Chapter 11 has a recipe *Creating a PayPal purchase form with the ReDirect plug-in* that looks at redirecting the user with some of the form data

Backing up and restoring your forms

We're going to complete this first chapter with a little security recipe and back up the form on which we worked so hard.

ChronoForms stores the Form information in the Joomla! database so it will get backed up whenever your database is backed up, but it's still often useful to take a backup copy.

This is also the best way of transferring a form from one site to another or to send it to someone else for help in debugging problems.

Getting ready

Any ChronoForms form will do fine.

How to do it...

1. Open the ChronoForms **Forms Manager** in your browser. Notice that towards the right of the Toolbar there is a group of three icons labeled **Backup Form**, **Backup Forms**, and **Restore**.

2. Next to the name of each form in the **Forms Manager** list is a checkbox that we use to select forms for actions like Backup. Check the box by **newsletter_signup**, and then click the **Backup Form** icon in the toolbar.

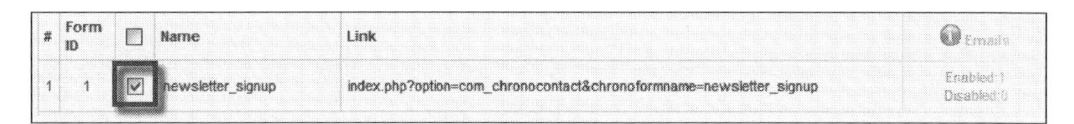

Chapter 1

3. The **Save File** dialogue from your browser will open and you can save the form backup file in a convenient local folder.

> ChronoForms backup files are named `form_name.cfbak`. They are plain text files and can be opened in Notepad or any text editor.

4. Now let's restore the form back into ChronoForms again. This will create a second form with the same name which is a potential problem, but we'll sort that out.

   Click the **Restore Form** icon in the toolbar and you'll see a new screen:

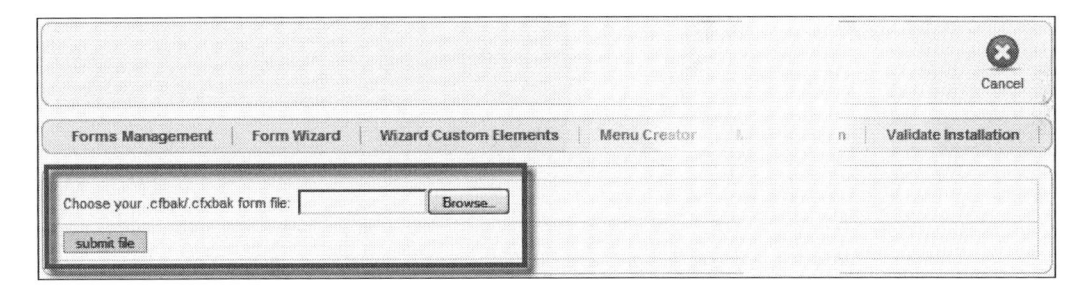

5. Click the **Browse...** button, navigate to the `newsletter_signup.cfbak` file that you just saved, and click the **submit file** button to restore the form.

> Notice the **Cancel** icon to the top right just in case you don't want to be here.

6. When the form is restored you are returned to the **Forms Manager**; there is a System Message saying **Restored Successfully** and there is a new entry in the Forms list. However, the new entry is almost identical to the previous one.

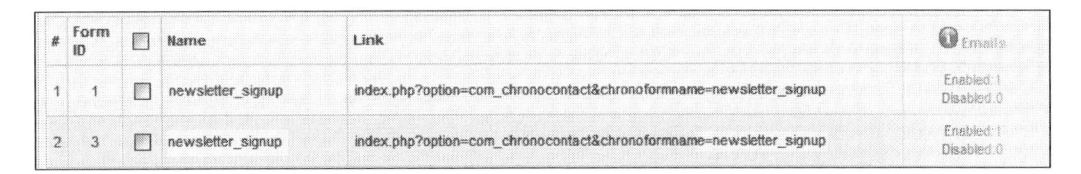

#	Form ID		Name	Link	Emails
1	1	☐	newsletter_signup	index.php?option=com_chronocontact&chronoformname=newsletter_signup	Enabled: 1 Disabled: 0
2	3	☐	newsletter_signup	index.php?option=com_chronocontact&chronoformname=newsletter_signup	Enabled: 1 Disabled: 0

ChronoForms can tell the difference between these two forms here because they have different Form IDs (here it is 1 and 3; yours may be 1 and 2). However, when the forms are in use on your site the names are used to distinguish them, not the IDs; so having two forms with the same name can be a real problem.

Creating a Simple Form

7. You can change the name by using Wizard Edit and resaving with a different name, or you can click the Form name link to open the **Form Editor**, change the name in the first box in the **General** tab, and resave the form.

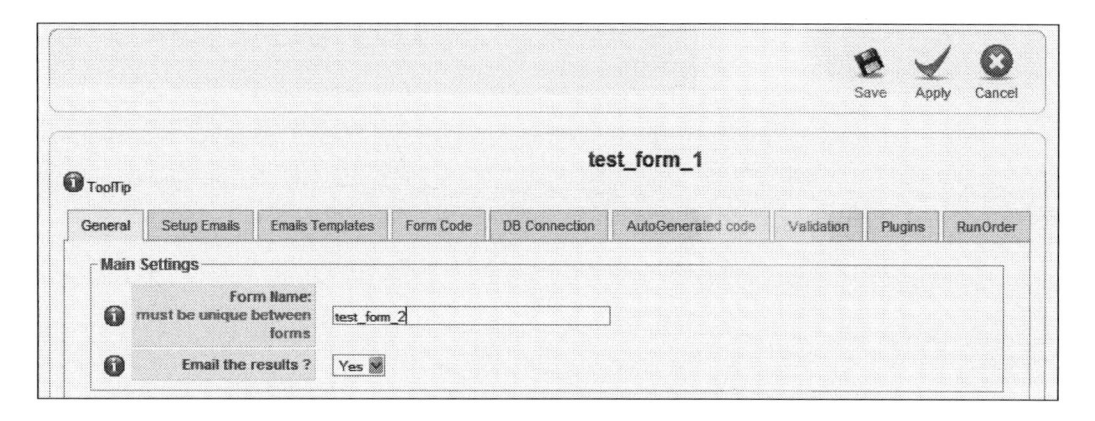

> Use the icons at the top right to save the renamed form—**Save** will save and return you to the **Form Manager**; **Apply** will save and keep you in the **Form Editor**; **Cancel** will return you to the **Form Manager** without saving any changes (since the last Apply or Save).

There's more...

You'll remember that there's also a **Backup Forms** icon. You can use this to backup several forms (or all of your forms) at the same time. Just select the forms using the checkboxes by the Form names and then click the **Backup Forms** icon. All of your forms will be backed up into a single `.cfxbak` file. This can be restored in just the same way as a `.cfbak` file for a single form.

Using Backup and Restore is a complicated way to make a copy of a form. You can use the **Copy Form** icon in the toolbar instead. Again, you must change the name of one of the two forms before trying to use them.

Lastly, if you end up with copies that you don't need, the **Delete** icon in the toolbar will delete one or more forms. There is no confirmation request and no undelete; so use with care!

2
E-mailing Form Results

In this chapter, we will cover:

- Replying to e-mails
- Getting your e-mails delivered safely
- Sending a "Thank you" e-mail to the form submitter
- Choosing e-mail addresses from a list
- Attaching uploaded files to the e-mail
- Attaching a "standard" file (for example, terms and conditions) to the e-mail
- Creating a "dynamic" subject line using information from the form

Introduction

One of the two main things that forms "do" when they are submitted, is to send e-mails. We saw in *Chapter 1*, *Creating a Simple Form* how to send an e-mail, including values from the form, to a site administrator.

In this chapter, we'll learn more about this and look at different ways of sending e-mails from your ChronoForms forms.

Replying to e-mails

Sending an e-mail to the site administrator is great, until he decides to reply. Then we have a problem. When you click **Reply**, the e-mail that opens is addressed to the site administrator (actually, we set it to `info@example.com` if you recall). So, he sends the e-mail to himself, and not to the person who submitted the form.

Yet their e-mail is right there in the e-mail text. Can't we put that in the **From Email** field? Then the reply will go just where we want it.

Well, yes we could put the e-mail in there (technically using a **Dynamic From Email** field). But then we find that the administrator no longer receives any e-mails at all!

This is most likely because the site ISP is checking for spammers and one of the checks that they run is to compare the site domain with the domain in the **From Email** header of the e-mail. If they don't match, the e-mail is marked as "likely spam" and dropped in the bin.

The answer is to use the **Reply To Name** and **Reply To Email** headers.

Getting ready

We're going to use the form from the end of *Chapter 1, Creating a Simple Form* which has **Name** and **Email** fields.

How to do it...

In *Chapter 1, Creating a Simple Form*, we used Wizard Edit to change our form; here we're going to start exploring the complexity of the **Form Editor**. Fortunately, in this case it is pretty much the same.

1. In the **Forms Manager** click the Form Name to open the Form Editor.

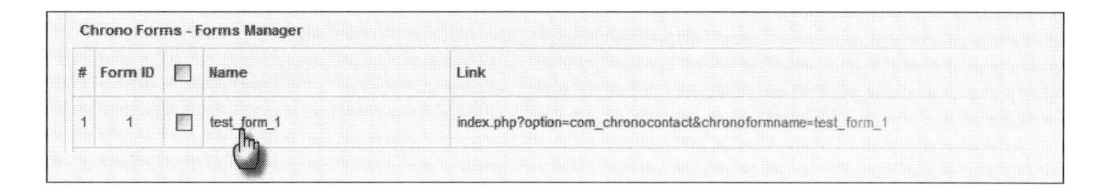

#	Form ID		Name	Link
1	1	☐	test_form_1	index.php?option=com_chronocontact&chronoformname=test_form_1

When the Form Editor opens, notice that there is a row of tabs starting with **General**, next to which is **Setup Emails**. This is the one that we want, so click the tab to open it.

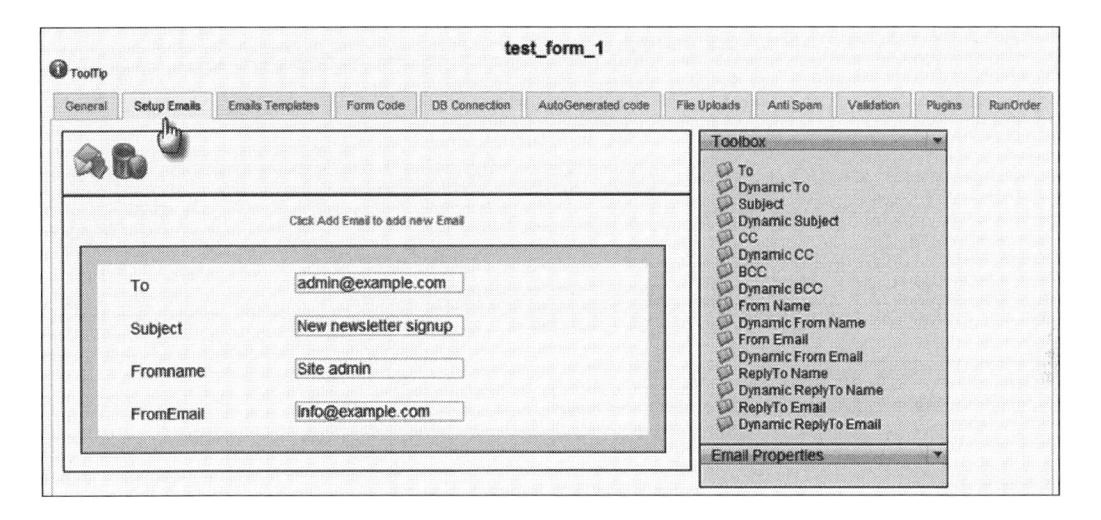

As expected, what is on this tab is pretty much identical to the Email Setup view from the Wizard Edit and what's more, there is all the data we entered in the Wizard Edit.

2. There, we already have the four elements that are required to enable an Email Setup. We are now going to add two more "Reply To" elements for the information that the user has submitted in the form.

    We need their name and their e-mail address and we already have these fields in our form; so far so good. But we can't just type the values in because they are going to be different each time the form is submitted.

    We call these changing values **dynamic** as opposed to the static unchanging values we have so far.

    And you'll notice that in the **Toolbox** there are two versions of each element—**To** and **Dynamic To**, **Subject** and **Dynamic Subject**, and so on.

    To capture values input from the form, we use the dynamic versions. And instead of static values we put field names into the boxes. Then when the form is submitted, ChronoForms will put in the values from the submitted form.

E-mailing Form Results

First drag the **Dynamic ReplyTo Name** and the **Dynamic ReplyTo Email** elements into the workspace.

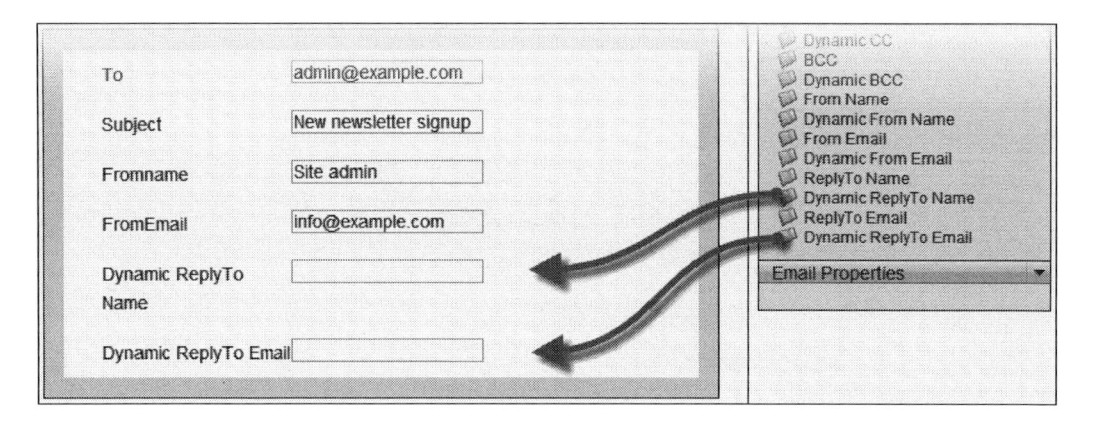

3. Now we just need to add in the field names for those two fields in the two boxes. They were `text_0` for the Subscriber Email input and `text_1` for the Subscriber Name input.

> **Important note**: We enter just the field names in the boxes with no quotes, no brackets, and no spaces.

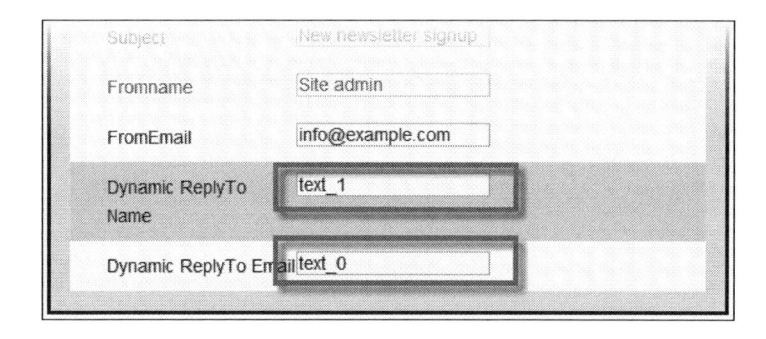

4. That's all we need for now, so let's save the Form using the **Save** icon in the Form Editor toolbar and return to the Forms Manager.

5. Click the Form link again to open the form; put some information into the boxes and submit the form.

When the e-mail arrives click the **Reply To** button and you should find that the **To...** address for the e-mail is set to the address of the new subscriber.

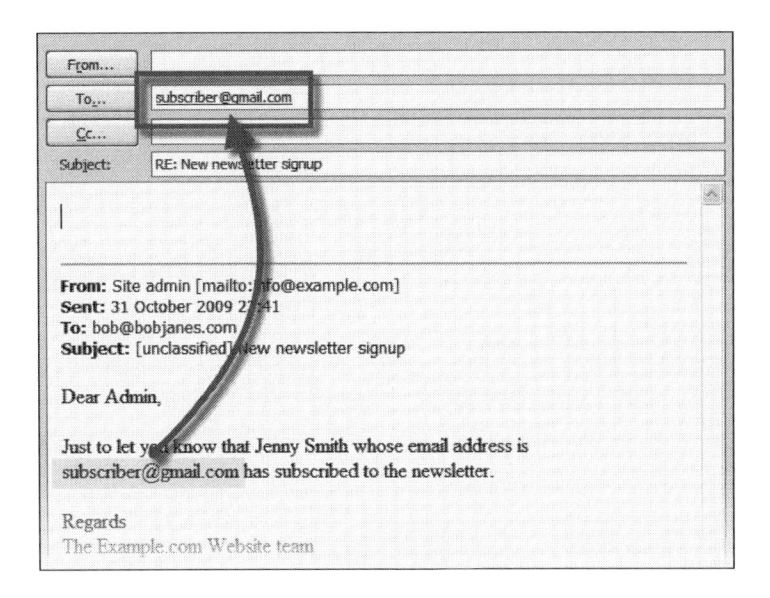

> The way that e-mail headers are handled differs a little between ISPs who send the e-mails and the mail readers that we use to read and reply to them. You may not see exactly the same result.

See also

- *Chapter 1, Creating a Simple Form*. The *Send your form results by e-mail* section describes how to use the Form Wizard to set up e-mails, and the *Format your e-mail* section talks about formatting the content of the e-mail.

Getting your e-mails delivered safely

We've seen how easy it is to set ChronoForms up to send e-mails in response to a form submission. The difficult part is to make sure that your e-mails are delivered safely. Here are four checks to ensure safe delivery.

E-mailing Form Results

How to do it...

1. Checking if your e-mail is working:

    Your Joomla! site needs to be configured to have access to a working mail-server. The easy way to check this is to browse to any article and look for the **email to a friend** icon.

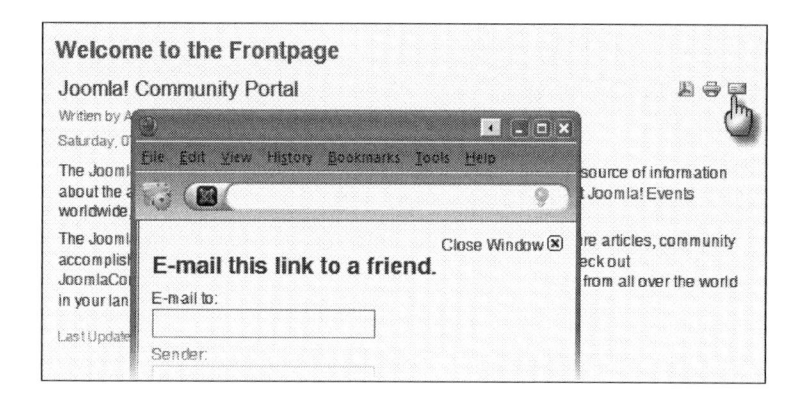

$$\left[\vphantom{\begin{array}{c}a\\a\\a\end{array}}\right.$$ These icons are turned on by default in Joomla!, if you don't see them you can enable them for an article in the **Article Editor** under the **Parameters (Advanced)** section, look for the **E-mail Icon** setting. $$\left.\vphantom{\begin{array}{c}a\\a\\a\end{array}}\right]$$

Enter your email in the **E-mail to** box, complete the other boxes with anything you like and click Send.

$$\left[\vphantom{\begin{array}{c}a\\a\\a\\a\\a\\a\end{array}}\right.$$ When testing e-mails like this, use a good working e-mail address that auto-filters e-mails as little as possible. You want to be testing the ability of the site to send e-mails, not the spam filters used by your e-mail provider. Please don't use e-mail addresses from Hotmail, Yahoo!, AOL, Live, or other similar services. Gmail is fine, but check your spam folder to see if the message has been diverted there. $$\left.\vphantom{\begin{array}{c}a\\a\\a\\a\\a\\a\end{array}}\right]$$

If you receive the e-mail from the **E-mail this link to a friend** then you can be sure that your site e-mail is working.

2. Check your Joomla! site e-mail setup:

    If you don't receive the test e-mail, the first place to check is your spam folder. After that check the site e-mail setup; this is in **Site Global Configuration | Server | Mail Settings**.

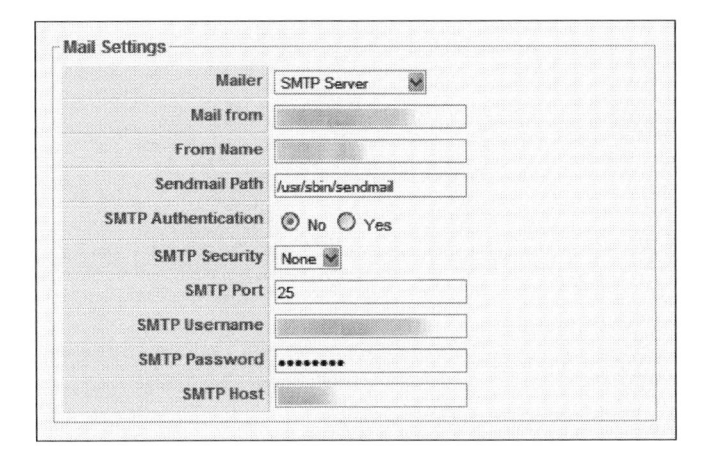

    [Mail Settings form showing fields: Mailer (SMTP Server), Mail from, From Name, Sendmail Path (/usr/sbin/sendmail), SMTP Authentication (No/Yes), SMTP Security (None), SMTP Port (25), SMTP Username, SMTP Password, SMTP Host]

    The exact settings to go in here depend on your site host and the way they have e-mail services setup. Check their help documents for the necessary information.

    If you have problems with your ISP service, then you can use the free Gmail SMTP server in here. You need a Gmail account and then you can get the settings from Gmail help (http://mail.google.com/support/bin/answer.py?hl=en&answer=13287).

    > If you use the PHP Mail Function as your Mailer then CC and BCC are not always supported. This appears to be related to some PHP security settings. If you encounter this problem then using an SMTP server on your site fixes this.

3. Checking the Administrator e-mail addresses:

    Just a little check here—make sure that the "To" and "From" addresses for your Admin e-mails are different. That's why we used `info@` and `admin@` in the earlier example. We've seen a few cases where e-mails that have the same address in both places are dropped by an ISP. After all, who'd send an e-mail to oneself?

4. Checking content filters:

    One more thing that can trigger spam filters is "inappropriate" content. This can be as simple as using HTML, using "free", having too many images, let alone a stack of other trigger words.

    If in doubt run, your e-mail subject line and body through a spam checker like the one at **Site Build It** (http://spamcheck.sitesell.com/).

How it works...

Not so much "how it works" but "why it works". ISPs recognize that spam is a big problem for their customers (not to mention that they end up processing it all). So they develop increasingly sophisticated ways to filter out spam early in the process. And the "best" spam filters are those used by the most popular sites—Yahoo!, AOL, and so on.

The most common reason for e-mails not being delivered is because they are inadvertently setting off a spam alarm and being filtered out and dropped.

Sending a "Thank you" e-mail to the form submitter

We've already sent e-mails to the administrator with the form information in it. Sometimes you also want to thank the form submitter too. These e-mails seem to fall into two broad groups—confirming the details on the submitted form, and simpler messages that say "thanks" with maybe a little extra info.

ChronoForms will do either (or a combination) quite happily. Here you are going to see how to create an e-mail from the second group.

How to do it...

1. We'll use the same form again. Go into the ChronoForms Form Manager, open up `newsletter_signup` in the Form Editor, and go to the **Setup Emails** tab. Now click the envelope icon to create a new e-mail setup.

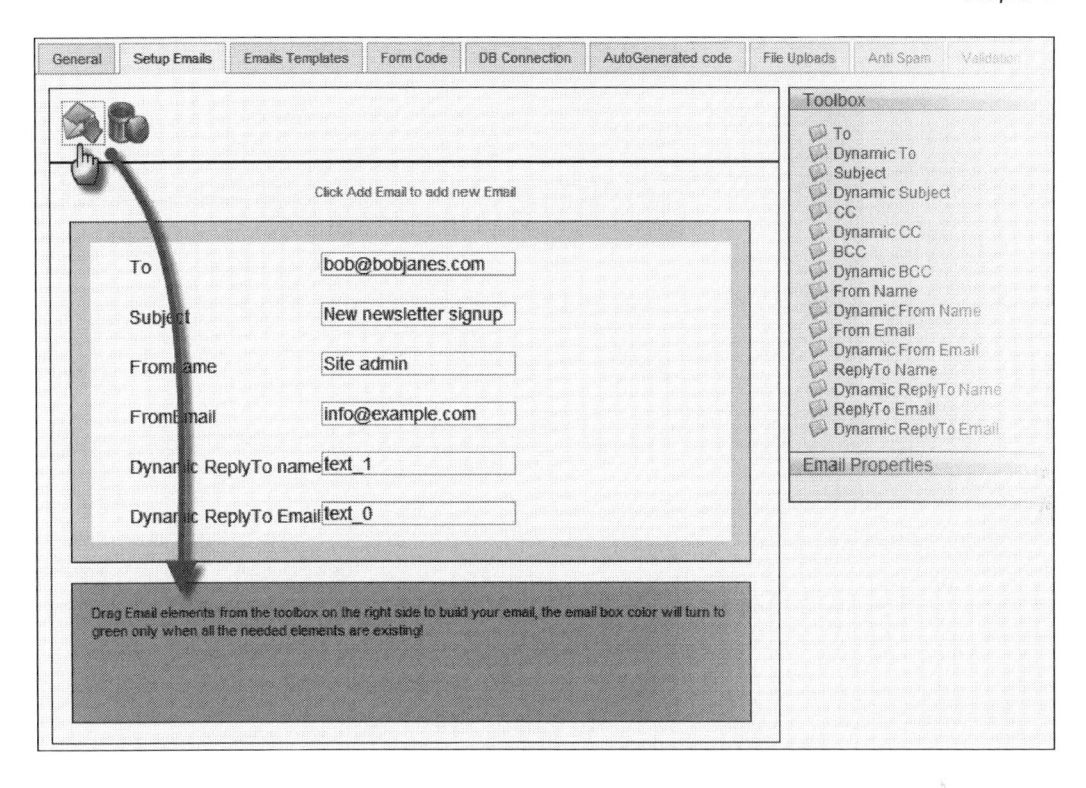

2. A new pink workspace opens up at the bottom of the screen. This works in the same way as the first one. We can drag elements on there and ChronoForms will "fill in the blanks" when the form is submitted, and send a second e-mail.

> You can keep on adding e-mail setups here though it's pretty unlikely in practice that you'll need more than two or three.

As we want to send an e-mail to the form user we need a **Dynamic To** element plus **Subject**, **From Name**, and **From Email**; all non-dynamic versions. We don't need to use **ReplyTo** fields because this time the e-mail will be from us and the **From Email** will work correctly if the user clicks **Reply**.

E-mailing Form Results

3. Enter the name of the e-mail input from the form into the **Dynamic To** element. Then add entries in the other inputs as we did in the earlier recipe.

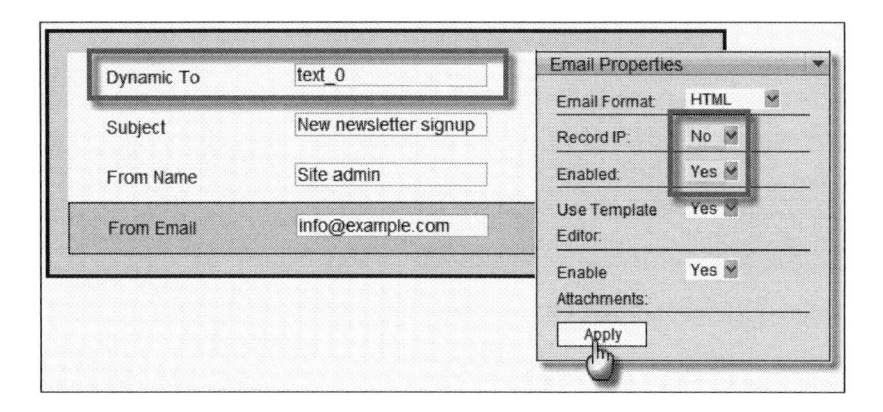

4. We'll set **Record IP** to **No** here as there is little purpose in sending the user's IP address back to them.

   And before finishing we need to enable the Email Setup.

5. Then complete the Email Setup by clicking **Apply** in the **Email Properties** tab to save your changes.

6. Now we need to switch to the **Email Templates** tab to create the message that we want to send.

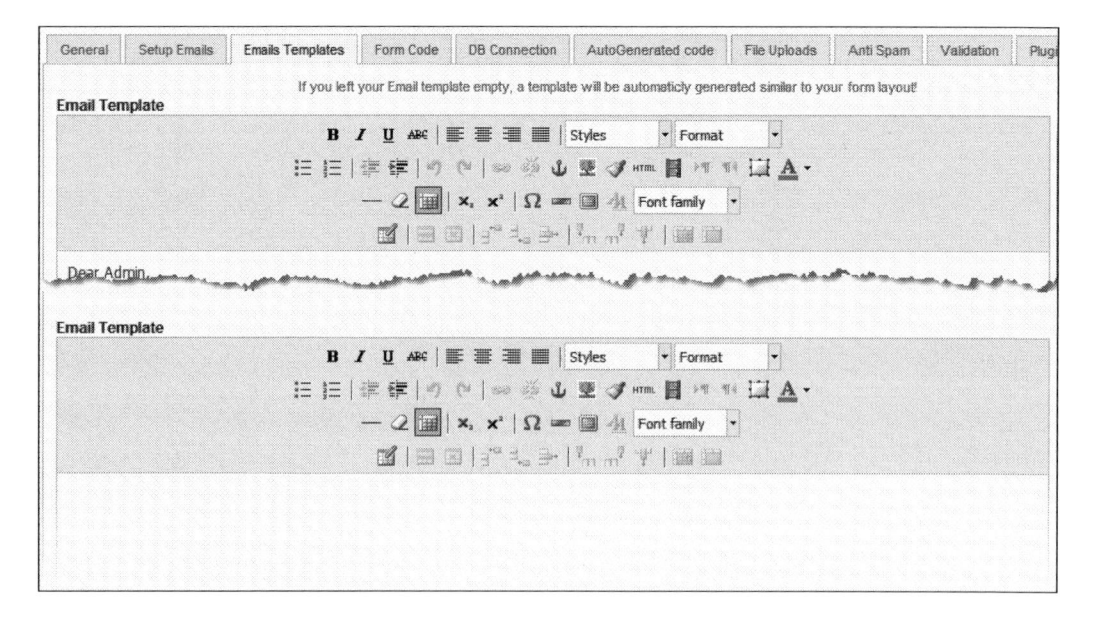

Note that ChronoForms has automatically created a second e-mail template for us to work with.

> Although neither e-mail setups nor templates are obviously named, they are related by the order in which they appear. The first Email Template links to the first Email Setup, and so on.

We can use the `{field_name}` syntax in here so let's add a quick thank you note:

```
Dear {text_1},

Thank you for subscribing to our newsletter, we hope that you
enjoy all of the future editions.

Regards
The example.com team
```

7. Save the form to save both the Email Setup and Email Template, then test the form to make sure that both e-mails are sent.

Choosing e-mail addresses from a list

You don't always want to send the e-mail to the site administrator. Sometimes you want to send it to different people depending on the information in the form. One example might be customer support where some queries are technical, some are sales related, and some are about billing queries.

We'll create a form that uses a set of radio buttons to choose a department to receive the e-mail. One easy way to do this is to put the e-mail addresses in the form code but we really, really don't want them to appear anywhere on the website (even if they aren't visible to human readers, the bots will find them). So we'll also add code to look up the correct e-mail address after the form is submitted and use that in the e-mail that is sent.

> Note: This recipe uses some PHP and Joomla! code and is more advanced than the earlier recipes.

Getting ready

We'll use that same form again, our old friend `newsletter_signup`.

Open it up in the **Form Editor | Email Setup** tab and disable the second e-mail setup if you have one; we don't need it for the moment and that will save you sending out random messages by mistake while we are testing.

E-mailing Form Results

Save the form and return to the Form Manager view.

> If you have made any changes to the Form HTML without using the Wizard Edit, then you may want to work on a copy, as the changes in the form will be lost.

How to do it...

1. Open the form with the **Wizard Edit** again. Remember that Wizard Edit is accessed from the icon on the toolbar.

   > If the form that opens up is empty then you may have used the Form Wizard (used for creating new forms) instead of the Wizard Edit.

   > ChronoForms keeps two completely separate copies of the Form HTML. One "encoded" version is used for the Wizard Edit, the other for the plain Form Editor. When you save from Wizard Edit both versions are updated, but changes in the Form Editor are not saved in the "encoded" version.

2. When the form opens at step 1, drag a **Radio Button** element into the workspace above the **Submit** button.

   > Dragging into the workspace is sometimes a little erratic, and if the element gets misplaced you can drag it up or down inside the workspace to get it back into place. Note that depending on your browser you may need to select the green "curly arrows" icon to drag an element.

   The default **RadioButton** element has three buttons labeled **Radio 1**, **Radio 2**, and **Radio 3**. In the **Properties** box is a text area where you can edit these labels, and also add more buttons if you need them, each on a new line.

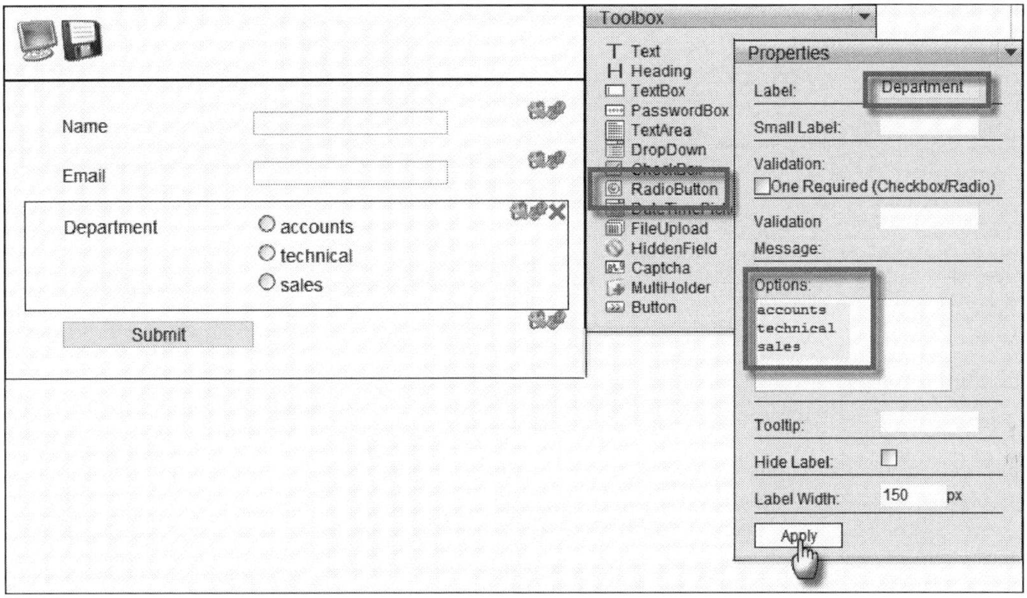
Name
Email
Department
accounts
technical
sales
Submit
Toolbox
Text
Heading
TextBox
PasswordBox
TextArea
DropDown
RadioButton
FileUpload
HiddenField
Captcha
MultiHolder
Button
Properties
Label:
Department
Small Label:
Validation:
One Required (Checkbox/Radio)
Validation
Message:
Options:
accounts
technical
sales
Tooltip:
Hide Label:
Label Width:
150
px
Apply

While you are in the **Properties** box change the **Label** element as well.

3. Click **Apply** to save the updated element, then save the form. It should now look like this in the front-end:

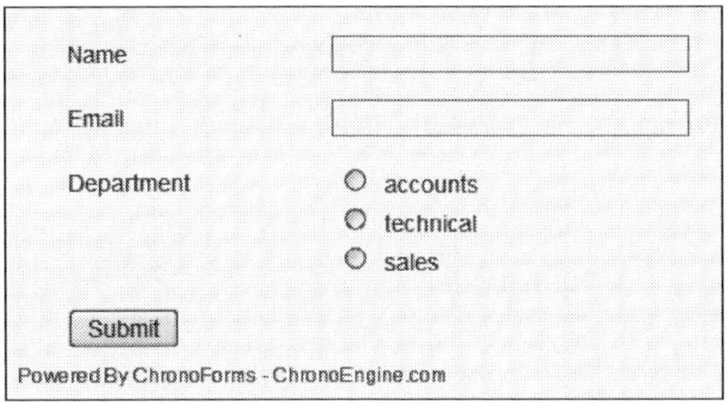
Name
Email
Department
accounts
technical
sales
Submit
Powered By ChronoForms - ChronoEngine.com

4. That looks good. Now we need to add the code to be run when the form is submitted to add the right e-mail address.

   To do that we need to know what the name of our radio box input is. Unlike the text inputs, ChronoForms didn't show us this when we created it (it might in a future version).

   There are several ways to do this, and we're going to turn on ChronoForm's useful **Debug Report** to find the answer.

E-mailing Form Results

> If the form that opens up is empty then you may have used the Form Wizard (used for creating new forms) instead of the Wizard Edit.

Go back to the ChronoForms Form Manager view and open the form in the Form Editor by clicking on the title of the form you want to edit.

On the **General** tab there is a group of **Other Form Settings** and **Debug** is about a third on the way down. Change the drop-down to **ON** and **Apply** or **Save** the form.

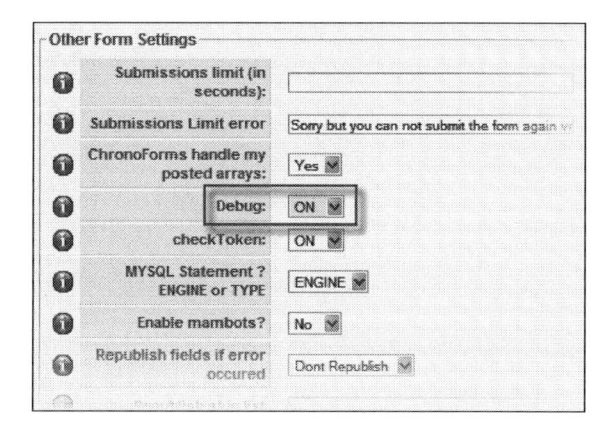

5. Now go back to the form; it really helps when working like this to keep the form and the Form Manager open in two browser tabs or windows. Enter some values and **Submit** the form.

   You should see a screen full of rather odd looking output:

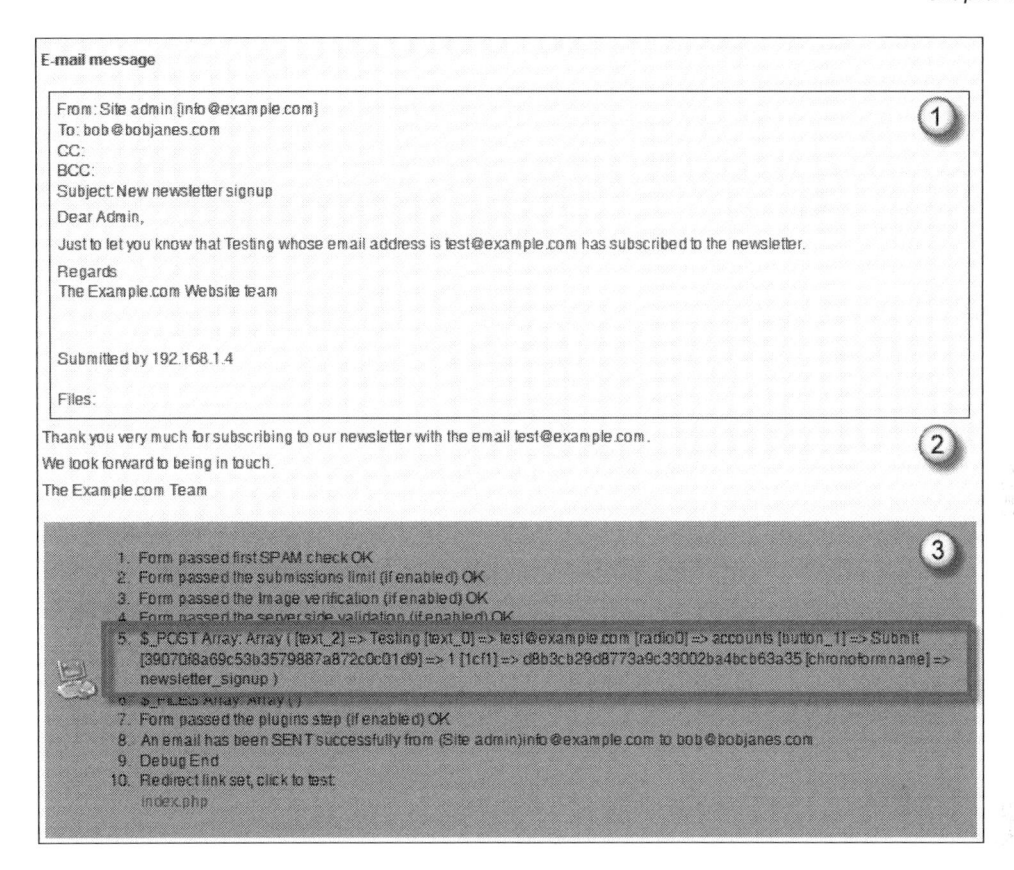

```
E-mail message

From: Site admin [info@example.com]
To: bob@bobjanes.com
CC:
BCC:
Subject: New newsletter signup

Dear Admin,

Just to let you know that Testing whose email address is test@example.com has subscribed to the newsletter.

Regards
The Example.com Website team


Submitted by 192.168.1.4

Files:
```
①

Thank you very much for subscribing to our newsletter with the email test@example.com.
We look forward to being in touch.
The Example.com Team

②

1. Form passed first SPAM check OK
2. Form passed the submissions limit (if enabled) OK
3. Form passed the image verification (if enabled) OK
4. Form passed the server side validation (if enabled) OK
5. $_POST Array: Array ([text_2] => Testing [text_0] => test@example.com [radio0] => accounts [button_1] => Submit [39070f8a69c53b3579887a872c0c01d9] => 1 [1cf1] => d8b3cb29d8773a9c33002ba4bcb63a35 [chronoformname] => newsletter_signup)
6. $_FILES Array: Array ( )
7. Form passed the plugins step (if enabled) OK
8. An email has been SENT successfully from (Site admin)info@example.com to bob@bobjanes.com
9. Debug End
10. Redirect link set, click to test:
    index.php

③

Breaking this into chunks:

- Section 1 is a "dummy" version of the e-mail that the form will send
- Section 2 is the "thank you" page that will display if there is no ReDirect set
- Section 3 is a series of Debug messages that track the progress of the form processing

Message 5 in Section 3 is the $_POST Array. This shows you the values that are submitted from the form back to the server. These are the "raw materials" that we will work with, save, and process in more complex forms. Here's what we see, with some added line-breaks for clarity:

```
$_POST Array:
Array (
    [text_2] => Testing
    [text_0] => test@example.com
    [radio0] => accounts
    [button_1] => Submit
```

```
            [39070f8a69c53b3579887a872c0c01d9] => 1
            [1cf1] => d8b3cb29d8773a9c33002ba4bcb63a35
            [chronoformname] => newsletter_signup
)
```

> **A little jargon**: Arrays are coder-speak for a group of pairs, each pair consists of a 'key' and a 'value' and the syntax here is `[key] => value`.

The first two entries in the array are the name and e-mail fields that we've been working with (notice that the name field here is `text_2` rather than `text_1`). The third entry is the one that we want here `[radio0] => accounts` tells us that the "key" or "name" for our radio button is `radio0`.

That's all we need from here.

> If this was a live site, we'd go straight back and turn off Debug now, but this is a test site so we're going to leave it turned on for a while longer.

6. Go back to the Form Editor (open the form from the Form Manager if necessary) and select the **Form Code** tab. You should see a page like the following:

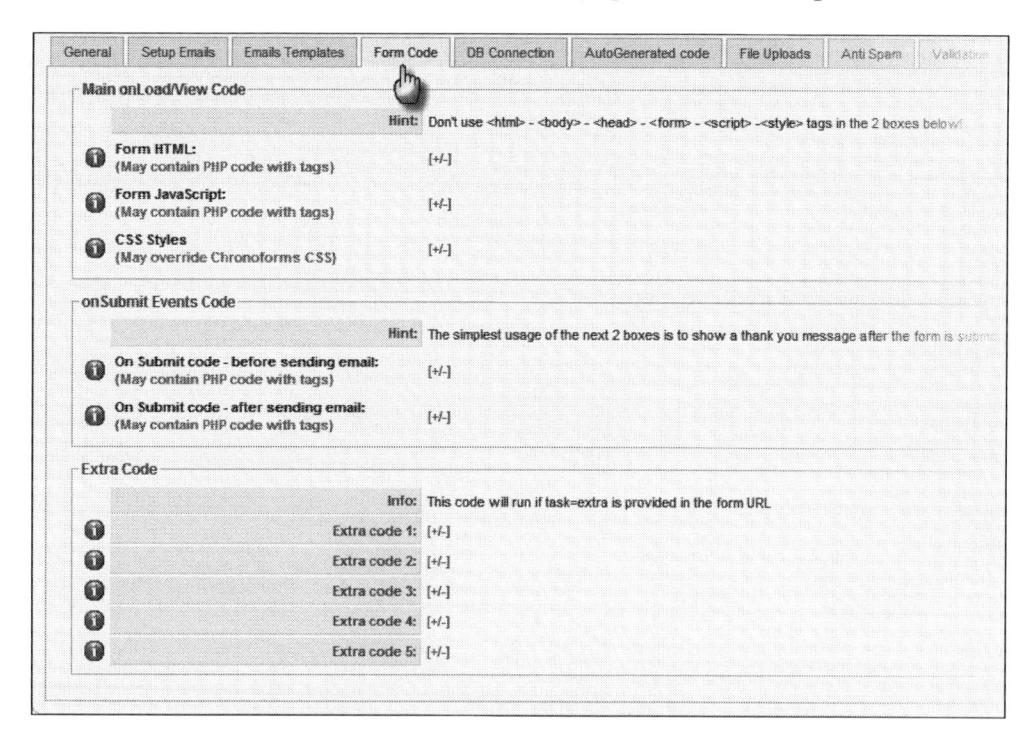

There are three blocks here again:

- **Main onLoad/View Code** contains the Form HTML with associated JavaScript and CSS – this block structures the visible form.
- **onSubmit Events Code** contains code that is run after the form is submitted.
- **Extra Code** contains code that is used for special purposes. Really, you can use this for whatever you want; we shall use one of these boxes for an AJAX interactive form later on.

For now click the **[+/-]** link after **On Submit Code – before sending email** (we'll call this **OnSubmit Before** from now on), and a text box will open like this:

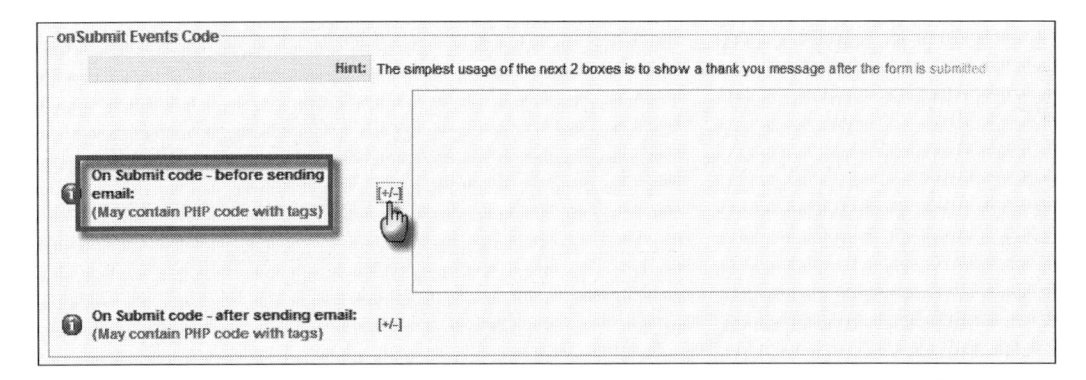

> If you look at the **Form HTML** or **OnSubmit code – after sending email** boxes in the same way, you will see the results of code that we created using Wizard Edit.

7. We're going to be entering some PHP code in here. PHP is the programming language that Joomla! is written in. If you aren't familiar with programming then some of this will look a little cryptic but you should be able to copy and paste the code and make the small edits that you need to get it to work for you.

   PHP code is marked out by PHP tags `<?php` and `?>`; anything between these is PHP and will be "processed" by the server. Anything outside these tags, and any output from the PHP will be treated as HTML and is usually sent to the browser as part of a web page.

   So we'll start out by putting a pair of PHP tags in the box:

   ```
   <?php

   ?>
   ```

E-mailing Form Results

We need to get the value of `radio0` from the `$_POST` array. Joomla! provides us with a way to do this which also offers some protection from malicious users entering potentially dangerous code into our forms. Wherever we can, we'll use this Joomla! code to get our form results.

```php
<?php
$radio0 = JRequest::getString('radio0', '', 'post');
?>
```

> In PHP, variable starting with $ so $radio0 is a new PHP variable. `JRequest::getString(. . .)` is a Joomla! function to get a text string result from a form (it will filter the result to remove anything that doesn't look like a text string, or that might be malicious). `radio0` tells the function which result to look for and "post" where to look for it.

There's a possibility that the user didn't select anything so `radio0` will be empty, or not be there at all. We still want to send an e-mail if this happens so we'll set a default value, and it can go to the administrator for them to sort out.

```php
<?php
$radio0 = JRequest::getString('radio0', 'admin', 'post');
?>
```

We also need to set an e-mail for each department and we'll do this with an array where the "key" is the department name from the form, and the "value" is the e-mail address:

```php
<?php
$radio0 = JRequest::getString('radio0', 'admin', 'post');
$emails = array (
   'accounts' => 'accounts@example.com',
   'technical' => 'technical@example.com',
   'sales' => 'sales@example.com',
   'admin' => 'admin@example.com'
);
?>
```

Now we know that `$radio0` must match one of the four keys so we just have to find out which. We select an array value by setting the "index" to `$radio0`.

```php
<?php
$radio0 = JRequest::getString('radio0', 'admin', 'post');
$emails = array (
   'accounts' => 'accounts@example.com',
   'technical' => 'technical@example.com',
   'sales' => 'sales@example.com',
```

```
    'admin' => 'admin@example.com'
);
$email_to_use = $emails[$radio0];
?>
```

Lastly, we have to pass this e-mail to ChronoForms to use. We're going to do this in two steps. First, by creating a new entry in the $_POST array using the Joomla! code `JRequest::setVar()`, which is like `JRequest::getString()` in reverse.

```
<?php
$radio0 = JRequest::getString('radio0', 'admin', 'post');
$emails = array (
  'accounts' => 'accounts@example.com',
  'technical' => 'technical@example.com',
  'sales' => 'sales@example.com',
  'admin' => 'admin@example.com'
);
$email_to_use = $emails[$radio0];
JRequest::setVar('email_to_use', $email_to_use);
?>
```

The two parameters in the function are the key and the value of the new pair.

> **Note**: We could simplify the last two lines into
> `JRequest::setVar('email_to_use', $emails[$radio0]);`

Apply the form to save our code entries in this box.

8. To tell ChronoForms to use this value we need to edit the Email Setup, so open that tab in the Form Editor. At present the Admin Email Setup looks something like the following:

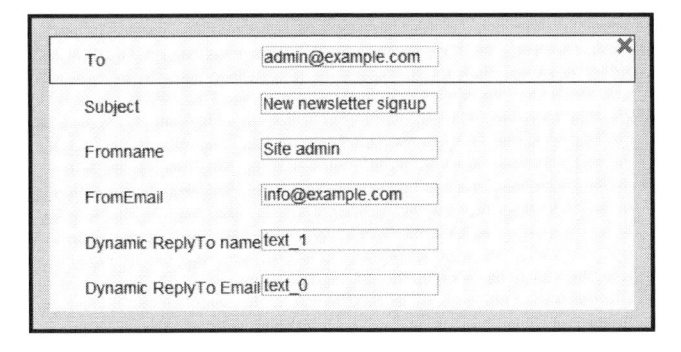

To	admin@example.com
Subject	New newsletter signup
Fromname	Site admin
FromEmail	info@example.com
Dynamic ReplyTo name	text_1
Dynamic ReplyTo Email	text_0

E-mailing Form Results

We now need to switch that **To** field from static—that always goes to the same address—and replace it with a **Dynamic To** linked to the `email_to_use` input.

Click the red cross in the corner of the **To** element to delete it. Notice that the Email Setup turns red because we've removed a required element.

Drag in a new **Dynamic To** element; it will go to the bottom but that is fine, as the order isn't important. Then, the Email Setup will turn green again.

> When you click on the **Dynamic To** element, Chrono Forms will display a version of the form, so that you can click a field to use in dynamic element. Just ignore this screen and enter the text directly into the element.

Now add the input name **email_to_use** into the **Dynamic To** box. Enter the string without any quotes or brackets.

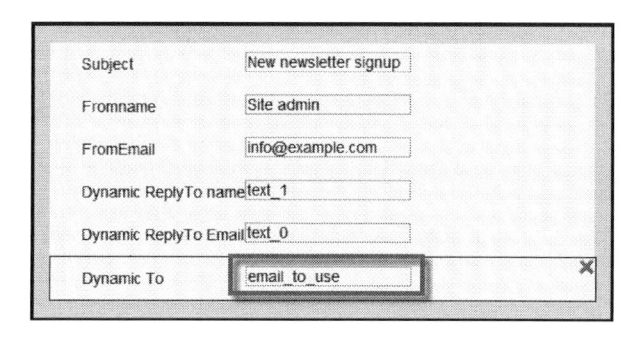

Check that the e-mail is "enabled" in the Email Properties box (ChronoForms may have disabled it when it turned red), set to **Yes**, and **Apply** if you need to. Then save the form in the editor, go to the form in the Front End and submit it to test.

9. Turn Debug on and complete the form, selecting **Technical** in the Radio Buttons. Here's the dummy e-mail:

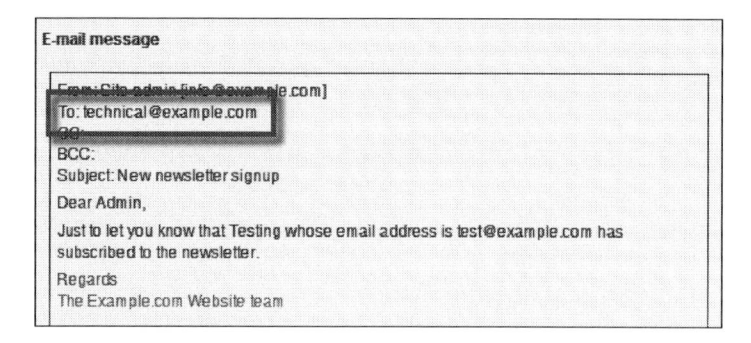

And there's the e-mail address for the technical department in the **To** field.

How it works...

In this recipe we've ventured a little deeper into the use of ChronoForms and we've added a few lines of PHP to "do something" with the results submitted from the form.

We'll see more complex examples of this as we go further.

There is a blurry edge between ChronoForms and the core Joomla! code. You might think of ChronoForms as a window into the core. You can use it "out of the box" to do quite a lot, or you can dig deeper and do "almost anything". How far you go really is up to you—your needs, knowledge, and experience.

There's more...

We chose to use radio buttons here because they are visually clear and straightforward. If you have more than a few "departments" then a drop-down may be a more useful interface. This will work just as well.

You could also keep the **To** field as well as the **Dynamic To**. Then the e-mail addresses will both end up in the e-mail **To** field, so the administrator will get every e-mail and each will also go to the selected department.

> You'd probably want to remove the default e-mail in this case so that the administrator doesn't get two copies.

See also

- *Chapter 12, Adding Advanced Features* looks at how you can enable and disable whole Email Setups in a similar way.

Attaching uploaded files to the e-mail

We'll be seeing later on in *Chapter 8, Uploading Files from your Forms* how to add file inputs to your forms and handle the files after the form is submitted. Here we are going to anticipate that and look at how to add an uploaded file to an e-mail.

Getting ready

Any form with a file input and an Email Setup will work.

E-mailing Form Results

How to do it...

1. Open the Email Setup by clicking the **Setup Emails** tab for the form and in the **Email Properties** box and set **Enable Attachments** to **Yes** (actually that's the default setting so you probably won't have to do anything).

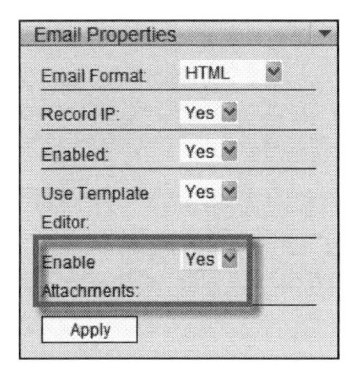

2. Test the form.

That's it!

See also

▶ Chapter 8, *Uploading Files From your Forms* is where we talk about uploading files from your forms. See the first recipe in that chapter to add a file input to your form.

Attaching a "standard" file to the e-mail

In the preceding recipe, we saw how to attach a file uploaded by the user, here we'll look at the similar task of attaching a file to an e-mail sent to the user. This time the file is not uploaded but is in a folder on the server somewhere.

Very often these are "terms and conditions" that you want to send out but we'll stay with the Newsletter theme and assume that we have a sample newsletter in a PDF file.

Getting ready

We'll be using the same form but this time, please make sure that the User Email Setup is enabled. You can also disable the administrator Email Setup if you like; we won't need it for this recipe.

> You can enable or disable an Email Setup in the **Email Properties** box for the setup. Set the **Enabled** drop-down to **YES** or **NO** and click **Apply**.

You'll also need a file to attach. We'll use a file called `newsletter.pdf` that's been uploaded to the site with the site Media Manager into the `root/images` folder (that's the default folder for the Media Manager).

How to do it...

1. ChronoForms doesn't have a box that you can fill in to do this so we need to add some code to the **OnSubmit Before** box in the Form Editor.

   > If you already have code in the box – we added some in a previous recipe – that's fine. This code block can go before (or after) that one in the box.

   ChronoForms adds the form attachments to a `$attachments` array and we are going to add an extra entry to that. The code is short, once you know what it is:

   ```php
   <?php
   $form_id = $MyForm->formrow->id;
   $MyUploads =& CFUploads::getInstance($form_id);
   $MyUploads->attachments[] = 'images'.DS.'newsletter.pdf';
   ?>
   ```

   Taking this line by line:

   - `$form_id = $MyForm->formrow->id;`

   This gets the form ID, the entry you see in the first column of the Forms Manager. This is the internal identifier for the form and must be unique.

   - `$MyUploads =& CFUploads::getInstance($form_id);`

   This gets a copy of a ChronoForms object that holds the uploads information for this form. In this case it's empty but if there had been files uploaded for the form, the information about them would be temporarily stored here.

   - `$MyUploads->attachments[] = 'images'.DS.'newsletter.pdf';`

   This adds a new "upload" entry to the **ChronoForms Uploads Object**, though in this case it's not an upload but our static file. ChronoForms isn't fussy and will quite happily accept this.

E-mailing Form Results

> Note that the path uses .DS. instead of / or \, because the **Default Separator** (**DS**) can vary depending on the server Joomla! adopts this more flexible version. We've used the partial path here `'images'.DS.'newsletter.pdf'`, to be a bit more thorough we could have added the fuller `JPATH_ROOT.DS.'images'.DS.'newsletter.pdf'`.

With those three lines in place ChronoForms will attach the sample newsletter file to each e-mail that it sends out.

> Note that if you have more than one e-mail setup then the file will be attached to both of them unless you disable attachments on one or the other. At the moment, there is no way of having two Email Setups with different file attachments (though it could be achieved by hand coding an e-mail setup).

How it works...

ChronoForms has built-in code to attach an uploaded file to an e-mail. We are hijacking that code to get it to send the standard file.

As we go on to more complex recipes we will quite often come back to this idea of "adopting and adapting" the standard features of ChronoForms.

See also

Creating a "dynamic" subject line using info from the form

Here's one more "hijacking" example to end this chapter. ChronoForms gives you two choices for your e-mail subject—either a fixed phrase using the "subject" element in the Email Setup, or a value returned from the form using the "dynamic subject" element.

It's a frequent request to have a subject line that's a bit of each—a fixed text with a variable element. We can do this with another code snippet in the OnSubmit Before box.

Getting ready

We'll use the same form and alter the Admin Email Setup to include the value of the name field.

How to do it...

1. In the Form Editor go to the Email Setup by clicking on the **Setup Emails** tab and find the setup for the e-mail to the site administrator, delete the **Subject** element and drag in a **Dynamic Subject** instead.

2. Put `subject` (no quotes, no brackets) into the **Dynamic Subject** box, **Enable** the Email Setup, and **Apply** the changes in the **Email Properties** box.

3. Go to the **Form Code** tab and open the **OnSubmit Before email** box. Add this snippet to any code that's already there:

```php
<?php
$name = JRequest::getString('text_1', '' ,'post');
$subject = "New subscription from $name";
JRequest::setVar('subject', $subject);
?>
```

Line by line:

- `$name = JRequest::getString('text_1', '' ,'post');`

This gets the value of the name input from the form results (remember the input name was `'text_0'`) and assigns it to the `$name` variable.

- `$subject = "New subscription from $name";`

This inserts the value of `$name` into the string, so the value of `$subject` might be **New subscription from Jenny Smith**

- `JRequest::setVar('subject', $subject);`

This takes out new subject line and saves it into the `$_POST` array where the ChronoForms e-mailer can find it.

How it works...

This is a fundamental building block in working with ChronoForms—get a result from the form, alter it, and add it back into the results array so that the next step in the form processing will use the altered value.

3
Styling your Form

In this chapter, we will cover:

- Using ChronoForms default style
- Switching styles with "Transform Form"
- Adding your own CSS styling
- Putting several inputs in one line
- Adding your own HTML

Introduction

Styling forms is more a subject for a book on Joomla! templating, but as not all templates handle it very well, ChronoForms has some basic formatting capabilities that we will look at here.

We'll look at two areas—applying CSS to change the "look and feel" of a form and some simple layout changes that may be helpful.

We'll be assuming here that you have some knowledge of both CSS and HTML.

Using ChronoForms default style

ChronoForms recognizes that many Joomla! templates are not strong in their provision of form styling, so it offers some default styling that you can apply (or not) and edit to suit your needs.

Styling your Form

Getting ready

It might be helpful to have a form to look at. Try creating a test form using the ChronoForms Wizard to add "one of each" of the main inputs to a new form and then save it.

How to do it...

Each of the five steps here describes a different way to style your forms. You can choose the one (or more) that best meets your needs:

1. When you create a form with the Wizard, ChronoForms does three things:
   - Adds some `<div>` tags to the form HTML to give basic structure
   - Adds classes to the `<div>` tags and to the input tags to allow CSS styling
   - Loads some default CSS that uses the classes to give the form a presentable layout

   If you look at the Form HTML created by the Wizard you will see something like this (this is a basic text input):

   ```
   <div class="form_item">
     <div class="form_element cf_textbox">
       <label class="cf_label" style="width: 150px;">
           Click Me to Edit</label>
       <input class="cf_inputbox" maxlength="150" size="30"
           title="" id="text_2" name="text_2" type="text" />
     </div>
     <div class="cfclear"> </div>
   </div>
   ```

   > This example uses the default values from the Wizard. The label text, size, and name may have been changed in the Wizard Properties box.

   There is a wrapper `<div>` with a class of `form_item`. Then, there is a second wrapper around the `<label>` and `<input>` tags with two classes—`form_element` and `cf_textbox`.

   There are the `<label>` and `<input>` tags themselves with classes of `cf_label` and `cf_inputbox` respectively.

Chapter 3

And lastly there is an "empty" `<div>` with a class of `cfclear` that is used to end any CSS floats used in styling the previous tags.

The coding for other types of input is very similar, and usually the only difference is the class of the input tag and the `<div>` tag wrapped around the label and the input.

There is nothing very special about any of this; it provides a basic framework for styling.

> You can't change the default styling used by the Wizard but you can use your own HTML, or edit the Form HTML created by the Wizard. If you change the class names or override the ChronoForms CSS styling with your own styles, then the ChronoForms CSS will no longer apply.

Here's what the test form looks like with the default ChronoForms styling:

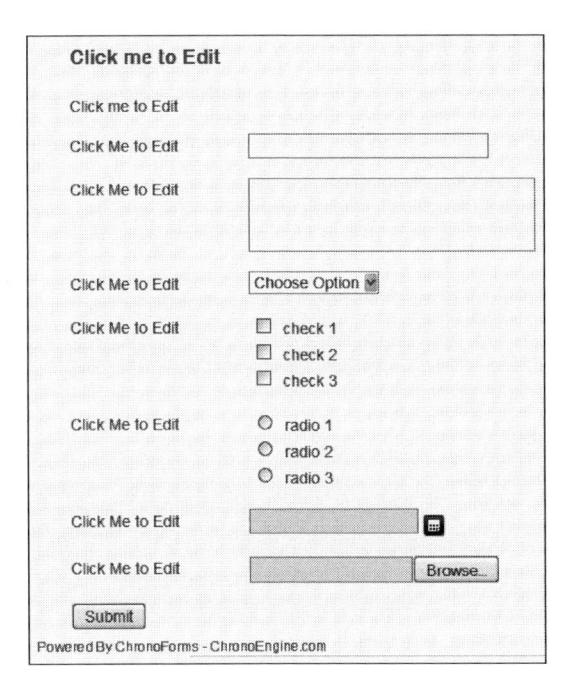

Styling your Form

2. To see the effect of the ChronoForms CSS, open the form in the Form Editor. Go to the **General** tab, open **Core/View Form Settings,** and change **Load Chronoforms CSS/JS Files** to **No**.

   Save the form and refresh the front-end view. Here is the same form without the ChronoForms CSS styling loaded. Not so pretty, but still fully functional.

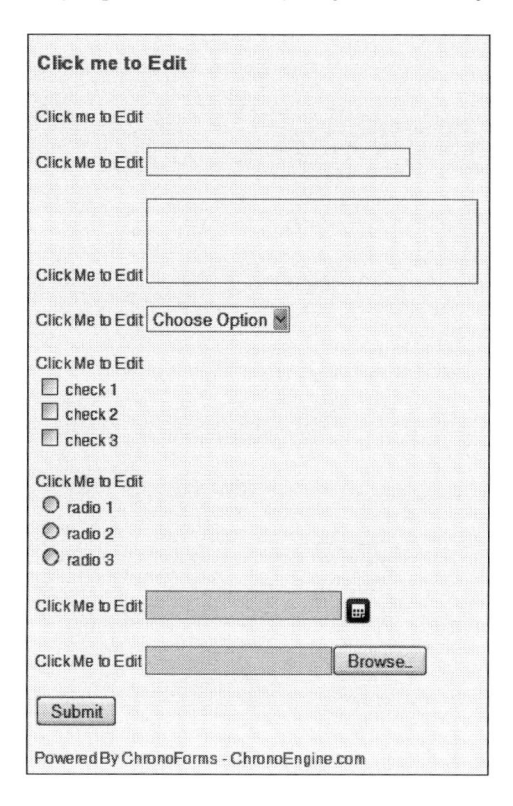

> Note: If you create your form in the Form Editor rather than the Wizard, the default setting for **Load Chronoforms CSS/JS Files** is **No.** So, you need to turn it on if you want to use the default styling.

See also

- Chapter 8, *Uploading Files from your Forms* in particular the *Moving a form with CSS* section
- W3Schools CSS tutorials and references at `http://www.w3schools.com/css/default.asp` provide a useful online introduction to CSS

Chapter 3

Switching styles with "Transform Form"

The ChronoForms default styling doesn't always suit. So, ChronoForms provides a basic form theming capability. There are only two themes provided—"default" and "theme1".

Getting ready

We're using the same form as in the previous recipe.

How to do it...

1. In the Forms Manager, check the box next to your form name and then click the **Transform Form** icon in the toolbar.

   You will see a warning that using Transform Form will overwrite any manual changes to the Form HTML and two form images—one for the "default" theme and one for "theme1".

   There's a radio button under each theme, and **Preview** and **Transform & Save** buttons at the bottom left.

   The **Preview** button allows you to see your form with the theme applied. This will not overwrite manual changes; **Transform & Save** will!

   > Warning: Using **Transform & Save** will recreate the Form HTML from the version that ChronoForms has saved in the database table. Any manual changes that you have made to the Form HTML will be lost.

2. Applying "theme1" changes the Form HTML structure significantly. Select the "theme1" radio button and click the **Preview** button to see the result.

   You can't see this from the preview screen but here's what the text input block now looks like:

   ```
   <div class="cf_item">
     <h3 class="cf_title" style="width: 150px;">
       Click Me to Edit</h3>
     <div class="cf_fields">
       <input name="text_2" type="text" value=""
   ```

```
            title="" class="cf_inputtext cf_inputbox"
            maxlength="150" size="30" id="text_2" />
        <br />
        <label class="cf_botLabel"></label>
    </div>
</div>
```

The wrapping `<div>` tags and the input are still the same; the old label is now an `<h3>` tag and there's a new `<label>` after the input with a `cf_botlabel` class. The `<div>` with the `cfclear` class has gone.

This theme may work better with forms that need narrower layouts or where the `cfclear` `<div>` tags cause large breaks in the form layout.

> Neither theme creates a very accessible form layout, and "theme1" is rather less accessible than the "default" theme. If this is important for you then you can create your own form theme.

How it works...

A ChronoForms theme has two parts—a PHP file that defines the form elements and a CSS file that sets the styling. The Transform Form gets the "Wizard" version of your form that is saved in the database, and regenerates the form HTML using the element structures from the PHP file. When the file is loaded, the theme CSS file will be loaded instead of the default ChronoForms CSS.

See also

- The article "Accessible Forms using WCAG 2.0" (http://www.usability.com.au/resources/wcag2/) is a practical introduction to the topic of web form accessibility.

Adding your own CSS styling

Many users will want to add their own styling to their forms. This is a short guide about ways to do that. It's not a guide to create the CSS.

> To add your own Form CSS, you will need to have a working knowledge of HTML and CSS.

Getting ready

You need nothing to follow the recipe, but when you come to it out, you'll need CSS and a form or two.

How to do it...

1. Adding CSS directly in the Form HTML:

   The quickest and least desirable way of styling is to add CSS directly to the Form HTML. The HTML is accessible on the **Form Code** tab in the Form Editor. You can type directly into the text area. For example:

   ```
   <input name="text_2" type="text" value=""
       title="" class="cf_inputtext cf_inputbox"
       maxlength="150" size="30" id="text_2"
       style="border: 1px solid blue;" />
   ```

   The only time when you might need to use this approach is to mark one or two inputs in some special way. Even then it might be better to use a class and define the style outside the Form HTML.

2. Using the Form CSS styles box:

   In the **Form Code** tab, ChronoForms has a **CSS Styles** box, which is opened by clicking the **[+/-]** link beside **CSS Styles**. You can add valid CSS definitions in this box (without `<style>` or `</style>` tags) and the CSS will be included in the page when it is loaded. For example, you could put this definition into the box:

   ```
   cf_inputbox {
      border: 1px solid blue;
   }
   ```

   This will add the following script snippet to the page. If you look at the page source for your form in the front-end you'll find it correctly loaded inside the `<head>` section.

   ```
   <style type="text/css">
   cf_inputbox {
      border: 1px solid blue;
   }
   </style>
   ```

3. Editing the ChronoForms default CSS:

   If you have **Load Chronoforms CSS/JS Files?** set to **Yes**, then ChronoForms will apply one of its themes, the default one unless you have picked another.

   The theme CSS files that are used in the front-end are in the `components/com_chronocontact/themes/{theme_name}/css/` folder. Usually there are three files in the folder.

   The `style1-ie6.css` file is loaded if the browser detected is IE6; `style1-ie7.css` is loaded as well for IE7 or IE8; `style1.css` is loaded for other browsers.

   If you edit the ChronoForms CSS, you may need to edit all three files.

   > Note: The themes are duplicated in the Administrator part of ChronoForms, but those files are used in the Transform Form page only.

4. Editing the template CSS:

   If you want to apply styling more broadly across your site then you may want to integrate the Form CSS with your template style sheets.

   This is entirely possible; the only thing to make sure of is that the classes in your Form HTML are reflected in the template CSS. You can either manually edit the Form HTML or add the ChronoForms classes to your template styles sheets.

   > Note that this is a much better approach than editing the ChronoForms theme CSS files. Upgrading ChronoForms could well overwrite the theme files. If you have the styles in your template's style sheets, this is not a problem.

5. Creating a new ChronoForms theme is a better solution than editing the default themes as it is protected against overwriting, and allows you to change the layout of the HTML elements in the form.

   The simplest way to do this is to copy one of the existing theme folders, rename the copy, and edit the files in the new folder.

   The CSS files are straightforward, but the `elements.php` file needs a little explanation. If you open the file in an editor, you will find a series of code blocks that define the way in which ChronoForms will structure each of the form elements in the Wizard. Here is an example of a text input:

```
<!--start_cf_textbox-->
<div class="form_item">
  <div class="form_element cf_textbox">
    <label class="cf_label"{cf_labeloptions}>{cf_labeltext}
    </label>
```

```
   <input class="{cf_class}" maxlength="{cf_maxlength}"
      size="{cf_size}" title="{cf_title}" id="{cf_id}"
      name="{cf_name}" type="{cf_type}" />
   {cf_tooltip}
   </div>
   <div class="cfclear"> </div>
</div>
<!--end_cf_textbox-->
```

The comment lines at the beginning and end mark out this element and must be left intact.

Between the comment lines you may add any valid HTML body tags that you like, except that the text input element must include `<input type='text' . . . />` and so on.

The entries in curly brackets, for example `{cf_labeltext}`, will be replaced by the corresponding values from the **Properties** box for this element in the Form Wizard. If they appear they must be exactly the same as the entries in the ChronoForms default theme.

Most of the time you will not need to create a new theme, but if you are building Joomla! applications, this provides a very flexible way of letting users create forms with a predetermined structure and style.

> Note that if you create a new theme, you need to ensure that the files are the same in both theme folders (`administrator/components/com_chronocontact/themes/` and `components/com_chronocontact/themes/`). Maybe a future version of ChronoForms will remove the duplication.

There's more...

Sometimes, you want to add "conditional" CSS, that is you want your styling to respond in some way to the information submitted on the form or to something else that changes from one session to another. The classic example we've already seen is to serve a different CSS file to users browsing with Internet Explorer.

Browser sniffing

Joomla! provides some code that can be used to detect the user's browser and we can adopt that to serve different files. First though, here is the basic code to load a CSS file from Joomla!:

```php
<?php
$doc =& JFactory::getDocument();
$doc->addStyleSheet('url_of_css_file');
?>
```

Inside the familiar `<?php . . .?>` tags we have two lines. The first of these gets us access to the Joomla! **Document Object**, which is a predefined group of variables and methods that Joomla! will use to build the final web page.

> The `=&` is important to make sure that we get access to the same object that Joomla! will use and don't create a new copy of our own.

The second line calls one of the Document Object methods to add a CSS file to the page. This file will be called from a CSS link placed in the page `<head>` tags. What you will see in the page source is:

```
<link href="url_of_css_file"
    rel="stylesheet" type="text/css" />
```

Now we need to find out what kind of browser is being used. Joomla! has a browser object for this, so we'll need to access that too:

```php
jimport('Joomla!.environment.browser');
$browser = JBrowser::getInstance();
```

This will get us an instance of the Joomla! browser object, We can get the browser type from this and set the CSS file to be loaded accordingly:

```php
if ( $browser->getBrowser() == 'msie' ) {
  $css_file = 'url_of_css_file_for_ie_browsers';
} else {
  $css_file = 'url_of_css_file_for_other_browsers';
}
```

> This example uses a PHP `if . . . else` to switch between IE and non-IE browsers; we could use a PHP "switch" statement to distinguish between several different groups of browsers. There is also browser version information available in the Joomla! browser object so, for example, we could have different files for different IE versions.

Putting all this together, our code snippet looks like this:

```php
<?php
jimport('Joomla!.environment.browser');
$browser = JBrowser::getInstance();
if ( $browser->getBrowser() == 'msie' ) {
  $css_file = 'url_of_css_file_for_ie_browsers';
} else {
  $css_file = 'url_of_css_file_for_other_browsers';
}
$doc =& JFactory::getDocument();
$doc->addStyleSheet($css_file);
?>
```

This code may look a bit cryptic at first glance, but broken down into small chunks it should make sense and will introduce you to some of the richer features of Joomla!.

Conditional CSS

Let's assume that our form is asking about babies and there is an input `boy_or_girl` that returns either "girl" or "boy". We want to display a pink or blue "thank you" message depending on the result.

Let's assume that in our thank-you HTML we have:

```
<div class='boy_or_girl'> . . . </div>
```

And we need to set the background color of this div. This will need a CSS snippet such as the following:

```
div.boy_or_girl {
  background-color: //color goes here
}
```

First, we need to get the value of the `boy_or_girl` field from the form:

```php
$boy_or_girl =
  JRequest::getString('boy_or_girl', 'boy', 'post');
```

Then we can use this to set the color:

```php
switch ($boy_or_girl ) {
  case 'boy':
  default:
    $color = '#8888FF';
  break;
  case 'girl':
    $color = '#FF8888';
  break;
}
```

Styling your Form

> We've used a "switch" statement to show its use; an `if . . . else` would have worked equally well.
>
> We also added a default case to our switch statement. It is always good programming practice to have a default in case the input is not one of the values that we were expecting.

We insert this color into a style snippet:

```
$style = "
div.boy_or_girl {
   background-color: $color ;
}
";
```

And insert into the page using the Joomla! document object again:

```
$doc->addStyleDeclaration($style);
```

Putting it all together, we get the following code snippet, which will go into the **OnSubmit After** code box so that it displays after the form is submitted:

```
<?php
$boy_or_girl =
   JRequest::getString('boy_or_girl', 'boy', 'post');

switch ($boy_or_girl ) {
  case 'boy':
  default:
     $color = '#8888FF';
  break;
  case 'girl':
     $color = '#FF8888';
  break;
}

$style = "
div.boy_or_girl {
   background-color: $color ;
}
";
$doc =& JFactory::getDocument();
$doc->addStyleDeclaration($style);
?>
<div class='boy_or_girl'> . . . </div>
```

Chapter 3

Putting several inputs in one line

The HTML produced by the ChronoForms Form Wizard puts each field into a single column. This works well for short forms but may not always be useful for longer or more complex forms. We'll see later how you can add your own HTML. Here, we'll look at one small way that ChronoForms can help.

Getting ready

We'll work with a form that has three short text fields intended to input a date (day, month, and year). Created with the Wizard it looks like this:

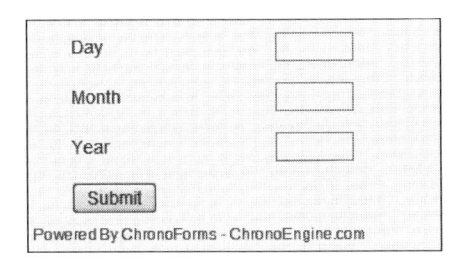

How to do it...

1. Open the form again with Wizard Edit then drag a **MultiHolder** into the workspace.

   > The MultiHolder needs to go after the elements that are to be placed into it.

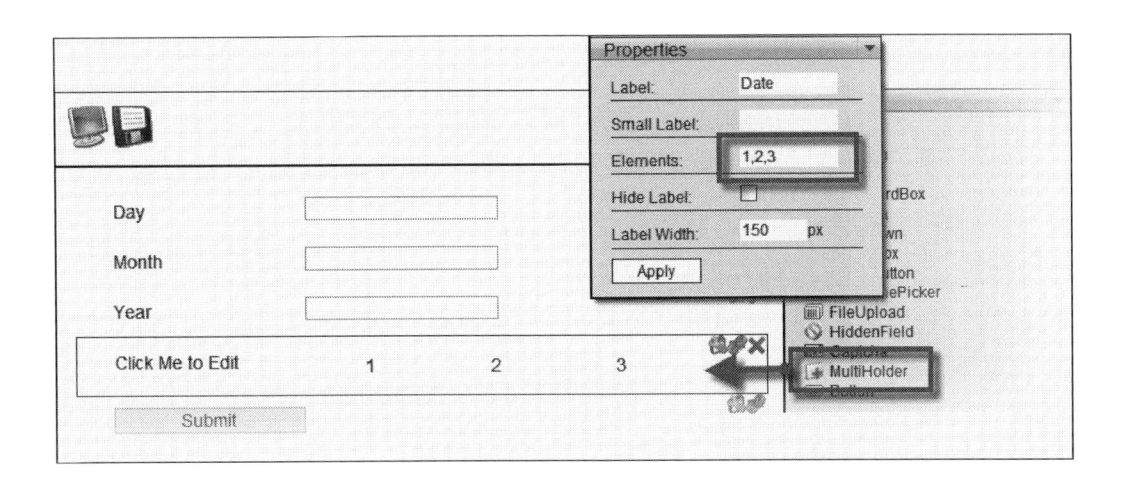

75

Styling your Form

2. In the **Properties** for the **MultiHolder** is an **Elements** box. You enter the numbers of the elements that you want to include in the MultiHolder here. Unfortunately, ChronoForms doesn't give you any easy way of finding out what these numbers are. They are the order in which elements were added, starting with 1, so a little trial and error is sometimes required.

3. Once the MultiHolder is applied, the form looks like this:

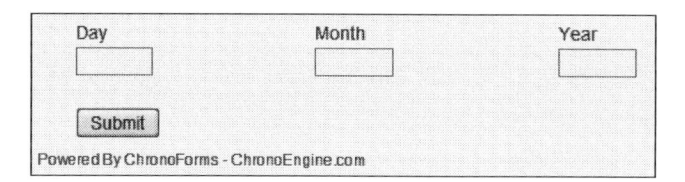

> Here we've used the **Hide Label** checkbox in the **Properties** box of the MultiHolder element to hide the **Click Me to Edit** text in the displayed form.

4. This is still not ideal but with a little more tweaking of the code and styling this can be very useful.

Adding your own HTML

The ultimate in form layout is to hand-craft your own HTML one way or another. We'll be looking at that in more detail in *Chapter 9, Writing Form HTML*. Here we'll just look at a quick way to change the layout.

> In order to add your own Form HTML, you will need to have a working knowledge of HTML and CSS.

Getting ready

You can start with any form created with the ChronoForms Wizard.

How to do it...

1. The Wizard is an easy way of getting the key form elements into your Form HTML and being reasonably sure that they will work with ChronoForms. But, as we've seen, it brings with it quite a lot of "framework" HTML that gives the ChronoForms its look and feel, but may not be what you want.

   So, you can strip away everything but the core HTML and rebuild your own framework around it. Here, we'll switch the date form in the previous recipe to use an HTML table.

   > HTML tables are anathema to purist coders but they have their practical uses and sometimes they are the easiest way to lay out complex forms.

   After we created the form from the Wizard (before using the MultiHolder), the code for each of the three input boxes looked like this:

   ```
   <div class="form_item">
     <div class="form_element cf_textbox">
       <label class="cf_label" style="width: 150px;">Day</label>
       <input class="cf_inputbox" maxlength="4" size="4" title=""
           id="text_0" name="text_0" type="text" />
     </div>
     <div class="cfclear"> </div>
   </div>
   ```

   The key line in here is the `<input>` tag:

   ```
   <input class="cf_inputbox" maxlength="4" size="4" title=""
       id="text_0" name="text_0" type="text" />
   ```

   That is the core code, we can throw the rest away.

2. If we use a table with four columns then we can neatly accommodate our three inputs:

   ```
   <table>
     <tr>
       <td>
         <label class="cf_label" style="width:150px;" >
           Date</label>
       </td>
       <td>
         <input class="cf_inputbox" maxlength="4" size="4"
             title="" id="text_0" name="text_0" type="text" />
       </td>
   ```

Styling your Form

```
      <td>
        <input class="cf_inputbox" maxlength="4" size="4"
          title="" id="text_1" name="text_1" type="text" />
      </td>
      <td>
        <input class="cf_inputbox" maxlength="4" size="4"
          title="" id="text_2" name="text_2" type="text" />
      </td>
    </tr>
</table>
```

The end result is a neatly formatted section of a form.

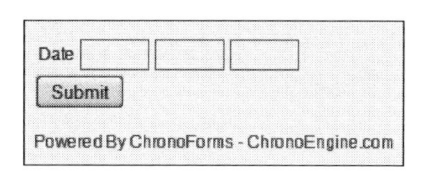

3. Clearly, this is a simple example. Add in a few text inputs, a couple of text areas, and a drop-down or two, and there has to be some careful tuning of the code to keep it looking good.

   The message to take from here is that you don't need to stick with ChronoForms code, except for the core tags.

> In practice, ChronoForms will work with almost any legal HTML. The key things to remember are:
>
> (a) That names are required and can only contain `a-z`, `A-Z`, `0-9`, and underscore '`_`'. No dashes, spaces, or other special characters.
>
> (b) `id` attributes are highly desirable if you want to use JavaScript with your form. The same naming rules apply plus `id` attributes must be unique in the page.
>
> (c) The input `type` attribute is required.

See also

- *Chapter 9, Writing Form HTML* looks at more ways that you can add Form HTML—from existing forms or from Dreamweaver or a similar HTML editor.

4
Saving Form Data in the Database

In this chapter, we will cover:

- Creating a table to save your results and linking your form to it
- Updating and changing DB Connections
- Viewing your saved form results
- Exporting your results to Excel or a CSV file

Introduction

E-mailing the form results gets us so far, but there soon comes a time when that isn't enough. We need to record the information in a more organised and accessible way.

Joomla! runs on a database and provides us with the framework to access it, so we can save our form data there too.

As we found with e-mails, ChronoForms also provides both a set of basic tools and the opportunity for more advanced and complex processing.

In this chapter, we'll explore the basic tool set. The advanced tools will increasingly show up in the later recipes.

Saving Form Data in the Database

Creating a table to save your results and linking your form to it

This recipe is the basic building block of connecting your form to a table in the database. A few quick definitions and explanations may be helpful before we start.

Joomla! almost always uses a database engine called MySQL, and the language that we use to give instructions (often called "queries") to the database engine is MySQL, or sometimes just SQL for short (though technically SQL is something a little different). A typical MySQL query looks something like this:

```
SELECT `column_1`, `column-2` FROM `table_name` WHERE `column_1` = 'some_value';.
```

The MySQL engine is capable of running many databases; Joomla! typically uses just one—sometimes called a **schema**, and this database has many **tables**. A default Joomla! installation has around 36 tables, and each extension that you install will add more.

A useful way to think of a table is as a grid of rows and columns; each row is one record in the database, and each column is a field in the record. Here we'll usually call them **records** and **columns**.

When we save data from a form to the database each input from the form will match up to a column, and each time the form is submitted, it will create a new record in the table.

Getting ready

We're going to use the same newsletter subscription form as we had in the earlier recipes. The form is called `newsletter_signup`.

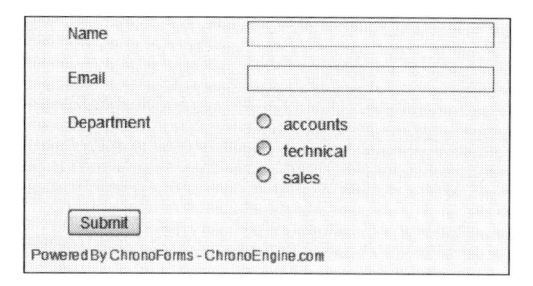

How to do it...

This is a three-step process. We're going to make some changes to the Form HTML to help us identify the data in the database, then create a database table from the form, and lastly, link the form to the new table.

1. Here's how we go about improving the Form HTML.

   Here are the key lines from the Form HTML (here, all of the `<div>` tags that are used for display have been removed, but this doesn't affect the data):

   ```
   <input class="cf_inputbox" maxlength="150" size="30"
      title="" id="text_1" name="text_1" type="text" />
   <input class="cf_inputbox" maxlength="150" size="30"
      title="" id="text_0" name="text_0" type="text" />

   <input value="accounts" title="" class="radio" id="radio00"
      name="radio0" type="radio" />
   <input value="technical" title="" class="radio" id="radio01"
      name="radio0" type="radio" />
   <input value="sales" title="" class="radio" id="radio02"
      name="radio0" type="radio" />

   <input value="Submit" name="button_1" type="submit" />
   ```

   You can see that we have two `text` inputs, then a group of three `radio` inputs, and lastly a `submit` input.

   Now, we could continue and work with this code exactly as it is, and if you just need to create a "quick and dirty" form to meet a short-term need, then that is exactly what you should do.

   We are going to take a little more time and tidy this code up a bit to make our lives easier down the road. Specifically, we're going to give the inputs more meaningful names. We are going to call the name input `name`, the e-mail one `email`, the radio buttons become `dept`, and the submit button is `submit`. These names will become the column names in our database table and it will be much easier to understand what `email` is than `text_0`.

   Here's the edited version; if you are keeping the `<div>` tags then they can stay unchanged.

   > Technically the `<label>` tags could take a `for='input_name'` attribute that would also change, but ChronoForms doesn't create those for you.

   ```
   <input class="cf_inputbox" maxlength="150" size="30"
      title="" id="name" name="name" type="text" />
   <input class="cf_inputbox" maxlength="150" size="30"
      title="" id="email" name="email" type="text" />
   ```

Saving Form Data in the Database

```
<input value="accounts" title="" class="radio" id="dept0"
  name="dept" type="radio" />
<input value="technical" title="" class="radio" id="dept1"
  name="dept" type="radio" />
<input value="sales" title="" class="radio" id="dept2"
  name="dept" type="radio" />

<input value="Submit" name="submit" type="submit" />
```

Here are a few things to keep in mind:

- We've used all lowercase names, for example, `name` and not `Name`. You are allowed to use capitals in names but they are a possible source of confusion so the better policy is to stay with all lowercase.
- We've used `email` and not `e-mail`. Dashes cause problems in MySQL column names (and with JavaScript) so it's best to develop a habit of avoiding them completely.
- The three radio buttons have the same name `dept` but different IDs—`dept1`, `dept2`, `dept3`. The name is used to return the value from the form and a group of radio buttons that share a name will only return one value (when you select one button the others are automatically unselected). The IDs are used to uniquely identify the input so they can't be the same.

That's it; save the form and return to the Forms Manager.

2. Next, we are going to create the database table:

   Check the box next to the form name and then click the **Create Table** icon in the toolbar. You'll get a new dialogue page like the following:

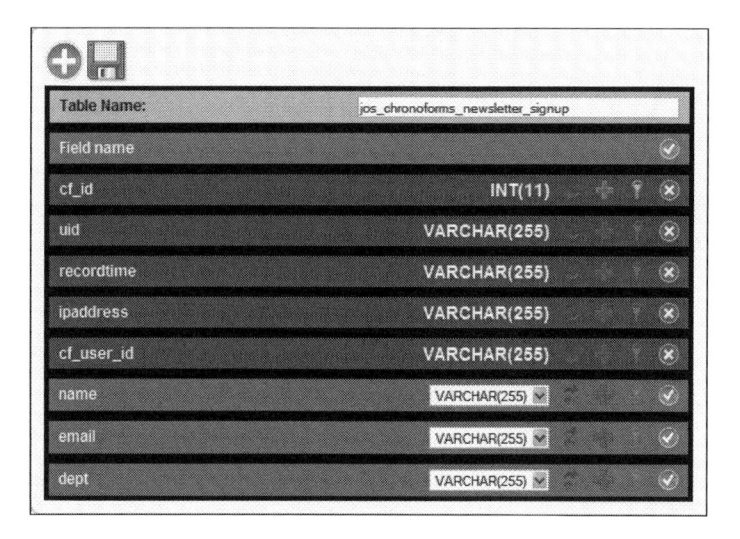

Table Name:	jos_chronoforms_newsletter_signup
Field name	
cf_id	INT(11)
uid	VARCHAR(255)
recordtime	VARCHAR(255)
ipaddress	VARCHAR(255)
cf_user_id	VARCHAR(255)
name	VARCHAR(255)
email	VARCHAR(255)
dept	VARCHAR(255)

Before starting to explain this dialogue, it's fair to say that it is not one of the ChronoForms' best and may change in some small but important details in future releases.

Note that there are two icons at the top. Also, there are two blue bars, five green ones, and then a group of red bars—three here, but that will vary with your form.

> ChronoForms reads your Form HTML and tries to find out the names that have been used for the `<input . . . >` tags in the form. If none of them appear or some are missing, then check your Form HTML to make sure that the inputs have valid names.

The green **+** icon at the top left allows you to add a new column to the table. Sometimes this is useful if, for example, you are creating a table from one step of a multi-page form.

The `disk` icon will save the table.

The first bar, labelled **Table name**, is the table name suggested by ChronoForms, and we can leave it unchanged as `newsletter_signup`. If you do change it, then make sure you leave the `jos_` prefix in place as Joomla! uses it to identify tables for this site.

The second blue bar, labelled **Field name**, is useful. At present the red bars are *not selected* and if you save now, they will not be included in the table. Click the "tick" icon in this bar to select all of the bars; you will almost always want to do this.

> The interface here is poorly designed in this ChronoForms release and users often go by the icon to the right of the bar. This shows the "action" from clicking the bar; the bar color shows the current "status".

The green bars are a block of standard entries that ChronoForms adds to the table. Mostly they are useful and we can leave them alone (see the *There's More...* section for more information on these bars).

The red bars at the bottom have the names of the three inputs from our form (ChronoForms has helpfully left out the `submit` input).

We want all three fields included in the table so go up and click on the "tick" icon to the right of the blue **Field name** bar. All of the bars will turn green. You can use this "action" icon to change the status of all the bars, or the icons on the individual bars to turn them on and off.

Saving Form Data in the Database

In each of the three bars that link to our field inputs, there is a drop-down that is pre-set to **varchar(255)**. This will tell MySQL the kind of data we expect to have in this column.

> VARCHAR is short for variable character, and basically describes a field that will be used for storing text entries of variable length—up to maximum of 255 characters in this case.

Although 255 characters is much longer than we need, we can accept the default entries here.

Double-check that all the bars are green and then click the "disk" icon to create the table. You will be returned to the Forms Manager and a systems message tells you that "Table has been created successfully".

3. Now we can link the form to the database table:

    Click the Form Name link to open the Form Editor and open the **DB Connection** tab.

    Near the top you'll see a select drop-down to **Enable Data storage**—set this to **Yes**. There's a second select box with a scroll bar containing a list of table names—select the name of our new table in here, here it is `jos_chronoforms_newsletter_signup`.

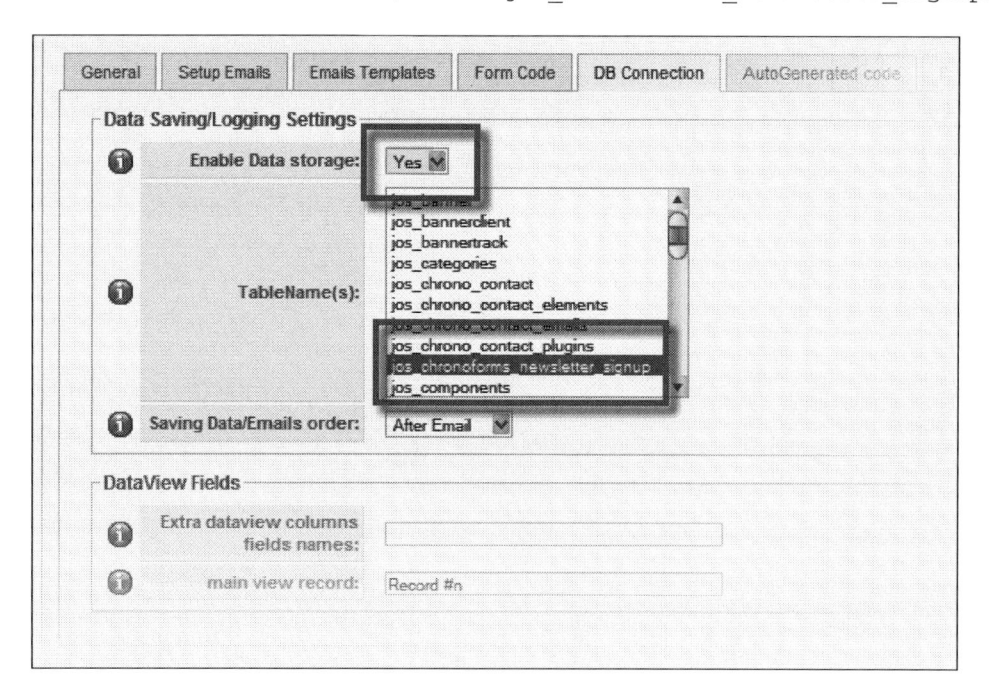

You can leave the other settings unchanged. Save the form and return to the Forms Manager.

The form is now "connected" to the database table and every time it is submitted, a new record will be created. Look toward the right of the Forms Manager and you'll see a new link entry in the **Tables Connected** column.

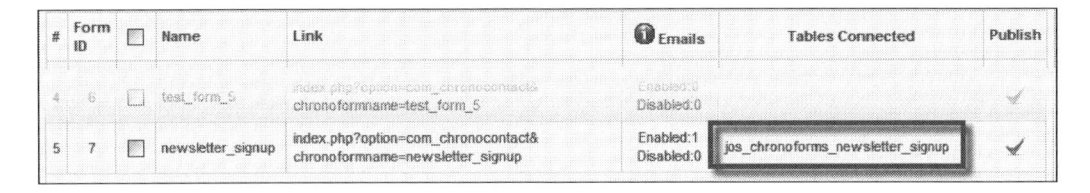

#	Form ID		Name	Link	Emails	Tables Connected	Publish
4	6	☐	test_form_5	index.php?option=com_chronocontact&chronoformname=test_form_5	Enabled:0 Disabled:0		✓
5	7	☐	newsletter_signup	index.php?option=com_chronocontact&chronoformname=newsletter_signup	Enabled:1 Disabled:0	jos_chronoforms_newsletter_signup	✓

4. Before we finish, we need to check that it works:

   Open the form in your browser and submit it a couple of times.

   > While testing, it is sometimes useful to set **Email the results?** to **No** in the Form General Tab. Note that this has the side-effect of preventing any "OnSubmit Before" code from running.

   When you submit the form nothing tells you if the data has been saved or not; this is a back-end function that is invisible to the front-end user. To see the results go to the next recipe—*View your saved form results*.

How it works...

Behind the scenes this is one of the more complex parts of ChronoForms. And correspondingly it is one of the most powerful; we've only just touched the surface with this simple form.

> You can see on the **DB Connection** tab that there is a long list of all of the tables in the Joomla! database. You can connect a form to any of them, but you do so at your peril! Making inappropriate changes to Joomla! tables can stop your site working or destroy important data. Always back up first, or work on a test site, and do be sure that you understand what you are doing. If in doubt...don't, is a good rule to follow here.

When you create a DB Connection in ChronoForms, a couple of things happen:

- ChronoForms creates a PHP code snippet that describes the table and saves it in the database. This will be used to link the data from the form to the table. (Technically this code is an extension of the Joomla! "Table" class.)

Saving Form Data in the Database

- ChronoForms creates a second PHP snippet, also saved in the database. This one is visible in the Form Editor under the **Autogenerated Code** tab. (Click the **[+/-]** link to open the textarea.) This snippet creates the ChronoForms data to add to the form data and does the actual save into the database.

Here's the autogenerated code for our form (there are added comments and the order of a few lines has been changed for clarity):

```php
<?php
// get the settings info for this form
$MyForm =& CFChronoForm::getInstance("newsletter_signup");

// Check the DB Connection is set to 'Yes'
if ( $MyForm->formparams("dbconnection") == "Yes" ){

  // get the User info
  $user = JFactory::getUser();
  JRequest::setVar( "cf_user_id",
    JRequest::getVar( "cf_user_id", $user->id, "post",
                                                     "int", "" ));;

  // create the random uid string
  $row =&
    JTable::getInstance("chronoforms_newsletter_signup", "Table");
  srand((double)microtime()*10000);
  $inum    =    "I" . substr(base64_encode(md5(rand())), 0, 16)
    .md5(uniqid(mt_rand(), true));
  JRequest::setVar( "uid",
    JRequest::getVar( "uid", $inum, "post", "string", "" ));

  // get the current date and time
  JRequest::setVar( "recordtime",
    JRequest::getVar( "recordtime", date("Y-m-d")."
      - ".date("H:i:s"), "post", "string", "" ));

  // get the user's IP address
  JRequest::setVar( "ipaddress",
    JRequest::getVar( "ipaddress", $_SERVER["REMOTE_ADDR"], "post",
      "string", "" ));
```

```
    //get the information submitted in the form
    $post = JRequest::get( "post" , JREQUEST_ALLOWRAW );

    // link the data to the database table
    if (!$row->bind( $post )) {
      JError::raiseWarning(100, $row->getError());
    }

    // store the data in the database table
    if (!$row->store()) {
      JError::raiseWarning(100, $row->getError());
    }

    // save the results in a temporary object
    $MyForm->tablerow["jos_chronoforms_newsletter_signup"] = $row;
  }
  ?>
```

If you are familiar with this kind of code you'll notice that there is no MySQL query here to save the data. Instead ChronoForms takes advantage of some of the Joomla! Framework code that partially automates this process. The code `$row->bind($post)` links the data from the form `$post` to the information about the table that was saved in the database. Then `$row->store()` executes the code to save the linked data.

This approach has several advantages—ChronoForms doesn't have to construct a precise MySQL query for each save; only the input data from inputs with names that match column names are saved. In the right circumstances, it's possible to update an existing record in the table rather than create a new one.

> In previous releases of ChronoForms this code was editable, and that is why it is shown on the **Autogenerated Code** tab. You can still edit the text area, but any changes there will be lost when the form is saved, so it's a waste of time. Above the box it says **Hint: The data below is auto generated by ChronoForms and will be regenerated every time the form is saved, editing it is worthless.**
>
> There's more to come...

Using the options in Create Table

As mentioned earlier, we'll explain some more of these options in this section:

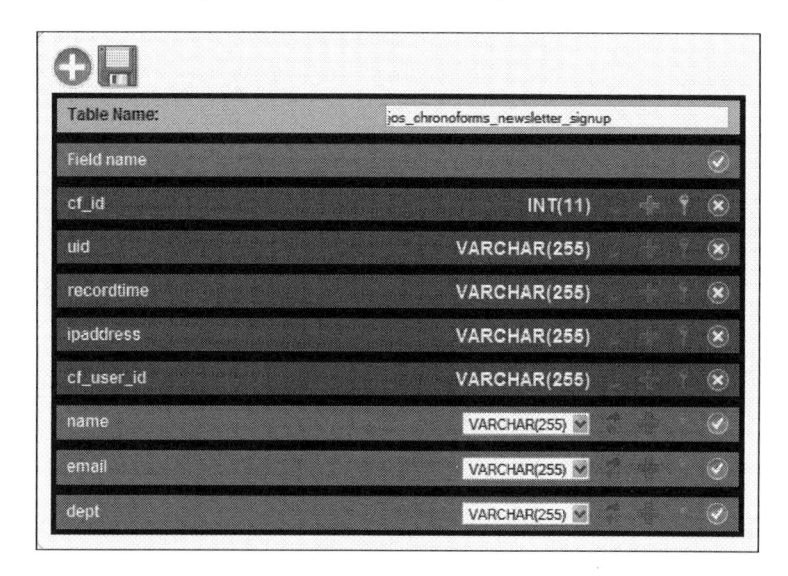

Each of the red and green bars has a group of four icons at the right end. These are:

- **Blue arrows**: These allow you to drag and drop the bars to change the order of the columns in the table. Usually this isn't terribly important but sometimes it's helpful to co-locate related fields.

- **Blue cross**: These make this field **auto-increment**. This only applies to integer fields and means that MySQL will automatically add one to the field value for each new record. Usually this is only used for record ID fields like `cf_id`, as you can see here.

- **Key**: These make this field the **primary key** for the table (there can only be one). That is the "main index" that will be used to identify records. Usually primary key records need to have unique values and the record id field is also the primary key.

- **Tick or cross**: These are the "action" icons for the bar—clicking the "cross" icon disables the bar; clicking the "tick" icon enables the bar. (Note: This is not consistent with the use of these icons elsewhere in Joomla! and may be changed in a future release of ChronoForms.)

The select drop-downs in the later rows show a long list of column types that you can specify for the table. The options here are—**VARCHAR(255), TINYINT, TEXT, DATE, SMALLINT, MEDIUMINT, INT(11), BIGINT, FLOAT, DOUBLE, DECIMAL, DATETIME, TIMESTAMP, TIME, YEAR, CHAR, TINYBLOB, TINYTEXT, BLOB, MEDIUMBLOB, MEDIUMTEXT, LONGBLOB, LONGTEXT, ENUM, SET, BIT, BOOL, BINARY, VARBINARY.**

You can look at the MySQL documentation at `http://dev.mysql.com/doc/` for the definitions of these. Most of them you will never need.

VARCHAR(255) is a good all purpose option; **DATETIME**, **DATE**, and so on are for date and time values; **TEXT** or **LONGTEXT** are good for `<textarea>` longer than 255 characters; the various **INT** options are for integer values; **BOOL** is for Boolean "yes/no" or "true/false" values.

While **VARCHAR** will usually work, it helps with data integrity and validation if you use a column type that matches your data. For example, if you have a field that should be an integer distance `VARCHAR` will happily accept `abcd` or `192km`; **INT** will not.

> Other values are possible in MySQL—you can, for example, specify **VARCHAR(16)** but the ChronoForms interface doesn't support these. If you need them, create the table with ChronoForms then fine tune the column definitions with another MySQL tool.

Checkbox groups and multi-select drop-downs

Most form inputs return a single value—a number, a text string, or a date. However, these two—**checkbox groups** and **multi-select drop-downs**—can return a list of values.

A checkbox group is a group of inputs with `type='checkbox'` and the same name. They are similar to the radio button group we used in this form; however, in a checkbox group more than one value can be selected.

A multi-select drop-down is a select drop-down where more than one value can be selected. The database table list on the **DB Connection** tab is an example.

These two kinds of inputs *must* be given array names—those are names ending in `[]` such as `table[]` or `dept[]`. If not, only the last value selected will be submitted from the form.

Unfortunately MySQL can't save arrays in the database table; they need to be converted back into strings first, so `array(item_1, item_2, item_3)` becomes `item_1, item_2, item_3`.

ChronoForms provides an option that will do that for you as far as it can. On the form **General** tab set, in the **Other Form Settings** area, set **ChronoForms handle my posted arrays** to **Yes** and this will work smoothly most of the time.

Saving Form Data in the Database

> ChronoForms converts the arrays to comma separated strings as in the example here. Sometimes this is not helpful. For instance, the popular Community Builder extension for Joomla! requires strings separated by `|*|` like `item_1|*|item_2|*|item_3`. At the moment, this has to be hand-coded by adding PHP to the ChronoForms **On Submit Before** box. Here's what the PHP might look like:
> ```
> <?php
> $select_0 = JRequest::getVar('select_0', '', 'post');
>  $select_0 = implode('|*|', $select_0);
>   JRequest::setVar('select_0', $select_0);
> ?>
> ```

See also

- In this recipe and in some of the earlier ones, we've referred to Joomla! code and Joomla! objects such as JUser and JTable. You can find detailed information about the Joomla! code in the Joomla! Official Documentation wiki at `http://docs.joomla.org/`. Use the search box in the left-hand column to look for information on a particular topic.

- For more experienced developers who are comfortable reading PHP there is also the Joomla! 1.5 API Reference at `http://api.joomla.org/`, which is a complete set of documentation extracted from the Joomla! code.

Viewing your saved form results

Once you have set up your form to save results in a database table you will want to look at them to see exactly what is being saved.

Getting ready

Save a few records from the newsletter with the DB Connection enabled that we created in the previous recipe.

Chapter 4

How to do it...

1. Go to the back-end Forms Manager view and click on the new link in the **Tables Connected** column to show the ChronoForms data viewer. This is a basic tool but is good enough for checking the data in simple forms.

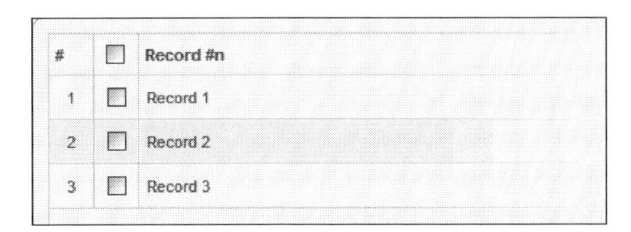

#		
#	☐	Record #n
1	☐	Record 1
2	☐	Record 2
3	☐	Record 3

2. Here you can see that three records have been saved in the table. Click **Record 1** to open it and you can see the details of that record.

Field name	Field Data
cf_id:	1
uid:	INTg0OGFkOTU5NTcwa05a2e7c070b213647c594fe5b80c241
recordtime:	2009-11-10 – 10:07:29
ipaddress:	192.168.1.4
cf_user_id:	0
name:	Tester 1
email:	tester_1@example.com
dept:	technical

The last three lines are the data that was entered in the form; the others are from the data that ChronoForms adds (if you leave those bars enabled when you create the table). They are:

- **cf_id**: The unique ID for the record in the table
- **uid**: A random string that ChronoForms uses for a little added security; sometimes it is useful to identify a record
- **recordtime**: The date and time the record was saved (this will use the site server clock)
- **ipaddress**: The IP address of the submitter if it is known
- **cf_user_if**: The Joomla! user ID of the submitter if they were logged in (the 0 here shows a guest user)

Saving Form Data in the Database

The ChronoForms data viewer only shows one record at a time, which isn't always useful. As you start working more with database tables and records you'll need a more versatile viewer.

- **PHPMyAdmin** is the most common tool and is usually provided by your ISP as part of the site hosting setup.
- **EasySQL** is a free Joomla! Administration Extension that allows you to view and work with database tables and records from the Site Admin. (The extension is—quite rightly—limited to SuperAdmin users only.)
- A personal preference is the free **Query Browser** from MySQL that is a part of their Administration Tools package. However, this will only work if the hosting site settings permit remote access to the database—some of the "cheaper" hosting packages don't include this feature.

> MySQL Query Browser is still available from the MySQL site but has now been replaced by the integrated set of tools in MySQL Workbench `http://dev.mysql.com/downloads/workbench/5.2.html`.

3. Here's the data table viewed in MySQL Query Browser so that you can see all of the records so far:

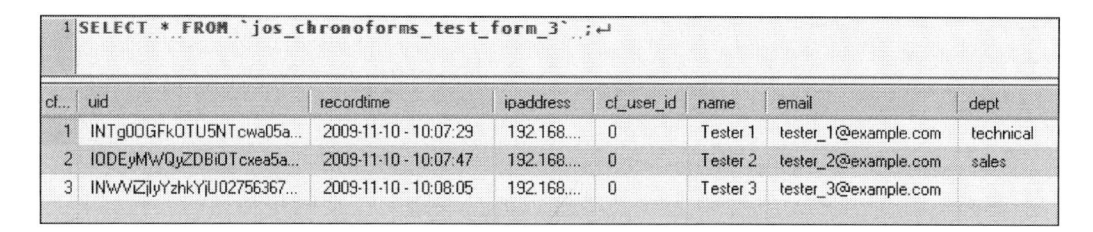

```
1 SELECT * FROM `jos_chronoforms_test_form_3`;
```

cf...	uid	recordtime	ipaddress	cf_user_id	name	email	dept
1	INTg00GFkOTU5NTcwa05a...	2009-11-10 - 10:07:29	192.168....	0	Tester 1	tester_1@example.com	technical
2	IODEyMWQyZDBiOTcxea5a...	2009-11-10 - 10:07:47	192.168....	0	Tester 2	tester_2@example.com	sales
3	INWViZjlyYzhkYjU02756367...	2009-11-10 - 10:08:05	192.168....	0	Tester 3	tester_3@example.com	

This layout shows you more clearly that we have the fields in "columns" and the data "records" in rows. You can also see the MySQL snippet used to create this report at the top of the image.

See also

- In *Chapter 11, Using Form Plugins*, the recipe *Showing and editing saved information using the Profile plug-in* talks about displaying a single database record in a form.
- ChronoConnectivity, a sister product to ChronoForms, can be used to display lists of records from a table to users though its use is beyond the scope of this book.

Updating and changing DB Connections

This is what usually happens—you get the form nicely set up and working when the client calls and says "Oh, just had a thought, can you add one more field in there?"

Here's how to do that.

Getting ready

Use any form with a DB Connection; we're going to use the newsletter form again. The request is to add a field for the client's location. Let's make it easy and just collect a two letter abbreviation for their state: AL = Alabama, AK = Alaska, and so on.

How to do it...

1. We've edited the form manually now so Wizard Edit will no longer work. Instead we can open the Form HTML box in the Form Editor and copy the block of text for the name field and re-paste the copy after the e-mail field.

2. We need to edit the copied block a little to handle the state code:

    ```
    <div class="form_item">
      <div class="form_element cf_textbox">
        <label class="cf_label" style="width: 150px;">
          State</label>
        <input class="cf_inputbox" maxlength="2" size="2"
          title="" id="state" name="state" type="text" />
      </div>
      <div class="cfclear"> </div>
    </div>
    ```

    We've changed the `name`, `id`, and the label text. We've also changed the settings for `maxlength='2'` and `size='2'` The `maxlength` attribute sets the maximum length of the result that can be typed into the input box. The `size` attribute sets the visible width of the input. This is often less than `maxlength`. In this case, we're setting both to two characters.

Saving Form Data in the Database

> In reality we'd probably use a select drop-down for the state list, as it pre-validates the codes that can be entered. We'll see an example of that kind of code later.

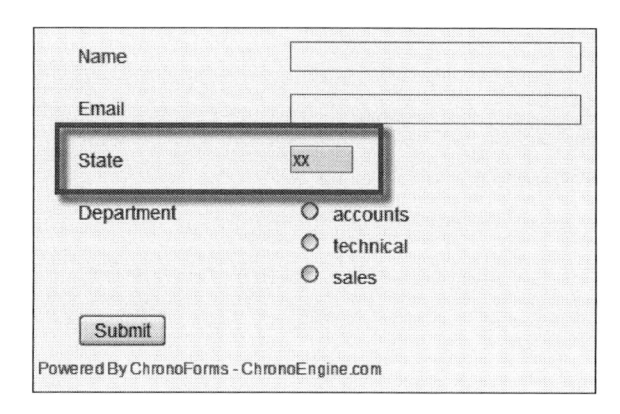

[Form image: Name, Email, State (xx) highlighted, Department with radio buttons (accounts, technical, sales), Submit button. Powered By ChronoForms - ChronoEngine.com]

That's the form part dealt with. Now we need to add a new field to the database table.

3. In the next step, we will be making changes to your site database. Please make a database backup before going any further.

> You can make a database backup with PHPMyAdmin or with the MySQL Workbench or you can use a specialized Joomla! extension like Akeeba Backup from `http://www.akeebabackup.com/`, which has replaced the older JoomPack extension.

4. Go to the Forms Manager and click the **Tables Manager** icon in the toolbar.

[Toolbar image: Delete, Transform Form, Wizard Edit, Create table, Tables Manager (highlighted), Backup Form, Backup Forms, Restore Form(s), Parameters]

This opens a new page with a list of all the tables in the Joomla! database each in a bar with three icons:

- A blue screen icon, to view the records in the table
- A yellow pencil icon, to edit the table
- A red "X" icon to delete the table

> **IMPORTANT**:
>
> Editing or deleting tables inappropriately can damage your site and/or delete site content. Act with great care!
>
> Please ensure that you have backed up your database before going any further.

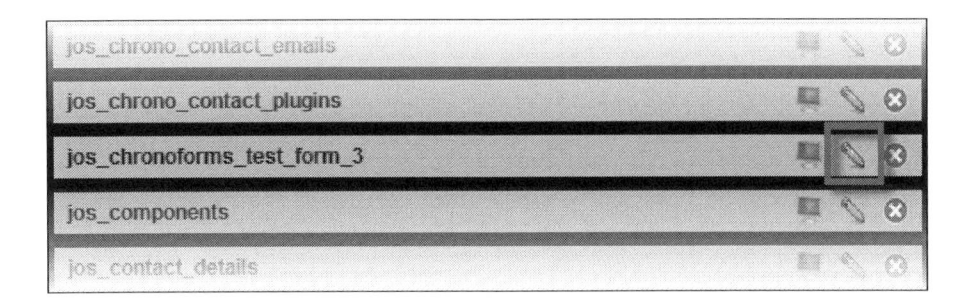

5. Choose the table that is connected to the form and click the "edit" icon. This will re-open the dialogue with the green and red bars that we used to create the table earlier.

6. To add a new column click the green "**+**" icon at the top of the table and a new bar will be created at the bottom of the dialogue. Enter the input name **state** and choose a column type of **TINYTEXT** from the select drop-down.

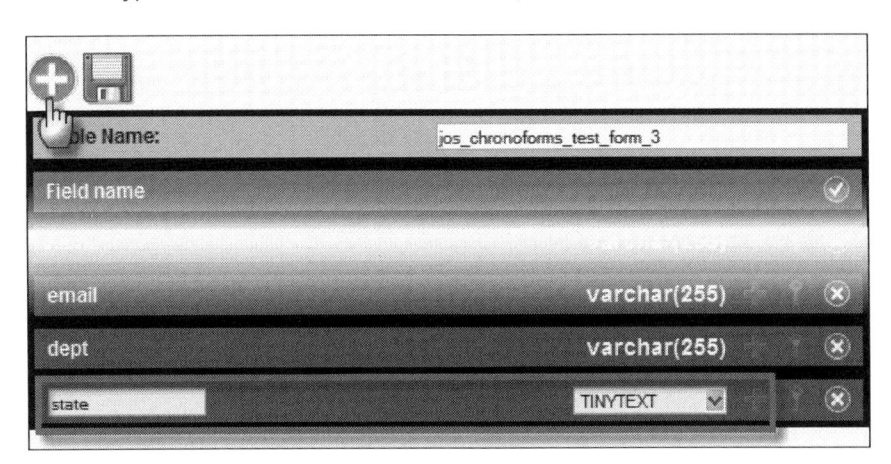

7. Click the "disk" icon to save the modified table.

8. There is one final step to this process; we need to refresh the information about the table that ChronoForms has stored with the form info in the database. There's no single button to do this and it's easily forgotten!

Saving Form Data in the Database

Open the form in the Form Editor and open the **DB Connection** tab. Set **Enable Data storage** to **No** and **Apply** the form to save it. Now re-open the **DB Connection** tab, change the setting back to **Yes** and save the form again. This forces ChronoForms to re-write the table information and the new field will now save correctly.

9. If we submit the form again and add an entry to the state field then this will save correctly to the database table.

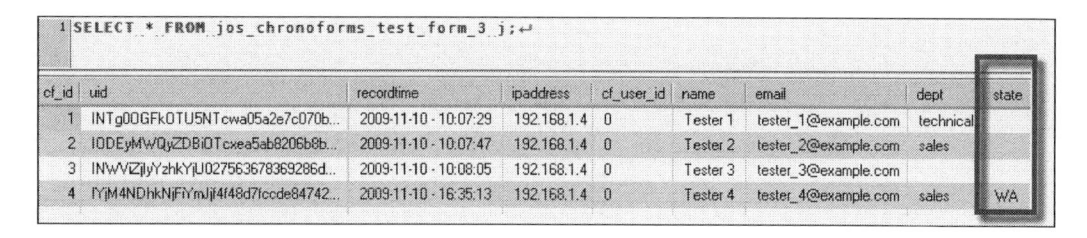

```
SELECT * FROM jos_chronoforms_test_form_3 j;
```

cf_id	uid	recordtime	ipaddress	cf_user_id	name	email	dept	state
1	INTg00GFkOTU5NTcwa05a2e7c070b...	2009-11-10 - 10:07:29	192.168.1.4	0	Tester 1	tester_1@example.com	technical	
2	IODEyMWQyZDBiOTcxea5ab8206b8b...	2009-11-10 - 10:07:47	192.168.1.4	0	Tester 2	tester_2@example.com	sales	
3	INwViZjlyYzhkYjU027563678369286d...	2009-11-10 - 10:08:05	192.168.1.4	0	Tester 3	tester_3@example.com		
4	IYjM4NDhkNjFiYmJjl4f48d7fccde84742...	2009-11-10 - 16:35:13	192.168.1.4	0	Tester 4	tester_4@example.com	sales	WA

There's more...

Removing an input

Deleting an input from a form is simpler. We can just remove or comment out the code from the Form HTML and leave the column in the database. Any future entries will either be empty or will take any default value that has been set.

If you want to remove a column from the database, then you can do that from **Tables Manager | Edit**. Note that any previously saved data for the deleted column will be lost.

Reordering columns

There's no easy way to do that in ChronoForms once the table has been created. You can do it in a MySQL editor if you really need to. See the MySQL documentation available from http://dev.mysql.com/doc/ for the necessary code.

Updating the e-mail template

We have covered this before but it's worth mentioning again here. If you add or remove an input you can either edit the template by hand, or you can force ChronoForms to recreate a default template by removing all text—including hidden HTML—from the template and saving the form.

Exporting your results to Excel or a CSV file

We've seen how to save the information from your forms in the MySQL database, but sometimes this isn't enough and you need to export the data from the table to a spreadsheet or to another database.

ChronoForms lets you export your data to either a CSV file or an Excel spreadsheet.

> The ChronoForms features are fairly simple and may not work with big tables or if you need to do any pre-processing of the data. There are other methods that you can use in these cases.

Getting ready

Any form that is connected to a database, and has at least a few records saved, will be fine to test this.

How to do it...

1. Open the ChronoForms Forms Manager and click the link in the **Tables Connected** column to open the Record Viewer. At the right end of the toolbar you'll see two icons—**Backup to Excel** and **Backup to CSV**.

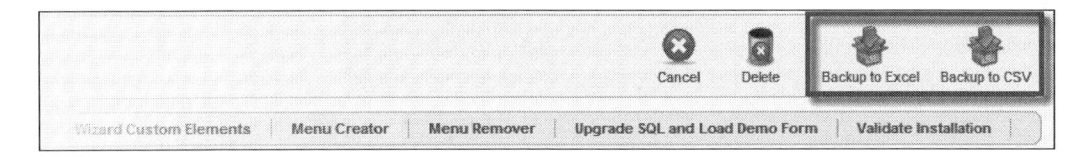

2. The standard browser download dialogue will open offering you the opportunity to either **Open** or **Save** the file. Usually **Save** is the better option to choose.

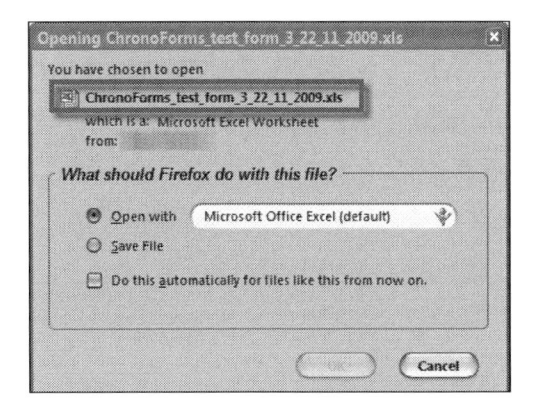

Saving Form Data in the Database

This is the result of clicking the **Backup to Excel** icon. Note that ChronoForms gives the file a longer name than we might expect. It has the format `ChronoForms_form_name_dd_mm_yyyy.xls`, which can be useful if you download more than one copy of the backup as it stops the later versions from over-writing the older ones.

3. Once you've saved the file, you can open it like any other spreadsheet file.

> There is usually little practical difference between using the Excel and CSV file formats. Excel will happily open the downloaded CSV files, though they have a little less formatting. There may be advantages to one or the other if you have particular needs.

How it works...

When you download an Excel file ChronoForms loads up quite a complex set of code libraries (the extension includes a version of the **PEAR ExcelWriter** package `http://pear.php.net/package/Spreadsheet_Excel_Writer`). ChronoForms only makes limited use of the library but having it available can be very useful for advanced ChronoForms users.

Downloading a CSV file uses much simpler PHP commands. If you have problems with the Excel download, then try CSV instead.

5
Form Validation and Security

In this chapter, we will cover:

- Making "required" fields
- Specifying the types of input that are allowed, that is, text, numbers, dates, and so on
- Customizing validation error messages
- Adding extra security with server-side validation of submitted information
- Getting the user to confirm their data before submission
- Adding an ImageVerification captcha/anti-spam check
- Adding a ReCaptcha anti-spam check
- Limiting form access to registered users

Introduction

Unless you are extraordinarily lucky, users are going to misuse, or worse, abuse your form. Typical misuse is entering the wrong kind of data, or leaving important fields blank. Typical abuse is submitting spam, or input designed to damage or take over your site.

In this chapter, we'll look at a range of different techniques for protecting your site. Which ones you need to implement will depend on your site. A quiet, private site with a few well-behaved visitors might get away with none; a popular high-visibility or controversial site might need everything here and more besides that.

Form Validation and Security

Making "required" fields

On most forms some fields are "required"; that is, the submitted data is useless without this content.

> We've all seen forms where almost every field is required; this is a temptation for all of us form creators. Take care when designing your form to make only the really essential fields "required", as each extra field that has to be completed reduces the chances of a user getting as far as clicking the submit button.

Getting ready

We'll be working with the newsletter form again, making the e-mail field "required". This really is essential as we can't send a newsletter without an e-mail address. (Ideally we'd like a name too, but we can send the newsletter without it so we won't make it a required field.)

How to do it...

Open the form in Wizard Edit, click on the e-mail text input element to open the element **Properties** box, and tick the **Required** box at the top of the **Validation** group.

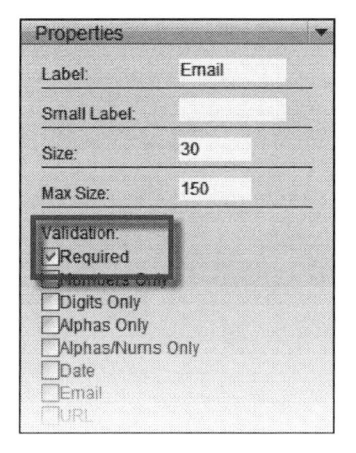

1. Click **Apply** at the bottom of the element **Properties** box to save the change, then save the Form using the **Apply** icon in the toolbar above.
2. Open the form **General** tab and make sure that **Load ChronoForms CSS/JS Files?** is set to **Yes**, then save the form.

3. Open the form in your browser. Leave the boxes empty and click **Submit**.

   If all is well, the form will not submit and you will see a red error message by the **Email** box.

> If the form submits and doesn't show the error message then most likely **Load ChronoForms CSS/JS Files?** is set to **No**. If that's not the problem, then some more serious debugging may be required. See the recipe *Trouble shooting problems with forms* in Chapter 12, *Adding Advanced Features*. Now type something (anything will do) into the **Email** field and try submitting again. As soon as there is at least one character in the field you will be allowed to submit the form.

Clearly this isn't checking for a valid e-mail address, just that the input isn't empty. We'll see how to check an e-mail address in the next recipe.

Notice that along with the red error message, the border of the input has turned red as well. It turns green when there is something in the input.

The validation is doing three things:

- Preventing the form from submitting
- Showing an error message in red
- Changing the color of the input border

How it works...

If you look at the Form HTML for the **Email** input you will see:

```
<input class="cf_inputbox required" maxlength="150"
  size="30" title="" id="text_0" name="text_0" type="text" />
```

Notice that the second value in the `class` attribute is `required`. Checking the box in the Form Element Properties makes ChronoForms add this value to the normal `cf_inputbox` styling.

When the form is loaded ChronoForms checks the Form HTML and adds a JavaScript snippet when it finds the `required` value. It's this snippet that does the validation which you are seeing in the form.

Form Validation and Security

> Behind the scenes ChronoForms uses the LiveValidation JavaScript library from `http://livevalidation.com/`. LiveValidation is a robust and flexible validation suite that can be extended to include custom validations as we'll see later.

There's more...

We set the validation by checking the box in the Wizard Edit element properties but, in effect all this does is add the "required" value to the attribute. You can get the same result by adding `class='required'` to any form input in the Form HTML.

There's also a **Validation** tab in the Form Editor. Here you can use the numbered input boxes to enter input names to specify the validation you require.

> This tab was originally developed for an earlier version of ChronoForms using a different validation suite; the **Validation Library** drop-down which lets you choose the MooTools or Prototype libraries is no longer used as ChronoForms has followed Joomla! in adopting the MooTools library.

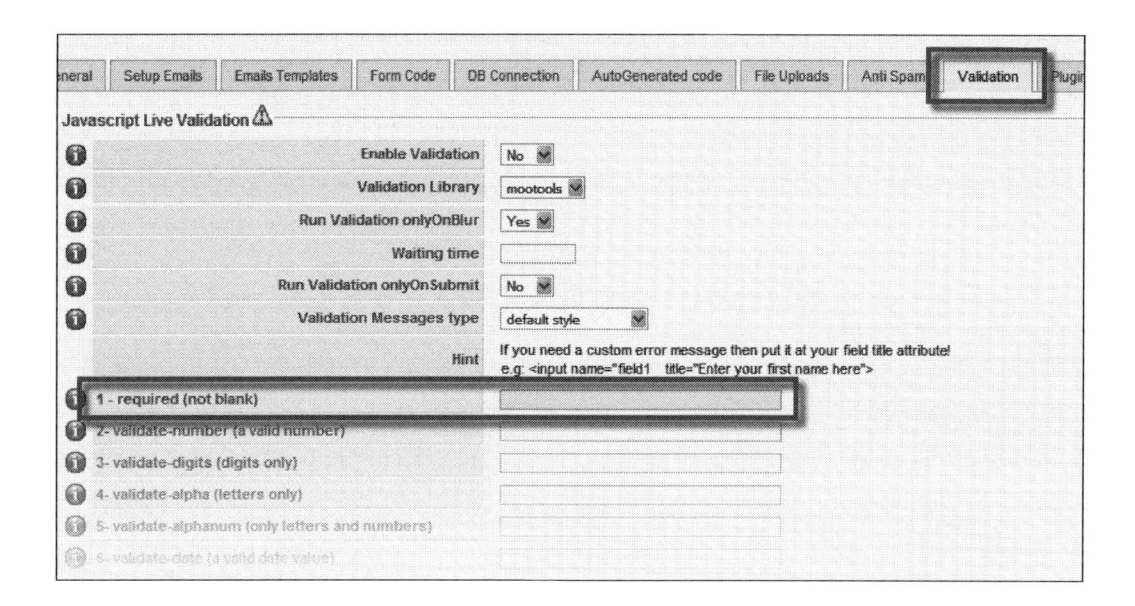

You need to enable validation here if you are specifying the input to be validated on this tab. The approach we used in the recipe above will work even if **Enable Validation** is set to **No** here.

The **Run Validation only On Blur** option specifies that the validation check is done when the user tabs or clicks out of the input (with an option delay set in the **Waiting Time** box); **Run Validation only On Submit** defers the checks until the **Submit** button is clicked.

The **Validation Messages type** option allows you to choose between the default messages that appear to the right of the input, or to specify your own message divs using `id='CF_LV_ERROR_field_id'` to link the input to the error message div (you'd replace `'field_id'` with the ID of the input being validated; for example, `id='CF_LV_ERROR_text_0'`).

See also

- *Customizing validation error messages* later in this chapter

Specifying the types of input that are allowed—text, numbers, dates, and so on

The previous recipe looked at making an input required, but as we saw with the e-mail input, that often is not enough. We need to be able to check the kind of input as well as checking that the input isn't empty.

ChronoForms has some built-in validations for common types of input and it's possible to add custom checks for many more.

Getting ready

We're going to check that there is an e-mail address in the newsletter form e-mail input.

Form Validation and Security

How to do it...

1. Open the form in Wizard Edit, click in the Email text input element to open the element **Properties** box, and check the **Email** box in the Validation group. Leave the **Required** box checked as well as we want both validations.

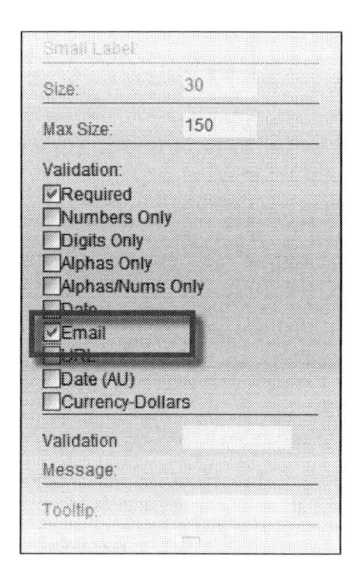

2. Click the **Apply** button in the Properties box to save the change to the element, then **Save** the form in the editor and re-open or refresh the newsletter form in your browser.

3. If you leave the **Email** field empty and submit the form, you should see the **This field is required** error message as before. However, if you type in some text that isn't an e-mail address, when you leave the input by tabbing or clicking outside the input box you will now see a different error message:

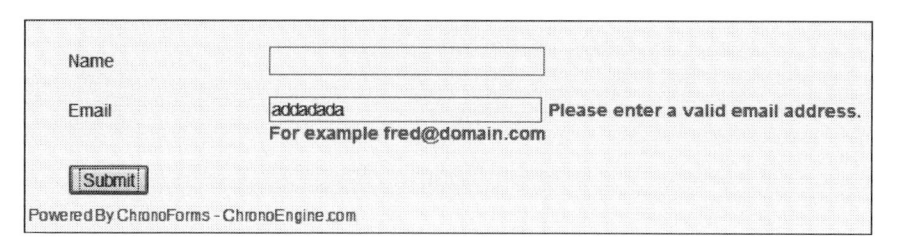

This isn't the world's most elegant error message, but we'll see in the next recipe how to improve that. For the moment, notice that we are now validating both whether there is an entry in the field and the type of entry.

> Notice that there is an example e-mail address **fred@domain.com** in the error message. This can cause a problem if you are displaying the form inside an article and you have the Joomla! Email Cloaking plugin enabled. The plugin finds the example address and tries to replace it with a cloaked version; the result is a mess of JavaScript showing in the form page. The fix is either to turn off the Email Cloaking plugin if you don't really need it, or to change the order of the plugins so that the ChronoForms plugin runs after the Email Cloaking plug-in.

How it works...

If you look at the Form HTML for the Email input you will see that we now have a third value in the class attribute:

```
<input class="cf_inputbox required validate-email"
   maxlength="150"    size="30" title="" id="text_0"
   name="text_0" type="text" />
```

This tells the LiveValidation script to check that this field is a valid e-mail address.

The nuts and bolts of the validation are supplied by the LiveValidation suite. If you dig into the code in `com_chronocontact/js_/livevalidation_standalone.js` you will find that the test uses a **Regular Expression** to check the e-mail:

```
/^([^@\s]+)@((?:[-a-z0-9]+\.)+[a-z]{2,})$/i
```

This may look rather cryptic, Regular Expressions often do, but it is a condensed description of the various combinations of characters that can make up valid e-mail addresses. Roughly decoded, it reads:

- Almost any combination of characters except "@"
- Followed by "@"
- Followed by a combination of letters and numbers
- Followed by "."
- Followed by two or more letters

> Regular expressions like this are an important part of form validation. You don't need to understand them unless you need to create your own validation tests. If you need more information, Regex Buddy at `http://www.regexbuddy.com` is a useful source.

Form Validation and Security

There's more...

In addition to the e-mail validation here, ChronoForms has built-in checks for the following input types:

- `validate-number`: It checks for a number, possibly including decimal places or in scientific notation.
- `validate-digits`: It checks for `0-9`.
- `validate-alpha`: It checks for `a-z, A-Z` only.
- `validate-alphanum`: It checks for `0-9, a-z, A-Z` only.
- `validate-date`: It checks for a date in the international `yyyy/mm/dd` format, for example, 2008-12-02, 1897 04 16.
- `validate-email`: It checks for a valid e-mail address.
- `validate-url`: It checks for common forms of URL (some more unusual forms will not validate and may need a custom validation).
- `validate-date-au`: It checks for a date in `dd/mm/yyyy` format.
- `validate-currency-dollar`: It checks for a valid dollar value (for example, `99`, or `99.99`, `$99.99`, `$9,999`).
- `validate-selection`: It checks that a drop-down box option with a value has been selected. (Note: For this to work the first option should have `value=""` otherwise the validation will always test true.)
- `validate-one-required`: It checks the radio button, or more often check-box arrays, to make sure that at least one box is checked, (Note: For this to work the buttons or boxes in the array should all have the same name and there should be a `<div>` or `<td>` tag that wraps the whole array.)

Any of these validations can be enabled from the Form Wizard or Wizard Edit by entering an input name (or a comma separated list of input names) on the Form Editor **Validation** tab, or by adding the values—for example `validate-one-required`—to the class of the input in the Form HTML.

There are some conspicuous omissions from this list—notably a US format mm/dd/yyyy date validation and alpha validations for alphabets with accented characters like "é".

These can both be added fairly easily with custom validations.

> The particular choice of built-in validations is a result of the history of ChronoForms. The first validation library used was "Really Easy Validation" developed by Andrew Tetlaw, an Australian, and the validations in that library have been carried forward for compatibility.

See also

- Check the LiveValidation documents at `http://livevalidation.com/`
- For the background to the validation options see Andrew Tetlaw's "Really Easy Field Validation" at `http://tetlaw.id.au/view/javascript/really-easy-field-validation` (Note: This library is still installed in ChronoForms but is not used in the present releases)

Customizing validation error messages

As we saw previously with the e-mail error message, they aren't always pretty. In this recipe we'll look at how to customize the messages and add your own versions.

Getting ready

We'll work with the same e-mail error message we saw in the previous recipe.

How to do it...

1. The simplest fix is to add a validation message to the e-mail text input. There's an entry for this in the element **Properties** box in the Wizard Edit.

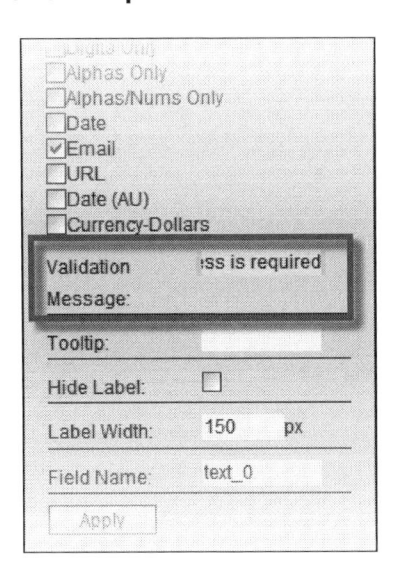

   There is only one validation message entry for the element—the same message will be used for each validation check—in this case, it is **Email address is required**.

Form Validation and Security

2. As usual, click **Apply** to save the element properties and save the Form.

> There is no equivalent place to enter messages on the **Validation** tab in the Form Editor, just a note to remind you that you can set a message by adding a title attribute to the input in the Form HTML.

How it works...

All that ChronoForms has done in the Wizard is to add the title attribute into the input tag. The ChronoForms validation script checks to see if this attribute is present, and if it is, sets it as the failure message for the validation check.

```
<input class="cf_inputbox required validate-email"
    maxlength="150" size="30" title="Email address is required"
    id="text_0" name="text_0" type="text" />
```

You can, of course, add or edit this manually in the Form HTML.

Adding extra security with "server-side" validation of submitted information

The validation we have looked at so far works by using JavaScript running in the user's browser. This is commonly called "client-side" validation. This makes it flexible and responsive as long as the browser has JavaScript installed and running and the user doesn't deliberately try to bypass or "mess" with it.

Today most users have JavaScript enabled (and indeed Joomla! loses some functionality if it isn't running). But for important inputs, we need to run "server-side" validation as well. This validation will only run after the form is submitted and the inputs have been sent back to the site server.

Chapter 5

> It is important to know that "client-side" validation using JavaScript will not protect your site against malicious attacks. To be secure, you must add server-side validation to any critical fields, and you must "filter" the data before it is saved into the database. ChronoForms does no validation or filtering by default.

ChronoForms makes it straight-forward to add basic server-side validation. But it does mean writing a little PHP.

Getting ready

We're going to work with that e-mail input on the newsletter form yet again.

How to do it...

1. There is no option to enter server-side validation using the Form Wizards; you need to open the Form Editor, click the **Validation** tab, and scroll down to see the **Server Side Validation** section.

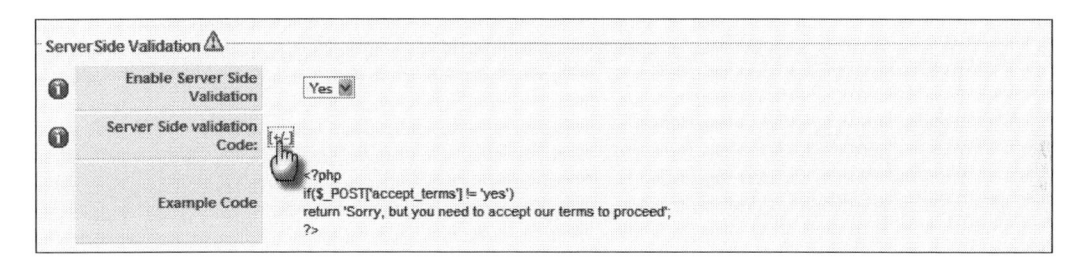

Server Side Validation	
Enable Server Side Validation	Yes
Server Side validation Code:	[+/-]

Example Code	`<?php`
	`if($_POST['accept_terms'] != 'yes')`
	`return 'Sorry, but you need to accept our terms to proceed';`
	`?>`

2. Click the **[+/-]** link to open an empty text area if it isn't already open.

   Notice that there is an **Example Code** below the text area; this is a useful memory jogger when you haven't used server-side validation for a while.

   The basic structure of a ChronoForms server-side validation is that you run a validation check—probably using the PHP `if` control as in the example—and, if the input fails the test, return with a message. (And if it passes, return with no message, which will happen at the end of this code anyhow.)

   We'll repeat the check on the e-mail input from the newsletter form.

3. First we need to get the input value:

   ```
   $email = JRequest::getString('email', '', 'post');
   ```

Form Validation and Security

We are using the Joomla!-filtered input here and are specifying that we expect a text string returned from the "post" array. This has the same result as the code in the example if the result is a good e-mail; it will prevent some possible "bad" results being processed.

4. Next, we need to check that the string is a valid e-mail address. PHP has a function that allows us to use a regular expression to do this.

   ```
   $pattern = '/^([^@\s]+)@((?:[-a-z0-9]+\.)+[a-z]{2,})$/i'
   preg_match($pattern, $email);
   ```

   The ChronoForms validation requires us to put the check inside an `if` condition, check if it is `not` valid, and show an error message if there is a problem.

   ```
   if ( !preg_match($pattern, $email) ) {
       return "Please enter a valid email address in the email box.";
   }
   ```

5. Putting it all together and adding the required `<?php ... ?>` tags we have:

   ```
   <?php
   $email = JRequest::getString('email', '', 'post');
   $pattern = '/^([^@\s]+)@((?:[-a-z0-9]+\.)+[a-z]{2,})$/i';
   if ( !preg_match($pattern, $email) ) {
       return "Please enter a valid email address in the email box.";
   }
   ?>
   ```

   Now when we submit the form with an invalid entry in the Email box, the form is redisplayed instead of being submitted with an added server-side error message.

   > Note that we have to remove the client-side valid e-mail validation to see this error. If that was still working, we would be unable to submit the form.

   ⊗ 1. Please enter a valid email address in the email box.

   Name
   Email
   [Submit]
   Powered By ChronoForms - ChronoEngine.com

The error message appears above the form; it's not linked to the field where the error occurred. ChronoForms doesn't know what that was. So, if this is a long form you need to make the messages very clear.

> The two forms of validation "client-side" and "server-side" may look similar but they perform two fundamentally different purposes. Client-side validation helps the user complete the form correctly. Server-side validation and data filtering protects your site from malicious damage; in a worst case scenario this could destroy your site database, but more often it will add spam links that redirect your users.

6. There's one problem here—the form that we are showing with the error message is blank so the user has to reenter all their data, with every chance that they will make a different error next time around.

    ChronoForms has a fix for this. Among the many options on the **General** tab in the Form Editor is **Republish fields if error occurs** with two choices—**Dont Republish** (the default) and **Try to Republish**.

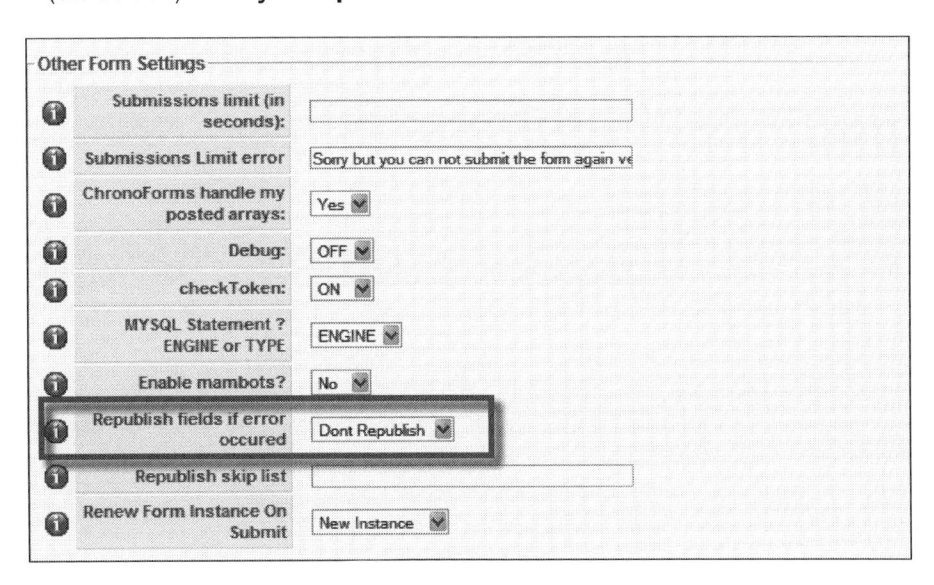

Form Validation and Security

Change this setting to **Try to Republish**, save the form, and resubmit.

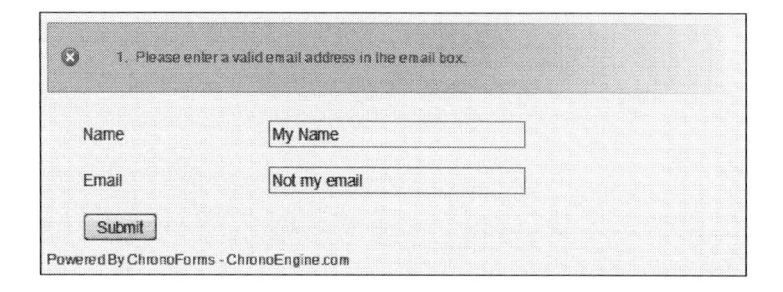

We still have the error message but now the input data has been preserved and is redisplayed.

How it works...

There really isn't much to say here. The code in the server-side validation is run as a function more or less as soon as the form is submitted. If the function returns a message string, then the form is redisplayed with the message.

There's more...

Adding several validations

It's rarely the case that we only want to check one input. But that is not a problem, as we can just add more `if` clauses to check the other inputs, or to run more than one check on the same input.

Here's an example where we check that neither input from our newsletter form is blank, and we check that the email field is a valid email as before:

```
<?php
$name = JRequest::getString('name', '', 'post');
if ( !$name ) {
  return "Please enter a name";
}
$email = JRequest::getString('email', '', 'post');
if ( !$email ) {
  return "Please enter an email address";
}
$pattern = '/^([^@\s]+)@((?:[-a-z0-9]+\.)+[a-z]{2,})$/i';
if ( !preg_match($pattern, $email) ) {
  return "Please enter a valid email address in the email box.";
}
?>
```

Combining error messages

There is a problem with this approach to adding several validations though. The server-side validation function will end when the first error is found and the others will go unreported.

We can solve this but we need some slightly more complex code to check all the validations before we return. We'll collect the error messages in an array and return them all at the end.

```
<?php
$messages = array();
$name = JRequest::getString('name', '', 'post');
if ( !$name ) {
  $messages[] = "Please enter a name";
}
$email = JRequest::getString('email', '', 'post');
if ( !$email ) {
  $messages[] = "Please enter an email address";
}
$pattern = '/^([^@\s]+)@((?:[-a-z0-9]+\.)+[a-z]{2,})$/i';
if ( !preg_match($pattern, $email) ) {
  $messages[] = "Please enter a valid email address in the email box.";
}
// check if there are any error messages and return
if ( count($messages) ) {
  return implode('<br />', $messages);
}
?>
```

A PHP array is a collection of values. Here we declare $messages as an empty array and then use $messages[] = . . . to add any error messages to the array.

At the end we check how many messages are in the array with count($messages). If there aren't any then all is well, and we do nothing; if the array isn't empty then we link the messages into a single string with <br /> tags to insert line-breaks between them and return this long message:

Styling error messages

The message box here is styled by ChronoForms and we will see it in various forms in later recipes. Sometimes the default style doesn't suit our template. We can change this by adding a little CSS to our form.

Looking at the page source tells us that the error messages are displayed in a `<span>` tag with `class='cf_alert'`. So we can use the `span.cf_alert` CSS selector to target this element on the page. Let's add this CSS to the CSS **Styles** box on the **Form Code** tab in the Form Editor:

```
span.cf_alert {
  background-color:yellow;
  border: 1px solid red;
  font-weight:bold;
}
```

This may not be the ideal choice but we can see the difference!

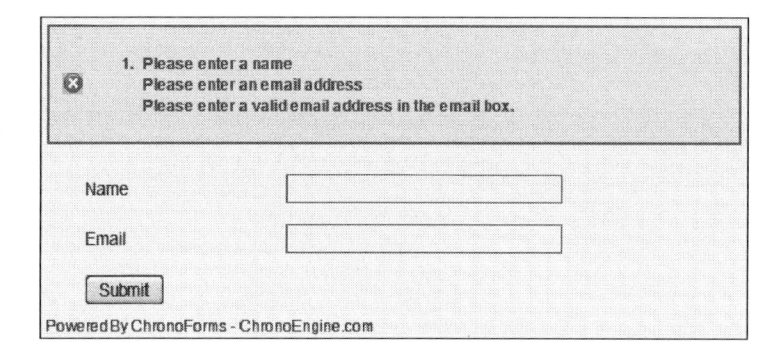

> Note: Adding CSS to the form will just change the display for this form. You can make similar changes to the ChronoForms or site templates if you want the changes to run across the site.

Checking the database in a validation

Most kinds of validation can be done using Regular Expressions or other simple PHP. Sometimes though we need to do things that are more complex.

A typical example using our newsletter, might be to check and see if the e-mail address is already listed in our newsletter database. See the recipe *Creating a table to save your results and linking your form to it* in *Chapter 4, Saving Form Data in the Database* to set up saving the form to a database table.

Still in the server-side validation box we can add code to check the database table:

```php
<?php
$db =& JFactory::getDBO();
$email = JRequest::getString('email', '', 'post');
$query = "
  SELECT COUNT(*)
    FROM `#__chronoforms_test_form_1`
    WHERE `email` = '$email' ;
";
$db->setQuery($query);
if ( $db->loadResult() ) {
  return "This email address is already listed";
}
?>
```

In this code snippet we get the e-mail address as before; look it up in the database using COUNT(*), which will return the number of times it was found.

If it is not found, then the count returned will be zero, which is equivalent to false for the if clause (any other number will be equivalent to true).

We really only want to run this check if we already know that the e-mail address is valid so we can combine the "not blank", "valid email", and "already in use" checks into one code block like this:

```php
<?php
$messages = array();

// start email validation check
$email = JRequest::getString('email', '', 'post');
$pattern = '/^([^@\s]+)@((?:[-a-z0-9]+\.)+[a-z]{2,})$/i';

if ( !$email ) {
  $messages[] = "Please enter an email address.";
} elseif ( !preg_match($pattern, $email) ) {
  $messages[] = "Please enter a valid email address.";
} else {
  $db =& JFactory::getDBO();
  $query = "
    SELECT COUNT(*)
      FROM `#__chronoforms_test_form_1`
      WHERE `email` = '$email' ;
  ";
  $db->setQuery($query);
  if ( $db->loadResult() ) {
```

Form Validation and Security

```
      return "This email address is already listed";
    }
  }
  // end email validation check

  // check if there are any error messages and return
  if ( count($messages) ) {
    return implode('\n', $messages);
  }
?>
```

Using the `if . . . elseif . . . else` control structure means that the later validation checks will only be run if the input passed the previous checks. Only one error message will be returned for this element.

Filtering form data

We saw previously that it is important to filter the data from your form before it is saved into the database. The major risk here is from **Cross-site Scripting** (XSS), which is an exploit that submits data that appears to be valid but in fact contains some MySQL commands that attempt to take control of your database.

In ChronoForms, the best place to add the filtering code is in the "OnSubmit Before" box.

Joomla! provides some methods that are designed for filtering data. They are built in to the `JRequest::getXxx(. . .)` code that you saw earlier in this recipe.

The basic form is:

```
$var_name = 
  JRequest::getVar('input_name', 'default value', 'source');
```

Here, source depends one where the data is being retrieved from. The common values are `post` for form values, `get` for URL values, or `cookie` for cookie data.

Other methods include:

- `getBool()` returns true or false values only
- `getCmd()` only allows the characters `[A-Za-z0-9.-_]`
- `getFloat()` only allows digits and periods e.g.`123.45`
- `getInt()` only allows digits
- `getString()` will allow all characters but removes 'bad' HTML
- `getWord()` only allows the characters `[A-Za-z_]`

A simple way to use on of these filters is to get the form data using the filter and to replace the input value with the filtered value.

For example, if we have an input that should only return an integer we might use this code:

```php
<?php
$input = JRequest::getInt('input_name', 0, 'post');
JRequest::setVar('input_name', $input);
?>
```

> An added benefit of doing this is that we can add default values to inputs where we want them.

See also

- The Wikipedia article **Cross-site scripting** at http://en.wikipedia.org/wiki/Cross-site_scripting has more information on the risks to your site.
- There is a short article **Retrieving and Filtering GET & POST requests with JRequest::getVar** in the Joomla! Documentation wiki at http://docs.joomla.org/Retrieving_data_from_GET_and_POST_requests.

Getting the user to confirm their data before submission

When a form includes important or complex information, it can be useful to give the user a chance to take a look and make sure that the details are correct before finally submitting the form. And, of course, this must include the ability to go back and correct any mistakes or omissions.

ChronoForms provides this functionality with a plugin, an extra that can be added to a form when it is needed. Several plugins are included in the standard ChronoForms installations and it is one of these—the "Confirmation Page" plugin, which we will be using in this recipe.

> ChronoForms plugins are quite distinct from Joomla! plugins although they unfortunately use the same name.

Getting ready

Once again we'll be working with the same newsletter form. By now you may have several versions, so create a new copy of the basic form with just the two inputs for name and e-mail.

Form Validation and Security

How to do it...

1. Open the ChronoForms **Forms Manager** and you'll notice that the left-hand column is headed **Plugins** and there are a dozen or so links in the column:

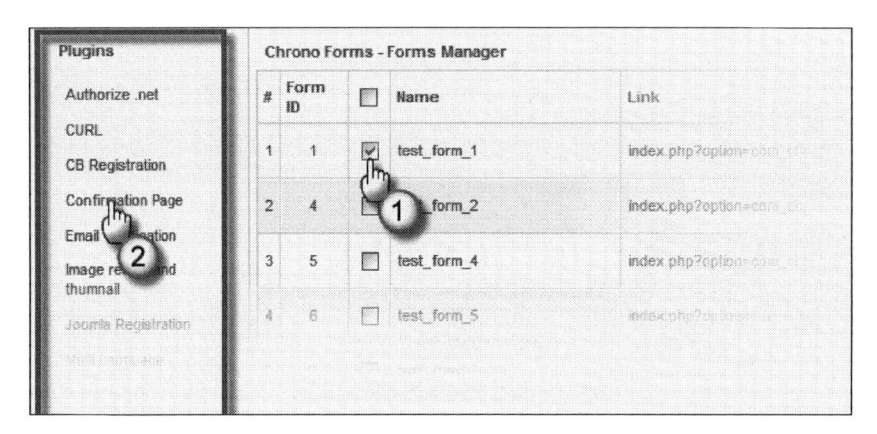

2. To setup the **Confirmation Page** plugin for our form first, click the check box just before the form name, then click the Confirmation Page plugin **Link**.

   The Confirmation Page plugin configuration page will open as follows:

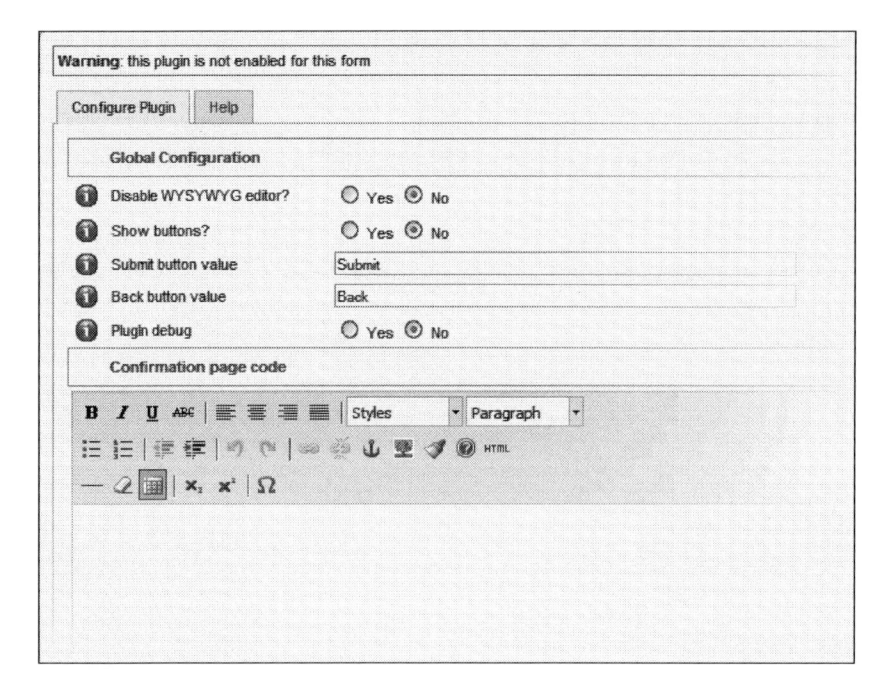

This is a fairly simple plugin with a warning message and just two tabs, the second one is a **Help** tab with a brief description of the plugin and its options.

> This image is from a beta version of the plugin release on the ChronoForms forums. The version you see may look a bit different.

The warning message at the top reminds us that as well as configuring the plugin here we will need to enable it in the Form Editor.

On the main **Global Configuration** tab there are a few options at the top and a "rich text" editor window at the bottom.

3. Click **Yes** next to the **Show buttons?** label and then click the **Save** icon on the toolbar to save the plugin configuration. We do need to add some content in the page editor but there is a quick cheat way to do that if we go back to the Form Editor.

4. In the Form Editor, click the **Setup Emails** tab and create a new setup if there isn't already one there. Enable the Email Setup, and then **Apply** the form. Click the **Email Template** tab and there is a plain vanilla template for your form in the template editor. Copy the text from the editor, cancel out of the Form Editor, and reopen the **Confirmation Page** plugin. Click the cursor in the editor window and paste the template code.

> This may seem long-winded for the two inputs we have in this form. It is a great help when you have a form with 50 inputs, all with obscure names.

5. Save the plugin configuration again, return to the Form Editor and click the **Plugins** tab.

   When the tab opens, you'll see a block of red bars, one for each of the ChronoForms plugins currently installed. If these look familiar, it's because they are just like the bars we saw in the Create Table dialogue in the last chapter.

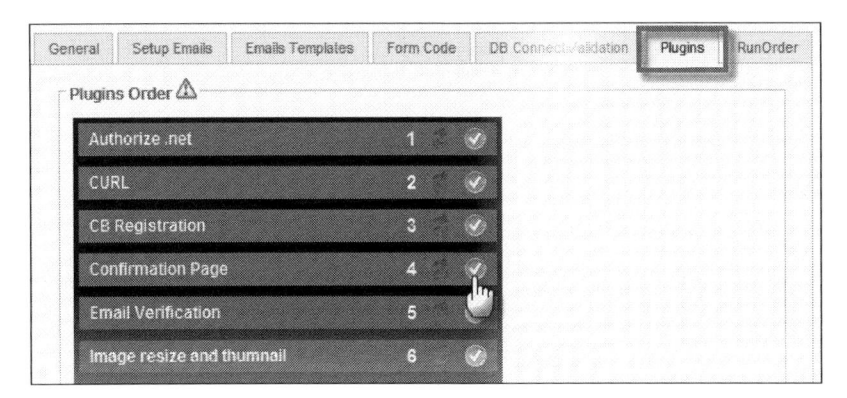

Form Validation and Security

> Remember, the color of the bar shows the plugin status—red is disabled, green is enabled. The icon to the right shows the "click action". Click the "tick" to enable the plugin, click the "x" to disable it.

6. Click the "tick" icon on the Confirmation Page bar to enable the plugin; the bar will turn green. Save the form in the Form Editor, make sure that it is published, then click the form Link in the Forms Manager to view it in a browser window.

7. Enter some values in the boxes and submit the form.

```
Name My name
Email my.email@example.com
 [ Submit ]  [ Back ]
```

Here is the "Confirmation Page". So far this shows the bare minimum, just the input labels and values. We'll fix that in the plugin configuration shortly.

8. Click the **Back** button and you will be taken back to the form; change one of the entries and resubmit the form. You'll see the confirmation page again with the new values displayed. Click the **Submit** button to finally submit the form.

9. If we go back to the plugin Configuration and add a few more lines in the editor we get a result like this:

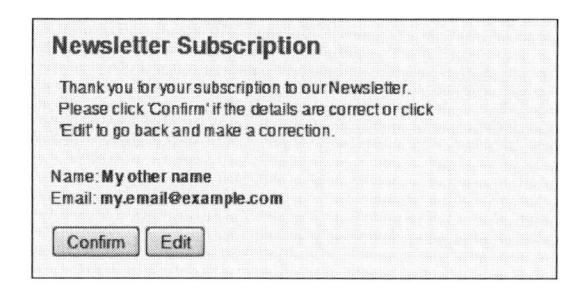

Newsletter Subscription

Thank you for your subscription to our Newsletter.
Please click 'Confirm' if the details are correct or click
'Edit' to go back and make a correction.

Name: **My other name**
Email: **my.email@example.com**

[Confirm] [Edit]

Here there is a title, a little more descriptive text, some simple CSS, and the button names have been changed from the default values to the more helpful **Confirm** and **Edit**.

How it works...

We'll see more about how plugins in general work in *Chapter 11, Using Form Plug-ins* later in the book. This particular plug-in is called when the form is submitted; it stores the form values temporarily, creates the confirmation page, and displays it just as we have seen.

See also

- *Chapter 11, Using Form Plug-ins* for other plugin applications.

Adding an ImageVerification captcha / anti-spam check

One of the most common features of forms are "Captcha" checks, which try and verify that the submitter is not a "spambot". There's a constant battle to try to keep out the spammers without blocking legitimate users.

ChronoForms has a built-in "imageverification Captcha check" and, as we'll see in the next recipe, there is also an option to use an external check instead.

Getting ready

As usual, we're going to add this to the newsletter form.

How to do it...

1. This is a two-step process—first we will add a "place-holder" to the Form HTML using the Wizard Edit, then we'll enable it in the Form Editor.

    Open the form using Wizard Edit, drag across a "Captcha" element, set the **Label** text in the **Properties** box, and click **Apply** to save it. Save the form and return to the Forms Manager.

Form Validation and Security

> If you prefer to edit the Form HTML directly, then you need to make sure that the {imageverification} placeholder is included where you want the Captcha check to appear.

> If there is a problem then you may still be able to use the **Without Fonts** option or talk to your ISP to get GD with FreeType and PNG support installed on your server.

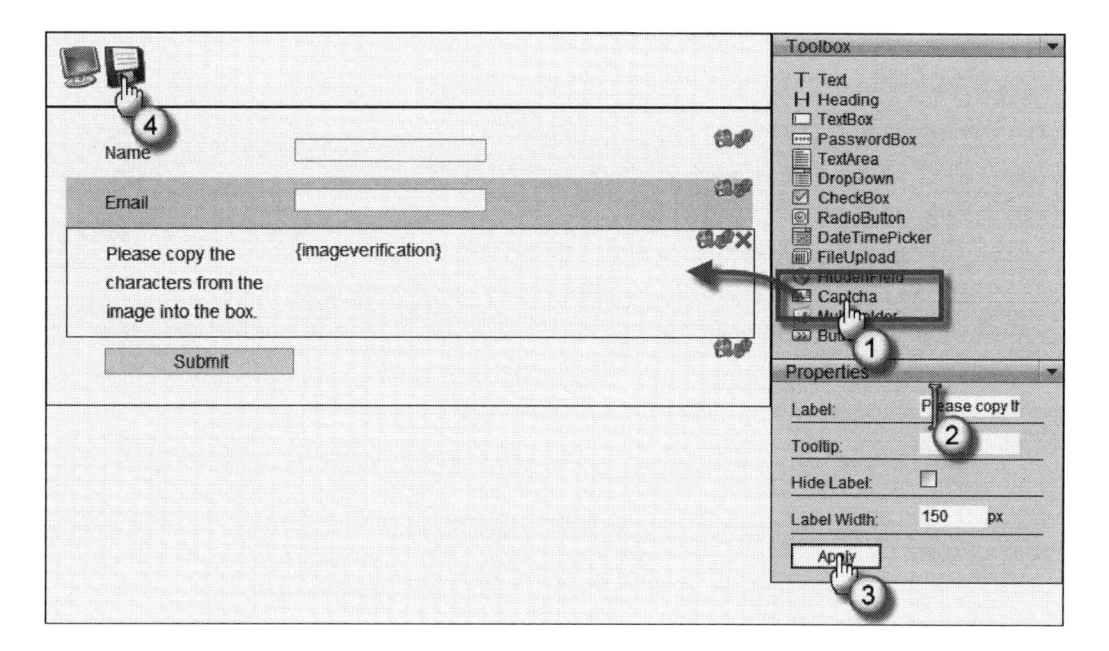

2. Now open the form in the Form Editor and click the **Anti Spam** tab.

   You'll see two blocks of settings. Check the lower **GD info** block first. The "Sample Image" will probably be blank but you should see either a version number or **Yes** against the other settings. These are confirming that you have the necessary "GD" graphics library installed to create the Captcha images. Unless you have a very old version of PHP on your server, these should be fine.

Chapter 5

3. Set **Use Image Verification** to **Yes** and **What type of image to show?** to **With Fonts** then **Apply** or **Save** the form. Reopen the **Anti Spam** tab and all being well you'll see a **Sample image** like the one shown here:

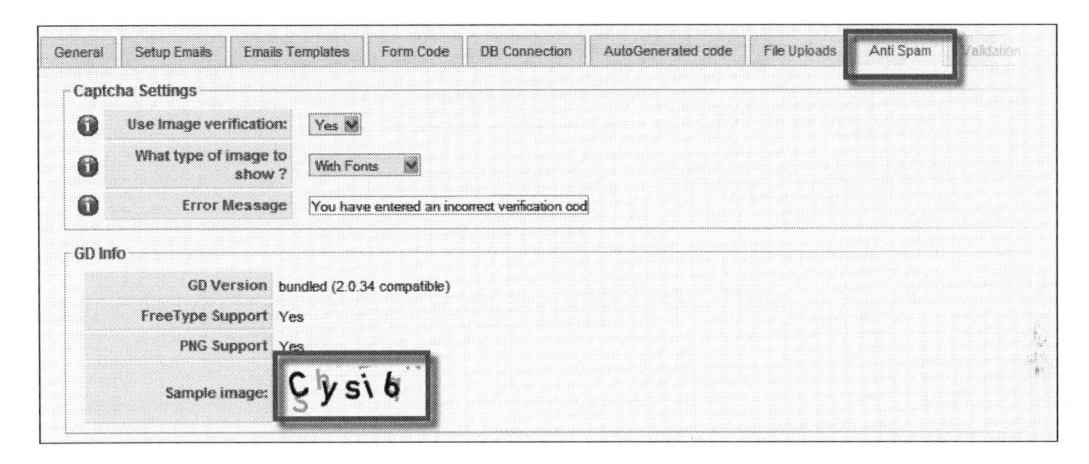

> Usually this is all that is required. If the image isn't there the cause is probably related to security hosting settings. There are a couple of things to check, see the *There's More...* section for some more information.

4. If all is well, open the form in a browser window and you will see something like this:

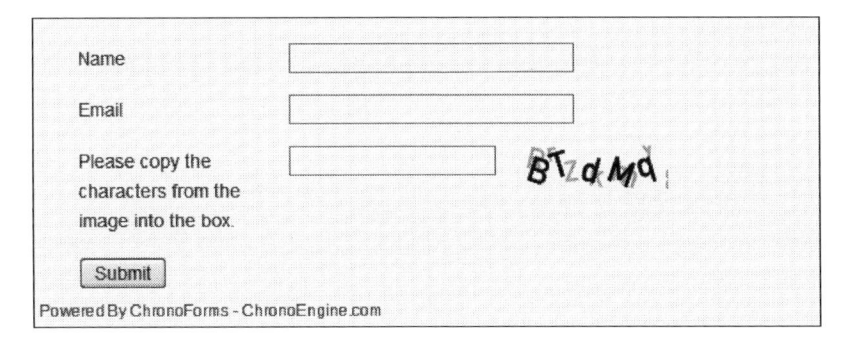

5. Try submitting the form without putting anything into the ImageVerification box; you will see a ChronoForms error message saying **You have entered an incorrect verification code at the bottom of the form.** and the image will have been regenerated with a different sequence of characters.

> You will probably have lost any entries in the other boxes when you did this. They will be re-displayed if **Republish fields if error occurred** is set to **Yes** in the form **General** tab.

Form Validation and Security

> Try submitting again with the correct sequence in the ImageVerification box (you can use all lowercase letters without any problem) and the form should submit correctly.

How it works...

ChronoForms has a separate file `chrono_verification.php` that generates the Captcha image. When it is called, this file creates a random text string, and embeds it in a PNG image with some other random characters in the background. It also saves a "key" to the random string in the user session information.

When the form is submitted, ChronoForms does a calculation on the value of the field and compares the result to the saved key. If the two match then the form is submitted; if they don't then the form is redisplayed with the error message.

There's more...

Debugging when the Captcha image won't display

If the image doesn't display then you can get more "informative" error reports if you change the header at line 17 of `chrono_verification.php` from `header("Content-type: image/png");` to `header("Content-type: text/html");`. Then point your browser directly to that file, that is, `http://www.example.com/components/com_chronocontact/chrono_verification.php`. This will show PHP errors on the page if there is something that PHP cannot handle and should provide enough input to fix the problem.

Remember to change the header back afterwards.

Debugging when you see a server error

If you see a server error reported, then there are a couple of causes that we have seen:

- The server isn't configured to allow the PNG file type
- The server permissions don't allow the image to be saved to a temporary folder for displaying

In either case, your server logs will probably give more information. You may need to speak to your ISP to find the exact cause and get it fixed.

Changing the layout of the ImageVerification element

The label for the Image Verification block can be changed in the Wizard Edit, or by editing the Form HTML. The layout of the input field and the image is hard-coded into ChronoForms. You can change it by finding this code in `components/com_chronocontact/chronocontact.html.php`; (in the current version it is around line 174):

```
if ( trim($MyForm->formparams('imagever')) == 'Yes' ) {
  $imver = '<input name="chrono_verification"
    style="vertical-align:top;" type="text" id="chrono_verification"
    value="" />   <img src="'.$CF_PATH
    .'components/com_chronocontact/chrono_verification.php?imtype='
    .$MyForm->formparams('imtype').'" alt="" />';
}
```

This shows the block layout is `<input . . . />  <img . . . />`. You can change the sequence or layout of these elements provided that you take care to preserve all the attribute code inside the tags.

> Any change you make here will affect all forms on your site and may be overwritten if you later upgrade ChronoForms.

Adding a "refresh" link to the Image Verification element

Although ChronoForms tries to avoid ambiguous characters in the Captcha image, sometimes it can be hard to be certain. This modification will add a **Refresh** link to the element to allow the user to generate a new image.

In the form HTML add this code to display a refresh button

```
<div class="form_item">
  <div class="form_element cf_button">
    <input value="Reload Image verfication" name="reload" id="reload" type="button" />
  </div>
  <div class="cfclear"> </div>
</div>
```

and add this script snippet to the Form JavaScript box

```
window.addEvent('domready', function() {
  $('reload').addEvent('click', reloadCaptcha);
});

function reloadCaptcha() {
  var img = $$('.cf_captcha img');
  img.setProperty('src', img.getProperty('src') + '&t=1');
};
```

Form Validation and Security

This will add a **Refresh** button after the Captcha image and when you click it the Captcha image will change. See the previous section to change the layout of the element.

> Any change you make here will affect all forms on your site and may be overwritten if you later upgrade ChronoForms.

See also

- For more about Captcha in general, see http://en.wikipedia.org/wiki/CAPTCHA
- To change the display of ChronoForms error messages, see *Customizing validation error messages* recipe earlier in this chapter

Adding a reCAPTCHA anti-spam check

Some users don't like the ChronoForms built-in Captcha for one reason or another, so there is a ChronoForms plugin to use the third-party Captcha system from reCAPTCHA (see http://recaptcha.net/).

Getting ready

We'll use our familiar newsletter form but please disable the ChronoForms Captcha in the **Anti Spam** tab of the Form Editor first.

How to do it...

1. In the Forms Manager click the check-box by the form name and click the **reCAPTCHA verification** link in the **Plugins** column at the left.

   You'll see the following **Configuration** tab. Leave all the settings as they are; just click the **Save** icon in the toolbar to save the default configuration.

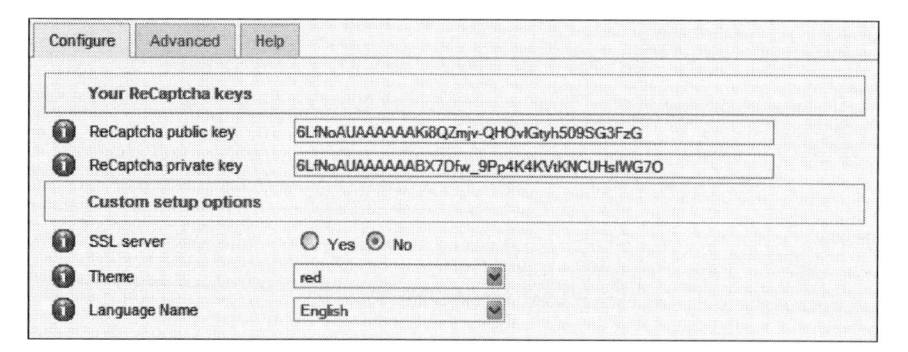

2. In the Form Editor, click the **Plugins** tab, and enable the reCAPTCHA verification plugin. Click the **Anti Spam** tab to make sure that **Use Image verification** is set to **No**.

3. Click the **Form Code** tab, open the Form HTML box, and find the {imageverification} placeholder if it is there, and remove the whole block. Then add an element block like this to the Form HTML (usually just before the **Submit** button block):

```
<div class="form_item">
  <div class="cf_captcha">
    <span>{ReCaptcha}</span>
  </div>
  <div class="cfclear"> </div>
</div>
```

4. Save the Form Editor and view the form in your browser.

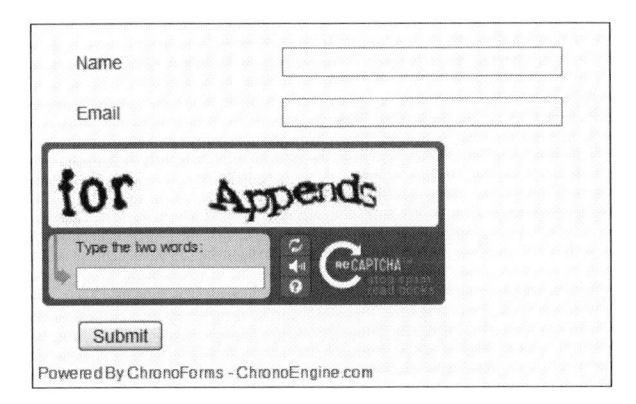

The default reCAPTCHA block has been inserted into your form. As before, if you submit without typing the correct words the form will redisplay with a ChronoForms error message: **The reCAPTCHA wasn't entered correctly. Go back and try it again (reCAPTCHA said: incorrect-captcha-sol)**

> The second line of this is a message from the reCAPTCHA server that may be useful if you have problems.

Notice that the reCAPTCHA block includes a refresh button, an audio link that validates using a spoken phrase, and a help button.

Form Validation and Security

How it works...

reCAPTCHA is a third-party Captcha system. When you load the page, the reCAPTCHA block and the check words are downloaded from a reCAPTCHA server. When the form is submitted ChronoForms sends the results back to a reCAPTCHA server for checking. The verification is pretty much independent of ChronoForms.

There's more...

Configuring the reCAPTCHA plug-in

reCAPTCHA keys

On the plug-in configuration, there are two reCAPTCHA keys. These are general keys issued to ChronoForms for use on any website. You are welcome to continue using them but we recommend that you go to the reCAPTCHA site and get your own keys tied to your domain; this will increase the Captcha security.

When you get them just copy and paste them into the **Configuration** tab in place of the default keys.

reCAPTCHA setup options

The rest of the **Configuration** tab has some reCAPTCHA options:

- Set **SSL server** to **Yes** if the form has an `https://` address
- Set the **Theme** drop-down to choose a different reCAPTCHA theme
- Set the **Language** drop-down to choose a different reCAPTCHA language

The choice of themes and languages is from reCAPTCHA, not from ChronoForms. If you find that there are new choices from the reCAPTCHA site, please let us know and we'll add them to the plug-in configuration.

Here's an example of reCAPTCHA with the "white" theme in Turkish.

Chapter 5

Problems with reCAPTCHA

There have been some reports of problems with reCAPTCHA in Internet Explorer. These are intermittent and seem to happen when the reCAPTCHA server is slow in serving some of the JavaScript. Please test your site carefully before using reCAPTCHA.

See also

- The reCaptcha FAQ is at `http://recaptcha.net/faq.html`

Limiting form access to registered users

Using Captcha is one way to stop your forms being abused, and another is not to show them to "strangers". If you have a Joomla! site where members can register, it may be better to restrict some forms to signed-in members.

Joomla! and ChronoForms together make this very simple.

Getting ready

While it's unlikely that you'd want to limit your newsletter signup form to registered members, it would be a shame to abandon it now—so that's the form we'll work with here.

How to do it...

1. We're going to add a little PHP into the Form HTML, so open the form in the Form Editor and click the **Form Code** tab.

2. At the beginning of the Form HTML add this code snippet:
   ```
   <?php
   if ( !$mainframe->isSite() ) { return; }
   // get the Joomla! User object
   $user = JFactory::getUser();
   // if there isn't a user_id found end the form display.
   if ( $user->id == 0 ) {
     return;
   }
   ?>
   ```

3. Save the form in the Form Editor, log out of the front-end if you are logged in, and then display the form in a browser window.

   All you see is the ChronoForms tag line.

Form Validation and Security

4. This isn't too friendly, so we'll add a little message:

```php
<?php
if ( !$mainframe->isSite() ) { return; }
// get the Joomla! User object
$user = JFactory::getUser();
// if there isn't a user_id found end the form display.
if ( $user->id == 0 ) {
  echo "<div style='border:1px solid red; padding:6px;' >
    Sorry, registered users only!</div>";
  return;
}
?>
```

> Sorry, registered users only!
> Powered By ChronoForms - ChronoEngine.com

That looks a bit better, and of course you can add a better message and style it however you like.

How it works...

Joomla! keeps information about the current user in a "User object"—a collection of information that we can call on. Among the information is the User ID—for a guest this will be 0, and for a logged in user it will be some integer greater than 0. The code simply checks that and if it finds a guest displays a message and ends.

> If it finds the user is logged in, then it will show the form exactly as our earlier examples. The first line in the code `if ( !$mainframe->isSite() ) { return; }` is there to prevent the code being evaluated in the Joomla! administration as that can prevent it saving correctly. This may have some side-effects on other form features; if in doubt try commenting it out temporarily.

There's more...

Redirecting the user

Instead of showing the message on the form page you can redirect the user to another page on the site. If you want to hide a form completely then redirecting to the home page is often useful.

```php
<?php
if ( !$mainframe->isSite() ) { return; }
$user = JFactory::getUser();
if ( $user->id == 0 ) {
   $mainframe->redirect('index.php');
}
?>
```

Redirecting the user with a message

Instead of showing the message on the form page, you can redirect the user to another page on the site. If you want to hide a form completely, then redirecting to the home page is often useful.

```php
<?php
if ( !$mainframe->isSite() ) { return; }
$user = JFactory::getUser();
if ( $user->id == 0 ) {
   $mainframe->redirect('index.php',
      'Sorry, that page isn''t available');
}
?>
```

This will return to the home page showing a Joomla! system message.

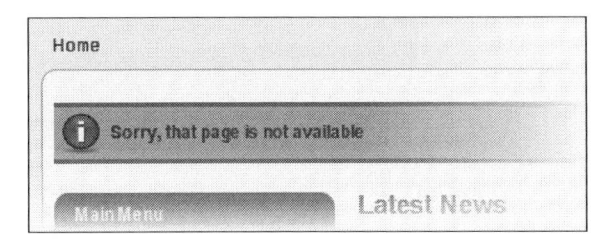

Form Validation and Security

The exact appearance of the messages will depend on the site template you are using. This shows a standard system message, and you can add a third parameter to the redirect to specify different message type—"message" (as shown previously), "error", or "alert".

```
$mainframe->redirect('index.php',
    'Sorry, that page isn't available', 'error');
```

> Not all Joomla! templates show Joomla! system messages correctly. If in doubt, please switch the site temporarily to one of the default templates.

See also

- The recipe in *Chapter 11, Using Form Plugins* about using the Watchman plugin provides a number of ways of controlling access to your forms.

6
Showing your Form in your Site

In this chapter, we will cover:

- Including your form in an article using the ChronoForms plugin
- Showing your form on selected pages using the ChronoForms module
- Linking to your form from Joomla! menus
- Using a form to create a Joomla! article
- Redirecting users to other Joomla! pages after submission

Introduction

So far we've looked at creating forms more or less in isolation; in this chapter, we'll start to integrate them more into our Joomla! website. There are many cases when it is perfectly good for a form to stand alone on its own web page, and there are others where it needs to work with existing content.

We'll look at two standard ChronoForms tools for embedding forms in a Joomla! page, either within an article or in a Joomla! module. We'll also look at ways to link forms from Joomla! menus, and how to redirect users after a form has been submitted. And lastly, in a slightly different direction, we'll explore how to take the information submitted in a form and redisplay it as a Joomla! article.

Showing your Form in your Site

Just for clarity, it will help if we start by defining some terminology:

- A Joomla! **article** is a page created or managed through the **Site Administrator | Content Menu**—these pages are the main content of a typical Joomla! site.
- A Joomla! **plug-in** (previously a Mambot) is an extension that can be used to alter or work with other Joomla! content. Search boxes and editors, among others, fall into this group. (Not to be confused with ChronoForms plug-ins which work only with ChronoForms forms.)
- A Joomla! **module** is a chunk of code that is displayed in one of a number of defined positions or "boxes" around a Joomla! page. Modules can be displayed on all pages, or just on selected pages. Module positions are determined by the Joomla! Template in use, though some are common to most templates.
- Joomla! **menus** are lists of links, typically to other pages on the site. They are usually displayed in menu modules.
- Joomla! **templates** are groups of files that between them determine the "look and feel" of a Joomla! site. Typically they include templates for page layout, CSS files for page styling, and possibly JavaScript files for "special effects".

> Note that not all modules or menus are visible to users. Some just work behind the scenes to manage how the site works. For example, a Google Analytics module loads scripts into the page.

Including your form in an article using the ChronoForms plugin

In this recipe, we'll look at inserting a form into an existing Joomla! article. Our newsletter article is the kind of form where it makes sense to insert a small form at a relevant point in a long article.

> Usually, it doesn't make sense to create an article primarily to contain a form. If you want short paragraphs of text to go before or after a form, then it is more practical to add the text into the Form HTML. All of the same formatting can be applied there if you use the site CSS.

Getting ready

At the risk of being very boring, we're going to use the same newsletter subscription form yet again.

How to do it...

1. Go to the ChronoForms site, click the **Downloads** menu item (http://chronoengine.com/downloads), and navigate to the current release of the ChronoForms plugin (also called the Mambot / Plugin).

2. Install the plugin from the **Joomla! Administration | Extensions | Install/Uninstall** page in exactly the same way as we did with the ChronoForms component in *Chapter 1, Creating a Simple Form*, in the *Downloading and installing ChronoForms* section. If all is well you will see the **Install Plugin Success** message.

3. Next, go to **Joomla! Administration | Extensions | Plugin Manager** and look for the **chronocontact** link. Usually, it's near the top of the list; use the **Filter** at the top left to search for "chrono" if it's not immediately visible.

4. Click the **chronocontact** link to open the plug-in configuration.

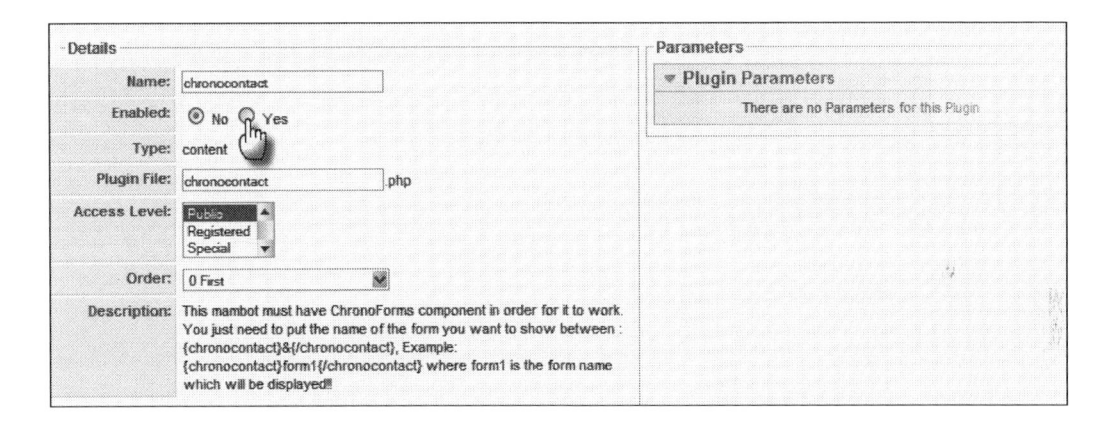

There really is only one thing of any importance here. In the description section is the syntax for inserting a form into an article: {chronocontact}form_name{/chronocontact}. When you can't remember exactly what syntax to use, this is a useful place to look.

While we are here, select **Yes** for the **Enabled** option to enable the plug-in (you can also do this directly from the Plugin Manager).

5. Click **Save** on the toolbar to save and close the Plugin Editor. Notice that the **chronocontact** entry in the **Enabled** column now shows a green "tick" icon.

6. Go to the **Content | Article Manager** menu item and scan down the list of articles to find a convenient one to test the newsletter form in. In a default Joomla! installation, we'll be using the **Joomla! License Guidelines** article but anything convenient will do.

7. Click the article title to open the Article Editor. We'll be working in the "rich editor" box on the left.

Showing your Form in your Site

Find a suitable place in the article text, insert the cursor, and use **Enter** to create a new paragraph. Type `{chronocontact}test_form_1{/chronocontact}` and use the name of your form in place of `test_form_1` if it is different.

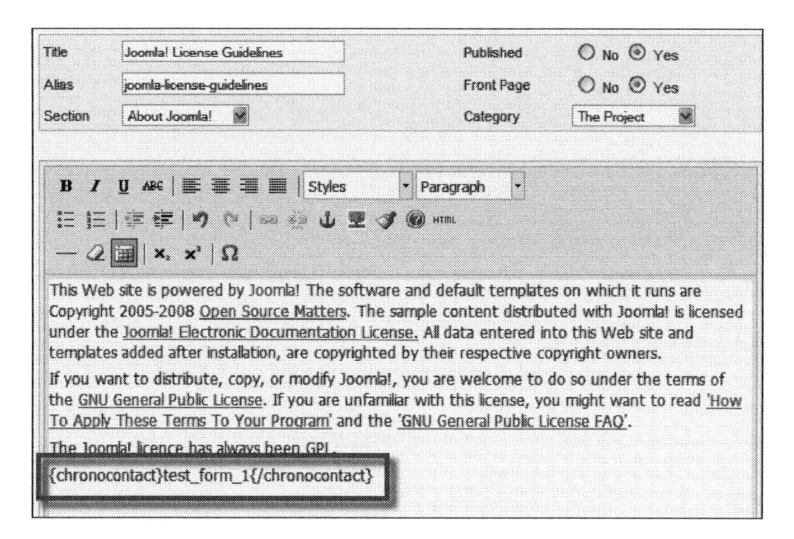

2. Click **Save** on the toolbar to save the article, then open the site in a new browser window and find the article with the form neatly embedded in it.

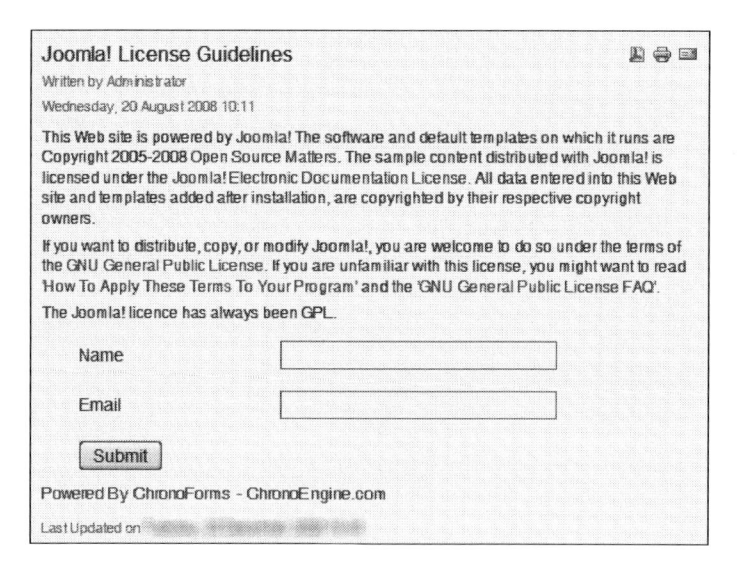

This will work with almost any form in any normal article. There may be problems if there are other Joomla! plug-ins enabled that conflict with the form code—we see this sometimes with the Email Cloaking plug-in but it's easily fixed (see the following section).

> When you submit a form from the plugin you will be returned to the "normal" ChronoForms "Thank You" page, not back to the article page. You need to be aware of this in planning your work-flow.

How it works...

The ChronoForms plug-in acts as a link back to the ChronoForms extension code and you are, more or less, running ChronoForms from the article page. The main difference is in the page URLs and this will cause some practical changes in the way the form works.

Many of the recipes in this book will work using the ChronoForms plug-in.

There's more...

Debugging the ChronoForms plugin

If all you see is the `{chronocontact}form_name{/chronocontact}` text in the article then either the plug-in isn't installed, or it's installed but not enabled.

If you see a large and rather strange block of JavaScript displaying near or instead of your form, then it's most likely that you have the Joomla! Email Cloaking plugin installed and it's trying to cloak a sample e-mail address inside the ChronoForms validation code. Turn the Email Cloaking plug-in off to check; if it is the problem then change the plugin order in the Plugin Manager so that the Email Cloaking plugin runs before the ChronoForms plug-in.

You can do this by changing the order of the plugins in the Joomla! Plugin Manager so the Email Cloaking plug-in is higher in the list than the ChronoContact plug-in.

See also

- See the Joomla! Documentation Wiki for more information on Joomla! plugins. **Joomla! Extensions Defined** is a useful place to start (`http://docs.joomla.org/Joomla!_Extensions_Defined`)

Showing your form on selected pages using the ChronoForms module

The ChronoForms module is similar to the ChronoForms plug-in except that it displays the form in one of the module positions in the template rather than inside an article.

Getting ready

Guess what? We'll be using the same newsletter subscription form here. Any suitably-sized form will work fine.

How to do it...

1. Go to the ChronoForms site, click the **Downloads** menu item (http://chronoengine.com/downloads) and navigate to the current release of the ChronoForms module.

2. Install the module from the **Joomla! Administration | Extensions | Install/Uninstall** page in exactly the same way as we did with the ChronoForms component in *Chapter 1, Creating a Simple Form*, in the *Downloading and installing ChronoForms* section (and the ChronoForms plugin the previous recipe). If all is well, you will see the **Install Module Success** message.

3. Next, go to **Joomla! Administration | Extensions | Module Manager** and look for the **ChronoForms** link; it will probably be with other modules that are in the left position.

> Use the **Filter** at the top left to search for "chrono" if it's not immediately visible.

4. Click the **ChronoForms** link to open the module configuration.

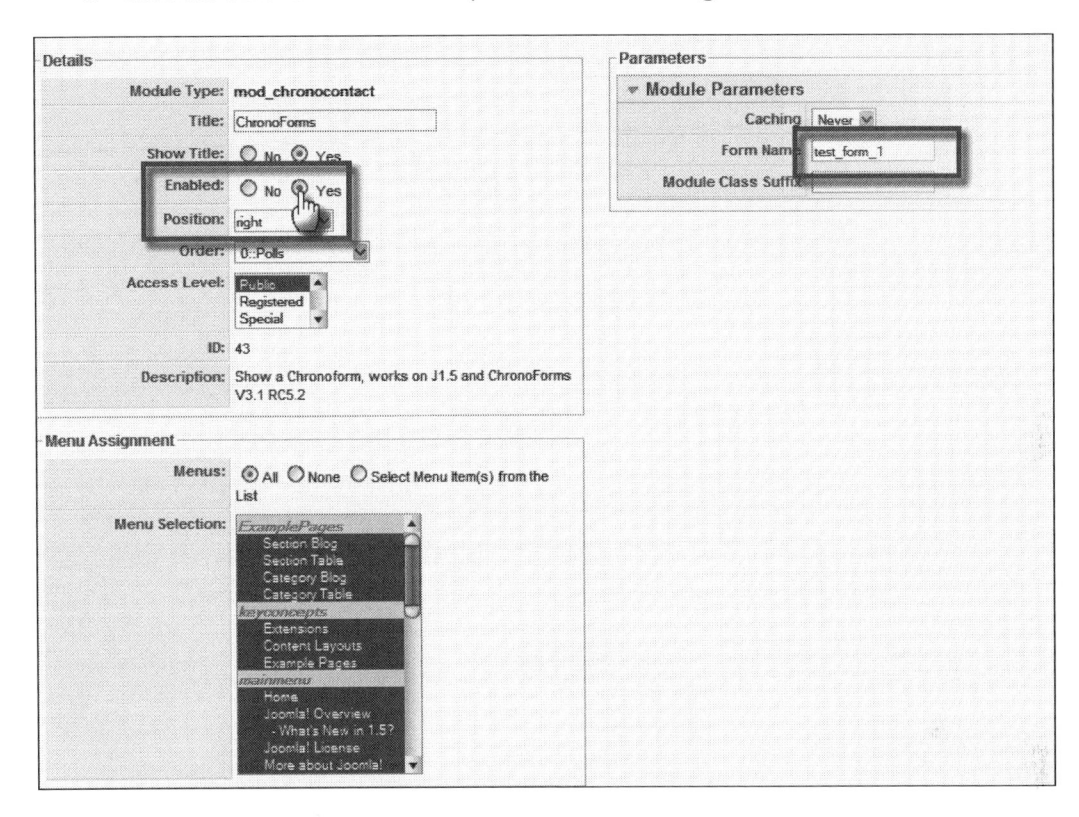

There are more settings here than there were for the ChronoForms plugin!

First, over to the right in the **Module Parameters | Form Name** box, enter the name of your form—`test_form_1` in this case.

> There's an important difference here between the plug-in and the module. Whereas the module will let you use any form in any article simply by changing the form name in the place holder tags, the module can only be used with one form in one module location. However, you can create many copies of the module to use with different forms in a different location.

Showing your Form in your Site

5. Over to the left, select the **Yes** for the **Enable** option to turn the module on. Then in the **Position** drop-down select the "right" module position to show the module in the right-hand column of the page.

> It is possible that your template does not have a "right" position and the form will not display. In that case use whatever position you want the module to be displayed in. You can usually see the available module positions by going to **Site Administration | Extensions | Template Manager**, clicking on the name of the current template (it has a yellow star in the **Default** column) and then clicking the **Preview** icon.

6. That's all for now, we'll come back to some other settings later. **Save** the module.
7. View the home page of your site in the browser, and refresh the page if necessary.

Latest News
- Joomla! License Guidelines
- Content Layouts
- The Joomla! Community
- Welcome to Joomla!
- Newsflash 4

Popular
- Joomla! Overview
- Extensions
- Joomla! License Guidelines
- Welcome to Joomla!
- What's New in 1.5?

Welcome to the Frontpage

Joomla! Community Portal

Written by Administrator
Saturday, 07 July 2007 09:54

The Joomla! Community Portal is now online. There, you will find a constant source of information about the activities of contributors powering the Joomla! Project. Learn about Joomla! Events worldwide, and see if there is a Joomla! User Group nearby.

The Joomla! Community Magazine promises an interesting overview of feature articles, community accomplishments, learning topics, and project updates each month. Also, check out JoomlaConnect™. This aggregated RSS feed brings together Joomla! news from all over the world in your language. Get the latest and greatest by clicking here.

Last Updated on Saturday, 07 July 2007 09:54

ChronoForms

Name

Email

[Submit]

Powered By ChronoForms - ChronoEngine.com

Polls

And there's our form at the top of the right-hand module block. It looks as though the CSS needs some adjustment to tighten it up and have it fit better in the space available. If you have some CSS experience, then that is not too difficult.

8. At present the module will show on every page of our site. Sometimes this is useful; more often, we want to be a little more selective. The first place to change the display settings is back in the Module Editor where the block at the bottom left allows us to link the module display to selected menu items.

The **Details** block above also lets us select the **Order** that the module will display in if there is more than one set in the same template position.

In the same block, we can also limit the display by **User Group**; in Joomla! 1.5 these are fairly crude: XE "ChronoForms module:form, displaying on selected pages"

- **Public**: Everyone
- **Registered**: All signed-in, registered members
- **Special**: Anyone with more permissions than registered members, for example authors, managers, or administrators

> If we need to, we can set up finer grained display limits in ChronoForms either by using the Watchman plugin or by adding PHP to the Form HTML box. There are some examples in the following *There's more...* section.

How it works...

The ChronoForms module acts as a link back to the ChronoForms extension code and you are, more or less, running ChronoForms from the module. The main difference is in the page URLs and this will cause some practical changes in the way the form works.

Most of the recipes in this book will work using the ChronoForms module; the exceptions are those where the form size or display isn't suitable.

There's more...

While many Joomla! modules are displayed on every page on your site, they come into their own when you display them selectively to relate to other content on the page. Here, we'll look at a couple of ways of doing this.

Controlling the display of a module

If a module has no content, then it will not display at all, and we can use this to hide our module if certain conditions are met.

> For it not to display at all the module must be completely empty, that is, no spaces, or empty `<div>` tags; they will show up as odd gaps in the page display. It pays to keep your coding tight and neat.
>
> The Module Title display must also be turned off in the Module Editor, and your copy of ChronoForms should be validated so that the ChronoForms strap-line doesn't display.

Showing your Form in your Site

The basic code to hide a module goes at the beginning of the Form HTML. In "pseudocode" it is:

```
<?php
if ( condition ) {
   return;
}?>
```

For example, if we want to show a module only to guests but hide it from registered users then we could write:

```
<?php
$user =& JFactory::getUser();
if ( $user->id > 0 ) {
   return;
}?>
```

This will hide the module if the current user ID is not zero, that is, the user is logged in.

The page URL can also be a useful source of information. The "option" parameter in the URL will tell us which component is being displayed. Let's hide the module if this is a ChronoContact page:

```
<?php
$option =& JRequest::getString('option', '' , 'get');
if ( $option == 'com_chronocontact' ) {
   reurn;
}?>
```

> JRequest::getVar() is a Joomla! method that allows us to get parameter values from the current page URL; using JRequest::getString() adds an extra requirement that we want a text string returned.

Using code snippets like this can give us that fine grained control over the module display.

Let's look at a more complex code snippet and say that we want to display our module on content pages only, but change the heading color depending on the category of the current page.

```
<?php
$catid =& JRequest::getInt('catid', '' , 'get');
switch ( $catid ) {
   case 25:
   case 29:
   case 30:
     $color = 'red';
     break;
   default:
```

```php
        $color = 'green';
        break;
}
?>
<h3 style='color:<?php echo $color; ?>; '>Heading</h3>
. . .
```

Now the module displays the heading in red if the current article category ID is 25, 29, or 30, and in green anywhere else.

> Notice the use of a PHP `switch` construct to execute a different block of code depending on the value of a control variable. This is a useful technique for creating active forms that change in some way depending on the user, the language, the article, and so on.

This example isn't an especially useful example except that it starts to introduce us to the idea of more interactive forms that use information that Joomla! makes available to influence the way our form is displayed.

We could, for example, have used this code structure to invite the user to subscribe to a different newsletter depending on the category article they are reading:

```php
<?php
$catid =& JRequest::getInt('catid', '' , 'get');
$article_id =& JRequest::getInt('id', '' , 'get');

switch ( $catid ) {
   case 25:
   case 29:
   case 30:
      $newsletter = 'Newsletter 1';
      $newsletter_id = 1;
      break;
. . .
   default:
      $newsletter = 'Newsletter 9';
      $newsletter_id = 9;
      break;
}
?>
<h3>Subscribe to <?php echo $newsletter'; ?></h3>
. . . // the remaining form HTML is here
<input type='hidden' name='newsletter_id'
   value='<?php echo $newsletter_id; ?> />
<input type='hidden' name='article_id'
   value='<?php echo $article_id; ?> />
. . .
```

Showing your Form in your Site

Now we are showing different headings, and we are collecting the values of the `newsletter_id` and the `article_id` so that we can use them to send a personalized e-mail on submission: Thank you for subscribing to Newsletter 9 while you were reading our article on 'Flying Pigs'....

> We've used the Joomla! category ID here. As the Joomla! hierarchy is such that "Sections" are the highest level; they contain "Categories" which in turn contain "Articles"; it might make more sense to use the section ID for this particular task. We didn't do so simply because the code to obtain the section ID is more complex and might distract from the main point of the example.

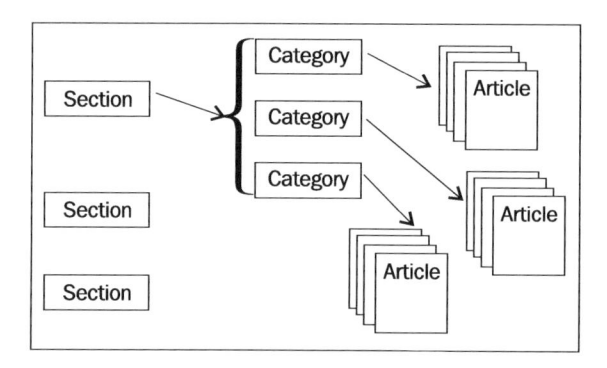

See also

- *Chapter 3, Styling your Form* for information on changing the layout.
- See the Joomla! Documentation Wiki for more information on Joomla! plugins. **Joomla! Extensions Defined** is a useful place to start: `http://docs.joomla.org/Joomla!_Extensions_Defined`.
- For an introduction to CSS see the W3Schools tutorials at `http://www.w3schools.com/css/`.

Linking to your form from Joomla! menus

If you don't show the form embedded in an article, or in a module, then you're going to need to give your users some way of navigating to it. We'll look at how to create a menu link to your form.

Getting ready

There's nothing to it really; any form will do, like that same old newsletter form for instance.

How to do it...

1. In the Site Administration area go to **Menus | Main Menu**, click the **New** icon, and then the **Chrono Forms** link.

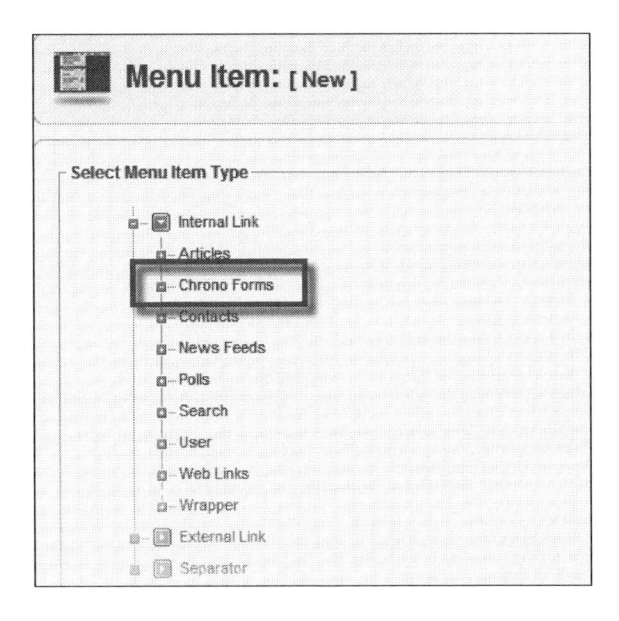

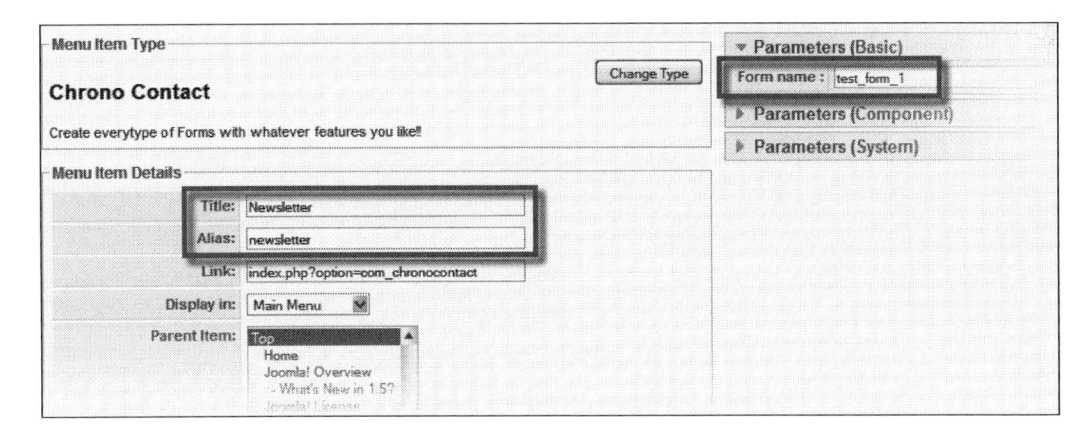

2. Add entries to the **Title** and **Alias** boxes and, most importantly, to the **Form name** box in the **Parameters (Basic)** area on the right. It's easy to overlook this but without it, the menu link won't work.

Showing your Form in your Site

> There are other settings further down the left-hand column that let you select the menu—set the position of the menu item in the menu, enable or disable the item, and set how the linked page is to display. These are all standard Joomla! settings.

3. That's all you need. **Save** the new menu item and test it.

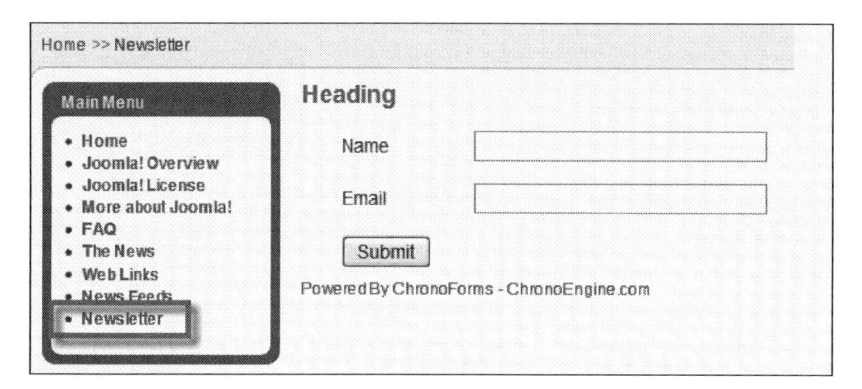

How it works...

There really isn't anything to say, this is just a completely conventional Joomla! menu link.

There's more...

Passing extra parameters

Sometimes you need to pass other parameters in the menu link. You can do this simply enough by using a Menu Item Type of **External** and adding the complete form link in the box there. For example:

```
index.php?option=com_chronocontact&chronoformname=test_form_1&my_param=abc
```

Changing the value of `my_param` would allow you to use a single form from different menu items and to tune the form display depending on the value of `my_param`. This is similar to the ways of controlling the display we saw in the last recipe.

Creating administrator menu items

We should mention briefly here that ChronoForms has two administrator links in the Forms Manager—**Menu Creator** and **Menu Remover**, which allow you to create (or remove) Administrator Menu Items to link to a list of saved data from your forms.

Using a form to create a Joomla! article

Surprisingly for a form application ChronoForms doesn't come with a big stock of forms. Over the years we have learnt that almost every user has a different set of needs and most of the common forms are easily created with the Form Wizard.

One that does come up quite frequently is the wish to take the information submitted in a form and use it to create a Joomla! article to be published on the site. For this, there is a form available.

Getting ready

This time we don't need anything special.

How to do it...

1. Go to the `ChronoEngine.com` Downloads area and navigate to **ChronoForms | ChronoForms Applications** and download the `submitcontent.cfbak` file.

> Notice that the file comes with a warning: **Pay Attention, misconfiguration of the form may put you at the risk of losing your content...!** And there's also a request that you pay a small fee if you use the form on a production site. There's no charge if you use it only for testing and development.

2. Restore the form into your Forms Manager and make sure that it is published.

> See *Backup and restore your forms* section in *Chapter 1, Creating a Simple Form* if you need help with this.

Showing your Form in your Site

3. Click on the Form link to open the form in a browser window.

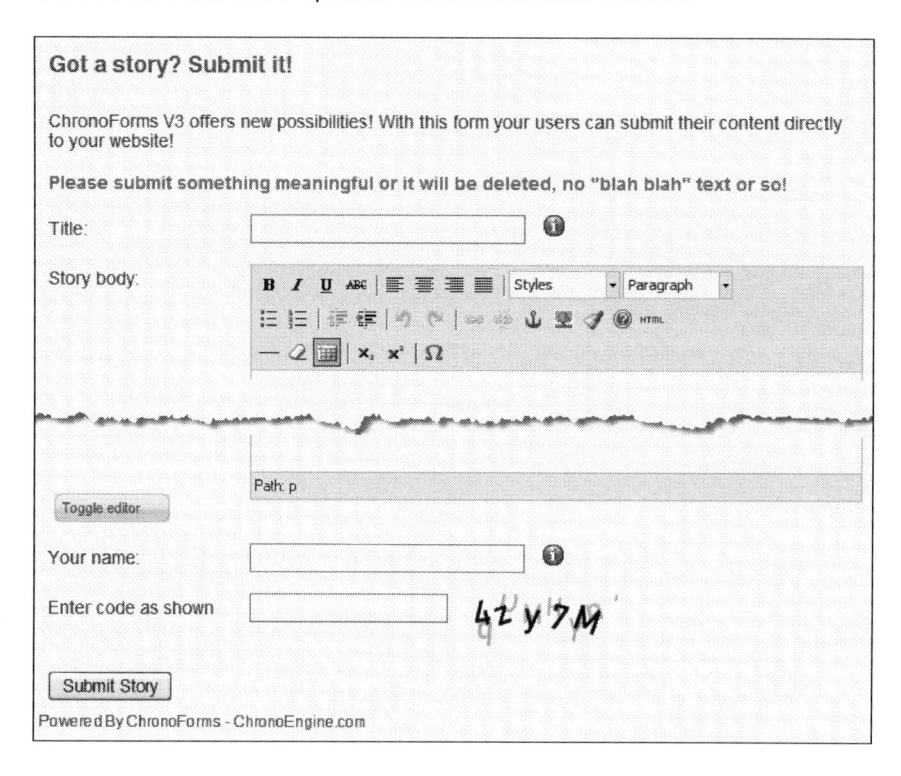

This is a very simple form with just three main inputs—**Title**, **Story body**, and **Your name**, which will be used for the article title, the article body, and the article author respectively.

4. Now enter some values into the form and click **Submit Story**. You will see a short "Thank You" message.

5. Open the site Administrator and go to **Content | Article Manager**, click on the heading of the **Date** column to sort the entries by date, and your new article should appear at the top of the list (if the column was already sorted it may take a second click).

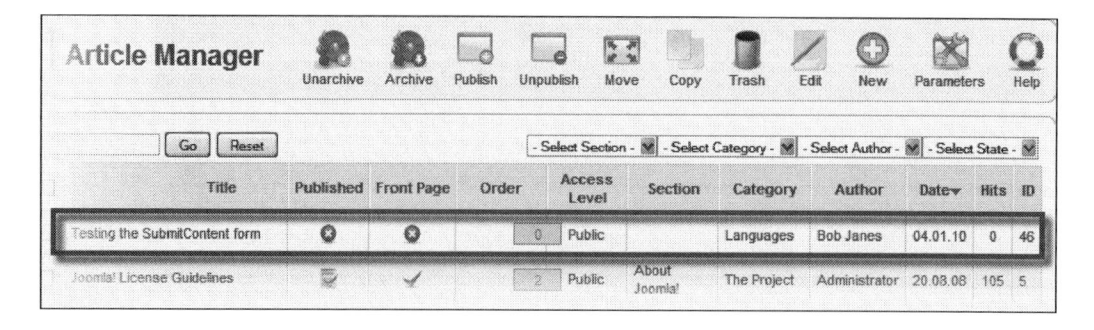

6. Click **Published** to approve the article and then browse to the article in the site front-end to have a look.

> **Testing the SubmitContent form**
> Written by Bob Janes
> Monday, 04 January 2010 21:35
>
> Class aptent taciti sociosqu ad litora torquent per conubia nostra, per inceptos himenaeos. Morbi iaculis mi quis tellus condimentum eu condimentum metus interdum. Vestibulum vel viverra dui. Nulla ante nulla, lobortis in ultrices at, accumsan sed eros. Cras porta; sem eget euismod sollicitudin, felis leo vehicula eros, non laoreet nulla ante ac enim. Ut laoreet metus at urna dictum sit amet egestas augue posuere. Duis sit amet faucibus nibh. Fusce leo sapien, malesuada ac eleifend sit amet; convallis id augue. Curabitur vulputate tincidunt erat mattis congue. Maecenas consequat, tortor sit amet aliquet cursus, augue justo dignissim ante, quis dictum libero erat ac ipsum. Duis dapibus ipsum vitae lectus euismod id condimentum eros vulputate. Vivamus tortor elit, iaculis vel bibendum id; luctus vel ligula. Sed orci nibh, consequat vel ullamcorper non, vehicula eu nisi. Phasellus justo ante, ultricies luctus bibendum viverra, interdum quis ante. Sed turpis sem, semper ac tincidunt quis, egestas in nisl. Praesent eget vulputate nisi. Maecenas quam nulla, adipiscing vel dapibus consequat, molestie at risus. Ut pretium diam metus, nec vehicula lorem! Curabitur non elit sed arcu gravida scelerisque!
>
> In hac habitasse platea dictumst. Aliquam congue luctus nisl eget imperdiet. Sed tellus elit, pharetra id mattis quis, feugiat id mauris. Fusce felis lectus, porta in varius eget; congue et arcu. Vestibulum venenatis leo in massa tincidunt faucibus. Vestibulum ullamcorper consectetur nibh imperdiet malesuada? Donec eu lacus id elit tristique ultrices. Pellentesque habitant morbi tristique senectus et netus et malesuada fames ac turpis egestas. Praesent eu lacus eros. Vivamus nibh lacus, tincidunt id ornare in, vehicula non enim. Vivamus turpis dolor, accumsan vitae tincidunt quis, feugiat eu ante. Etiam ac consequat sapien. Ut congue libero at tellus tristique vitae suscipit ante consequat. Nam placerat mattis fermentum. Vestibulum dictum volutpat risus, quis tincidunt tellus tempus vel.
>
> Aliquam erat volutpat. Nullam ut urna orci, non varius metus. Phasellus pretium est lacinia odio pellentesque eget hendrerit arcu imperdiet! Aliquam lectus metus, feugiat at aliquam vitae, posuere et velit. Pellentesque dapibus ligula eget libero bibendum ac gravida ipsum feugiat. In interdum dolor quis libero accumsan porta? Maecenas viverra elit, eu pretium diam pharetra nec. Nam nibh mi, scelerisque eu blandit in, gravida id metus. Aliquam lorem quam; malesuada nec porta vitae, lobortis nec nisi. Phasellus id felis libero. Aliquam aliquam nunc vel orci auctor quis facilisis velit tincidunt? Etiam id massa sed augue luctus aliquet sed luctus mi. Vestibulum ante ipsum primis in faucibus orci luctus et ultrices posuere cubilia Curae;
>
> Last Updated on Monday, 04 January 2010 20:45

And there are your magic words transformed into a published article. Simple isn't it?

In practice there are a few more options that you'll need to consider. We'll look at those in the following *There's More...* section.

How it works...

A Joomla! Article is—like most of the content in Joomla!—saved as a record in a database table, usually `jos_content`. What this form does is to take the form input and create a correctly structured record in the the `jos_content` table.

The most important thing that the form manages is to match the input names with the column names from the table so that the data is stored in the "right" locations.

Showing your Form in your Site

Also, behind the scenes, the form creates some other settings that are needed to set up an article correctly. Let's take a look in the **OnSubmit code – after sending email** box on the **Form Code** tab. The code in there looks like this:

```
<div style='border:1px solid silver; padding:6px; margin:6px;' >
<div style='color: blue; ' >Thank you for submitting your story, we
will review it shortly and if approved it will be published!</div>
<div>Cheers<br />
the ChronoEngine.com team! </div>
<div style='font-style: italic; border:1px solid silver; padding:3px;'
>Note: Edit the OnSubmit After code box to change this message</div>
</div>
<?php
JRequest::setVar('sectionid', '1', 'post');
JRequest::setVar('catid', '1', 'post');
JRequest::setVar('id', '', 'post');
JRequest::setVar('state', '0', 'post');
JRequest::setVar('created', date("Y-m-d H:i:s"), 'post');
?>
```

The first few lines simply show a "Thank you" message after the form is submitted. You will certainly want to change these but for the moment we can ignore them.

The block of lines inside the `<?php . . .?>` tags are the more interesting entries for us. They are setting the other article parameters. The first two set the IDs for the section and category—here they are both set to 1 which will be the "News / Latest" combination in a default Joomla! installation. Change the default values here to suit your site configuration.

The article `id` is left blank so that Joomla! will assign the next available ID. You might set a value here if you want to overwrite an existing article (updating a user bio, for example).

The `state` parameter sets the article to "unpublished", and this requires an administrator to approve the article and publish it. Change the value to 1 to automatically publish the article.

Lastly, the `created` parameter is set to the current date and time.

See also

- The recipe *Building a complex multi-page form* in *Chapter 12, Adding Advanced Features* describes how to build a more complex article using a series of linked forms.

Redirecting users to other Joomla! pages after submission

ChronoForms makes it easy to show a "Thank You" message to your users after they submit a form, but sometimes you want to send them somewhere else on your site or to another site.

ChronoForms makes this easy too.

Getting ready

That newsletter form yet again.

How to do it...

1. Let's suppose that we want to redirect users to the site home page after the form is submitted.

    Open the **Form Editor | General** tab and scroll down to the **Form URLs** section. Enter `index.php` in the **Redirect URL** box, then **Save** or **Apply** the form and test the form submission.

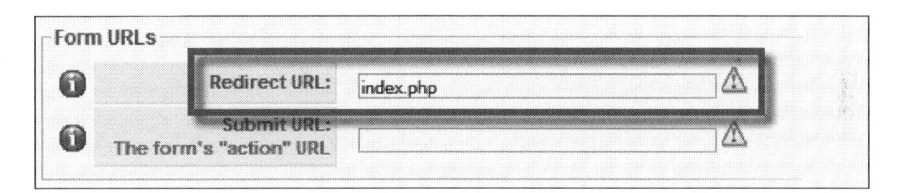

    When the form is submitted the user is redirected to the site home page as we requested.

2. Just to show how this is working try a different URL like `index.php?option=com_user&view=register`. Now the user is redirected to the registration page.

3. One more; this time use `http://google.com`. Now the user is redirected off the site completely to the Google home page.

    If you check the saved data you will find that ChronoForms saved the form data and sent any e-mails before the redirection so all the functionality is still working.

Showing your Form in your Site

> Important: The second box in the **Form URLs** section is the **Submit URL**. If you enter a URL in here then the form output is sent directly to that URL; ChronoForms will never see it and cannot process it in any way. Sometimes this is useful, but not all that often. The warning tooltip for this box says **Don't put anything here unless you know what you are doing**. Please remember that when a form stops working.

How it works...

There is really very little to say; ChronoForms processes the form data as usual and then, instead of displaying the HTML in the OnSubmit Boxes, redirects the user to the specified page.

There's more...

Showing a message after redirection

It can still be useful to show a thank you message to the user on the page that you've redirected them to, provided that they are still on your Joomla! site. You can do this by adding a "System Message".

Change the **ReDirect URL** back to `index.php` and add the following code in the OnSubmit After box:

```
<?php
$mainframe->enqueuemessage('Thanks for submitting our form.');
?>
```

Now when you submit the form, a message is displayed on the new page.

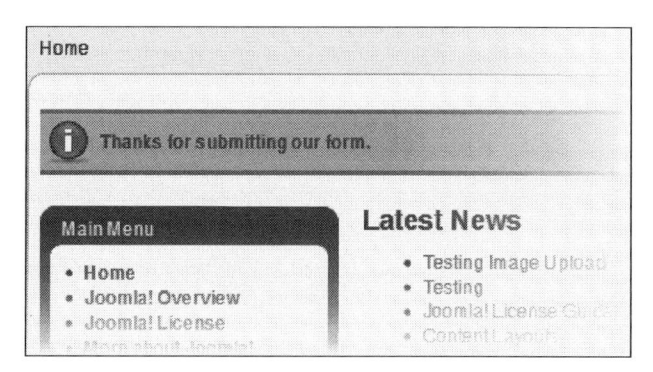

> Not all templates display Joomla! System Messages correctly (or at all). If the message doesn't display for you set your site temporarily to use one of the default Joomla! templates to check. You can add System Messages to a template by including `<jdoc:include type="message" />` in the `index.php` layout file for the template.

Showing a message before redirection

If you are redirecting the user to another site then the system message approach won't work. Instead you can display the normal ChronoForms "Thank You" message before redirecting. To use this method you need to leave the **ReDirect URL** box empty and add the full redirect code to the **OnSubmit** box.

```
<div>Thanks for submitting the form,
   we will redirect you in 5 seconds.</div>
<?php
$doc =& JFactory::getDocument();
$doc->setMetaData('refresh', '5;index.php', 'true');
?>
```

This uses the Joomla! Document class `setMetaData()` method to add a page header that will redirect the page. The critical part is `5;index.php`—5 specifies the delay in seconds and `index.php` the URL to redirect the user to.

Because this sets the page header directly, it will stop ChronoForms when it executes. It's important that everything we want ChronoForms to do is complete before this code line is reached. So it should be the last code in the OnSubmit After code block, and the Run Order should be set in the **RunOrder** tab so that **Order** of **OnSubmit Block** is 3, that is, after the **Plug-ins block** and the **Autogenerated block**.

Redirecting conditionally

Sometimes it is useful to send the user to different pages on your site depending on the information submitted in the form. We can do this once more by adding a code snippet to one of the **OnSubmit Code** boxes.

There isn't an obvious example of this except for the newsletter form so this example directs `John` to one article with `id = 19`, `Jenny` to another with `id = 3`, and everyone else to the site home page.

```
<?php
// get the value of 'name'
$name = JRequest::getString('name', '', 'post');
$name = strtolower($name);
// set the value of $id depending on the 'name' value
```

```
switch ($name) {
  case 'john':
    $id = 19;
    break;
  case 'jenny':
    $id = 3;
    break;
  default:
    $id = '';
    break;
}
// create the redirect url
if ( $id ) {
  $url = 'index.php?option=com_content&view=article&id='.$id;
} else {
  $url = 'index.php';
}
// set the ChronoForms ReDirect URL to the new value
$MyForm->formrow->redirecturl = $url;
?>
```

The first couple of lines get the value of the `name` field and switch it to all lower case; then the `switch` statement sets the article ID depending on the name; and finally we set a redirect URL to include the article ID if there is one, or to `index.php` if there isn't.

This snippet is only about 20 lines of code but it includes several useful tools for building flexible, responsive forms.

> The redirect URLs used here are very simple; it is possible to build complex URLs with query strings using several form values. However, the ChronoForms ReDirect plug-in is a better way of doing this as we shall see later.

See also

- There's a practical redirection application in Chapter 11, *Using Form Plug-ins*, in the *Creating a PayPal purchase form with the ReDirect plug-in* section.

7
Adding Features to your Form

In this chapter, we will cover:

- Adding a validated checkbox
- Adding an "other" box to a drop-down
- Sending an SMS message on submission
- Signing up to a newsletter service
- Adding a conversion-tracking script
- Showing a YouTube video
- Adding a bar-code to a form e-mail
- Adding a character counter to a textarea
- Creating a "double drop-down"

Introduction

We have so far mostly worked with fairly standard forms where the user is shown some inputs, enters some data, and the results are e-mailed and/or saved to a database table. Many forms are just like this, and some have other features added. These features can be of many different kinds and the recipes in this chapter are correspondingly a mixture.

Some, like *Adding a validated checkbox*, change the way the form works. Others, like *Signing up to a newsletter service* change what happens after the form is submitted. The *Showing a YouTube video* recipe isn't a form at all, but makes use of some of ChronoForms' abilities to use HTML code in different ways.

Adding Features to your Form

While you can use these recipes as they are presented, they are just as useful as suggestions for ways to use ChronoForms to solve a wide range of user interactions on your site.

Adding a validated checkbox

Checkboxes are less often used on forms than most of the other elements and they have some slightly unusual behavior that we need to manage. ChronoForms will do a little to help us, but not everything that we need.

In this recipe, we'll look at one of the most common applications—a stand alone checkbox that the user is asked to click to ensure that they've accepted some terms and conditions. We want to make sure that the form is not submitted unless the box is checked.

Getting ready

We'll just add one more element to our basic newsletter form. It's probably going to be best to recreate a new version of the form using the Form Wizard to make sure that we have a clean starting point.

How to do it...

1. In the Form Wizard, create a new form with two **TextBox** elements. In the **Properties** box, add the **Labels** "Name" and "Email" and the **Field Names** "name" and "email" respectively.
2. Now drag in a **CheckBox** element.

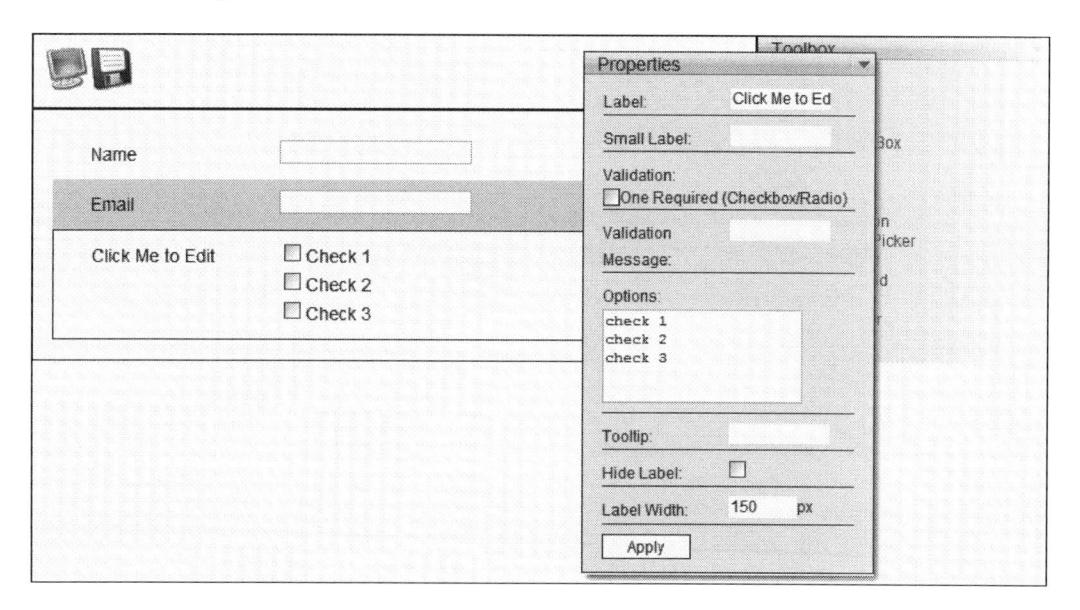

You'll see that ChronoForms inserts the element with three checkboxes and we only need one. In the **Properties** box remove the default values and type in "I agree".

While you are there change the label to "Terms and Conditions".

Lastly, we want to make sure that this box is checked so check the **Validation | One Required** checkbox and add "please confirm your agreement" in the **Validation Message** box. **Apply** the changes to the Properties.

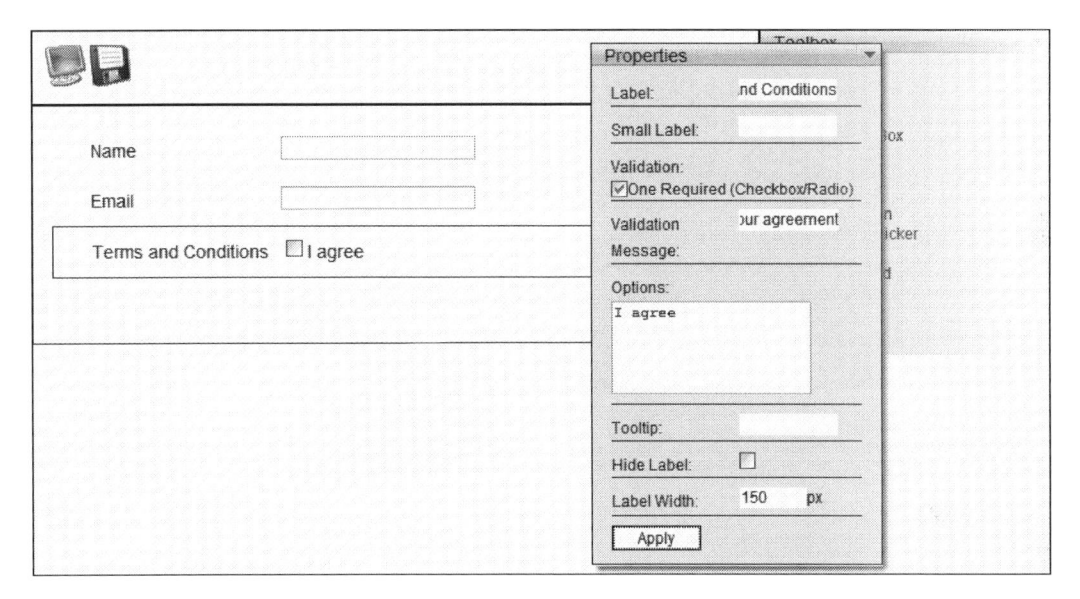

3. To complete the form add the **Button** element, then save your form, publish it, and view it in your browser.
4. To test, click the **Submit** button without entering anything. You should find that the form does not submit and an error message is displayed.

Adding Features to your Form

How it works...

The only special thing to notice about this is that the validation we used was `validate-one-required` and not the more familiar `required`. Checkbox arrays, radio button groups, and select drop-downs will not work with the `required` option as they always have a value set, at least from the perspective of the JavaScript that is running the validation.

There's more...

Validating the checkbox server-side

If the checkbox is really important to us, then we may want to confirm that it has been checked using the server-side validation box.

We want to check and, if our box isn't checked, then create the error message. However, there is a little problem—an unchecked checkbox doesn't return anything at all, there is just no entry in the form results array.

Joomla! has some functionality that will help us out though; the `JRequest::getVar()` function that we use to get the form results allows us to set a default value. If nothing is found in the form results, then the default value will be used instead.

So we can add this code block to the server-side validation box:

```php
<?php
$agree = JRequest::getString('check0[]', 'empty', 'post');
if ( $agree == 'empty' ) {
   return 'Please check the box to confirm your agreement';
}
?>
```

> Note: To test this, we need to remove the `validate-one-required` class from the input in the Form HTML.

Now when we submit the empty form, we see the ChronoForms error message.

> Notice that the input name in the code snippet is `check0[]`. ChronoForms doesn't give you the option of setting the name of a checkbox element in the **Form Wizard | Properties** box. It assigns a `check0`, `check1`, and so on value for you. (You can edit this in the Form Editor if you like.)
>
> And because checkboxes often come in arrays of several linked boxes with the same name, ChronoForms also adds the `[]` to create an array name. If this isn't done then only the value of the last checked box will be returned.

Locking the Submit button until the box is checked

If we want to make the point about terms and conditions even more strongly then we can add some JavaScript to the form to disable the **Submit** button until the box is checked.

We need to make one change to the Form HTML to make this task a little easier. ChronoForms does not add ID attributes to the **Submit** button input; so open the form in the Form Editor, find the line near the end of the Form HTML and alter it to read:

```
<input value="Submit" name="submit" id='submit'
  type="submit" />
```

This will allow us to use the MooTools `$('input_id')` syntax to address the input.

Now add the following snippet into the Form JavaScript box:

```
// stop the code executing
// until the page is loaded in the browser
window.addEvent('load', function() {
  // function to enable and disable the submit button
  function agree() {
    if ( $('check00').checked == true ) {
      $('submit').disabled = false;
    } else {
      $('submit').disabled = true;
```

```
        }
    };
    // disable the submit button on load
    $('submit').disabled = true;
    //execute the function when the checkbox is clicked
    $('check00').addEvent('click', agree);
});
```

Apply or save the form and view it in your browser.

Now as you tick or untick the checkbox, the submit button will be enabled and disabled.

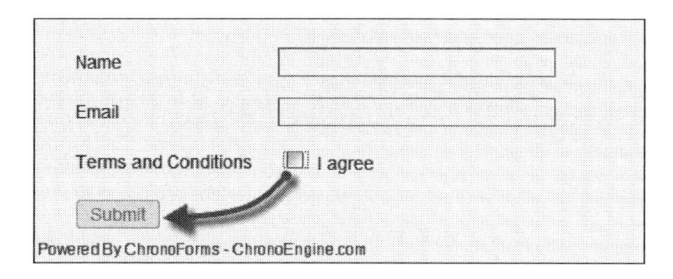

This is a simple example of adding a custom script to a form to add a useful feature. If you are reasonably competent in JavaScript, you will find that there is quite a lot more that you can do.

> There are different styles of laying out both JavaScript and PHP and sometimes fierce debates about where line breaks and spaces should go. We've adopted a style here that is hopefully fairly clear, reasonably compact, and more or less the same for both JavaScript and PHP. If it's not the style you are accustomed to, then we're sorry.

See also

- Chapter 5, *Form Validation and Security*, the *Adding extra security with "server-side" validation of submitted information* section

Adding an "other" box to a drop-down

Drop-downs are a valuable way of offering a list of choices to your user to select from. And sometimes it just isn't possible to make the list complete, there's always another option that someone will want to add. So we add an "other" option to the drop-down. But that tells us nothing, so we need to add an input to tell us what "other" means here.

Getting ready

We'll just add one more element to our basic newsletter form. We haven't used a drop-down before but it is very similar to the check-box element from the previous recipe and the radio button array we used in *Chapter 2, E-mailing Form Results*.

How to do it...

1. Use the Form Wizard to create a form with two **TextBox** elements, a **DropDown** element, and a **Button** element.

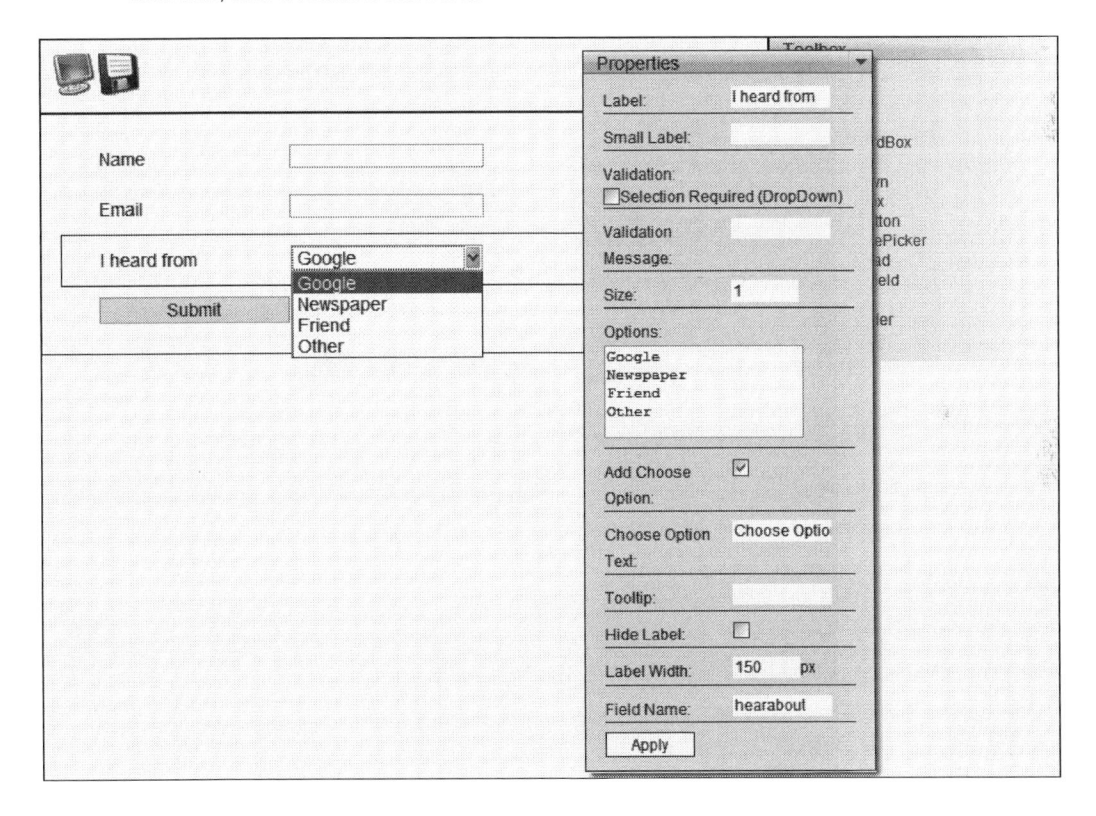

2. The changes to make in the element are:
   - Add "I heard from" in the **Label**
   - Change the **Field Name** to "hearabout"
   - Add some options to the **Options** box—"Google", "Newspaper", "Friend", and "Other"

   Leave the **Add Choose Option** box checked and leave **Choose Option** in the **Choose Option Text** box. **Apply** the **Properties** box.

Adding Features to your Form

3. Make any other changes you need to the form elements; then save the form, publish it, and view it in your browser.

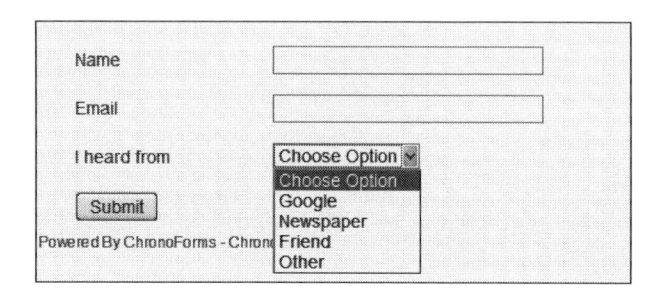

Notice that as well as the four options we added the **Choose Option** entry is at the top of the list. That comes from the checkbox and text field that we left with their default values.

> It's important to have a "null" option like this in a drop-down for two reasons. First, so that it is obvious to a user that no choice has been made. Otherwise it's very easy for them to leave the first option showing and this value—**Google** in this case—will be returned by default. Second, so that we can validate `select-one-required` if necessary. The "null" option has no value set and so can be detected by validation script.

4. Now we just need one more text box to collect details if **Other** is selected.

   Open the form in the Wizard Edit; add one more **TextBox** element after the DropDown element. Give it the Label **please add details** and the name "other".

   Even though we set the name to "other", ChronoForms will have left the input ID attribute as `text_4` or something similar. Open the Form in the Form Editor and change the ID to "other" as well. The same is true of the drop-down. The ID there is `select_2`, change that to `hearabout`.

5. Now we need a script snippet to enable and disable the "other" text box if the **Other** option is selected in the drop-down. Here's the code to put in the **Form JavaScript** box:

```
window.addEvent('domready', function() {
  $('hearabout').addEvent('change', function() {
    if ($('hearabout').value == 'Other' ) {
      $('other').disabled = false;
    } else {
      $('other').disabled = true;
    }
  });
  $('other').disabled = true;
});
```

This is very similar to the code in the last recipe except that it's been condensed a little more by merging the function directly into the `addEvent()`.

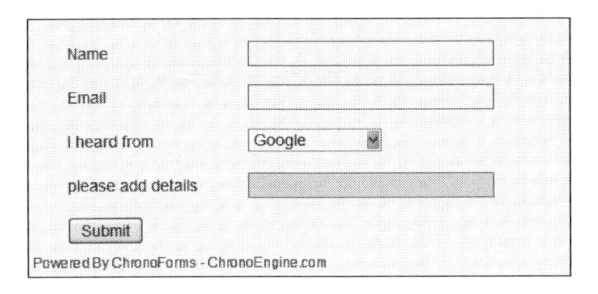

6. When you view the form you will see that the text box for **please add details** is grayed out and blocked until you select **Other** in the drop-down.

> Make sure that you don't make the **please add details** input required. It's an easy mistake to make but it stops the form working correctly as you have to select **Other** in the drop-down to be able to submit it.

How it works...

Once again, this is a little JavaScript that is checking for changes in one part of the form in order to alter the display of another part of the form.

There's more...

Hiding the whole input

It looks a little untidy to have the disabled box showing on the form when it is not required. Let's change the script a little to hide and unhide the input instead of disabling and enabling it.

To make this work we need a way of recognizing the input together with its label. We could deal with both separately, but let's make our lives simpler. In the Form Editor, open the **Form HTML** box and look near the end for the **other** input block:

```
<div class="form_item">
  <div class="form_element cf_textbox">
    <label class="cf_label"
      style="width: 150px;">please add details</label>
    <input class="cf_inputbox" maxlength="150" size="30"
      title="" id="other" name="other" type="text" />
  </div>
  <div class="cfclear"> </div>
</div>
```

Adding Features to your Form

That `<div class="form_element cf_textbox">` looks like it is just what we need so let's add an ID attribute to make it visible to the JavaScript:

```
<div class="form_element cf_textbox" id="other_input">
```

Now we'll modify our script snippet to use this:

```
window.addEvent('domready', function() {
  $('hearabout').addEvent('change', function() {
    if ($('hearabout').value == 'Other' ) {
      $('other_input').setStyle('display', 'block');
    } else {
      $('other_input').setStyle('display', 'none');
    }
  });
  // initialise the display
  if ($('hearabout').value == 'Other' ) {
    $('other_input').setStyle('display', 'block');
  } else {
    $('other_input').setStyle('display', 'none');
  }
});
```

Apply or save the form and view it in your browser. Now the input is invisible see the following screenshot labeled **1** until you select '**Other**' from the drop-down see the following screenshot labeled **2**.

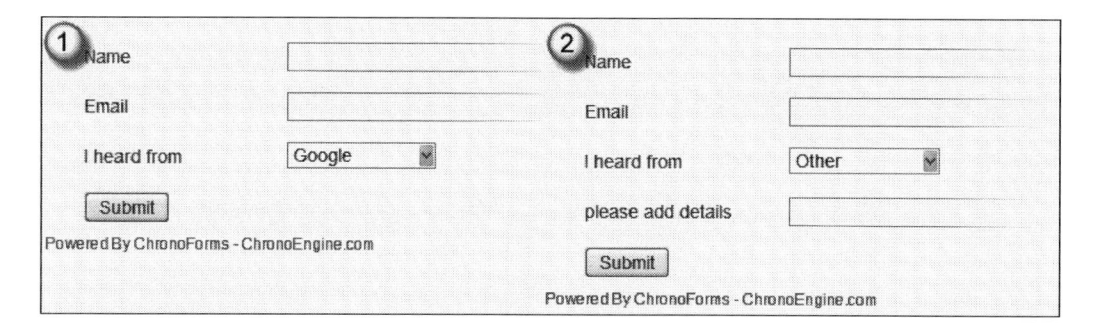

The disadvantage of this approach is that the form can appear to "jump around" as extra fields appear. You can overcome this with a little thought, for example by leaving an empty space.

See also

- *Creating a double drop-down* later in this chapter
- In some of the script here we are using shortcuts from the MooTools JavaScript framework. Version 1.1 of MooTools is installed with Joomla! 1.5 and is usually loaded by ChronoForms. You can find the documentation for MooTools v1.1 at `http://docs111.mootools.net/`

> Version 1.1 is not the latest version of MooTools and many of the more recent MooTools script will not run with the earlier version. Joomla 1.6 is expected to use the latest release.

Sending an SMS message on submission

We looked at the built-in ability of ChronoForms to send e-mails in *Chapter 2, E-mailing Form Results*. Sometimes though you need something more immediate—like a text message sent to a mobile phone. This isn't a built in feature, but it's not hard to add.

Getting ready

You'll need to find a web service that will send SMSes for you. It's possible that your phone provider has a service; but for this example we'll use the **API** from Clickatell (`http://www.clickatell.com`) who claim to cover over 800 networks in more than 220 countries.

You'll need to sign up to a service and find the specific details of its API. Clickatell offers ten free credits for testing.

You'll need a simple form to test with; if you don't have one then our standard newsletter form will do perfectly well.

How to do it...

1. We are going to use the ChronoForms **cURL** plug-in for this recipe. This is one of the ChronoForms plug-ins that comes with the installation and is accessed from the left hand column of the Forms Manager. The cURL and **ReDirect** plug-ins are siblings. Both enable us to send form data to other websites. Use the cURL plug-in when only the data needs to be transferred and the ReDirect plug-in when you need to send the user to the other site as well. You usually need to send the user when they have to authorize something, for example to sign in to a payment site like PayPal.

   Here, we just need to send data to Clickatell so the cURL plug-in is the one to use.

Adding Features to your Form

2. You can access the plug-in configuration by checking the box beside the form name and clicking the plug-in name in the left hand column. Here is the cURL plug-in configuration dialogue.

> We have no connection with or experience of Clickatell and they are used here as an example, not in any way as a recommendation.
>
> **API (Application Programming Interface)** is a set of functions that are made available to allow external users to interact with the service.

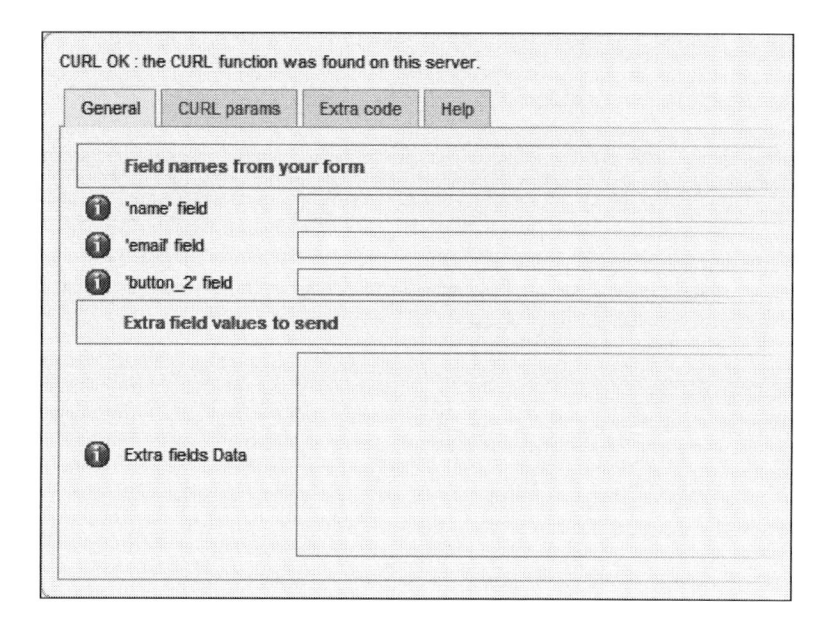

```
CURL OK : the CURL function was found on this server.

  General    CURL params    Extra code    Help

    Field names from your form
    (i) 'name' field          [                    ]
    (i) 'email' field         [                    ]
    (i) 'button_2' field      [                    ]

    Extra field values to send



    (i) Extra fields Data
```

Notice that there is a message at the top of the dialogue telling us that **the cURL function was found on the server**. cURL is an optional part of PHP and though most sites will have it installed, a few may not and will not be able to use this plug-in. (If this happens to you, talk to your ISP who can probably arrange to turn it on.)

This tab—one of four in the dialog—contains a section at the top with inputs that ChronoForms has created, matching the inputs in our form. (Here "button_2" is the submit button.) Below that is a text area where we can add other data that we want to send.

3. If you click the **cURL params** tab and take a quick look, you will see that the top box is "Target URL" which is where we will tell ChronoForms where we want to send the data.

   With that in mind, let's get some information about the Clickatell API.

Let's assume that we have a client who wants to receive a SMS message saying "Form submitted, check your mail now" when this form is submitted on their website. In this case we need to call the same phone number every time.

Clickatell have a range of ways that you can connect to their service. We'll use the simplest here—connecting through a URL, their HTTP/S service. We're going to use the test instructions from their site which say:

- Have the number you wish to send to ready in international format, for example 448311234567
- Open your browser (for example, Internet Explorer), and type in your info in the address bar in the following sequence:
  `http://api.clickatell.com/http/sendmsg?user=xxxxx&password=xxxxx&api_id=xxxxx&to=448311234567&text=Meet+me+at+home`
- The text of your message must be formatted so that + signs replace spaces between words as shown here

We need to break that long URL up into its separate parts. The formal structure of a **URL** is formally defined in a document called RFC3986. Here's an example from that document:

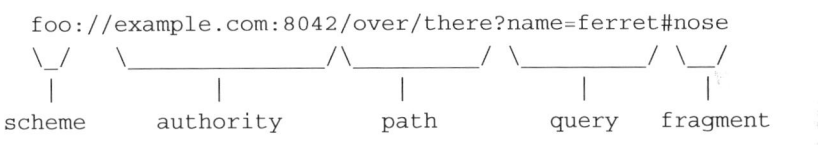

```
 foo://example.com:8042/over/there?name=ferret#nose
 \_/   _____/_____/ _____/ \__/
  |           |             |           |        |
scheme    authority        path       query   fragment
```

In the Clickatell URL we have the **scheme** and **path** before the ? and the **query** after it.

4. In the cURL plug-in dialogue put the scheme and path—`http://api.clickatell.com/http/sendmsg` in the **Target URL** box on the **cURL params** tab and, while you are there set the **Flow control** to **After Email**.

> The only reason for doing so in this case is that if the plug-in is set to **Before Email** it will not run unless **Send Emails** is set to **Yes** on the Form **General** tab.

5. Then we break the query part up into separate **parameter+value** pairs by splitting it at the & signs. We get this list:

```
user=xxxxx
password=xxxxx
api_id=xxxxx
to=448311234567
text=Meet+me+at+home
```

Adding Features to your Form

The `user`, `password`, and `api_id` will take the values you got when you signed up at Clickatell; the value of `to` is the client's phone number in international format (44 is the UK country code, it would be 1 for North America, and so on); and the value of `text` is the message.

All of these values stay the same each time a form is submitted. As they have constant values, we can enter them all into the textarea part of the **General** tab in the cURL plug-in configuration, remembering to replace the spaces in the message with +.

Here's an example we can use for a first test; those used previously aren't real values, so the test won't actually send a message though:

```
user=greyhead
password=mysecret
api_id=987xx123
to=1234567890
text=Form+submitted+-+check+your+mail+now
```

Remember to keep the message all on one line:

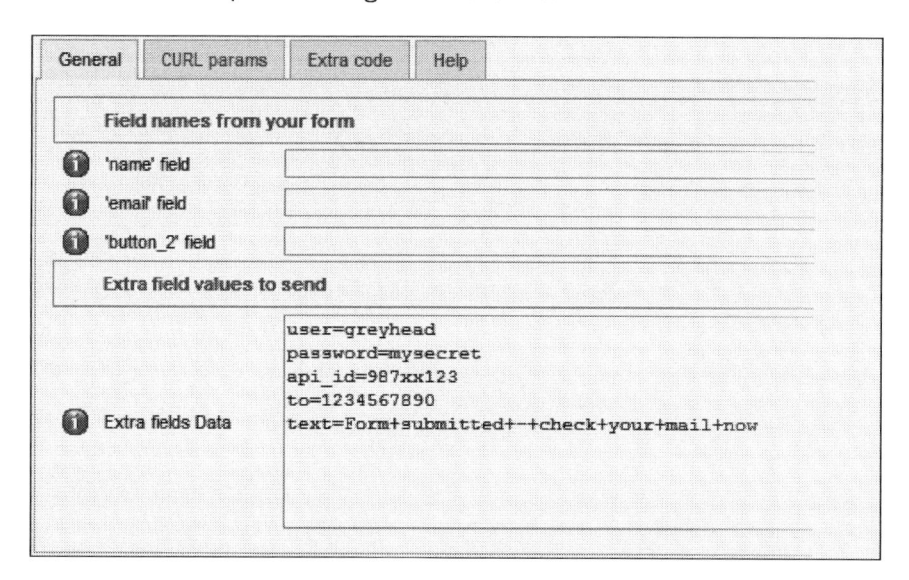

| General | CURL params | Extra code | Help |

Field names from your form

- 'name' field
- 'email' field
- 'button_2' field

Extra field values to send

Extra fields Data
```
user=greyhead
password=mysecret
api_id=987xx123
to=1234567890
text=Form+submitted+-+check+your+mail+now
```

6. Set **Debug** to **On** for the plug-in so that we can see the output, save the plug-in configuration, enable the plug-in in the Form **Plugins** tab if necessary, and then go to the form and submit it.

7. Here's the result from submitting exactly the data used previously:

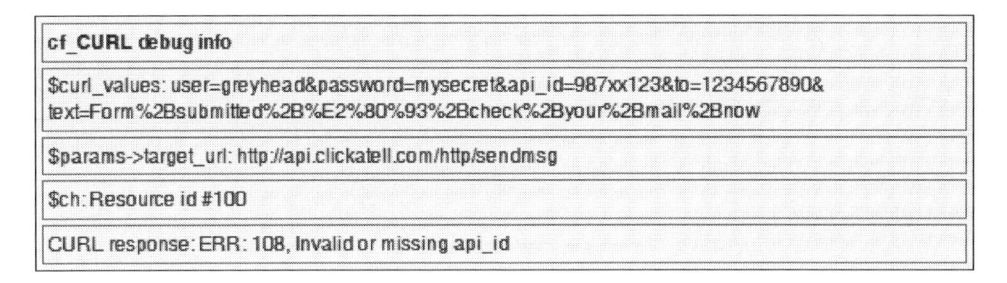

cf_CURL debug info
$curl_values: user=greyhead&password=mysecret&api_id=987xx123&to=1234567890& text=Form%2Bsubmitted%2B%E2%80%93%2Bcheck%2Byour%2Bmail%2Bnow
$params->target_url: http://api.clickatell.com/http/sendmsg
$ch: Resource id #100
CURL response: ERR: 108, Invalid or missing api_id

8. Now we haven't got a valid `api_id` for this test, so the message is not sent. But we do get an error message back from Clickatell (see the last line of the debug listing) so we know that we delivered our data successfully to their API.

How it works...

The cURL functionality is a set of PHP code that is built to allow just this kind of interaction between one computer and another over the internet using some standard protocols, in particular the HTTP POST protocol used by forms.

The ChronoForms cURL plug-in provides a simple way to use a small part of the cURL functionality with our forms and form data. There are many cURL options, most of which aren't accessible through the plug-in (see the PHP documentation at http://php.net/manual/en/book.curl.php for much more information).

Signing up to a newsletter service

We've been using that newsletter form for a long time now but haven't yet mentioned how we are going to send out the newsletters. One way to do this is to use a hosted newsletter service. There are many of these available each with slightly different offerings. Some familiar names include Aweber, MailChimp, Constant Contact, iContact, and half a dozen or so others.

Each of these services will have an API that can be accessed to update records. Some of these can be very rich and complex, others almost non-existent. However, all of them have suggestions for a form that you can include on your website for newsletter signups. This form code will give us enough to sign up our user automatically to the service.

We will work with iContact here but the same principals will apply to any of the other services.

Adding Features to your Form

Getting ready

We first need to find the "sign-up" form code for our newsletter service provider. iContact has a little wizard that generates a form in two versions—the Manual Sign-up Form is the one we want as it shows all of the form information.

How to do it...

1. Here's the HTML code the iContact sign-up wizard produces, with some styling and validation code removed:

```html
<form method=post
  action="https://app.icontact.com/icp/signup.php"
  name="icpsignup" id="icpsignup636" accept-charset="UTF-8" >
<input type=hidden name=redirect
  value="http://www.icontact.com/www/signup/thanks.html" />
<input type=hidden name=errorredirect
  value="http://www.icontact.com/www/signup/error.html" />

<div id="SignUp">
  <table width="260" class="signupframe" border="0"
      cellspacing="0" cellpadding="5">
    <tr>
      <td valign=top align=right>Email</td>
      <td align=left>
        <input type=text name="fields_email">
      </td>
    </tr>
    <tr>
      <td valign=top align=right>Last Name</td>
      <td align=left>
        <input type=text name="fields_lname">
      </td>
    </tr>
    <input type=hidden name="listid" value="9999">
    <input type=hidden name="specialid:9999" value="XAPD ">
    <input type=hidden name=clientid value="123456">
    <input type=hidden name=formid value="777">
```

```
      <input type=hidden name=reallistid value="1">
      <input type=hidden name=doubleopt value="0">
      <tr>
        <td> </td>
        <td>
          <input type="submit" name="Submit" value="Submit">
        </td>
      </tr>
    </table>
  </div>
</form>
```

The parts that interests us are—the form **Action URL** `https://app.icontact.com/icp/signup.php`, and then the list of input names and values which we can extract from the surrounding HTML:

- `fields_email`
- `fields_lname`
- `redirect=http://www.icontact.com/www/signup/thanks.html`
- `errorredirect="http://www.icontact.com/www/signup/error.html`
- `listid=9999`
- `specialid:9999=XAPD`
- `clientid=123456`
- `formid=777`
- `reallistid=1`
- `doubleopt=0`

The first two match up to the two fields in our form, the remainder have the same values whatever values are entered into the form.

The `redirect` and `errorredirect` inputs will not have any effect working with cURL so we can leave those out.

Adding Features to your Form

2. So we can use the cURL plug-in just as we did in the last recipe, but this time we will link the first two input names here to the corresponding form fields.

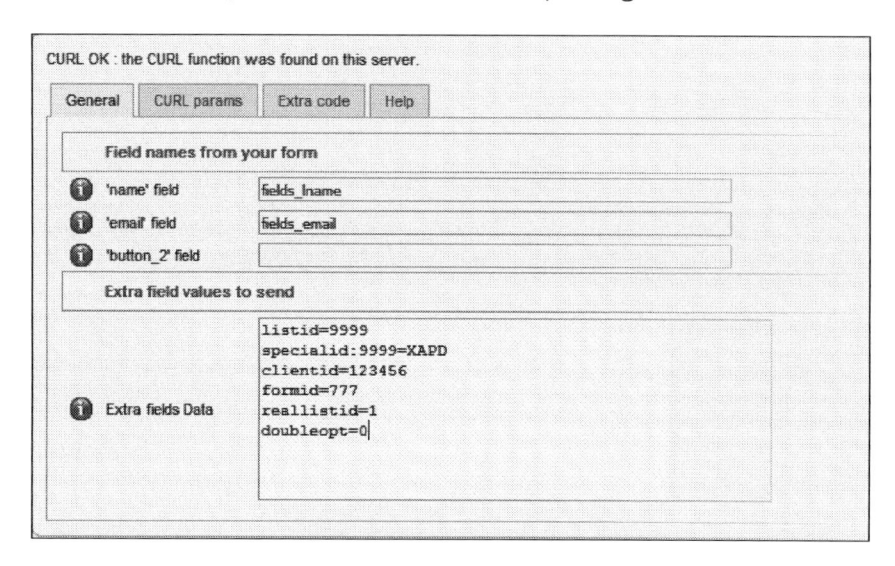

```
CURL OK : the CURL function was found on this server.

[ General ] [ CURL params ] [ Extra code ] [ Help ]

Field names from your form
  (i) 'name' field      [fields_lname                    ]
  (i) 'email' field     [fields_email                    ]
  (i) 'button_2' field  [                                ]

Extra field values to send

  (i) Extra fields Data
                        listid=9999
                        specialid:9999=XAPD
                        clientid=123456
                        formid=777
                        reallistid=1
                        doubleopt=0
```

Remember to add the **Target URL** on the second tab, then save the plug-in configuration. Open the form in the Form Editor, enable the plug-in on the **Plugins** tab and **Apply** or **Save** the form.

3. View the form in your browser and test it.

> Note that the IDs shown here are not valid so this exact data will not work. However, with the correct IDs this form successfully adds a new record to the iContact database, except that here iContact is setup to use **First Name** and **Last Name** fields and we've put both parts into the **Last Name** field. It would be simple to add an extra input to our form to handle this.

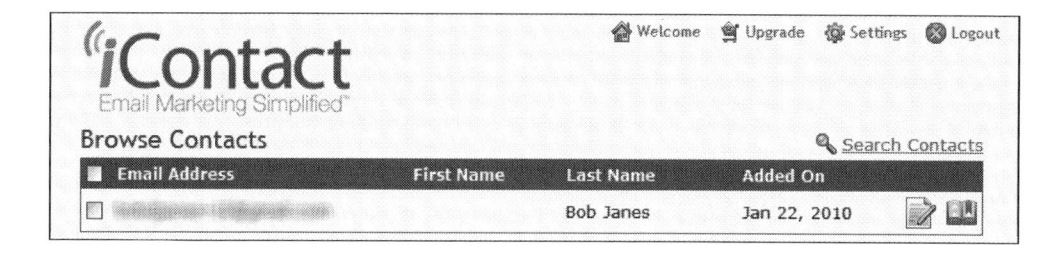

```
((( iContact                          Welcome  Upgrade  Settings  Logout
    Email Marketing Simplified®
Browse Contacts                                     Search Contacts
  [ ] Email Address         First Name    Last Name    Added On
  [ ] ...................                 Bob Janes    Jan 22, 2010
```

How it works...

We are pulling out the critical information from the form that the iContact wizard created and using the cURL plug-in to submit that as though it was coming from a form on our site.

See also

- The previous recipe in this chapter shows another way of using the cURL plug-in.
- The recipe *Creating a simple newsletter signup* in Chapter 10, *Creating Common Forms* shows how to create the underlying form and save it in the database. Also, the *Creating a form to link to Acajoom* recipe in the same chapter looks at a similar application within Joomla!

Adding a conversion tracking script

If you are running a commercial site then you may want to use one of the conversion tracking services to record the customer action after submission. Here we'll use the Google tracking code as an example; others will be very similar.

> Google Conversion Tracking is not the same as Analytics which track every page on your site. Google Analytics (and other similar services) need the code on every page and the best way to do this is either with a custom module (for example, the gh Google Analytics module), or by adding the code to your template.

Getting ready

You can use this with any form but you will need to have the ID codes for your own Google AdWords account to use it.

How to do it...

1. The conversion tracking code has one slightly different requirement to other form scripts. We only want to show it after conversion so we don't want the code in the Form HTML, but in one of the OnSubmit After boxes instead. The **OnSubmit After** box is preferred but the **OnSubmit Before** will work as well, as long as you have **Send Emails** set to **Yes** on the Form **General** tab.

Adding Features to your Form

2. Here's one of the example scripts from the Google AdWords™ Conversion Tracking Setup Guide:

```
<!-- Google Code for Purchase Conversion Page -->
<script language="JavaScript" type="text/javascript">
<!--
var google_conversion_id = 1234567890;
var google_conversion_language = "en_US";
var google_conversion_format = "1";
var google_conversion_color = "666666";
if (5.0) {
  var google_conversion_value = 5.0;
}
var google_conversion_label = "Purchase";
//-->
</script>

<script language="JavaScript"
  src="http://www.googleadservices.com/pagead/conversion.js">
</script>

<noscript>
<img height=1 width=1 border=0
src="http://www.googleadservices.com/pagead/conversion/1234567890/
  ?value=5.0&label=Purchase&script=0">
</noscript>
```

You'll see that there are three parts to this script:

- A JavaScript that sets some parameter values
- A link to download a script from Google
- A "noscript" script to allow conversion tracking for users without JavaScript enabled

You could just put this code as it is into the OnSubmit box and it will work fine most of the time.

If you want to be a little more elegant then you can use a little PHP to load the first two parts from the page head rather than the body. Note that you can't use the ChronoForms JavaScript box as that only works when the form is displayed and that's not what we want here.

```
<?php
$script = "
var google_conversion_id = 1234567890;
var google_conversion_language = "en_US";
```

```
        var google_conversion_format = "1";
        var google_conversion_color = "666666";
        if (5.0) {
                var google_conversion_value = 5.0;
        }
        ";
        $doc =& JFactory::getDocument();
        $doc->addScriptDeclaration($script);[/code]
        $doc->addScript( "http://www.googleadservices.com/pagead/
           conversion.js" );
        ?>

        <noscript>
        <div style="display:inline;">
        <img height=1 width=1 border=0 src="http://www.googleadservices.
           com/pagead/conversion/1234567890/?value=5.0&label=Purchase&scri
           pt=0">
        </div>
        </noscript>
```

3. That really is all that is required except to note that you must make sure that the ChronoForms "Thank you" page is displayed in order for the script to be delivered. See *Chapter 6, Showing your Form in your Site,* the *Redirecting users to other Joomla! Pages after submission* recipe for a way to show the page and then to redirect the user.

Showing a YouTube video

This is the "not really a form" recipe in this book, it just opens a little door to some of the other, more unexpected, capabilities of ChronoForms.

For the most part Joomla! protects the content you can display on your pages; it's easy to show HTML + CSS formatted content, more difficult to show PHP and JavaScript. There are many modules, plug-ins and extensions that can help with this but if you have ChronoForms installed then it may be able to help.

ChronoForms is designed to show pages that use HTML, CSS, PHP, and JavaScript working together. Most often the pages created are forms but nothing actually requires that any form inputs are included so we can add any code that we like.

> ChronoForms will wrap our code inside `<form>. . .</form>` tags which means that we can't embed a form (why would we want to?), but otherwise most things are possible.

Adding Features to your Form

Getting ready

You will need the ID of the YouTube video that you want to display. We're going to use a video from a conference at Ashridge Business School, but any video will work in essentially the same way.

> This recipe was developed for this particular video to force display of the HD version. At that time HD was a new option on YouTube and was not readily accessible as it is now.

How to do it...

1. Find the video you want on YouTube and look for the links boxes in the right hand column. Here we've clicked the "customize" icon—the little gear wheel—to open up the options menu.

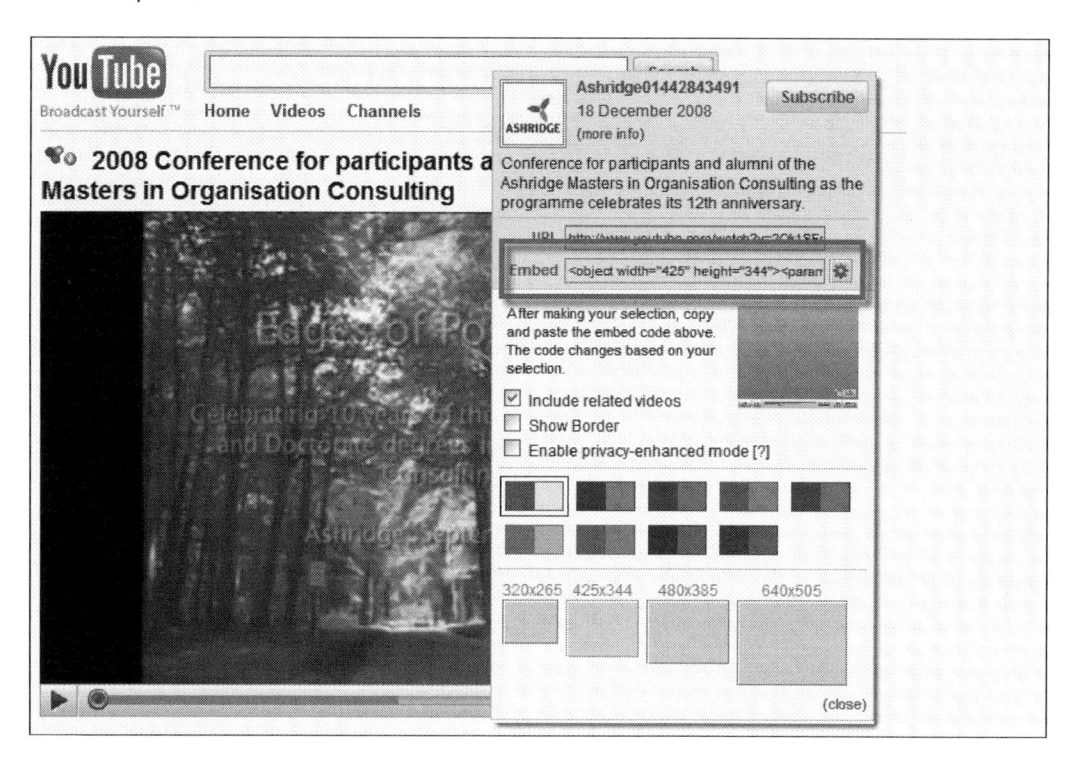

2. When you've set the options you want copy the code from the **Embed** box. Here is the code from this video with some added line breaks for clarity:

```
<object width="425" height="344">
<param name="movie"
   value="http://www.youtube.com/v/2Ok1SFnMS4E&hl=en_GB&fs=1&">
</param>
<param name="allowFullScreen" value="true"></param>
<param name="allowscriptaccess" value="always"></param>
<embed src="http://www.youtube.com/v/2Ok1SFnMS4E&hl=en_GB&fs=1&"
   type="application/x-shockwave-flash" allowscriptaccess="always"
   allowfullscreen="true" width="425" height="344">
</embed>
</object>
```

3. To create a good looking page, we are going to add some HTML before and after this snippet:

```
<h3>Video Postcards from the Edge</h3>
<div>The video of the 2008 AMOC Conference</div>
<div style='margin:6px; padding:0px; border:6px solid silver;
width:425px;'>
<object width="425" height="344">
<param name="movie" value="http://www.youtube.com/v/2Ok1SFnMS4E&hl
   =en&fs=1&ap=%2526fmt%3D18"></param>
<param name="allowFullScreen" value="true"></param>
<param name="allowscriptaccess" value="always"></param>
<embed src="http://www.youtube.com/v/2Ok1SFnMS4E&hl=en&fs
   =1&ap=%2526fmt%3D18" type="application/x-shockwave-flash"
   allowscriptaccess="always" allowfullscreen="true" width="425"
   height="344"></embed></object>
</div>
<div>Some more text . . .</div>
```

> If you look closely, you'll see that there is also a new parameter in the URL—&ap=%2526fmt%3D18—which is there to force the HD version of the video to be used.

Adding Features to your Form

4. Paste this code into the Form HTML box of a new form, save, and publish it.

> Of course, it would be entirely possible to embed the video and to add form inputs in the same page, maybe to ask for comments or reviews.

How it works...

Very simply ChronoForms allows you to embed scripts into the page HTML that are not permitted in standard Joomla! articles.

Adding a barcode to a form e-mail

Sometimes it's important to add a unique identifier to the form response, for example travel or event tickets. In this recipe we will look at generating a "random" identifier and adding it to the form e-mail as a scannable barcode.

Chapter 7

Getting ready

We're going to need a simple form. Our newsletter form will be perfect although we'll be adding to the code in the Form HTML box.

We'll need a simple function to create the "random identifier" which we will see shortly.

Lastly we"ll need code to generate a barcode. Rather than taking time reinventing this particular wheel, we're going to use a PHP program created by Charles J Scheffold and made available for use or download from `http://www.sid6581.net/cs/php-scripts/barcode/`.

How to do it...

1. First, grab a copy of the `barcode.php` file from `sid6581.net`.
2. We'll need to make this file accessible to our form. So let's create a new folder inside the ChronoForms front-end folder.

   You'll probably need to use an FTP client to do this, or install the "exTplorer" Joomla! extension which will allow you to create folders from within the Joomla! Site Admin interface.

   - Browse to `[root]/components/com_chronocontact` and create a new `includes` folder
   - Copy the standard Joomla! `index.html` file from the `com_chronocontact` folder into the new folder
   - Upload the `barcode.php` file into the new `includes` folder

3. Now, we are going to add the function to create a "random" identifier to the Form HTML. This is a small function that creates an alphanumeric string when it is called.

```
<?php
if ( !$mainframe->isSite() ) { return; }
/*
 function to generate a random alpha-numeric code
 using a specified pattern
 *
 * @param $pattern string
 * @return string
 */
function generateIdent($pattern='AA9999A')
{
  $alpha = array("A","B","C","D","E","F","G","H",
    "J","K","L","M","N","P","Q","R","S","T","U","V","W",
    "X","Y","Z");
  $digit = array("1","2","3","4","5","6","7","8","9");
```

Adding Features to your Form

```php
    $return = "";
    $pattern_array = str_split($pattern, 1);
    foreach ( $pattern_array as $v ) {
      if ( is_numeric($v) ) {
        $return .= $digit[array_rand($digit)];
      } elseif ( in_array(strtoupper($v), $alpha) ) {
        $return .= $alpha[array_rand($alpha)];
      } else {
        $return .= " ";
      }
    }
    return $return;
}
?>
```

We call this function using `generateIdent()` or `generateIdent('pattern')` where the pattern is a string of `A`s and `9`s that defines the shape of the ident we want. The default is `AA9999A`, giving idents like `KX4629G`. This will be perfectly fine for our example here.

We also want to add the ident into the form and we'll use a hidden field to do that, but to make it visible we'll also display the value.

```php
<?php
$ident = generateIdent();
echo "<div>Ident is $ident</div>";
?>

<input type='hidden' name='ident' id='ident'
  value='<?php echo $ident; ?>' />
```

> In day to day use we probably wouldn't generate the ident until after the form is submitted. There is often no useful value in displaying it on the form and essentially the same code will work in the OnSubmit boxes. However, here it makes the process clearer to generate it in the form HTML.

4. We can add both these code snippets to our form just before the submit button element. Then apply or save the form and view it in your browser.

The layout may not be very elegant but the **Ident** is there. Refresh the browser a few times to be sure that it is different each time.

> It's simpler and tempting to use serial numbers to identify records. If you are saving data in a table then these are generated for you as record IDs. It does create some problems though; in particular, it can make it very easy to guess what other IDs are valid and if, as we often do, we include the ID in a URL it may well be possible to guess what other URLs will be valid. Using a random string like this makes that kind of security breach more difficult and less likely.

5. We said though that we'd generate a barcode, so let's develop this form one more step and show the barcode in the form.

    If you look at the code in `barcode.php`, it shows a list of parameters and says what we can use. For example:

    ```
    <img src="barcode.php?barcode=123456&width=320&height=200">
    ```

6. We need to modify this a little to link to the new folder for the file and to add our generated ident value:

    ```
    <img src="/components/com_chronocontact/includes/barcode.php?barcode=<? php echo $ident;?>&width=320&height=8">
    ```

    This code can go in place of the "echo" line we used to display the ident value:

    ```
    <?php
    $ident = generateIdent();
    echo "<img src='".JURI::base()
    ."components/com_chronocontact/includes/barcode.php?barcode="
    .$ident."&width=320&height=80' />";
    ?>
    ```

Adding Features to your Form

7. Apply or save the form and view it in your browser.

   There we have it—a bar code in our form showing the random ident that we have created.

   > If you don't see any graphic and the code appears to be correct then you may not have the PHP GD graphics library installed. Check on the **AntiSpam** tab for any of your forms and you will see a **GD Info** box. The GD library is now included in the vast majority of PHP installations. If you don't have it then check with your ISP to see if the library can be enabled.

8. Now that's actually not of much use except to show that it works, you can't scan a bar code off the screen. Where we want it is in our Email template.

   The code to add to the template is:

   ```
   <div>Your code: {ident}</div>
   <img src="<?php echo JURI::base().'components/com_chronocontact/
     includes/'; ?>barcode.php?barcode={ident}&width=280&height=100"
     />
   ```

9. As this includes some PHP, we can't add it using the Rich Text Editor. First we need to go to the **Email Setup | Properties** box and set **Use Template Editor** to **No**, apply the Properties, then apply the form and go to the **Email Template** tab.

   > To avoid an "oddity" in the current release of ChronoForms it may be necessary to comment out the `generateIdent()` function code block in the Form HTML, while you create an Email Setup. Just put `/* & */` before and after the block if you get a blank page or see a PHP Error message about re-declaring the function.

10. Now click the **Email Template** tab and paste the code at the end of the textarea.

11. Submit the form to test.

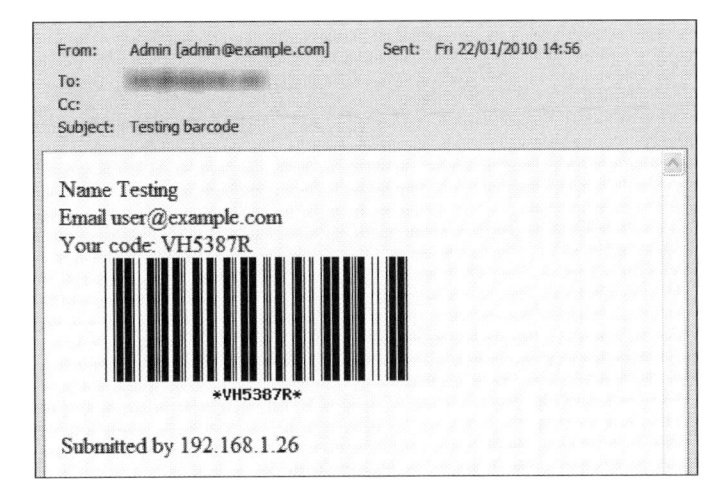

```
From:    Admin [admin@example.com]      Sent: Fri 22/01/2010 14:56
To:      ▓▓▓▓▓▓▓▓▓▓
Cc:
Subject: Testing barcode

Name Testing
Email user@example.com
Your code: VH5387R

[|||||| barcode |||||||]
       *VH5387R*

Submitted by 192.168.1.26
```

We now have a printable e-mail complete with a barcode showing our random ident.

How it works...

In this recipe we did a couple of things. We added some more complex PHP to the Form HTML that we had before and we imported a PHP script found on the internet and successfully used that in combination with ChronoForms.

There are many hundreds of useful scripts available for almost any conceivable function. Not all are of good quality and not all will work in this way but, with a little work, a surprising number will function perfectly well.

There's more...

We said earlier that it might be better to generate the ident after the form is submitted. Here's the code to use in the **OnSubmit Before** code box to get the same result in the e-mail:

```php
<?php
if ( ! $mainframe->isSite() ) { return; }
JRequest::setVar('ident', generateIdent());

/*
function to generate a random alpha-numeric code
using a specified pattern
*
* @param $pattern string
* @return string
```

Adding Features to your Form

```
    */
    function generateIdent($pattern='AA9999A')
    {
      $alpha = array("A","B","C","D","E","F","G","H",
        "J","K","L","M","N","P","Q","R","S","T","U","V","W",
        "X","Y","Z");
      $digit = array("1","2","3","4","5","6","7","8","9");
      $return = "";
      $pattern_array = str_split($pattern, 1);
      foreach ( $pattern_array as $v ) {
        if ( is_numeric($v) ) {
          $return .= $digit[array_rand($digit)];
        } elseif ( in_array(strtoupper($v), $alpha) ) {
          $return .= $alpha[array_rand($alpha)];
        } else {
          $return .= " ";
        }
      }
      return $return;
    }
    ?>
```

If you use this, then you can remove all of the additional code from the Form HTML box leaving just the basic HTML generated by the Form Wizard. The Email template code remains as we created it previously.

Adding a character counter to a textarea

Some users can get just a bit long-winded when presented with a text area to type into. When that happens it would be useful to be able to show the number of characters remaining and to block the input of extra characters if the limit is exceeded.

Getting ready

We'll use a very simple form created by the **Form Wizard** with just two elements—a **TextArea** and a **Button**. We will need to know the ID of the text area; by default it will be `text_0`, the same as the element name.

Chapter 7

How to do it...

1. Create the form, save it, and view it in your browser.

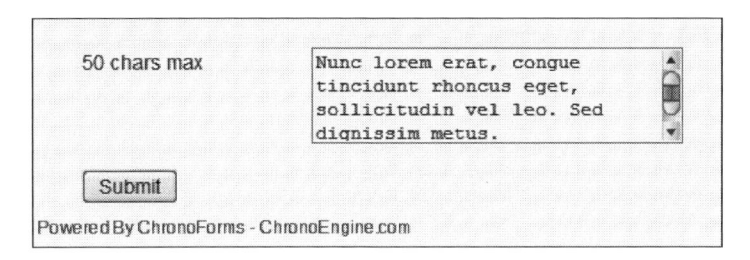

2. Notice that although we've labeled the textarea **50 chars max** it takes nearly 100 without complaint. In fact you could keep on typing for a long time and the textarea would just scroll down and accept the input.

3. We're going to add some JavaScript to the Form JavaScript box to count the characters:

```
window.addEvent('load', function() {
  // execute the check after each keystroke
  $('text_0').addEvent('keyup', function() {
    // set the maximum number of characters
    max_chars = 50;
    // get the current value of the input field
    current_value = $('text_0').value;
    // get current character count
    current_length = current_value.length;
    // calculate remaining chars
    remaining_chars = max_chars current_length;
    // show the remaining characters
    $('counter').innerHTML = remaining_chars;
  });
});
```

4. We would want to show the results of our calculation on the form somewhere, so we'll add some extra text to the textarea label:

```
<label class="cf_label" style="width: 150px;">50 chars max
<br /><span id='counter'>50</span> chars left</label>
```

185

Adding Features to your Form

That span, with `id='counter'` is where we'll show the characters remaining.

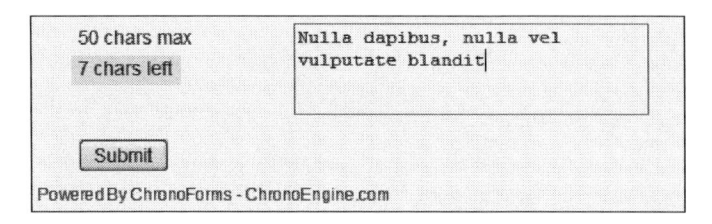

```
50 chars max        Nulla dapibus, nulla vel
7 chars left        vulputate blandit


 Submit
Powered By ChronoForms - ChronoEngine.com
```

This works very nicely to count the remaining characters. Unfortunately, it does nothing to stop more characters being entered, all that happens is that we quickly show a negative number of characters remaining.

5. We need some actions to block more characters being entered. We could disable the input as we did for the **Submit** button in an earlier recipe, but this stops the user editing their entry. What we will do is to trim the entry to 50 characters and show a warning.

   We need to add some more script in place of the `innerHTML` line previously shown:

   ```
   // Change color if remaining chars are five or less
   if ( remaining_chars <= 5 ) {
     $('text_0').setStyle('background-color', '#F88');
     $('text_0').value
       = $('text_0').value.substring(0, max_chars-1);
     if ( remaining_chars <= 0 ) {
       remaining_chars = 0;
     }
   } else {
     $('text_0').setStyle('background-color', 'white');
   }
   $('counter').innerHTML = remaining_chars;
   });
   ```

   This script does nothing much if there are more than five characters left except to clear any warnings. If there are less than five characters left, it changes the text area background to a reddish color; if there are no characters left it will trim the text to 50 characters preventing anything new being added.

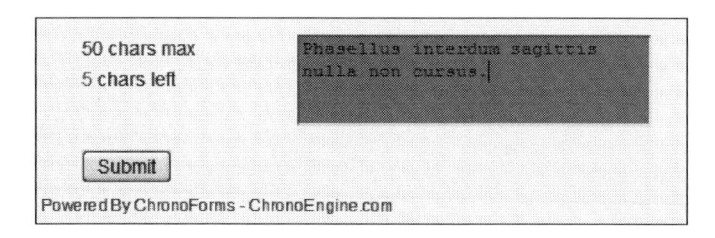

```
50 chars max        Phasellus interdum sagittis
5 chars left        nulla non cursus.


 Submit
Powered By ChronoForms - ChronoEngine.com
```

6. This is a fairly simple variant of this kind of script, more elaborate versions can show "thermometer" indicators of the characters left in place of the simple count here. And we could have more subtle messages too!

How it works...

The JavaScript runs a little function to count the characters each time a key click is recorded in the textarea. When the count gets near 50, it shows a warning and then acts when the count reaches 50.

This, like the last recipe, is an example of taking a script published on the Internet for free use and modifying it to work with a ChronoForms Form.

Creating a double drop-down

A 'double drop-down' is a pair of linked drop downs where the options in the second drop-down depend on the selection in the first drop-down.

As an example, this cookbook has a series of chapters, each of which contain several recipes. We might have a list of chapters in the first drop-down and then show the recipes from the selected chapter in the second drop-down.

For simplicity here we'll just use two chapters each with three recipes:

- Chapter 1: Recipe a, recipe b, and recipe c
- Chapter 2: Recipe x, recipe y, and recipe z

There are two fundamentally different ways of approaching this recipe. The first is to load all of the options into the Form HTML before the page is sent to the browser and to hide the unwanted options; the second is to load none of the options but to use an AJAX request to get the options we need when we need them.

Both approaches are useful in different situations. Where there are relatively few options, as there are with the book, the "load all" approach is easier and that is what we will use here.

Getting ready

We will need the code for a form with two **DropDown**s. You can create this with the **Form Wizard** though we will then edit the code in the **Form HTML** box.

Adding Features to your Form

How to do it...

1. Here's the Form HTML we will start with:

```html
<div class="form_item">
  <div class="form_element cf_dropdown">
    <label class="cf_label"
      style="width: 150px;">Chapter</label>
    <select class="cf_inputbox" id="chapter" size="1"
      title="" name="chapter">
      <option value="">Choose Option</option>
      <option value="1">Chapter 1</option>
      <option value="2">Chapter 2</option>
    </select>
  </div>
  <div class="cfclear"> </div>
</div>

<div class="form_item">
  <div class="form_element cf_dropdown">
    <label class="cf_label"
      style="width: 150px;">Recipe</label>
    <select class="cf_inputbox" id="recipe" size="1"
      title="" name="recipe">
      <option value="">Choose Option</option>
      <option value="a">Recipe a</option>
      <option value="b">Recipe b</option>
      <option value="c">Recipe c</option>
      <option value="x">Recipe x</option>
      <option value="y">Recipe y</option>
      <option value="z">Recipe z</option>
    </select>
  </div>
  <div class="cfclear"> </div>
</div>

<div class="form_item">
  <div class="form_element cf_button">
    <input value="Submit" name="submit"
      id="submit" type="submit" />
  </div>
  <div class="cfclear"> </div>
</div>
```

The Wizard code has been edited to add more meaningful names and IDs to the input elements and to change the option values to simple numbers or letters. Both of these changes make it easier to work with the code using JavaScript.

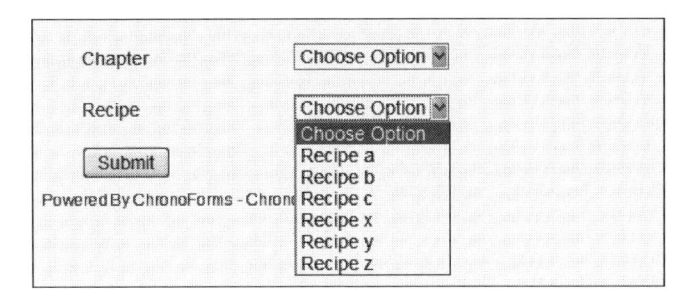

As you can see, at the moment all of the recipes are being displayed.

2. We will now edit the Form HTML to add option groups to the recipe options list:

```html
<optgroup label="Chapter 1" id="ch_1"
    disabled="disabled" >
  <option value="a">Recipe a</option>
  <option value="b">Recipe b</option>
  <option value="c">Recipe c</option>
</optgroup>
<optgroup label="Chapter 2" id="ch_2"
    disabled="disabled" >
  <option value="x">Recipe x</option>
  <option value="y">Recipe y</option>
  <option value="z">Recipe z</option>
</optgroup>
```

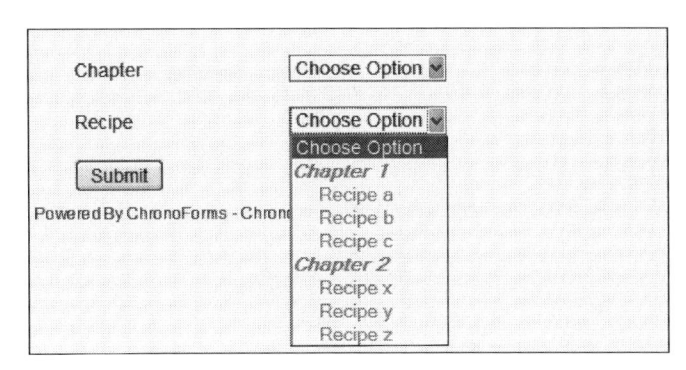

Now we have our recipes grouped by chapter and they are all disabled as no chapter is selected.

Adding Features to your Form

> You cannot disable individual options in a drop-down list but, as we see, you can disable option groups which makes them very useful for this kind of form.

3. Next we need to add a little script to check the chapters and enable the corresponding recipe option group:

```
window.addEvent('load', function() {
  // set the chapter count
  var num_chapters = 2
  // code to execute when the chapter changes
  $('chapter').addEvent('blur', function() {
    var chapter = $('chapter').value;
    var optgroup = 0;
    // loop through the chapters
    for ( var i = 1; i <= num_chapters; i++ ) {
      if ( i == chapter ) {
        // if this chapter is selected
        $('ch_'+i).disabled = false;
      } else {
        // if this chapter is not selected
        $('ch_'+i).disabled = true;
      }
    }
  });
});
```

Most of this script is self evident except perhaps for `'ch_'+i` – this is adding the current chapter number to `ch_` to give us `ch_1`, `ch_2`, and so on, which are the IDs of the recipe option groups.

4. Add this script snippet to the **Form JavaScript** box, apply or save the form, and reload it in your browser window.

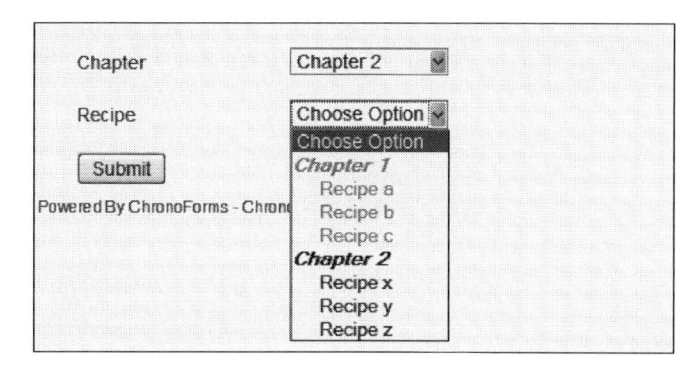

Now the corresponding option group is enabled when we choose a chapter and if we reselect **Choose Option** in the **Chapter** box, then all of the recipe options are disabled again.

5. We can take this one step further by hiding the disabled option groups with a few more lines in the script:

```
window.addEvent('load', function() {
  var num_chapters = 2
  // hide all the recipes to start with
  for ( var i = 1; i <= num_chapters; i++ ) {
    $('ch_'+i).setStyle('display', 'none');
  }
  $('chapter').addEvent('blur', function() {
    var chapter = $('chapter').value;
    var optgroup = 0;
    for ( var i = 1; i <= num_chapters; i++ ) {
      if ( i == chapter ) {
        $('ch_'+i).disabled = false;
        $('ch_'+i).setStyle('display', 'block');
      } else {
        $('ch_'+i).disabled = true;
        $('ch_'+i).setStyle('display', 'none');
      }
    }
  });
});
```

Here we are using `.setStyle('display', 'none')` and `.setStyle('display', 'block')` to hide and unhide the option groups.

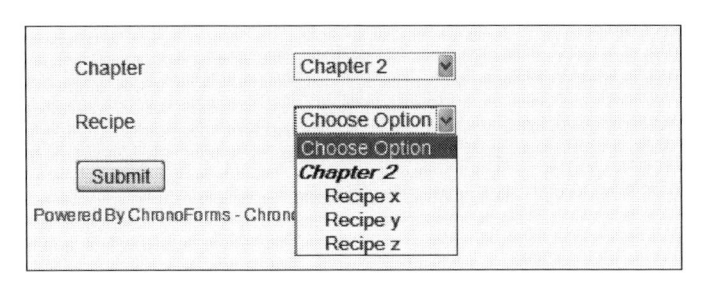

Adding Features to your Form

6. Now we have a working double-drop down. Because we have kept all of the options in place the standard ChronoForms "validate-selection" will work as usual.

> There are other ways of doing this by hiding and unhiding whole drop-downs, or by rewriting all of the options in a drop-down using a script. These can be made to work but are all more complex than this approach using option groups.

There's more...

At the beginning we mentioned the "load none" AJAX approach. This is more useful if there are many options, or the choice of options is more complex, for example if values are read from a database table depending on values in the form.

We'll explore ChronoForms support for AJAX more fully in a later chapter.

See also

- See the recipe *Using AJAX to look up e-mail addresses* in *Chapter 12, Adding Advanced Features* for one application of AJAX. The code there will show you the basics of using AJAX to get information from the server based on a user action.

8
Uploading Files from your Forms

In this chapter, we will cover:

- Adding a file upload field to your form and setting the allowed types and sizes
- Saving files to different folders
- Renaming files
- Linking files to e-mails
- Resizing and copying image files
- Displaying images in e-mails and articles
- Accessing uploaded files
- Trouble-shooting problems with files

Introduction

In the recipe *Attaching uploaded files to the e-mail* back in *Chapter 2, Emailing Form Results* we looked at attaching uploaded files to an e-mail, but we skipped over the bit about uploading the file in the first instance. It's not especially difficult, though there are a few pitfalls that can make it seem so. We'll try to cover all of these in this chapter. If you hit unexpected problems, then check out the troubleshooting recipe at the end of this chapter.

Uploading Files from your Forms

Adding a file upload field to your form and setting the allowed types and sizes

We're going to start out with the basics—adding a file upload input to your form for a simple image file. We'll work with JPG and PNG files, but exactly the same process will work with PDF and DOC, or MP3 and FLV files.

Getting ready

We're going to create a new form but before we do that, it will be really useful if you have some way of looking at the folders on your site, their contents, and the file and folder permissions.

Pretty much any FTP tool will let you do this; so will the excellent **exTplorer** Joomla! extension from `http://extplorer.sourceforge.net/` which lets you view and edit files and folders from the site administration.

> **Caution**: Extensions like exTplorer are very useful. However, because they let you edit site files, they also offer security risks. Make sure that they are only accessible to SuperAdmin users and that you control SuperAdmin access.
>
> And remember to take backups before changing the Joomla! files—we won't be doing that here but FTP or exTplorer access will let you damage your site if you don't take care.

How to do it...

1. Go to the ChronoForms Forms Manager and use the Form Wizard to create a new form. Drag in the **TextBox**, **FileUpload**, and **Button** elements. Change the name of the **TextBox** to **Description** and the **FileUpload** to **File upload**.

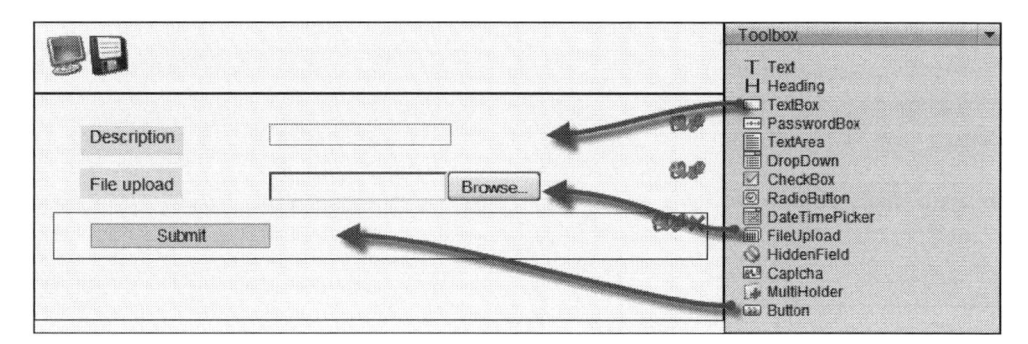

194

2. Save the form, publish it, and view it in your browser.

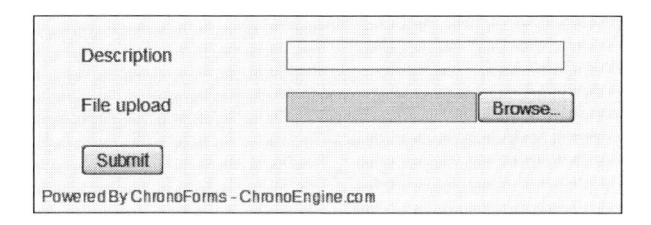

Notice that the **File upload** input is different from the normal text input. When you click the **File Upload** input box or the **Browse** button, your local file explorer will open for you to browse to the file that you want to upload.

You can experiment with this now, though the file won't upload correctly until we have entered some more settings in the ChronoForms Form Editor.

3. We'll go back to the Form Editor now and click the **File Uploads** tab:

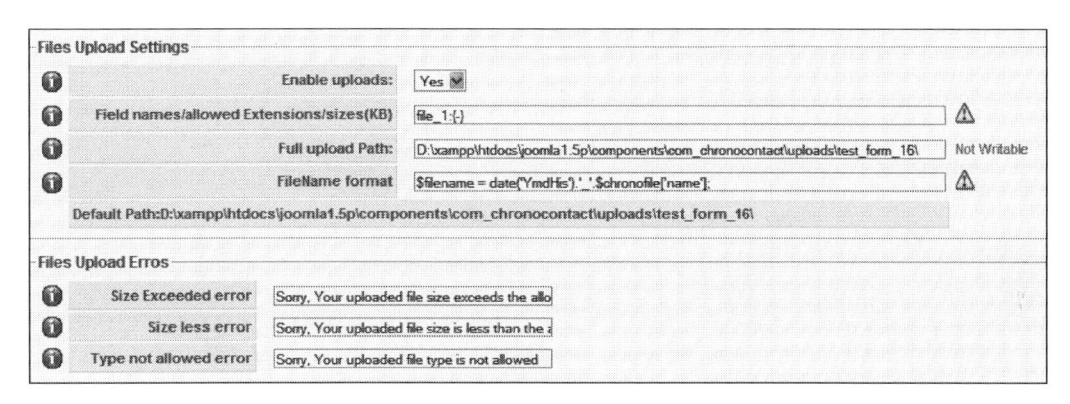

Firstly, take a quick look at the bottom block of three inputs in the **File Upload Errors** section. You can enter text messages here that will be displayed if ChronoForms finds any problems with the uploaded file. The defaults are fine for us.

> Notice that this is one of the places where you can change the text in the error message, including changing the language if your form is not in English.

The top section **Files Upload Settings** is the one that interests us right now.

Uploading Files from your Forms

4. The first drop-down **Enable uploads** needs to be set to **Yes** for ChronoForms to handle your file uploads. If you leave this set to **No**, then the File Upload input will still appear on your form, the files will still be uploaded to your site's temporary folder, but that's all; ChronoForms will not relocate or rename them, nor will it attach them to e-mails or save their name in the database.

5. The second input **Field names/allowed Extensions/sizes(KB)** is where you specify the type and size of uploads that you will allow for your form. The default value here will not work as it is; you must edit this setting.

   The syntax is:
   - The file upload input name—for example, `file_1`—followed by a colon (":")
   - A list of acceptable file extensions separated by vertical bars "|", for example, `png|jpg`
   - The allowable file sizes in kilobytes as `{max-min}`; for example `{1000-10}` meaning maximum 1000 KB, minimum 10 KB
   - If you have more than one file upload, you can repeat the sequence several times separated by commas

   Putting all that together, we get a sequence for our file upload input of:

   `file_1:jpg|png{1000-10}`

   > It can be easy to make small mistakes in this, so double-check each time.

6. The third box is **Full upload path**. This is the full path to the folder that you want ChronoForms to put the uploaded files into. Note that this is a path, not a URL.

   When ChronoForms is installed a folder is created at `components/com_chronocontact/uploads/` and ChronoForms suggests that files for this form are uploaded to a sub-folder in here, named after the form.

   For the moment we will accept this suggestion. But notice that there is an error flag besides the box saying **Not writable**, that is, ChronoForms has checked this folder and is unable to write a file into it at present.

   This could be because the folder doesn't exist, or because the current folder permissions don't permit writing new files. In this case the folder doesn't exist.

Chapter 8

You will need to access your site folder structure with your FTP tool or with exTplorer and create a new sub-folder to use for this form. Copy the small `index.html` file from one of the other folders into it as a security measure. (This stops the folder directory from being accessed from a web browser.)

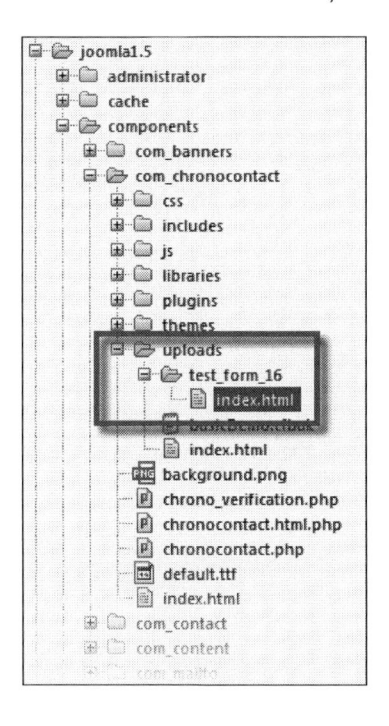

7. The fourth box in the section lets us set the file name that will be used. For the moment, we'll leave this unchanged. We'll look at this in more detail in a later recipe.
8. Apply the form to save it and click the **File Uploads** tab again.

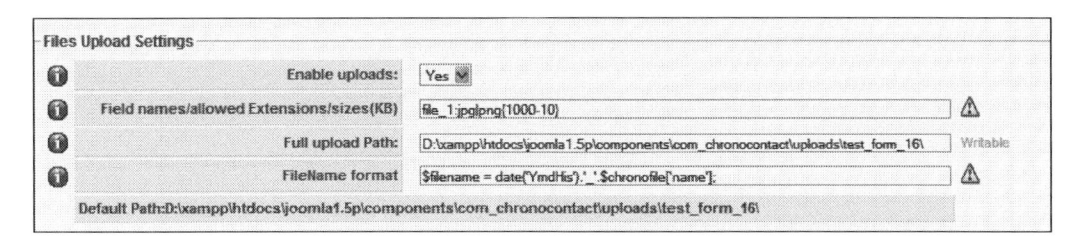

Notice that the error message has gone and is replaced with a **Writable** message confirming that ChronoForms can write to the folder.

Uploading Files from your Forms

9. Save the form and then open it in a browser window so that you can test the file upload. In the example here we used a file called `test_image.jpg`.

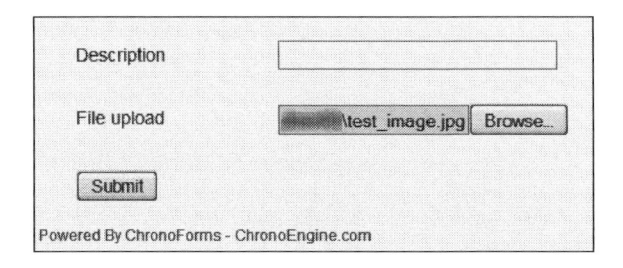

10. Here's the uploaded image file in the correct folder:

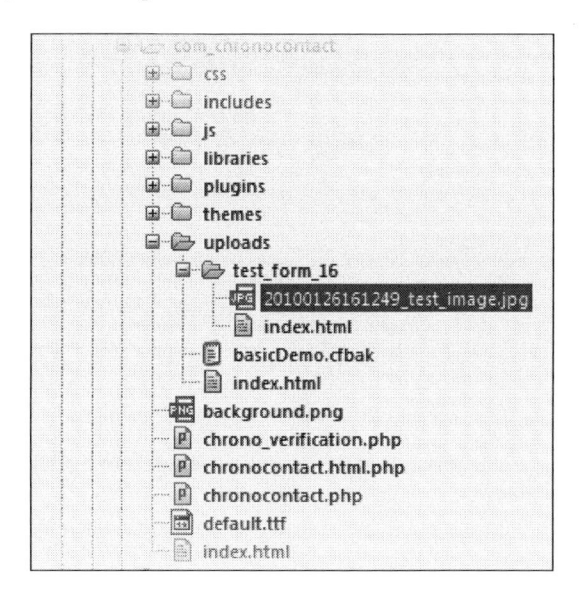

ChronoForms added the date and time (2010-01-26, 16:12:49, if you are curious) to the front of the file name `test_image.jpg` to avoid any problems with uploads having the same name. We'll see later how to change this if you need to.

That's it; we now have a form with a working file upload.

How it works...

It's helpful to remember that there is a two-stage process involved in a file upload. The initial stage—which is managed by the browser and server without any intervention from ChronoForms—uploads the file to a temporary folder on the server.

ChronoForms then takes over; checks if the file meets our specifications and, if it does, moves it to the folder we requested, probably renaming it at the same time. If there's an error in this process, ChronoForms will redisplay the form with an error message.

Try uploading the "wrong" kind of file for instance (this was a PDF):

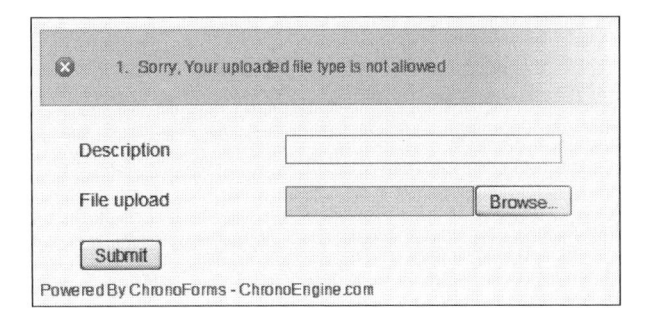

You'll see a ChronoForms error message with the text from the **Type not allowed error** box on the **File Uploads** configuration tab. Take a moment to go back, change the message and resubmit the form to confirm that this is working.

See also

> - The recipe *Attaching uploaded files to the e-mail* in Chapter 2, *E-mailing Form Results* looks at one way of sending an uploaded file by e-mail.

Saving files to different folders

By default, ChronoForms saves uploaded files to a sub-folder of the ChronoForms component folder. This is convenient for files that are only used with ChronoForms but not so good if; for example, you want to upload images to be included in articles. It's much more useful if they are stored in the Joomla! `images/stories/` folder.

Getting ready

We'll use the same form as last time, and for convenience we'll add a new subfolder inside `images/stories` to save our uploaded images.

Uploading Files from your Forms

How to do it...

1. In your site admin, go to **Site | Media Manager** and create a new subfolder:

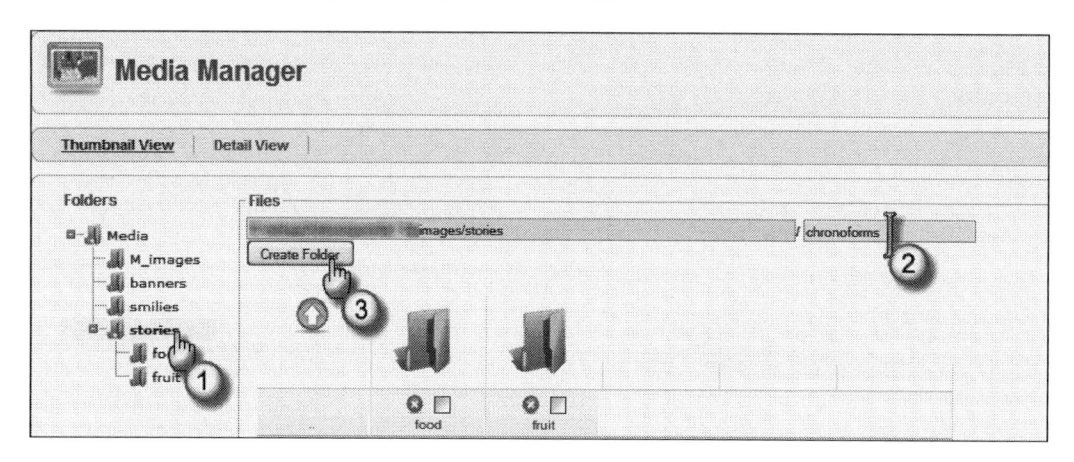

   Notice that the first part of the **Files** box entry (blurred out here because yours will be different) will be the path to the root folder of your site. Make a note of this root path as we will need to know what it is later. We'll call it `{root_path}`, when you see that in code here replace it with your root path.

   The `images/stories` part at the end should be there, whatever your root path is, once you've clicked the **stories** folder link at the left.

2. Type `chronoforms` in the box and click the **Create Folder** button to create the new folder. You will see it appear in the **Folders** tree under the **stories** entry.

3. Now go back to the ChronoForms Forms Manager, open the Form Editor for your form and click the **File Uploads** tab.

   In the **File uploads Path** box you will see that it says `{root_path}\components\com_chronocontact\uploads\{form_name}` Replace everything after the `{root_path}` with `\images\stories\chronoforms\` taking care to keep the slashes correct. You should now have `{root_path}\images\stories\chronoforms\`.

4. Apply or save your form, switch to view the form and resubmit it. Now go back to the Media Manager and view the `stories/chronoforms` folder, you should find your image there.

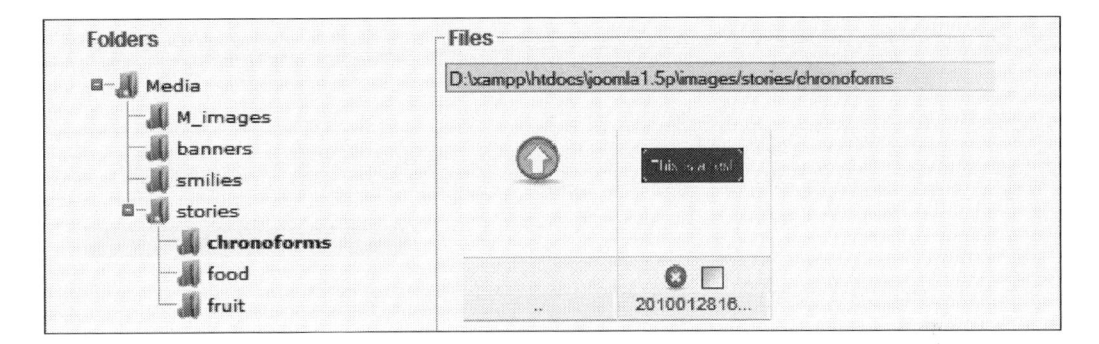

[Screenshot of Media Manager showing Folders tree with Media > M_images, banners, smilies, stories > chronoforms, food, fruit; and Files panel showing path D:\xampp\htdocs\joomla1.5p\images/stories/chronoforms with an uploaded file 20100128 16...]

> If your image isn't there, then go back and check the path in the **File Uploads** tab. In particular, check that the **Writeable** message is displayed.

5. Once you have a file uploaded into the `images/stories` folder it can be added to any article through the usual **Image** button.

How it works...

In the second stage of the upload process we described in the last recipe, ChronoForms moves the file from the site temporary folder into the folder you specify on the file uploads tab. Provided that the folder exists, and is writable, the process is very smooth and reliable.

There's more...

We've tested two folders, both inside the Joomla! folder structure. However, the upload folder doesn't have to be inside the Joomla! structure. You may want to upload your files into a folder outside the Joomla! structure so that it cannot be browsed to.

Whether you can do this or not will depend on your hosting arrangements. You will need to have access to the folder containing your website folder. This will usually be one step back up the `{root_path}`.

> Check your hosting Control Panel and documentation to see if this is possible. Access varies widely. You may need to set up **Secure Shell** (**SSH**) or **SSH FTP** (**SFTP**) access to get to these folders.

Uploading Files from your Forms

Create a new folder in there, check the permissions and add the path to that folder in the **File Uploads** tab. Check for the **Writeable** message after you apply the form.

Test the form again and see if the upload works.

Note that because this folder is outside your site domain you will not be able to access the files directly by URL, but will have to use some code to make them accessible to users.

Renaming files

In the last recipe we changed the upload folder to `images/stories/chronoforms` but we are still getting the default image names—in this case `20100126161249_test_image.jpg`. In this recipe, we'll look at ways to change the file names to more useful values for your application.

Getting ready

We'll continue with the same form as in the previous recipe.

How to do it...

1. Go back to the Form Editor and click the **File Uploads** tab.

   In the **FileName Format** box you'll see an entry like this:

   ```
   $filename = date('YmdHis').'_'.$chronofile['name'];
   ```

   This is a PHP snippet that sets the value of the `$filename` variable that ChronoForms will use to rename the uploaded file.

   There are two main pieces to it, joined by an underscore '_':

   - The first piece is `date('YmdHis')`. This is a PHP command to get the current date and time in the format set by `'YmdHis'`.
   - The second piece is `$chronofile['name']` which is the temporary variable that holds the original name of the uploaded file.
   - Lastly there's a semi-colon ";" at the end there to tell ChronoForms that this is the end of the expression.

   > Notice that this box has a yellow warning triangle next to it with a message that says **Warning: this field should contain valid PHP . . . without tags or it may break the whole form.** One easy way to break the form is to leave that semi-colon off the end. You have been warned!

2. As an example, we're going to give our file uploads names like `image` followed by a random string of five digits. This is simple enough to demonstrate what needs to be done.

   Before we build up our PHP code, we need to know how to generate that 5-digit string. To keep it simple we'll use numbers between 10,000 and 99,999, this means that we can use the built-in PHP function `rand()` in the form `rand(10000, 99999)`.

   > There's a reason why we add this random string, or the date + time string that ChronoForms uses. If users upload more than one image with the same name; or we use a constant name like "image" then we don't want to run into problems with two files having the same name. We'd have to add extra code to handle that, so it is best to avoid it somehow. (And yes, we could run into problems with these five digits but they'll work fine for the demonstration here.)

   So to build up the whole code snippet we have:
   - `$filename =`
   - `'image_'` NB we've included the underscore here
   - `.` —a dot to join the segments together (it's the PHP concatenation operator)
   - `rand(10000, 99999)`
   - `;` —don't forget the semi-colon!

   And putting this together we get:

   `$filename = 'image_'.rand(10000, 99999);`

   We can copy and paste this into the **FileName format** box.

3. If you test this, you'll find that it works nicely, but there is a little problem—our file has lost its suffix and is now called something like `image_87956` instead of `image_87956.jpg` or `image_87956.png`. If we had only allowed one type of file to be uploaded we could just stick `.jpg` on the end and all would be well. However, we allowed both `.png` and `.jpg` uploads so we need to do more.

   Here's one solution using PHP string functions. First we need to find the position of the last "." in the file name which we can do with this code:

   `$position = strrpos($chronofile['name'], '.');`

   Then we need to pick off the characters after the dot:

   `$suffix = substr($chronofile['name'], $position);`

Uploading Files from your Forms

For compactness we can merge these two together into:

```
$suffix = substr($chronofile['name'],
   strrpos($chronofile['name'], '.'));
```

And then add that into our code snippet with a dot :

```
$filename = 'image_'.rand(10000, 99999)
  .substr($chronofile['name'],
   strrpos($chronofile['name'], '.'));
```

This may seem too long for the box but fortunately it will all fit in, even though we can't see it all.

> Note: The line breaks in the codes above are just to fit the code on the page here. Otherwise, all the code goes on one line.

4. Now when we submit, we get the names we chose with the correct suffixes added to our files.

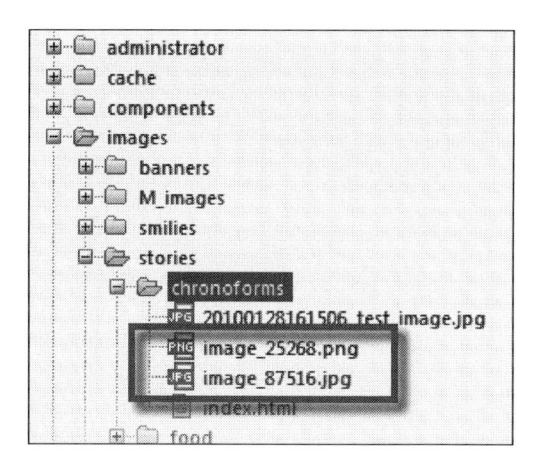

How it works...

ChronoForms takes the PHP snippet we entered in the **FileName format** box and passes it to the PHP processor after the form submits; then uses the resulting variable `$filename` to rename the file.

As we can see, quite a lot of the features of ChronoForms make use of this ability to execute snippets or chunks of PHP in processing both the form HTML and the form data.

Chapter 8

Linking files to e-mails

In *Chapter 2, E-mailing Form Results* we looked at attaching uploaded and "standard" files to e-mails, so there is no need to repeat that process here. Sometimes though what we want to do is to include a link to the file in an e-mail, so that the user can access it if they need it. This keeps e-mail size down and can be a useful technique to have in the kitbag.

Getting ready

We'll use the same small file upload form as we have in the last couple of recipes and we'll be linking to files uploaded to the `images/stories/chronoforms` folder. (The same technique can be applied to any other folder – except those outside the Joomla! folder structure.)

How to do it...

1. We need an **Email Setup** for the form, something very simple will be enough, then we'll work in the **Email Template**. You'll need to save or apply the form to get ChronoForms to create the template. When you reopen the **Email Template** tab you should see something dramatic like this:

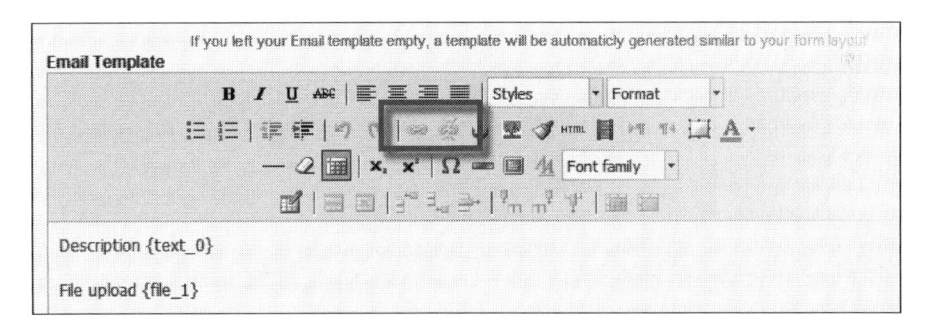

    Notice that there are a couple of link items in the editor toolbar, currently they are grayed out but they'll come to life when we select some text.

2. Type "Download file" in the editor window and select the text. The icons will spring into life and we can click **create link**—the left hand icon (the right hand icon is **break link**).

205

Uploading Files from your Forms

3. A new window will pop-up with the Link dialogue for us to complete.

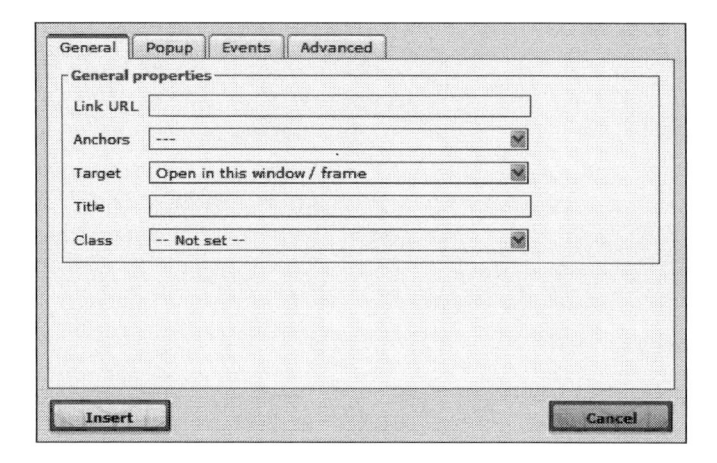

There are four tabs with options here, but because all we need is a link in an e-mail we'll just use the first box on the first tab.

4. Type the path to an existing file into the **Link URL** box. We'll use `images/stories/chronoforms/myfileupload.jpg` which is a file from the previous section.

5. Click **Insert** to save the link in the Email Template. Click the **General** tab in the Form Editor, set **Email the Results** to **Yes**; then scroll down to the **Other Form Settings** section and set **Debug** to **ON**.

6. Apply or save the form then view it in a browser window. Submit the form (you don't need to add any values in the boxes).

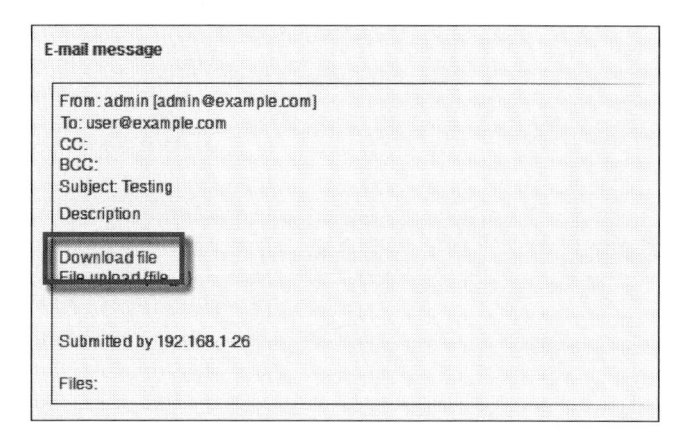

7. Check that the link works by clicking on it and the image will open in your browser.

This demonstrates how to create a link to the same file in every e-mail; but we want to link to the file uploaded when *this* form was submitted. We need some more work for this to add the current file upload name to the e-mail.

8. Go back to the Form Editor, click the **Form Code** tab and then open the **OnSubmit code – before sending email** text area. We're going to add some code in here (check the comments to see what the each line of code does):

```php
<?php
// get the form uploads information
$MyUploads =& CFUploads::getInstance($MyForm->formrow->id);
// extract the file path
$file_path = $MyUploads->attachments[file_1];
// remove the 'root folder' from the beginning
$file_url = substr($file_path, strlen(JPATH_SITE)+1);
//correct any mis-directed separators
$file_url = str_replace(DS, '/', $file_url);
// add the domain name to the beginning
$file_url = JURI::base().$file_url;
// save the URL into the form results
JRequest::setVar('file_url', $file_url);
?>
```

9. We now need to click the **Email Templates** tab and change the link in the URL there. Place your cursor in the link so that the **link icons** are highlighted and click the left hand icon again. Replace the entry in **Link URL** with `{file_url}` then apply or save the form and test it once again.

    Now the link in the debug e-mail will link to the file you just uploaded.

10. Test by sending an e-mail and make sure that the link works from there too.

How it works...

What we did here was to use the information that ChronoForms has about the file path and convert this into a URL that we can include in an e-mail. The steps of this process are in the last code snippet:

1. Get the file path `{root_path}/images/stories/chronoforms/myfileupload.jpg`.
2. Remove the `{root_path}` piece leaving `/images/stories/chronoforms/myfileupload.jpg`.
3. Switch the slashes if necessary.
4. Add the domain to the front `http://example.com/images/stories/chronoforms/myfileupload.jpg`.

5. Having got this url we then add to the data input to the form using `JRequest::setVar()` so that we can use the `{file_url}` syntax in the e-mail template.

> It would have been possible to enter this code snippet directly in the Email Template box by turning off the Rich Text editor. Keeping the code separate is a little neater and easier.

Resizing and copying image files

Image files are probably the most commonly uploaded files and often you want to use these files in your site. However, users are not always good at following directions about the sizes or types that you want.

Emmanuel Danan wrote the ChronoForms plug-in that can handle image resizing and a few other useful things. The plug-in has been updated to work with the current versions of ChronoForms and is included as a part of the installation package.

> Just to avoid any problems later, the plug-in will only work with one file upload input on any form. If you have multiple files to be uploaded then some more work will be required.

Getting ready

We already have a form with a file upload field that will accept `jpg` and `png` image files, so we'll use a new copy of that.

> Please ensure that you have a recent version of the plug-in; some of the earlier versions have a bug in the way they handle file names.

You should also check that your site has the PHP GD Graphics library installed (most do). The information is shown on the **Anti Spam** tab of the Form Editor as the same library is used to create the ChronoForms Captcha images.

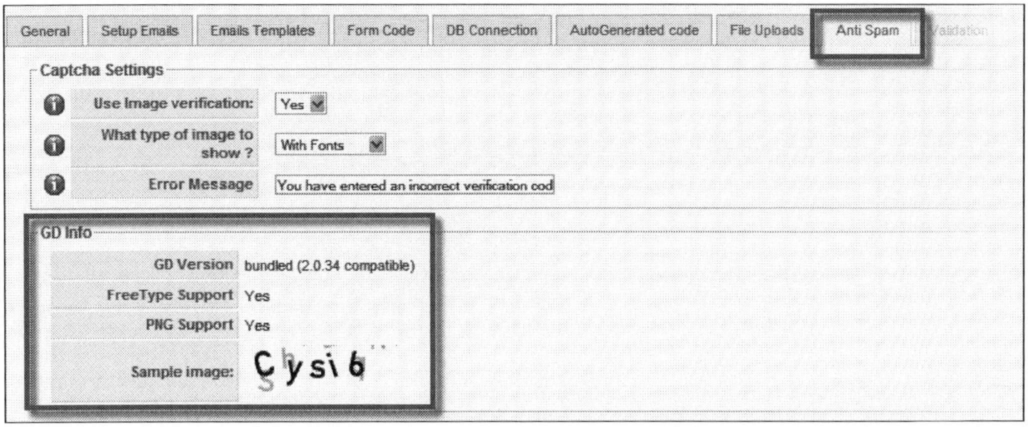

If you don't see a **GD Version** for the library then this plug-in probably won't work on your site. Talk to your host about getting the PHP GD library enabled.

How to do it...

1. In the Forms Manager, click the checkbox just in front of the form name; then click the **Image resize and thumbnail** link in the plug-ins column on the left-hand side of the page.

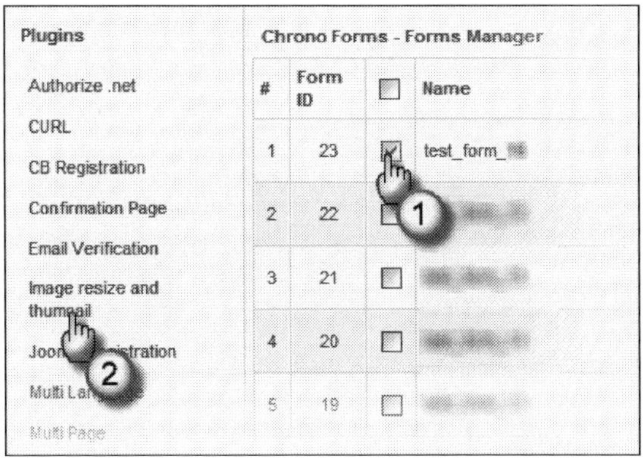

Uploading Files from your Forms

2. The **Image resize and thumbnail** plug-in tab configuration page will open. You will see several tabs: **General** and **Help** at the ends, and three image sizes—**Large Image**, **Medium Image**, and **Small Image** in between.

> Note that although we label the images "large", "medium", and "small" in fact you can set any size on any tab. They all behave in the same way and the **Large Image** tab will create a thumbnail just as well as the **Small Image** tab. The only restraint is that you must use the **Large Image** tab, the other two are optional.

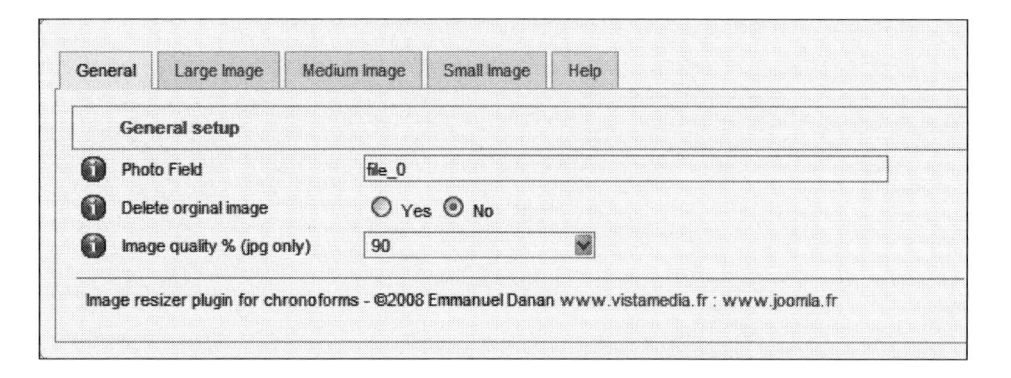

3. There are three boxes on the **General** tab and for our form we can leave all but one unchanged. The **Photo Field** box has `file_0` in it. This will probably not be correct unless the file upload input is the first element in the form. In our case, we need to change this to `file_1`.

4. Click the **Large Image** tab to see the details for specifying a resize.

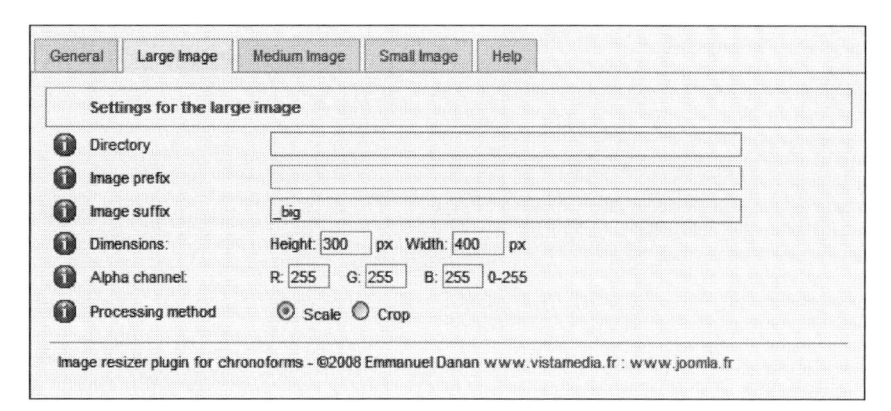

When you've had a quick look, click the **Medium Image** and **Small Image** tabs and notice that they are identical to the **Large Image** tab apart from the **Create xxx image?** radio buttons on each tab.

We can leave all the settings here exactly as they are, but it's worth briefly mentioning what they do.

- The **Directory** box is used to set a folder to save the resized image. If you leave it blank then ChronoForms will use the same folder as you specified in the **File Uploads** tab.
- The **Image prefix** and **Image suffix** boxes are used to enter strings that ChronoForms will add before and/or after the image names so that you can refer to the different sized images later. We'll leave the default **_big** suffix in place.
- The **Dimensions** box is to specify the resizing window that you want to use
- The **Alpha channel** can be used to set the background color for transparent PNG images
- And lastly, **Processing method** specifies if the image is to be resized to fit the whole image inside the window, which means that there may be white-space at the top or sides; or cropped so that the image window is full but the top or sides may be cut off

5. Save the Plug-in configuration; then return to the **Form Editor | Plugins** tab and enable the plug-in. Make sure that there's a green bar for this plug-in.
6. Apply or save the form, and submit the form to check the actions of the plug-in.

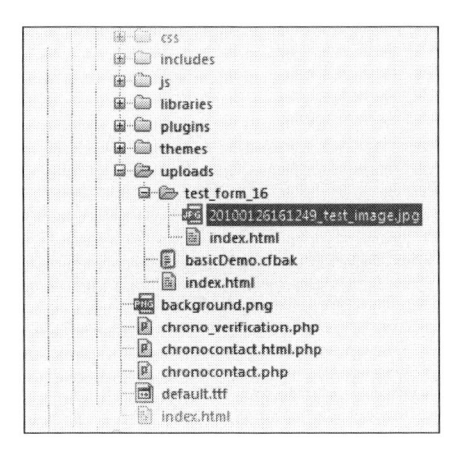

Uploading Files from your Forms

You can see here that we have both the original uploaded file `testresize.png` and the resized version `testresize_big.png`. In this case the re-sized version is bigger than the original!

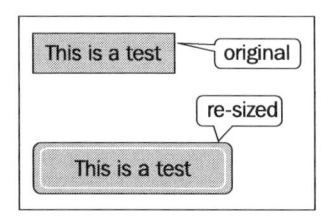

The original test image has been expanded from 200 x 68 pixels to 400 x 168 to fit inside the 400 x 300 window we specified.

> If you specify more than one image then you will get multiple versions saved at the same time. This can be really useful if you want say, a thumbnail to display in a list, a preview image for a more detailed view, and a large image to use in a pop-up.

How it works...

Behind the scenes the plug-in uses the PHP GD library to do the resizing; there is really nothing more that is useful to say without getting terribly technical.

See also

- If you want more technical information on the GD Library, check the PHP Manual at http://php.net/manual/en/book.image.php, in particular the section on Installing/configuring

Displaying images in e-mails and articles

We've already covered much of this in earlier recipes so this will be a variation on a theme. We'll look at the more difficult task of adding an uploaded image into an e-mail.

> Actually we're going to add a link to the image into the e-mail. This means that some users may not see it if they are not connected to the Internet or if their e-mail reader blocks images by default.
>
> It is technically possible to embed images in an e-mail but is beyond our abilities here.

Getting ready

We'll use the same form and include the image link alongside the download link that we created earlier.

How to do it...

1. Open the form in the Form Editor; click the **Form Code** tab and open the **On Submit code – before email** box. Check that the code from the previous recipe is still there, if it isn't then please add it:

    ```php
    <?php
    // get the form uploads information
    $MyUploads =& CFUploads::getInstance($MyForm->formrow->id);
    // extract the file path
    $file_path = $MyUploads->attachments[file_1];
    // remove the 'root folder' from the beginning
    $file_url = substr($file_path, strlen(JPATH_SITE)+1);
    //correct any mis-directed separators
    $file_url = str_replace(DS, '/', $file_url);
    // add the domain name to the beginning
    $file_url = JURI::base().$file_url;
    // save the URL into the form results
    JRequest::setVar('file_url', $file_url);
    ?>
    ```

2. Now click the **Email Templates** tab, create an empty line under the **Download file** link, and click the Image icon:

Uploading Files from your Forms

The editor Image dialogue will open, very much like the link dialogue we saw earlier:

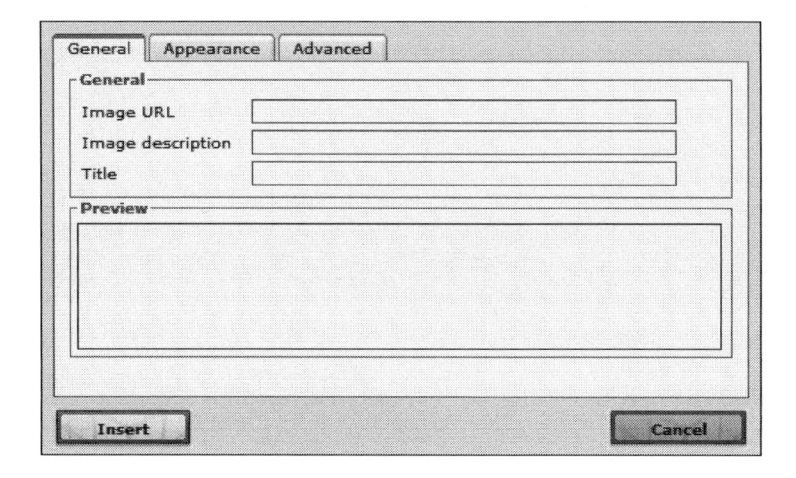

3. Again, type {file_url} into the **Image URL** box and add some suitable words in the **Image description** box. Click **Insert** to save the setting.

   You won't see anything in the template except a little image placeholder; that image URL doesn't yet link to any particular image.

4. Apply or save the form and submit the form from your browser window.

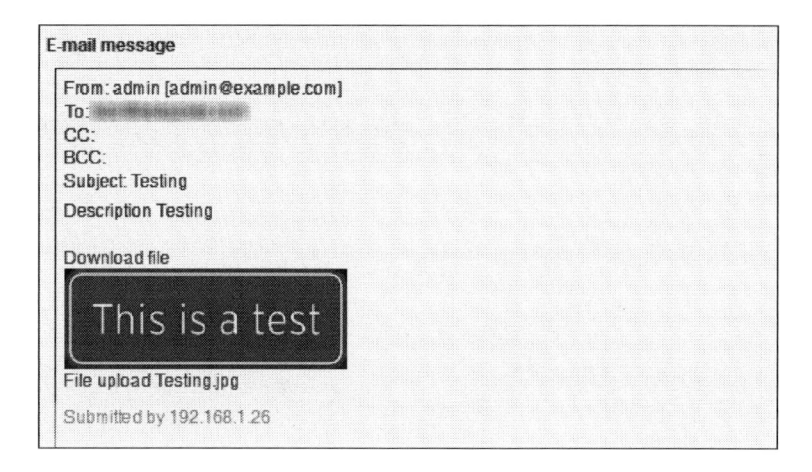

Here's the debug version of the e-mail with both the download link, and the linked image.

> In practice, the download link is probably more useful for documents, and the image for, well, images, though you could combine the two and include a small preview image here with a link back to a larger version.

There's more...

Adding an image to an article

Once an image is uploaded to the Joomla! `images/stories` folder it can be added to any article from the **Image** button in the **Article Editor.**

If you have an image in another folder outside the `images/stories` folder then it won't be visible from the media manager, but you can add it by using the URL in the **Image** dialogue.

See also

- If you are creating the article from the form data then see the recipe *Using a form to create a Joomla! article* from *Chapter 6, Showing your Form in your Site*
- The *Adding a barcode to form e-mail* recipe in Chapter 7, *Adding Features to your Form* may also be useful.

Troubleshooting problems with files

File uploads are really useful when they work smoothly, and can be a real problem when they don't. The upload process is quite different from the way the rest of the form data is handled and the upload itself is managed by PHP, before ChronoForms gets to see the form.

So, this recipe is the one to follow when your file uploads aren't behaving the way that you would like them to.

Getting ready

Keeping it simple, we'll follow through using a simple form with one file upload input and a submit button.

Here's the Form HTML of the form created with the Form Wizard:

```
<div class="form_item">
  <div class="form_element cf_fileupload">
    <label class="cf_label" style="width: 150px;">File upload</label>
    <input class="cf_fileinput cf_inputbox" title="" size="20"
      id="file_0" name="file_0" type="file" />
  </div>
  <div class="cfclear"> </div>
</div>

<div class="form_item">
```

Uploading Files from your Forms

```
    <div class="form_element cf_button">
      <input value="Submit" name="button_1" type="submit" />
    </div>
    <div class="cfclear"> </div>
</div>
```

Notice that the file input is named `file_0`, we may need that later.

How to do it...

The problem that we need to troubleshoot is the most common one—"My form won't upload files". This doesn't tell us much, so we'll go through step by step checking the possible causes.

1. Checking that there is a file input in the form:

   Bizarre as it may seem it does happen—fortunately, very rarely—that someone creates a form with a text input, labels it **File upload** and wonders why it doesn't work.

   So first we take a look at the form:

   File upload   [   ] [Browse...]
   [Submit]
   Powered By ChronoForms - ChronoEngine.com

   It's the **Browse** button that confirms that we do indeed have a File upload input in the form. While you are here, click the button, or in the input area, and the local file finder should open so that you can select a file to upload.

2. Checking the form HTML:

   We created the HTML above with the Form Wizard which usually creates good code, but sometimes HTML is hand-coded or copied and pasted in from elsewhere.

   Here's a file upload input tag with a few potential problems:

   ```
   <input name = '001-my file" type='file ' disabled />
   ```

   How many can you spot?

   Here's what I found:

   - The input is disabled (strictly that should be `disabled='disabled'` too).
   - There are curly quotes around the `file` entry. Quotes in HTML should always be straight quotes—either " " or ' '.
   - The quotes round `001-my file` are straight but don't match. They should either both be single or both double.

- In the `type=` attribute, there's a space after `file`. Sometimes this will be fine, sometimes it won't. So, it's always best to be safe.
- While we are looking at spaces, there are spaces round the `=` in `name = ;` they shouldn't be there
- There's yet another space inside the value of the `name` attribute—`001-my file`, that isn't allowed either
- And that dash "`-`" is technically legal but will cause problems in ChronoForms as it gives the database instructions indigestion. Avoid dashes (and spaces) and use underscores instead
- Lastly, the value of the name attribute starts with a number. That isn't allowed in HTML. ID and Name values should start with a letter. Safe characters are `a-z`, `A-Z`, `0-9` and underscore, no spaces or other special or accented characters. (You'll see here that we usually stick to all lower case too, that removes another possible source of a mismatch.)

A corrected version might look like this:

```
<input name='my_file_001' type='file' />
```

> There may well be other attributes inside the `<input . . . />` tag but `name` and `type` are the only two that are required.

The remainder of the surrounding `<div>` tags and the `<label>` in the Form HTML in the preceding example are only used to manage the display of the form on the page, so any errors there shouldn't affect the file upload itself.

3. Checking the File Uploads settings:

   Next stop is the **File Uploads** tab in the Forms Manager. There are several places here where it's easy to let a typo slip in.

   Firstly, check that **Enable Uploads** is set to **Yes**. It's easy to overlook if you are focusing on Permissions, Upload Paths, and Filenames.

   Secondly, look carefully at the next box—the file permissions (titled **Field names/allowed Extensions/sizes(KB)**).

   - Does the file name match the input name (remember we said we'd need that) exactly? This is case sensitive. `File_0` is not an exact match to `file_0`.
   - Is there a colon "`:`" after the file name (not a semi-colon "`;`", a dot "`.`", a comma "`,`", or a space "` `")?
   - Are the file extensions correct (these are not case sensitive, so `jpg` will match both `JPG` and `jpg`)?

Uploading Files from your Forms

- Is the separator between the extensions correct? It should be a vertical bar "|" (not an exclamation mark "!", or a broken bar "¦"). Also check that there is no separator at the end of the list, or files without any extension may be accepted.

- Are the brackets around the maximum and minimum sizes correct { . . . } (not (. . .) or [. . .])?

- Are the maximum and minimum sizes shown as integers separated by a dash; for example, `1000-1` or `999999-0`? There should be no commas, spaces, or other punctuation. Nor should there be any units shown—use `1000`, not `1000kb` or `1mb`.

- Are the limits the right way round—max then min—so the bigger number comes first?

- Do the limits make sense (the implied units are KB)? Setting the lower limit too high can block some files.

- Check that the **Writable** message shows against the **Full upload Path** box. If it doesn't then you may need to create the folder or modify the file permissions. Also check that the path has a "\" at the end. If in doubt check the **Default Path** that ChronoForms displays at the end of this section.

- Does the filename format make sense? If in doubt, reset the default or use something very simple for testing like `$filename = 'XXX';` Check that the structure is correct:

    `$filename = . . . some code . . . ;`

If this sounds like a long list—it is, but it's worth taking the time to check. More than half of the problems with file uploads are from these settings.

Have one final check of these before we move on!

4. Checking the file upload process

    Go to the form **General** tab in the Form Editor and scroll down to the **Other Form Settings** section. Set **Debug** to **ON** and apply or save the form.

    View the form in your browser, select a file to upload and submit the form. You will see a page of debug output that includes some useful information about our upload.

Chapter 8

```
1. Form passed first SPAM check OK
2. Form passed the submissions limit (if enabled) OK
3. Form passed the image verification (if enabled) OK
4. Form passed the server side validation (if enabled) OK
5. $_POST Array: Array ( [button_1] => Submit [15d3e5b83982fa731360cb7fa984d8d1] =>
   1 [1cf1] => 00c18d561ae976c1dea7037ec508de8 [chronoformname] => test_form_10 )
6. $_FILES Array: Array ( [file_0] => Array ( [name] => test_image.jpg [type] => image/jpeg
   [tmp_name] => D:\xampp\tmp\php64.tmp [error] => 0 [size] => 12597 ) )
7. Upload routine started for file upload by : file_0
8. D:\xampp\htdocs\joomla1.5p\components\com_chronocontact\uploads\test_form_18
   \20100205142041_test_image.jpg has been uploaded OK
9. Form passed the plugins step (if enabled) OK
10. Debug End
```

The messages outlined **6**, **7**, and **8** here are the ones that tell us about the file upload process. We'll look at them in turn. Here's the first with a few line-breaks and spaces added for clarity.

```
$_FILES Array:
Array (
   [file_0] => Array (
      [name]     => test_image.jpg
      [type]     => image/jpeg
      [tmp_name] => D:\xampp\tmp\php64.tmp
      [error]    => 0
      [size]     => 12597
) )
```

Several of these entries can be useful. Most obvious is the `[error] => 0`, which tells us that PHP didn't report any errors with this upload (so in this case the problem is further on in the process). However, if there is a number other than zero in here then it needs investigation.

The PHP File Upload errors can be a little technically obscure but they are still worth looking into. The list of errors is in the **PHP Manual** at http://www.php.net/manual/en/features.file-upload.errors.php and it is the "value" of the error that is being reported here.

We can't go into the depths of all of these here beyond a few notes:

- Error 1 is a file-size error, this does not relate to the file-size set in the Form Editor but is a server setting, usually defined by your ISP. You can see the current value on the **Site Admin | System Info | PHP Info** page. You may need to talk to your ISP if this is not big enough.

- Errors 6 and 7 relate to the folder that PHP uses to store temporary files. You can see the path to it in the `[tmp_name]` value in the Debug report. Check that the folder exists and that the Joomla! user has permission to write to it.

219

Uploading Files from your Forms

> With increased security on websites ISPs are increasingly tightening up folder site and security. One problem with Joomla! is that sometimes an FTP system user is used to create the site and given owner folder permissions, but this is not the same as the Joomla! system user, used for the site's operation. (Note: "System users" here are users on the host server, this has nothing to do with users registered in Joomla!.)

If you do not see an obvious problem and solution here then you should check with your ISP's help and support service, as these are server related issues rather than Joomla! or ChronoForms issues. Within reason (that is files of reasonable sizes and types) it should be possible for you to upload files to your server from a form on your site.

Going back to the Debug report, messages 7 and 8 report the second part of the upload process, where ChronoForms picks up the file, moves, and renames it. Here are the messages, again edited a little for clarity:

```
7: Upload routine started for file upload by : file_0
8: {root_path}\components\com_chronocontact\
uploads\test_form_18\20100205142041_test_image.jpg
has been uploaded OK
```

Message 7 simply reports that the ChronoForms process has started; message 8 reports that it has been completed successfully.

The main thing to check here is the file path in message 8. Look carefully at this. Sometimes slashes have been missed, or folder names mistyped. Use your FTP file browser to track down this folder step by step and make sure that it is correct.

It's a common problem that files are uploaded successfully but end up in an unexpected location.

The last thing to check, still in message 8, is that the file name is correct. As this is driven by a formula it's quite easy for a mistake to creep in and the file to end up with a garbled name.

That's it. Good hunting.

See also

- There's a more general form trouble-shooting recipe right at the end of this book in Chapter 12, *Adding Advanced Features*

9
Writing Form HTML

In this chapter, we will cover:

- Moving an existing form to ChronoForms
- Moving a form with CSS
- Moving a form with JavaScript
- Creating a form with Wufoo
- Creating a form in Dreamweaver

Introduction

For most of the recipes so far, we've used the ChronoForms Form Wizard to create our forms. This is quick and simple, and sometimes it just doesn't do what we need. For example, if the form needs a different layout, if we already have a form on an old site, if we need something more complex that takes too long with the Wizard, or if we just enjoy hand-coding HTML. In any of these cases, we need other ways of getting our HTML to work with ChronoForms.

With very few limits, ChronoForms will quite happily accept any HTML from any source; it doesn't have to be created in ChronoForms.

It will help here if we make some distinctions to be clear just what we are talking about as we go forward. A web form has several parts:

- **The Page HTML**: All of the HTML code that goes into creating the web page.
- **The Form HTML**: Those parts of the HTML that are specifically linked to the way this form works. Mostly these are the form controls—`<input>`, `<select>`, `<option>`, `<textarea>`, and `<submit>` tags that are used to collect user input. Closely linked to these are the `<label>`, `<fieldset>`, and `<legend>` tags that are used specifically to organize form layout but not for user input.

Writing Form HTML

- **The Form JavaScript**: Script snippets or files that are used to make the form more interactive; typically to validate, to add or remove fields, or to get extra information from the server.
- **The Form CSS**: Style snippets or files that are used to change the "look and feel" of the form.
- **The Form PHP**: Code that is used before the form is shown to the user to customize it in some way. This may be just to add a name, or to respond to some previous input, or sometimes to generate form HTML.
- **The Form backend**: More PHP, some managed by ChronoForms, some by Joomla!, and some that we can enter into ChronoForms that affects the way the form data is processed; this includes saving the data and sending e-mails.

In this chapter, we will be focusing mainly on the Form HTML, and to a lesser extent the Form JavaScript, CSS, and PHP. We will not be looking much at the rest of the page HTML, nor at the Form backend.

Moving an existing form to ChronoForms

When we think about a web form, we often have something in mind such as, "I'd like a form like that", or we have an existing form on another site that we want to move over into this site and into ChronoForms.

Usually it's fairly easy to get the functionality moved over. It may take a while to work through all the wrinkles though!

Getting ready

We're going to create a "functional" copy of an existing form inside ChronoForms. All we need to do to prepare, is to go to **Google** and find their famous home page:

This is the familiar Google Classic home page. It is, of course, a form. Now we don't have access to the backend functionality that Google uses so we won't be creating a functional Google search form, just the frontend part of it.

How to do it...

1. In your web browser, find the **View Source** option. Right-click on the page and select **View Source** in Internet Explorer 8 or Safari, **View Page Source** in Firefox or Chrome, or just plain Source in Opera.

   Depending on your browser, the page source will be displayed in a text window of some kind and you'll see that there is quite a lot of it. This is the View Source display from FireFox:

   You probably can't read that clearly here. Fortunately, we only want a small chunk of this, the piece between the `<form . . . >` and `</form>` tags, which is the segment selected in the image.

   > If you want to include the Google logo too, then you will need to expand the extract to the <center> and </center> tags surrounding this block. We're really only concerned about the form section here.

2. Here's what that code looks like out of the page and with a few line-breaks and spaces added:

   ```
   <form action="/search" name=f onsubmit="google.fade=null">
   <table cellpadding=0 cellspacing=0>
     <tr valign=top>
   ```

223

Writing Form HTML

```
            <td width=25%> </td>
            <td align=center nowrap>
              <input type=hidden name=rls value="ig">
              <input name=hl type=hidden value=en>
              <input name=source type=hidden value=hp>
              <input autocomplete="off"
                onblur="google&&google.fade&&google.fade()"
                maxlength=2048 name=q size=55 class=lst
                title="Google Search" value="">
              <br>
              <input name=btnG type=submit value="Google Search"
                class=lsb onclick="this.checked=1">
              <input name=btnI type=submit
                value="I&#39;m Feeling Lucky"
                class=lsb onclick="this.checked=1">
            </td>
            <td nowrap width=25% align=left id=sbl>
              <font size=-2>  
                <a href="/advanced_search?hl=en">Advanced Search</a>
                <br>  
                <a href="/language_tools?hl=en">Language Tools</a>
              </font>
            </td>
          </tr>
        </table>
      </form>
```

> Adding spaces and line breaks like this probably doesn't have too much effect on the form layout (the browser collapses white-space down to at most a single space). Google is much more concerned about using densely packed code to reduce the size of the page load than we are here.

3. In the ChronoForms Forms Manager, click the **New** icon to open the Form Editor for a new form.

4. On the **General** tab put `search_form` in the **Form Name** box. Then click the **Form Code** tab and open the **Form HTML** textarea.

5. Copy the Google code, leaving out the `<form . . .>` and `</form>` tags, so just from `<table>` to `</table>`, and paste it into the **Form HTML** box.

6. Save the form, publish it, and view it in your browser.

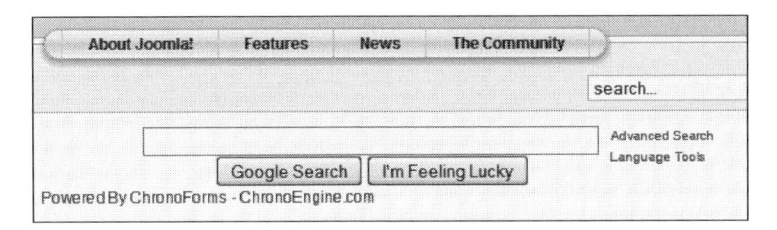

7. And there is the Google search box inside our Joomla! site. Now, the form won't function; it won't even link back to Google unless we were to make more changes in the Form HTML. And that isn't the point, we have achieved what we set out to do, to take the form HTML from an existing form on another site and put it into ChronoForms.

8. The next task would be to work on the backend to change or rebuild the functionality there to make this into a working form. Maybe another day.

How it works...

ChronoForms will accept any valid form HTML in the Form HTML field; indeed it will accept any valid HTML (or invalid HTML come to that) with one exception. You cannot enter `<form . . .>` or `</form>` tags; if you do then you will get an error message when you view the form. This is because ChronoForms adds its own `<form . . .>` and `</form>` tags around the form HTML when the form is viewed and nested form tags are not allowed in HTML.

So, you can import any form following the method we used here. Now many forms are more complex than this, but the same principle applies.

Moving a form with JavaScript

You can get Google Site Search for your site by signing up at Google `http://www.google.com/cse/` and paying an annual fee or accepting adverts in the results page. What you get isn't technically a form, but it will be a useful way for us to explore the way in which you might move the script and styles associated with a form into ChronoForms.

Getting ready

If you want to follow this through, then go to the Google site and sign up for a free (ad supported) Google search box. You'll need a Google account to do this.

Writing Form HTML

How to do it...

1. When we have followed through the Google instructions we get to click the **Get Code** link and will see something like this in the HTML box waiting to be copied:

```
<div id="cse" style="width: 100%;">Loading</div>
<script src="http://www.google.com/jsapi"
  type="text/javascript"></script>
<script type="text/javascript">
  google.load('search', '1', {language : 'en'});
  google.setOnLoadCallback(function(){
    var customSearchControl = new
      google.search.CustomSearchControl(
      '009999999999999999999:0aaaaaaa010' );
    customSearchControl.setResultSetSize(
      google.search.Search.FILTERED_CSE_RESULTSET );
    customSearchControl.draw('cse');
  }, true);
</script>
<link rel="stylesheet"
  href=http://www.google.com/cse/style/look/minimalist.css
  type="text/css" />
```

The original code is for a Google search of the ChronoEngine.com site, though I've masked the ID string in the middle of the code snippet shown here.

As we've seen, ChronoForms is quite happy to accept valid HTML even though it isn't a form. So, we'll first try copying and pasting this code into the Form HTML box of a new form named google_search.

Save and publish the form then view it in your browser. Here's what you might see searching ChronoEngine.com for javascript:

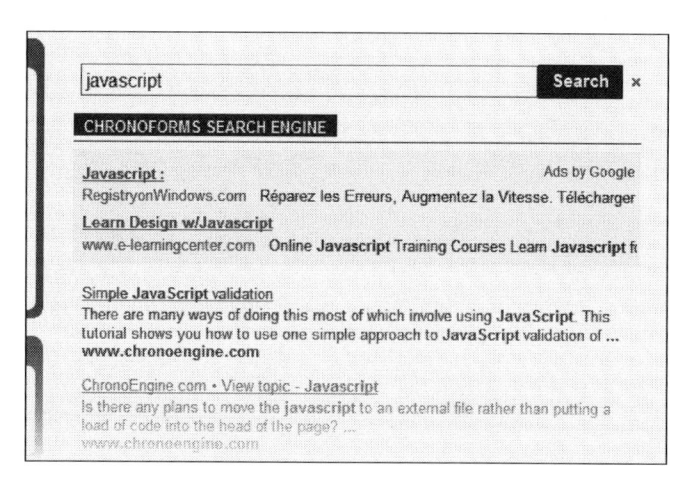

There we have a perfectly good, functioning Google Custom Search running inside ChronoForms so we could stop right here. But this recipe is about moving the JavaScript over and we haven't mentioned that yet.

2. In fact, most of this script is JavaScript related. This line is importing a base script `http://www.google.com/jsapi` from the Google site:

   ```
   <script src="http://www.google.com/jsapi"
   type="text/javascript"></script>
   ```

   And these lines are including a script snippet into our page code:

   ```
   <script type="text/javascript">
     google.load('search', '1', {language : 'en'});
     google.setOnLoadCallback(function(){
       var customSearchControl = new
         google.search.CustomSearchControl(
         '009999999999999999999:0aaaaaaa010' );
       customSearchControl.setResultSetSize(
         google.search.Search.FILTERED_CSE_RESULTSET );
       customSearchControl.draw('cse');
     }, true);
   </script>
   ```

   The form works so we can see that it's perfectly acceptable to include both script links and script snippets into the Form HTML. Particularly when you are testing, this is a quick and easy way to copy over a script from another site.

3. It does though take up some space inside the Form HTML box and we can be a little more elegant with the snippet by putting that into ChronoForms Form JavaScript box.

   Like the form code in the previous recipe we only want the code between the `<script . . . >` and `</script>` tags so copy that, paste it into the **Form JavaScript** box just below the Form HTML box, then delete the snippet, and the script tags, from the Form HTML box.

   Apply or save the form and refresh the view in the browser, and we find that the form no longer works! All that it shows up is **Loading**:

   > Loading
   > Powered By ChronoForms - ChronoEngine.com

4. What has happened is only apparent if you look at the page source code for our new form. A web page has two main parts—a head, marked out with `<head> . . . </head>` tags, and a body, marked out with `<body> . . . </body>` tags.

Writing Form HTML

When we put the code snippet inside the Form HTML, the code is included in the middle of the page in the body section. However, when we put the snippet into the Form JavaScript box ChronoForms changes the sequence and loads the snippet before the library is called in the Form HTML.

5. The answer to this is to use some Joomla! code to move the link to the base script into the header as well.

   To do this we need another Joomla! object; this time it's the Document object where all the information about the page is assembled and stored until it is ready to display. We get access to the Document object with this code which is starting to look familiar:

   ```
   $doc =& JFactory::getDocument();
   ```

   Then we can use one of the methods to load the script into the head of the page:

   ```
   $doc->addScript('http://www.google.com/jsapi');
   ```

   This code has to stay in the Form HTML, as at present ChronoForms has no direct support for linking script files. We'll also need the `isSite()` test line to prevent us hitting the ChronoForms evaluation error. So the whole snippet looks like:

   ```
   <?php
   if ( !$mainframe->isSite() ) { return; }
   $doc =& JFactory::getDocument();
   $doc->addScript('http://www.google.com/jsapi');
   ?>
   ```

   Put this into the Form HTML box to replace this line:

   ```
   <script src="http://www.google.com/jsapi"
   type="text/javascript"></script>
   ```

   Apply or save the form and refresh the browser view. Now our search box should be displaying correctly again.

   Now, we've seen how to add both JavaScript snippets and linked JavaScript files from another source into ChronoForms.

There's more...

When we come to move more complex Java Script into ChronoForms there are a few extra wrinkles that we have to look out for.

Changing the form name in ChronoForms

On simple web pages it's quite common for JavaScript to refer to a form, or field in the form using `document.form`, or `document.form_name` (where `form_name` is the value of the name attribute in the `<form . . . >` tag; for example, `<form name='my_form' . . . >`; or sometimes just `this`, or `this.form`).

In Joomla! there may be several forms on the page so it's helpful to specify which one your script refers to by using the form name. However, there's a little catch to look out for—ChronoForms changes the form name to make sure that it is unique. Our form in this recipe was called `google_search` in the Form Editor. If you look in the page source code you'll find that the form tag reads as follows:

```
<form . . . name='ChronoContact_google_search' . . .>
```

And this is the name that you will need to use in your JavaScript.

Most scripts can be adapted to work in ChronoForms provided that you keep this change in mind. If the script has many references to a `document.form`, then it may be useful to define a JavaScript variable for the form name and then use search and replace in a text editor to update the script:

```
var form_name = 'ChronoContact_google_search';
```

Beyond this stage, you need more JavaScript knowledge than we can include here.

Fixing conflicts with scripts using jQuery

Some more complex scripts use a JavaScript library to aid their functionality. There are several in common use including **Prototype**, **MooTools**, and **jQuery**. The MooTools library is used extensively by Joomla! in the back-end—the site administration pages—and is also used in the frontend though mostly for image captions. ChronoForms uses the MooTools library to add form functionality in several place including validation, republishing, and date-time pickers.

jQuery is increasingly being used to add functional enhancements to forms and templates in Joomla!. Unfortunately, out of the box, jQuery and MooTools are mutually incompatible and using them both usually means that they both stop working somewhere.

There is a fix for this that works well, that is to put jQuery into **noConflict** mode. This is done by adding the following script snippet into the page after both libraries have loaded:

```
jQuery.noConflict();
```

Joomla! loads script links before script snippets so that any required library files are available before any snippets that use them. So, adding the snippet to the ChronoForms Form JavaScript box should be sufficient.

If this doesn't work then some more advanced JavaScript debugging may be required (the FireBug extension for Firefox is an invaluable tool for this).

See the jQuery documents for more advanced options at `http://docs.jquery.com/Using_jQuery_with_Other_Libraries`.

Writing Form HTML

Loading snippets into the page head

We saw above how to use the document object method to load the script link from the page head. You can do the same for snippets using the `addScriptDeclaration()` method.

This can be useful if you want to create script snippets using PHP and therefore load them from the Form HTML box. The basic syntax is:

```
<?php
$doc =& JFactory::getDocument();
$doc->addScriptDeclaration('insert script here');
?>
```

Although it quickly becomes messy adding anything more than the briefest script in that space, a better approach is to create a `$script` string variable and to insert that at the end of the code section:

```
$script = "
  google.load('search', '1', {language : 'en'});
  google.setOnLoadCallback(function(){
    var customSearchControl = new
      google.search.CustomSearchControl(
      '009999999999999999999:0aaaaaaa010' );
    customSearchControl.setResultSetSize(
      google.search.Search.FILTERED_CSE_RESULTSET );
    customSearchControl.draw('cse');
  }, true);
";
$doc->addScriptDeclaration($script);
```

> Note that we've left out the `$doc =& JFactory::getDocument();` line here. It is only needed once in the Form HTML and we're assuming that is was included earlier. (If it is added twice then that normally does no harm.)

If you have several script snippets to add from different places in your form code then you can aggregate them like this:

```
$script  = "";
. . .
$script .= "/* a script snippet */";
. . .
$script .= "/* another script snippet */";
. . .
$doc->addScriptDeclaration($script);
```

Moving a form with CSS

Well the JavaScript was the difficult one so now we have a gentle walk through doing the same with CSS.

> If you have come directly to this recipe then we suggest that you take a quick look at the previous recipe—*Moving a form with JavaScript*—before reading on, as the two are closely related and we'll refer back sometimes to save repeating too much.

Getting ready

We'll use the same Google Custom Search form, using the "Minimal" styling option (chosen in the setup configuration).

How to do it...

1. If you look at the script you'll see that there is a CSS file linked but no snippet. This is fairly normal as CSS code is usually static and more amenable to being loaded from cached files than those parts of JavaScript that change depending on the form code. Here's the linked file:

   ```
   <link rel="stylesheet"
     href=http://www.google.com/cse/style/look/minimalist.css
     type="text/css" />
   ```

   We've already seen that this works perfectly well from the Form HTML box. And it's tidier to load it from the page head as we did with the JavaScript file in the last recipe. Again the Joomla! Document object has a method we can use:

   ```
   <?php
   $doc =& JFactory::getDocument();
   $doc->addStyleSheet(
      'http://www.google.com/cse/style/look/minimalist.css');
   ?>
   ```

   This is just the same as `addScript()` but now we have `addStyleSheet()`.

> We are getting a little ahead of ourselves here but this was a useful place to introduce some concepts that are valuable both in adapting scripts to ChronoForms and in writing more complex forms using PHP.

2. Replace the link in the Form HTML with this code.

> Make sure that the `$doc =& JFactory::getDocument();` line appears once before any of the `$doc->` . . . lines and all the PHP code is inside `<?php` . . . `?>` tags. Any time you find `?>` `<?php` tags with nothing but white space between them they can both be deleted.

3. If you find a form with CSS snippets then these can be pasted into the ChronoForms Form CSS box in the same way as we did with the JavaScript snippet.

   Let's try an experiment. Here's a small snippet from the `minimalist.css` file that we just linked to:

   ```
   .cse .gsc-branding, .gsc-branding {
     display : none;
   }
   ```

   We'll make a little change to this and put the changed snippet into the Form CSS box:

   ```
   .cse .gsc-branding, .gsc-branding {
     display : block;
   }
   ```

   Enter the code, apply, or save the form then refresh the browser view.

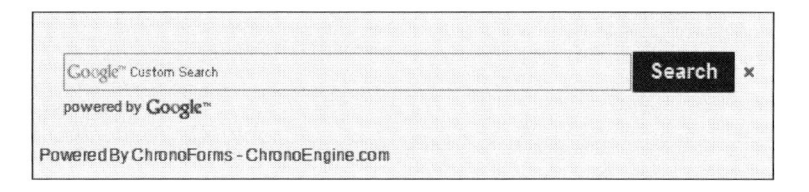

4. And you can see that the CSS snippet has "turned on" the **powered by Google** branding under the search box.

> The Google CSS file that we are linking to has the CSS set to hide the branding. Our CSS snippet over-rides that and turns the display on. That's a consequence of the "cascading" effect of stylesheets.

There's more...

Loading snippets into the page head
Again, as with the JavaScript, instead of using the Form CSS box we can add code into the Form HTML box to load the CSS snippet into the page head. Here's the longer version:

```
$style = "
cse .gsc-branding, .gsc-branding {
  display : block;
}
";
$doc->addStyleDeclaration($style);
```

Loading browser-specific CSS files into the page head
One thing that does change with CSS files is that we may want to use slightly different files for different browsers (older versions of Internet Explorer in particular).

It won't surprise you to know that Joomla! has some code that can help with this. There's what is called a "browser sniffer" included that will do its best to tell us which browser is being used.

> We're saying "do its best" because browser sniffing is not 100% accurate and it is very easy for a knowledgeable user to disguise or hide the browser type. Fortunately, most ordinary users don't do these things.

The following code imports and then loads the Joomla! browser object:

```
<?php
jimport('Joomla!.environment.browser');
$browser = JBrowser::getInstance();
```

Then we set `$style` to different style sheets depending on which browser is found:

```
switch ( $browser->getBrowser() ) {
  case 'msie':
    // Browser is Internet Explorer
    $style = 'shiny.css';
    break;
  case 'mozilla':
    // Browser is FireFox
    $style = 'minimalist.css';
    break;
  case 'konqueror':
```

Writing Form HTML

```
      // browser is Safari or Chrome
      $style = 'bubblegum.css';
      break;
   default:
      // browser is something else
      $style = 'default.css';
}
```

Finally we use the same code as before to load the style sheet set by the switch statement:

```
$doc =& JFactory::getDocument();
$doc->addStyleSheet(
   'http://www.google.com/cse/style/look/'.$style);
?>
```

If we add this code to the Form HTML in place of the single stylesheet link we had before, then we can try viewing the form in different browsers:

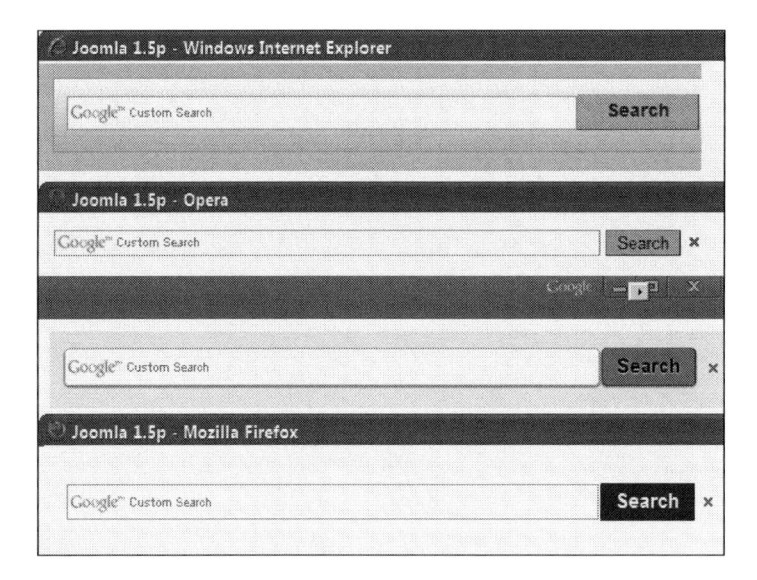

And you can see that each of these four browsers—Internet Explorer, Opera, Chrome, and Firefox is showing the search box with a different stylesheet.

Perhaps this isn't the most practical application, but it does clearly show the capability.

Chapter 9

Creating a form with Wufoo

Sometimes the ChronoForms Wizard doesn't quite do what you want and you need to look for another way to create your form code.

One route is to use an online form creator. **Wufoo** is one of the best we know and in this recipe, we'll look at creating a form in Wufoo and moving it across to ChronoForms in Joomla!.

Getting ready

Sign up for a free account at wufoo.com. Doing this will allow you to create three forms and host them at wufoo.com. If you do as we are going to do and move them elsewhere, then you can edit and replace those three to create more.

Of course, wufoo.com would really prefer that you host your forms with them so they don't let you take everything away with you, but there's enough.

Now create a form. We're going to use a form designed to collect online testimonials. You can see it at http://greyhead.wufoo.com/forms/testimonial/. While you could just copy the page HTML from here, if you create your own account then Wufoo makes the code access easier.

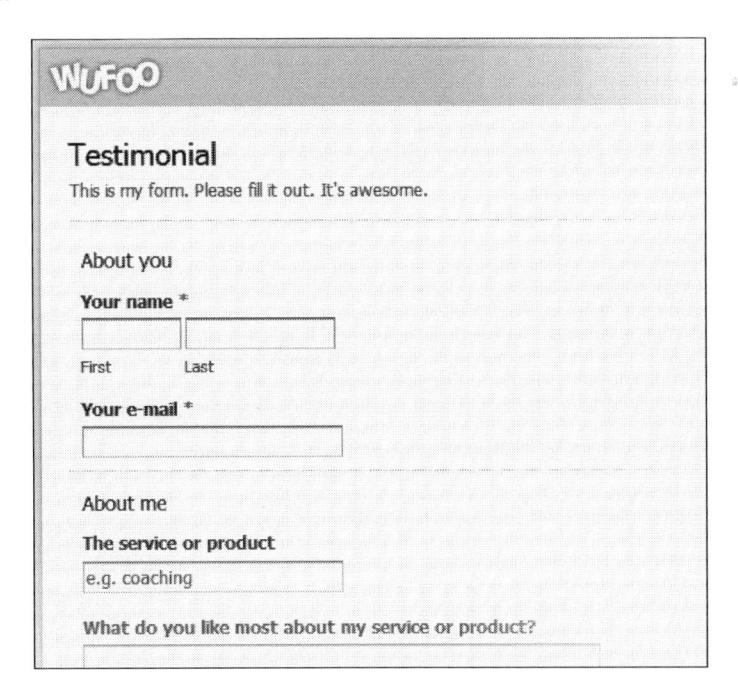

Writing Form HTML

We won't go into the process of creating a form at Wufoo here. It's a nice drag-and-drop process and they have their own excellent tutorials to show you how to do it.

How to do it...

1. Once you have created your form on Wufoo, you'll need to sign in, go to the Wufoo Forms Manager, and click the **Code** link for the form you want to transfer to ChronoForms.

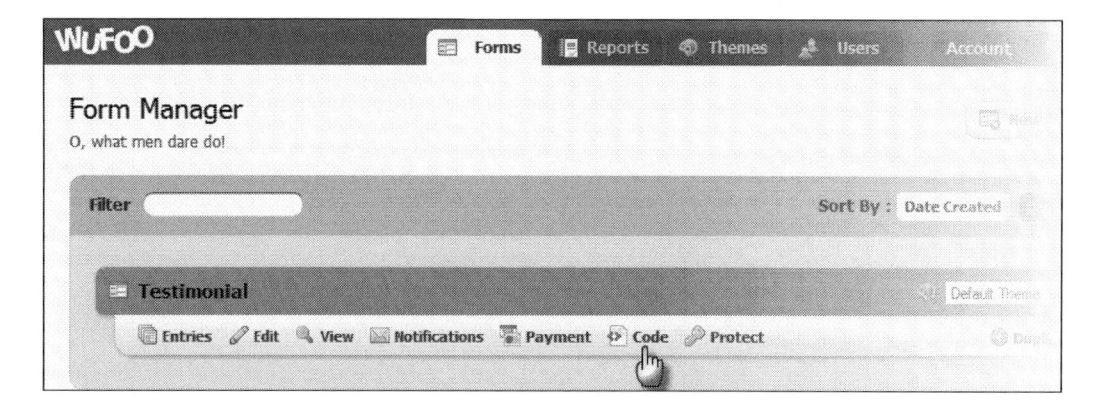

2. In the Code page, you'll see that Wufoo offers you several options for exporting your form or links to it. The last one is an **Email a friend** message, and the first three all offer ways to link back to the Wufoo hosted form from another site. We want the fourth option, **XHTML/CSS Code**.

> The link-back versions of the form will work perfectly well from Joomla!, and from ChronoForms, but they will send the data back to Wufoo rather than letting ChronoForms process it so we won't explore them any further here.

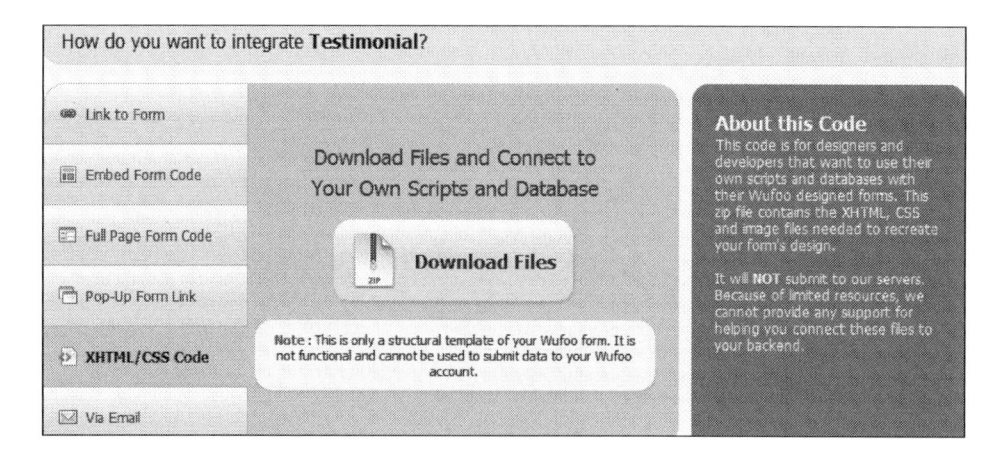

Chapter 9

3. Click the big **Download Files** button to get a zipped package of the form files.

> Note the messages that Wufoo shows here. These files are limited and will not submit to the Wufoo servers. There's also a message lower down saying **All code on this page is provided under a Creative Commons Attribution 3.0 License http://creativecommons.org/licenses/by/3.0/us/**.

When we open the ZIP file we find that there are quite a lot of files inside. As well as the main `index.html` file there is a JavaScript file, three CSS stylesheet files, six files in an `images` folder, and lastly there's a `README.txt` file.

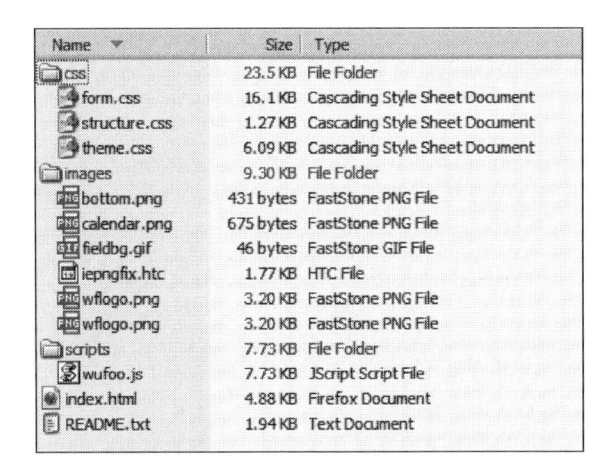

Name	Size	Type
css	23.5 KB	File Folder
form.css	16.1 KB	Cascading Style Sheet Document
structure.css	1.27 KB	Cascading Style Sheet Document
theme.css	6.09 KB	Cascading Style Sheet Document
images	9.30 KB	File Folder
bottom.png	431 bytes	FastStone PNG File
calendar.png	675 bytes	FastStone PNG File
fieldbg.gif	46 bytes	FastStone GIF File
iepngfix.htc	1.77 KB	HTC File
wflogo.png	3.20 KB	FastStone PNG File
wflogo.png	3.20 KB	FastStone PNG File
scripts	7.73 KB	File Folder
wufoo.js	7.73 KB	JScript Script File
index.html	4.88 KB	Firefox Document
README.txt	1.94 KB	Text Document

We'll assume that we need all of these, except perhaps the last. It also looks as though all of them except the `index.html` file are part of a "standard" Wufoo package that comes with all forms. So, we'll put them into a new `wufoo` folder.

4. Using your FTP tool create a new `wufoo` folder inside `{root_path}/components/com_chronocontact`.

[237]

Writing Form HTML

5. Now copy all the folders and their contents from the Wufoo package (but not the `index.html` or `README.txt` files) into the folder. To finish, copy the little Joomla! `index.html` file into the `wufoo` folder and each of the subfolders. Here's the structure we want to create:

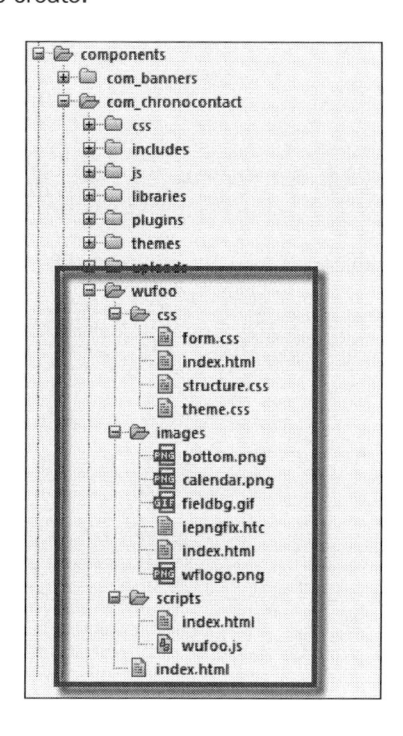

```
components
├── com_banners
├── com_chronocontact
│   ├── css
│   ├── includes
│   ├── js
│   ├── libraries
│   ├── plugins
│   ├── themes
│   └── uploads
└── wufoo
    ├── css
    │   ├── form.css
    │   ├── index.html
    │   ├── structure.css
    │   └── theme.css
    ├── images
    │   ├── bottom.png
    │   ├── calendar.png
    │   ├── fieldbg.gif
    │   ├── iepngfix.htc
    │   ├── index.html
    │   └── wflogo.png
    ├── scripts
    │   ├── index.html
    │   └── wufoo.js
    └── index.html
```

6. Now open up the ChronoForms Forms Manager and click the **New** icon to create a new form. Give it the name `wufoo_1`.

7. Open the Form HTML textarea. We want to paste an edited version of the Wufoo `index.html` in here, but it's quite a long file to edit in the small textarea space so you may find it easier to make the changes in a text editor first.

    Here's what we need to do:

    - First make a backup copy of the original file because we may need to go back to it. In particular we'll need the names of the CSS and JavaScript files that are linked near the beginning.
    - Delete the lines highlighted here from the beginning of the file:

```
<!DOCTYPE html PUBLIC "-//W3C//DTD XHTML 1.0 Transitional//EN"
"http://www.w3.org/TR/xhtml1/DTD/xhtml1-transitional.dtd">

<html xmlns="http://www.w3.org/1999/xhtml">
<head>
```

```html
<title>
Testimonial
</title>

<!-- Meta Tags -->
<meta http-equiv="Content-Type" content="text/html;
  charset=utf-8" />
<meta name="generator" content="Wufoo.com" />

<!-- CSS -->
<link rel="stylesheet" href="css/structure.css"
  type="text/css" />
<link rel="stylesheet" href="css/form.css" type="text/css" />

<!-- JavaScript -->
<script type="text/javascript"
  src="scripts/wufoo.js"></script>
</head>

<body id="public">
<div id="container">

<h1 id="logo">
  <a href="http://wufoo.com" title="Powered by Wufoo">Wufoo</a>
</h1>

<form id="form1" name="form1" class="wufoo   page"
  autocomplete="off" enctype="multipart/form-data"
  method="post" action="#public">
. . .
```

Now go to the end of the form and remove a few more lines:

```html
</ul>
</form>

</div><!--container-->
<img id="bottom" src="images/bottom.png" alt="" />

<a href="http://wufoo.com" title="Designed with Wufoo">
  <img src="/images/powerlogo.png" alt="Designed with Wufoo">
</a>
</body>
</html>
```

Writing Form HTML

- Back at the beginning we're going to replace those link lines with a little PHP:

```php
<?php
if ( !$mainframe->isSite()) { return; }

// define a url for the 'wufoo' folder
$wufoo_url = JURI::base()
   .'components/com_chronocontact/wufoo/';

// define a path for the 'wufoo' folder
$wufoo_path = JPATH_SITE.DS
   .DS.'components'.DS.'com_chronocontact'.DS.'wufoo'.DS;
$styles = $scripts = array();

// access the Joomla! Document object
$doc =& JFactory::getDocument();

// Add the CSS files
$doc->addStyleSheet($wufoo_url.'css/structure.css');
$doc->addStyleSheet($wufoo_url.'css/form.css');

// Add the JavaScript file
$doc->addScript($wufoo_url.'scripts/wufoo.js');
?>
```

- Add this PHP at the beginning of the file.
- Now go back down to the end of the file where there are two image links and amend those to add the new `wufoo` folder URL:

```html
</div><!--container-->
<img id="bottom" src="<?php echo $wufoo_url; ?>images/
   bottom.png" alt="" />

<a href="http://wufoo.com" title="Designed with Wufoo">
   <img src="http://wufoo.com/images/powerlogo.png"
      alt="Designed with Wufoo">
</a>
```

> The `powerlogo.png` image isn't in the Wufoo file package for some reason so we're linking back to their site for that one.

8. Copy the amended file and paste it into the Form HTML box in the form.

9. Save the form and publish it. Now click the link to view the form in your browser.

   If all is well, it should be looking pretty good, but it's not quite right. We have one more set of changes to make.

10. Open up each of the three CSS files in an editor and search for the image links (searching for "images" should find them). There aren't many.

11. In each case, replace `/images` with `/components/com_chronocontact/wufoo/images`.

> If you prefer you can put the full domain in here: `http://www.example.com/components/...` If your site is in a sub-domain then you may need to add the subdomain name in any case, for example `/subdomain/components/...`

12. Save the files again and reload them to your site if you edited them locally.
13. Refresh the form in your browser and it should now be complete.

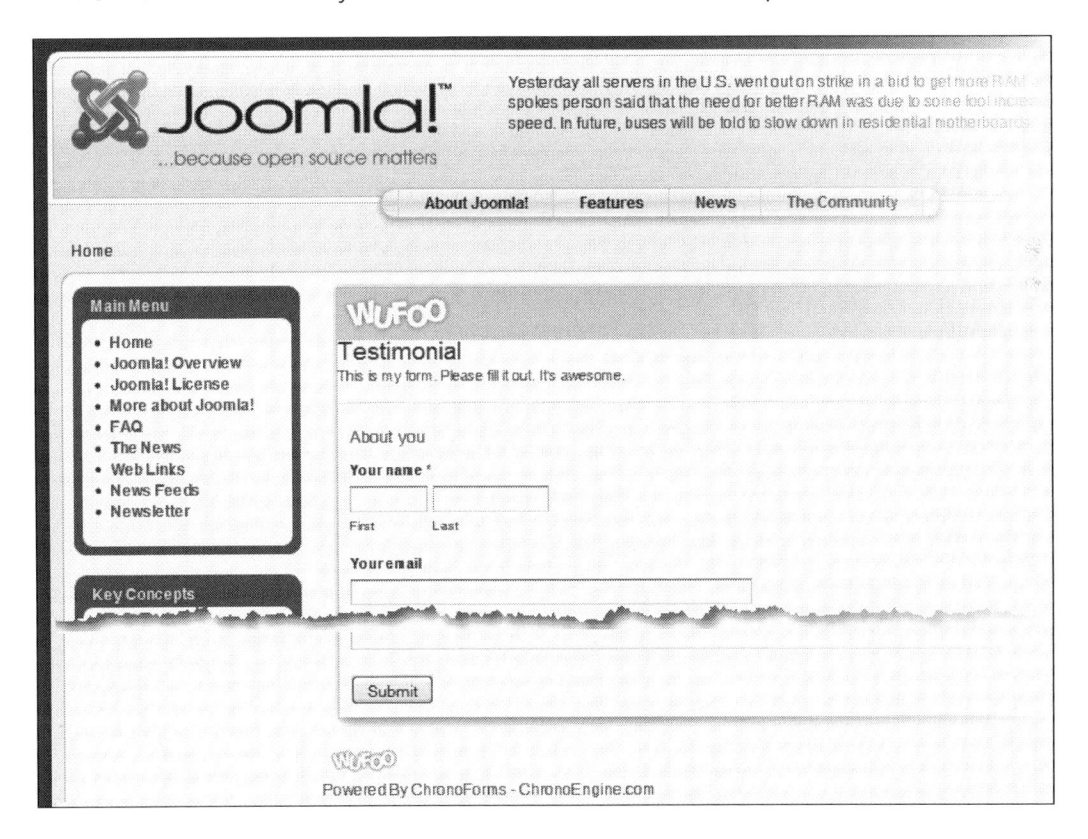

Writing Form HTML

There's a Wufoo created and styled form working inside Joomla! as a ChronoForms form. Check that the field high-lighting works.

14. Turn **Debug** on in the **Form Editor | General** tab and check that the form submits OK. The `$_POST` array entries should be displayed just as they are for a form created wholly in ChronoForms. The main difference is that the Wufoo input names are `Field1`, `Field2`, `Field3`, and so on instead of `text_0`, `text_1`, and so on.

How it works...

In the end, web forms are combinations of HTML, CSS, and JavaScript, provided that we set these up so that the parts work together.

What we have done here is to take the code from another source, make those few small adaptations so that the links from one part to another work inside our Joomla! folder structure and the form works perfectly.

There's more...

Changing the Wufoo theme template

1. Wufoo has developed a theme gallery of fifty or so CSS theme packages for their forms. The gallery is at `http://wufoo.com/gallery/designs/`. Go there and pick a theme that takes your fancy. We'll work with **Baked** from **Tab 3** but any of them will work in the same way.

2. When you've made your choice click the **Download CSS** button under the theme name and you will download a ZIP file very similar to the one we got for our form. But this time we only need one file.

3. Unzip the package and extract the `theme.css` file. Make the same changes we did previously to change the image URLs.

4. Then copy the file into the `wufoo/css` folder in place of the existing `theme.css` file (you might want to rename that to `theme1.css` for safekeeping).

5. Reload the form, and nothing changes!

   The Wufoo form HTML doesn't actually load the `theme.css` file so we need to add it ourselves. Open up the Form HTML again and insert the extra `$doc->addStyleSheet()` line:

   ```
   // Add the CSS files
   $doc->addStyleSheet($wufoo_url.'css/structure.css');
   $doc->addStyleSheet($wufoo_url.'css/form.css');
   $doc->addStyleSheet($wufoo_url.'css/theme.css');
   ```

6. Apply or save the form and refresh it in the browser and now our new theme will be working.

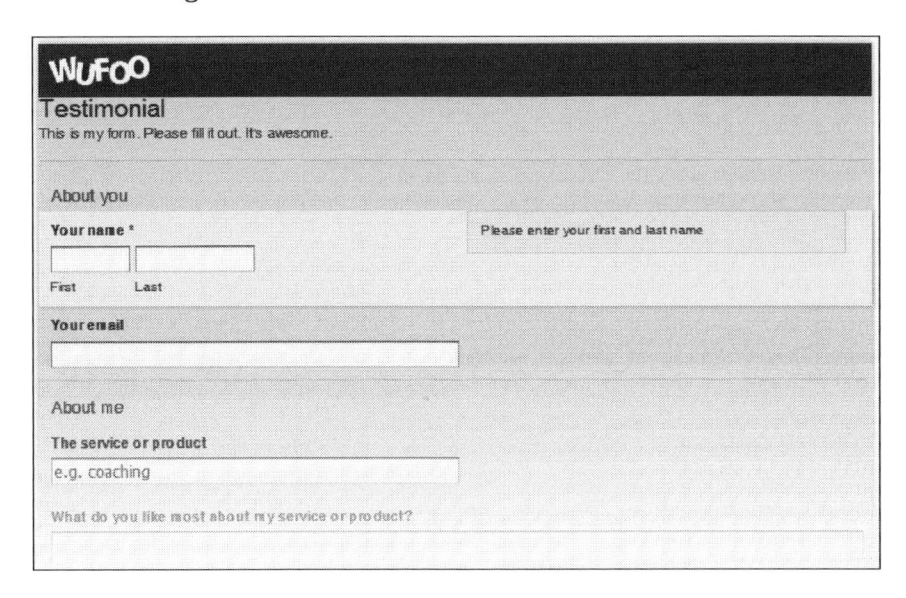

Here's the restyled form complete with field highlighting and tooltips.

> Note: To get the Wufoo tooltip to show in that location requires a small change to the `form.css` file. Around line 584 change `left:100%` to `left:50%` in this style:
>
> ```
> form li.focused .instruct, form li:hover .instruct{
>   left:50%; /* Prevent scrollbars for IE Instruct fix */
>   visibility:visible;
> }
> ```

Writing Form HTML

Using a form from the Wufoo gallery

There's also The Wufoo Form Gallery at `http://wufoo.com/gallery/templates` where there are close to 80 "typical" forms that you can view and download.

1. We'll download the **T-Shirt Order Form** from the **Online Orders** page but the same process can be used with any of the other forms there.

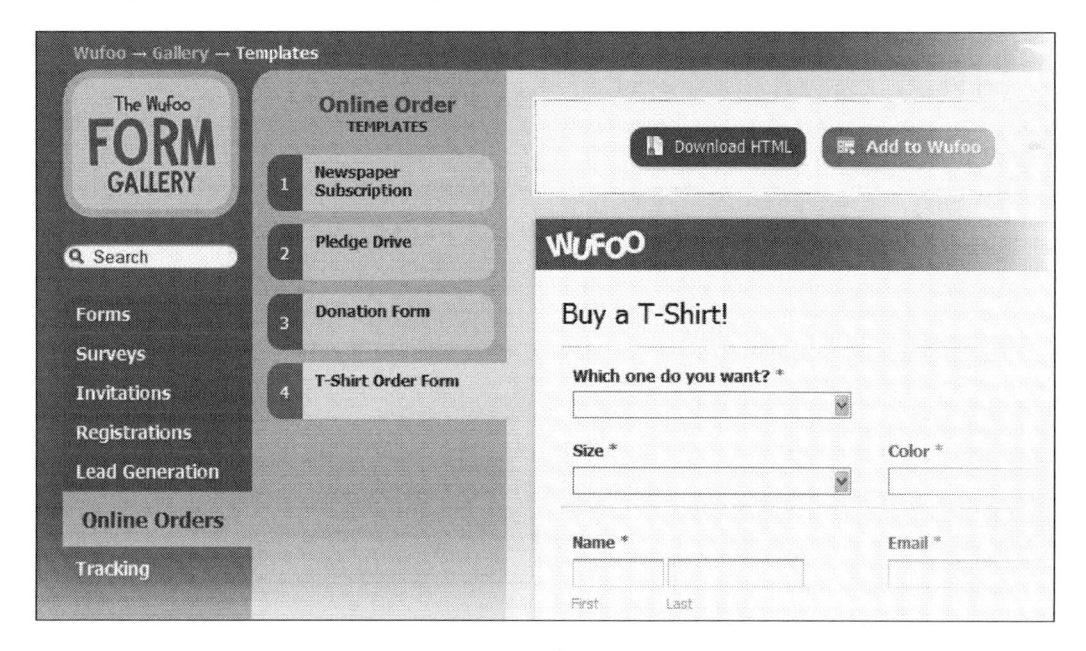

2. Click the **Download HTML** button to get the zipped file package.
3. In the ChronoForms Forms Manager check the box by the `wufoo_1` form and then click the **Copy Form** icon in the Toolbar. Open the newly created copy form to edit it and change the name to `wufoo_2`.

Chapter 9

> Caution: ChronoForms gives copied forms the same name as the original. It will not complain if there are two (or more) forms with the same name. However, when you open the form for viewing you will only get one of them, usually the one with the lowest Form ID. It can be a bit baffling when the changes you've made to the form code don't show up in the browser. This may be the cause.

4. Copying the existing form means that most of the changes we made to the Form HTML are already in place. Unzip the form package and open the `index.html` file in your text editor.

5. Select the code between the `<form . . . >` and `</form>` tags (but not the tags themselves) and paste it into the **Form HTML** textarea to replace the corresponding section of the code that is already there. You will be replacing the section with the beginning and end highlighted here:

```
. . .
<div id="container">

<h1 id="logo">
   <a href="http://wufoo.com" title="Powered by Wufoo">Wufoo</a>
</h1>

<div class="info">
   <h2>Buy a T-Shirt!</h2>
. . .
// Most of the file is here
. . .
   <input type="hidden" id="idstamp" name="idstamp" value="" />
   </li>
   </ul>
</div><!--container-->
. . .
```

Writing Form HTML

6. Save the form in the Form Editor and click the link to view it in a browser window:

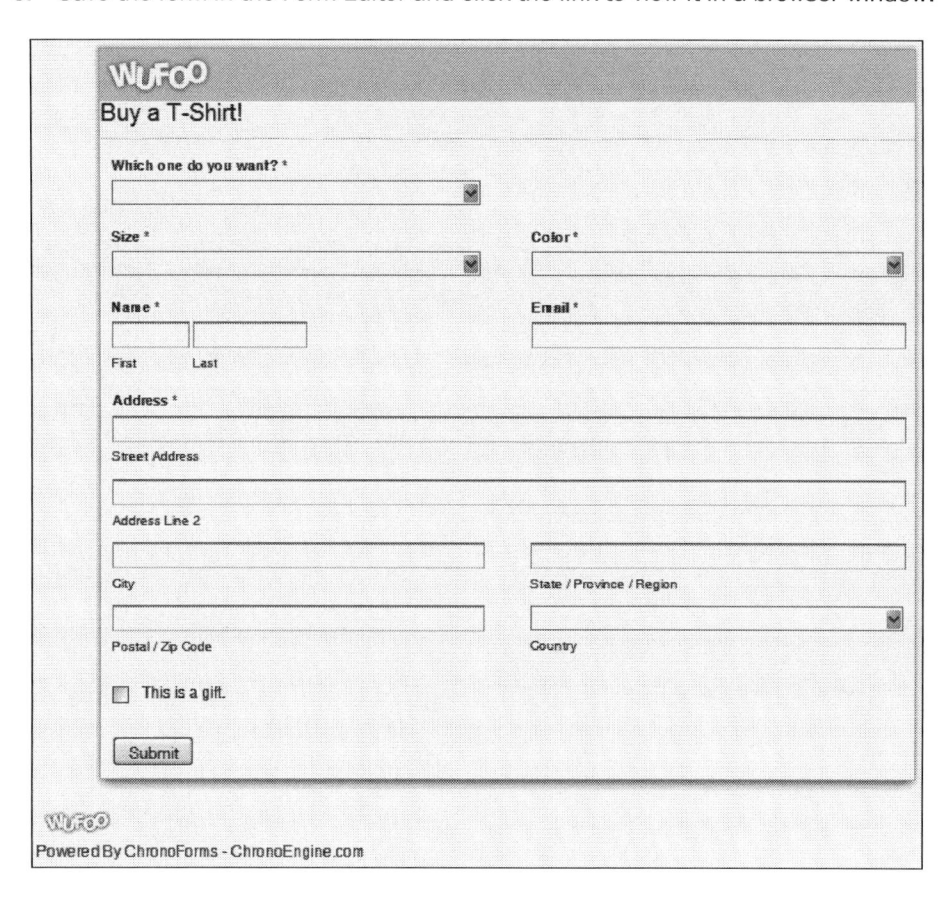

And you have a neat T-Shirt order form in ChronoForms.

Adding validation to a Wufoo Form

There doesn't appear to be any validation built into these forms; or if there is, it doesn't work in ChronoForms. We can however add ChronoForms validation with a little extra work.

1. There are two conflicts between the Wufoo supplied JavaScript file and the MooTools and/or ChronoForms JavaScript files. We'll make two edits to the Wufoo file to correct these.

    Open `wufoo.js` in a text editor and look for the line starting `addEvent(...` at about line 10. Change it to:

    `addEventWu(activeForm, 'submit', disableSubmitButton);`

Adding in the `Wu` distinguishes it from the MooTools `addEvents()` function.

2. Make the same change in the line starting `function addEvent(...` about ten lines from the end of the file so it becomes:

   `function addEventWu( obj, type, fn ) {`

3. Now add this line near the beginning of the form just before the `function initForm() {` line:

   ```
   // add the next line
   function handleInput() {};
   
   function addEventWu( obj, type, fn ) {
   ```

   This empty function prevents errors from code that is in the Wufoo Form HTML. It's easier to add the empty function than to find and remove every reference in the Wufoo code. Save the `wufoo.js` file back to the site.

4. Now open the form in the ChronoForms Form Editor; in the Form HTML find the `<input . . . >` tag for the Email input and add `required validate-email` to the class attribute:

   ```
   <li id="foli11" class="rightHalf" >
     <label class="desc" id="title11" for="Field11">
       Email
       <span id="req_11" class="req">*</span>
     </label>
     <div>
       <input id="Field11" name="Field11" type="text"
         class="field text medium required validate-email"
         value="" maxlength="255" tabindex="6"
         onkeyup="handleInput(this);"
         onchange="handleInput(this);" />
     </div>
   </li>
   ```

5. Lastly click the **Validation** tab and set **Enable Validation** to **Yes**.

Writing Form HTML

6. Apply or save the Form Editor and refresh the view of the form in the browser window.

   Test the validation in the Email field and it should be working fine. Check that both the `required` and the `validate-email` validations are working correctly.

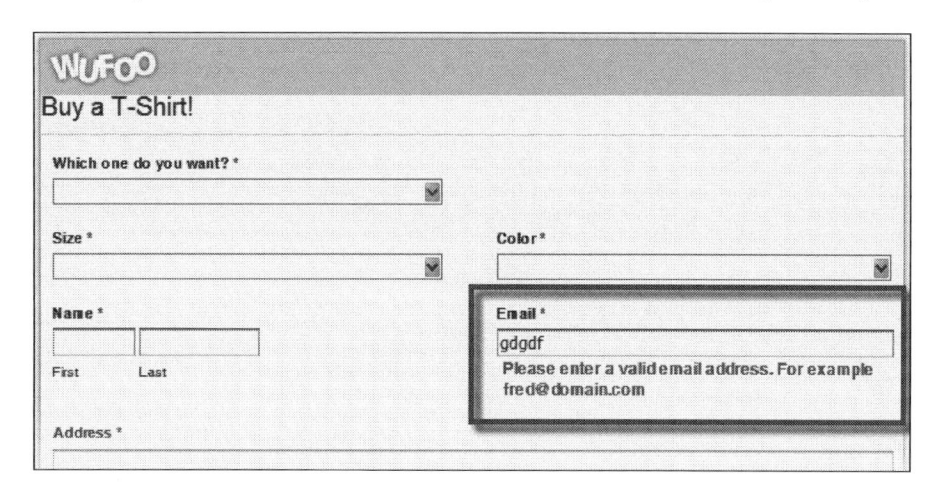

You can add more validations by adding the appropriate classes to the Form HTML.

Creating a form in Dreamweaver

Dreamweaver is a popular website development tool that can easily be used to create the HTML for a form. If you don't have Dreamweaver then you can use most other website development tools in a similar way.

Getting ready

We're going to use a simple example of a form created in Dreamweaver following the **Creating a Form** tutorial by Joseph Lowery and available from Adobe at `http://www.adobe.com/designcenter/video_workshop/?id=vid0160`.

Once again, this is a simple form as our intention here is to show you how to use the HTML in ChronoForms. There are many tutorials on the Adobe site and elsewhere that can teach you how to use Dreamweaver to create form code.

How to do it...

1. Here's what the form looks like in Dreamweaver:

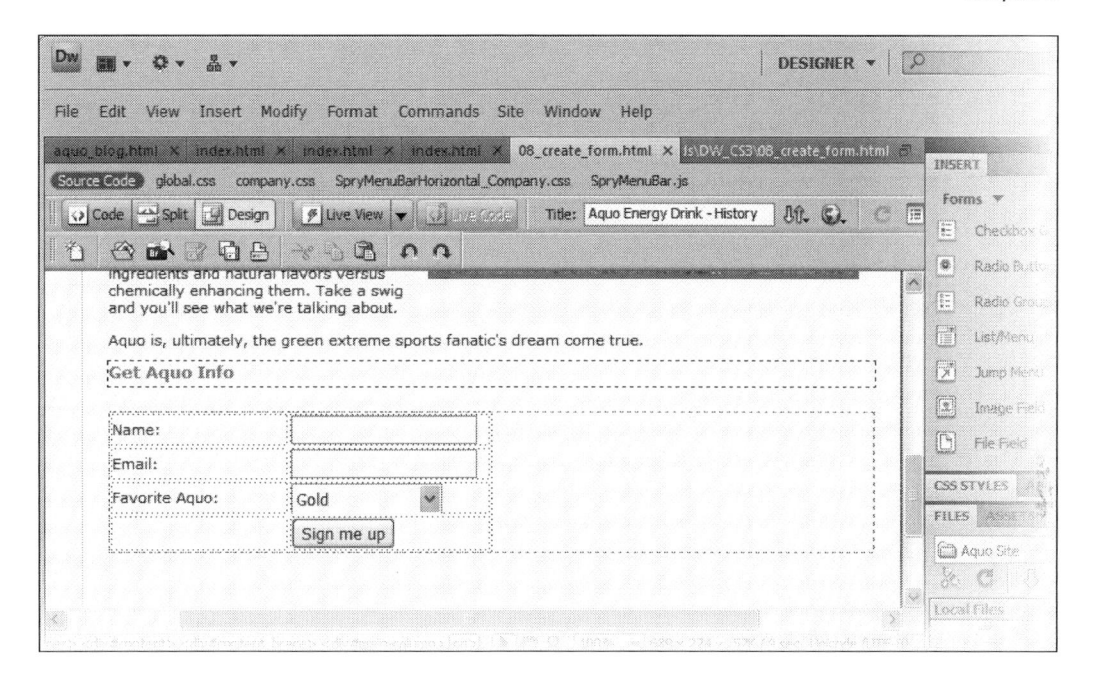

Switch to the code view in Dreamweaver and find the form code in the HTML. It's this section, including the 'Get Aquo Info' header just before the `<form . . . >` tag.

```html
<h2>Get Aquo Info</h2>
<p> </p>
<form id="form1" name="form1" method="post" action="">
  <table width="300" border="0">
    <tr>
      <td width="137">Name:</td>
      <td width="153"><input type="text" name="nameText" id="nameText" /></td>
    </tr>
    <tr>
      <td>Email:</td>
      <td><input type="text" name="emailText" id="emailText" /></td>
    </tr>
    <tr>
      <td>Favorite Aquo:</td>
      <td><select name="favMenu" id="favMenu">
        <option value="gold" selected="selected">Gold</option>
        <option value="red">Red</option>
        <option value="green">Green</option>
        <option value="clear">Clear</option>
        <option value="never">Never Tried It</option>
      </select></td>
    </tr>
    <tr>
      <td> </td>
      <td><input type="submit" name="submit" id="submit" value="Sign me up" /></td>
    </tr>
  </table>
</form>
```

Writing Form HTML

Copy the whole of this block.

2. Open the ChronoForms Forms Manager and click the '**New Form**' icon; give the form a name like `'aquo_dw_1'` and then open the **Form HTML** textarea on the **Form Code** tab.

    Paste in the code copied from Dreamweaver; find the `<form . . . >` tag near the beginning and delete the whole tag; then find `</form>` at the end and delete that.

3. Save the form and publish it; click the link to view the form in your browser:

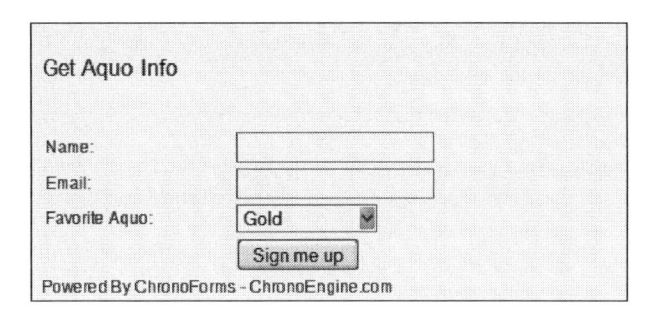

    Get Aquo Info

    Name:
    Email:
    Favorite Aquo: Gold
    Sign me up
    Powered By ChronoForms - ChronoEngine.com

And the form is there in ChronoForms complete with the drop-down and the customized submit button.

> If you have CSS or JavaScript created in Dreamweaver then you can also copy that over in much the same way as we did in the Wufoo recipe here. In both cases some debugging and tweaking may be needed to get the code working comfortably alongside the Joomla! template and ChronoForms CSS and JavaScript.

10
Creating Common Forms

In this chapter, we will cover:

- Creating a simple newsletter signup
- Creating a form to link to Acajoom
- Creating a form to publish a Joomla! article
- Creating a "Contact us" form
- Creating an image or document upload form
- Creating a multi-page form

Introduction

This is really Chapter 1—everything that went before was just preparation; maybe you skipped over all of that and came straight here anyway.

In this chapter, we're going to work through some common forms; the kind of application that more than half of ChronoForms users start out to achieve. Some of this will repeat forms that we've used in previous chapters. Most of the first few chapters used that little newsletter signup form, but here we'll just go through producing the form step-by-step, assuming that you already have a basic familiarity with ChronoForms. If you need more information, or more explanation; then it's probably somewhere in those chapters you skipped over!

Creating Common Forms

Creating a simple newsletter signup

Our newsletter signup form has text inputs for name and e-mail, and a checkbox to agree to the terms and conditions. All three fields are required, and the e-mail is validated as an e-mail address.

On submission, a confirmation e-mail is sent to the person signing up; the data is saved in a database table and a simple thank you message is shown to the user.

Getting ready

We're starting from scratch, so no preparation is required.

How to do it...

1. Creating the form:

    Open the ChronoForms Forms Manager and click the **Form Wizard** link.

    Drag in a **TextBox**, change the **Label** to **Your name** and the **Field Name** to "name", click the **Required** Validation, and **Apply** the **Properties**.

    Drag in a second TextBox, change the **Label** to **Your email** and the **Field Name** to "email", click the **Required** and **Email** Validations, and **Apply** the **Properties**.

    Drag in a **CheckBox**; change the **Label** to **Terms and conditions**; change the first **Option** to **I agree** and delete the other two; click the **One Required** Validation; **Apply** the **Properties**.

    Drag in a button, change the label to **Subscribe**, and **Apply** the **Properties**.

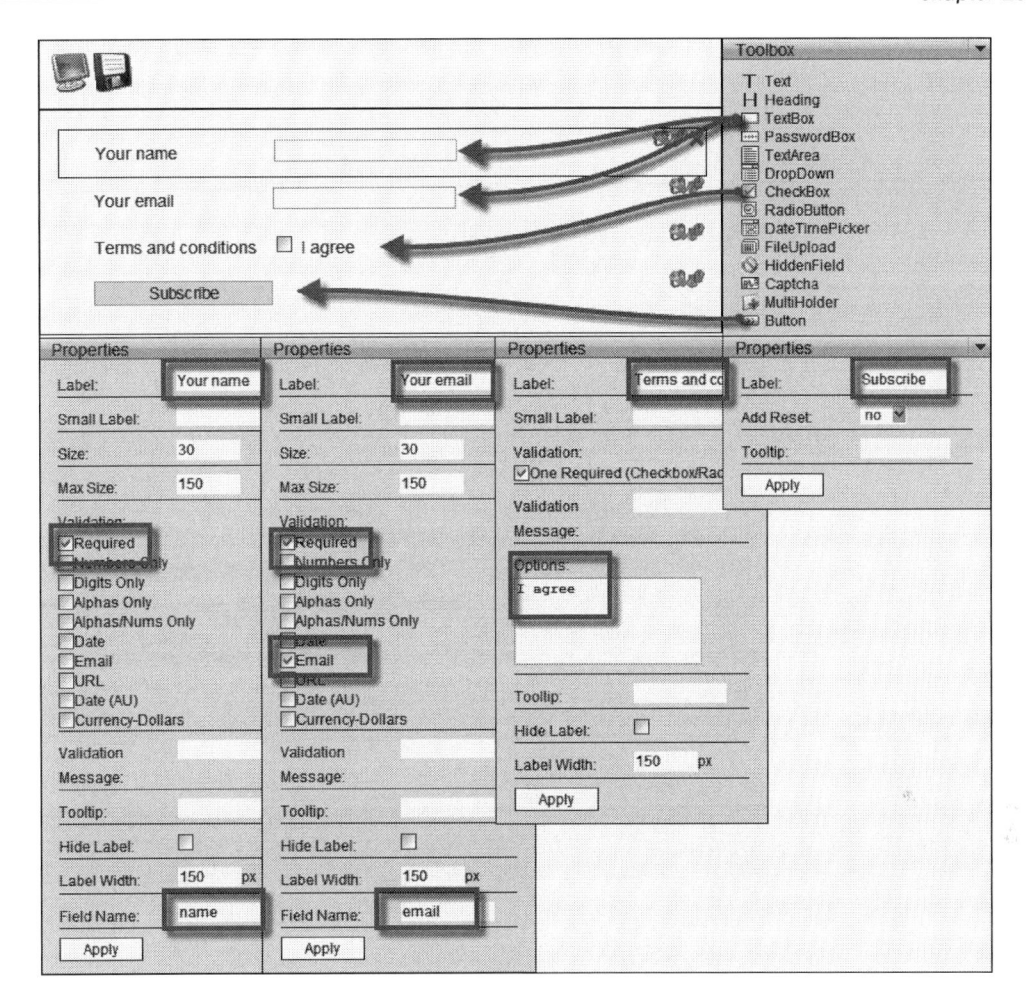

Click the disk icon to save the new form and give it a suitable name like `newsletter_1`.

In the Forms Manager click the button in the right hand column to **Publish** the form; then click the **Link** entry to view it in a browser window.

Creating Common Forms

2. Adding the e-mail:

   Now that the form HTML is done, we need to head back to the Form Manager for the rest of the work.

   Click the checkbox by your form name, then the **Wizard Edit** icon in the toolbar. Close the warning message that shows up.

   Now click **Step 2 Choose Email(s) Settings**.

   Drag four elements into the red box—**Dynamic To**, **Subject**, **From Name** and **From Email**.

   Click in the **Dynamic To** box and select the **email** box from the pop-up. Enter suitable values for your site in the other boxes.

   In the **Email Setup | Properties** box set **Enabled?** to **Yes** and **Enable Attachments** to **No**.

   Click **Apply** in the **Properties** box.

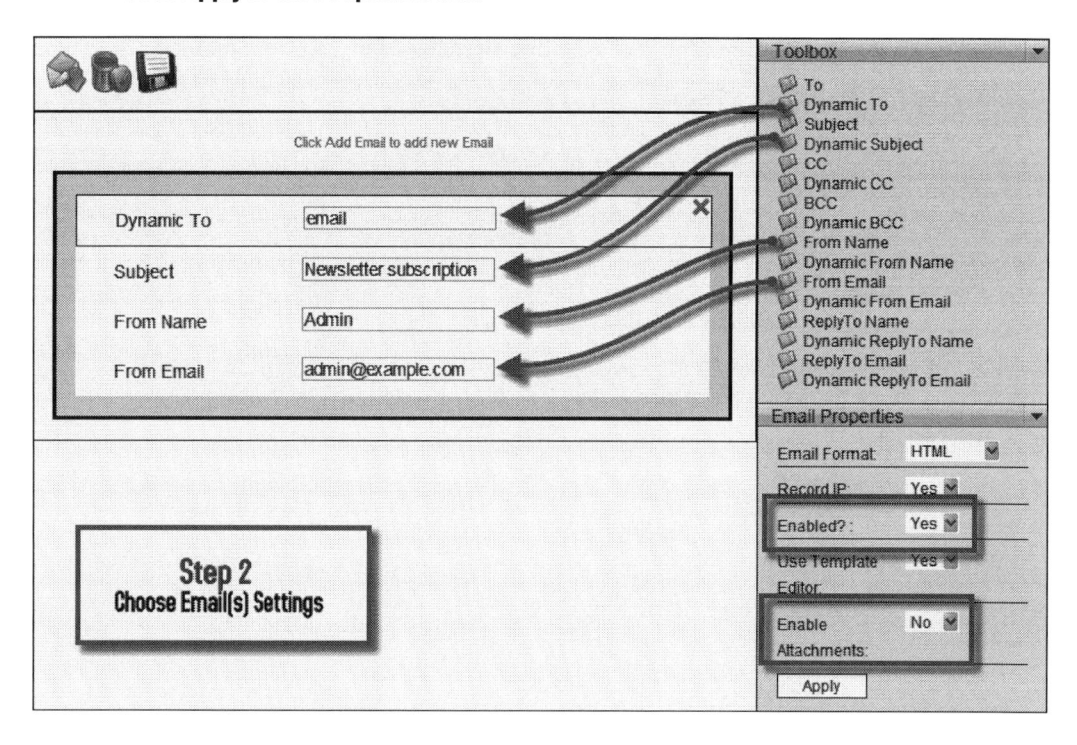

   Next, in the Email Template, click **Step 3** in the Wizard. You'll see a lot of code in the box which we don't need to send back to the subscriber, so select and delete all of it.

Instead we'll add a simple message:

```
<p>Hi </p>
<p>Thank you for subscribing to our newsletter. Look out for our first email soon.</p>
<p>Regards<br />The example.com team</p>
```

It might be better if we personalized this a bit, so place your cursor after "Hi" and type in {name}.

> There's also the "pen and pad icon" that you can use to do this. It works for Step 4, but not for Step 3.

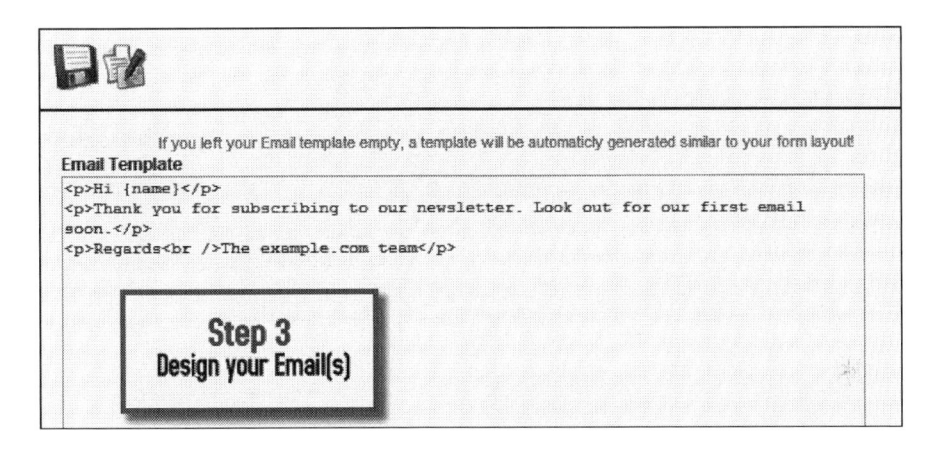

If you left your Email template empty, a template will be automaticly generated similar to your form layout!

Email Template
```
<p>Hi {name}</p>
<p>Thank you for subscribing to our newsletter. Look out for our first email soon.</p>
<p>Regards<br />The example.com team</p>
```

Step 3 Design your Email(s)

3. Adding the thank you page:

   While we're in the wizard, click **Step 4** and add a suitable message there.

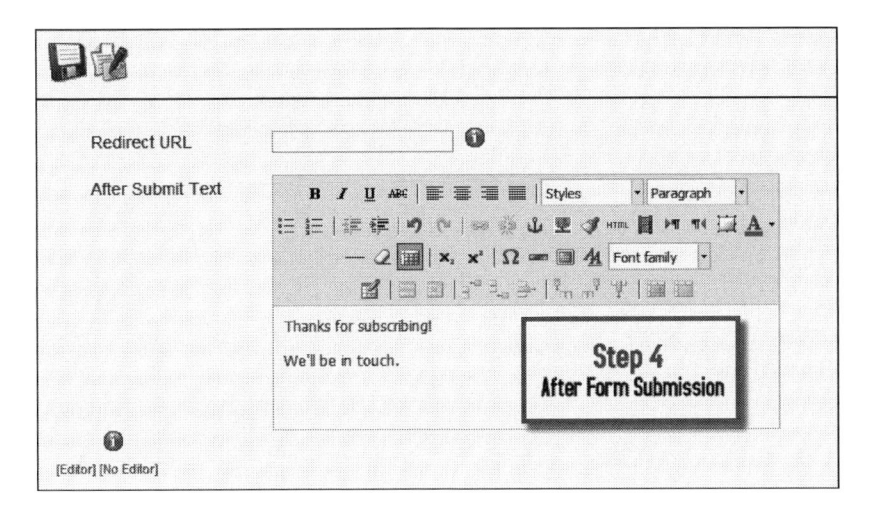

   Thanks for subscribing!
   We'll be in touch.

   Step 4 After Form Submission

Creating Common Forms

Finish off this stage by saving the form and closing the wizard.

4. Saving to the database:

   Go back to the Forms Manager, check the box by your form name and click the **Create Table** icon.

   When the dialog opens notice that the three bottom bars are red; these are the data fields for your form. Click the "tick" icon in the blue bar at the top left to select them and turn the bars green.

   Note the **Table Name**, it will be something like `jos_chronoforms_newsletter_1`.

   Click the "disk" icon to create the table.

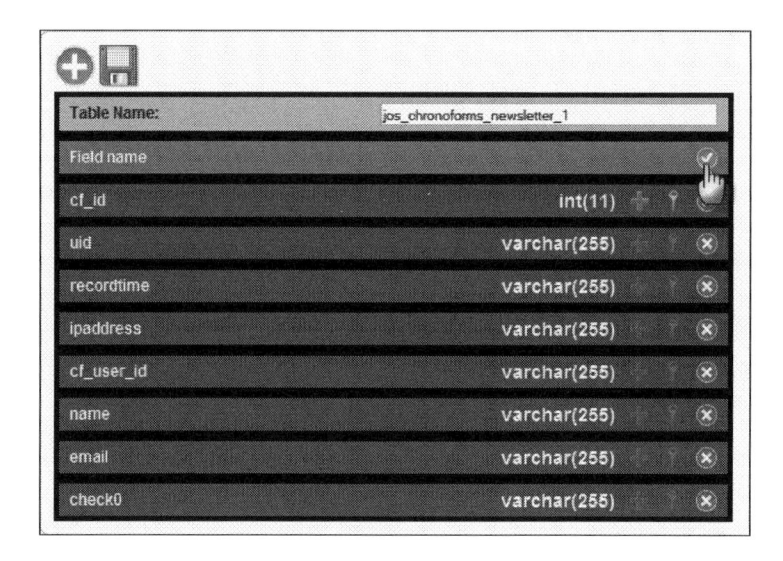

   Open the form in the Form Editor and click the **DB Connection** tab.

   Set **Enable Data storage** to **Yes** and select the new table in the dropdown.

5. Finishing up:

   There's one last thing to do in the Form Editor. Click the **General** tab and set **Email the results?** to **Yes**.

   Save your form and check that the **Emails** column shows **Enabled:1**, and that the table name appears in the **Tables Connected** column.

6. Test your form, and we're done.

See also

- If you need more information about any of these steps, or if your form needs a slightly different approach then please see the earlier chapters of this book. You'll find recipes there for each of these steps.

Chapter 10

Creating a form to link to Acajoom

Acajoom is a popular Newsletter extension for Joomla! that will allow you to create subscriber lists and send out newsletters. It comes in several versions; here we will be working with the free version that you can download from `http://www.ijoobi.com/`.

If you use a different extension you can probably use a similar approach by following the steps here, and tuning them to the needs of the extension.

Getting ready

You will need to have Acajoom installed, with at least one List set up, and the Acajoom subscriber module published and visible (the default setting is '**Menus: none**' so you'll need to change it).

How to do it...

1. Finding the information we need:

    View a page with the Acajoom module visible:

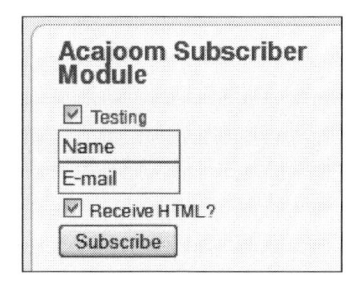

    Acajoom Subscriber Module

    ☑ Testing
    Name
    E-mail
    ☑ Receive HTML?
    [Subscribe]

    Also, look at the page source to find the HTML for the module. Here is the version we found (cleaned up a little for clarity):

    > Note that some of the formatting breaks a URL by adding some spaces in the middle, so the code won't work unless you fix that.

    ```
    <h3>Acajoom Subscriber Module</h3>
    <!-- Beginning Module : Acajoom News 6.0.0  -->
    <div class="aca_module">
    <script language="javascript" type="text/javascript">
    <!--
    function submitAcajoommod1(formname) {
      var form = eval('document.'+formname);
    ```

257

Creating Common Forms

```
      if(!form.elements)
        form = form[1];
    var place = form.email.value.indexOf("@",1);
    var point = form.email.value.indexOf(".",place+1);
    if (form.name.value == "" || form.name.value == "Name") {
      alert( "Please enter your name." );return false;
    }
    if (form.email.value == ""
        || form.email.value == "E-mail") {
      alert( "Please enter a valid e-mail address." );
      return false;
    } else {
      if ((place > -1)
          &&(form.email.value.length >2)
          &&(point > 1)) {
        form.submit();
        return true;
      } else {
        alert( "Please enter a valid e-mail address." );
        return false;
      }
    }
  }
  //-->
  </script>
  <form action="index.php?option=com_Acajoom"
    method="post" name="modAcajoomForm1">
  <input id="wz_31" type="checkbox" class="inputbox" value="1"
    name="subscribed[1]" checked="checked" />
  <input type="hidden" name="sub_list_id[1]" value="17" />
  <span class="aca_list_name">
    <span class="editlinktip hasTip" title="Testing::" >
    <a href="/index.php?option=com_Acajoom&amp;Itemid=999
      &amp;act=mailing&amp;task=archive&amp;listid=17
      &amp;listype=1">Testing</a>
    </span>
  </span>
  <br />
  <input type="hidden" name="acc_level[1]" value="0" />
  <input id="wz_11" type="text" size="10" value="Name"
    class="inputbox" name="name"
    onblur="if(this.value=='') this.value='Name';"
    onfocus="if(this.value=='Name') this.value='' ; " />
  <br />
```

```
<input id="wz_12" type="text" size="10" value="E-mail"
    class="inputbox" name="email"
    onblur="if(this.value=='') this.value='E-mail';"
    onfocus="if(this.value=='E-mail') this.value='' ; " />
<br />
<input id="wz_2" type="checkbox" class="inputbox" value="1"
    name="receive_html" checked="checked" /> Receive HTML?
<br />
<input id="aca_22" type="button" value="Subscribe"
    class="button" name="Subscribe"
    onclick="return submitAcajoommod1('modAcajoomForm1');" />
<br />
<input type="hidden" name="act" value="subscribe" />
<input type="hidden" name="redirectlink" value="" />
<input type="hidden" name="listname" value="1" />
<input type="hidden" name="passwordA" value="PaTcQBUT1lokM" />
<input type="hidden" name="fromSubscribe" value="1" />
</form>
</div>
<!--  End Module : Acajoom News 6.0.0   -->
```

The first chunk of this code is a JavaScript snippet for validating the form, and there are several script snippets, classes, and other stuff in the rest to make the form pretty as well as than functional. If we strip the code back to the bare bones we can see the parts we need more clearly.

Here's what we are left with:

The `<form . . . >` tag:

```
<form action="index.php?option=com_Acajoom"
    method="post" name="modAcajoomForm1" >
```

Four input tags that are used to collect information:

```
<input type="checkbox" value="1" name="subscribed[1]" />
<input type="text" value="Name" name="name" />
<input type="text" value="E-mail" name="email" />
<input type="checkbox" value="1" name="receive_html" />
```

And seven hidden tags that are passing fixed information:

```
<input type="hidden" name="sub_list_id[1]" value="17" />
<input type="hidden" name="acc_level[1]" value="0" />
<input type="hidden" name="act" value="subscribe" />
<input type="hidden" name="redirectlink" value="" />
<input type="hidden" name="listname" value="1" />
<input type="hidden" name="passwordA" value="PaTcQBUT1lokM" />
<input type="hidden" name="fromSubscribe" value="1" />
```

Creating Common Forms

2. Creating the form:

    Now we'll create a ChronoForms form with those four information collecting inputs.

    Open up the ChronoForms Form Wizard and drag in two **Checkbox** and two **TextBox** elements, plus a **Button** (you'll need to go back to the form or the full form code to find some of the labels to apply).

    Notice that there are some important things that we can't set in the Form Wizard, in particular the values and names of the Checkboxes; we'll fix that shortly. Meanwhile, here is the Wizard Preview view of the form we are creating (click the "screen" icon to see this at any stage while you are building the form).

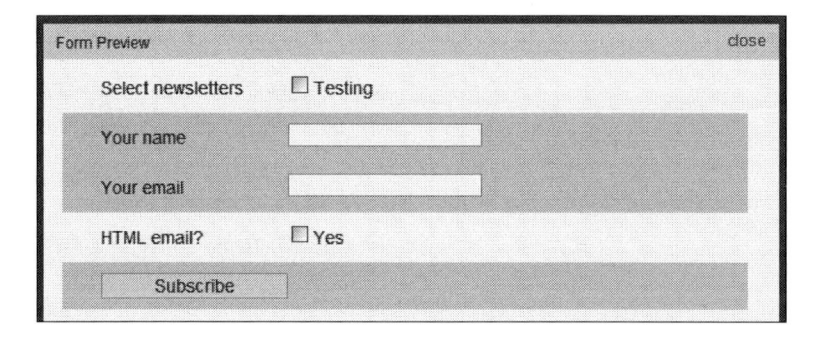

    Add validation to each of the fields—**required** for the TextBoxes and **validate-one-required** for the checkboxes. Save the form and give it a name like "Acajoom_1".

    Now reopen it in the Form Editor so that we can do some more work on it.

    Let's look first at the **Select newsletters** checkbox code. What ChronoForms gives us is a bit limited. Here's the input tag:

    ```
    <input value="Testing" title=""
      class="radio validate-one-required"
      id="check00" name="check0[]" type="checkbox" />
    ```

    Now go back and look at the Acajoom code. You'll see that we need to change the value and name of this input:

    ```
    <input value="1" title=""
      class="radio validate-one-required"
      id="subscribed_01" name="subscribed[1]" type="checkbox" />
    ```

We'll also change the ID to match.

> If you think that there is something odd about having a single checkbox here when there's only one newsletter to subscribe to, then you are correct. If you have several newsletters set up then there will be a checkbox for each of them.

Here are the corresponding changes to the **HTML email?** input:

```
<input value="1" title=""
  class="radio validate-one-required"
  id="receive_html " name="receive_html" type="checkbox"
  checked="checked" />
```

There will never be more than one checkbox in this array, so we don't need the array name; and we've set the box to default to checked.

The textbox inputs are fine as they are but we'll keep tidy and change the IDs to match the names (name and e-mail).

Turn on **Debug** in the Form **General** tab; save the form, publish it and click the link to view it in a browser window. Here's the first part of the **$_POST Array** from the Debug information:

```
$_POST Array:
  Array ( [subscribed] => Array ( [1] => 1 )
  [name] => tester
  [email] => test@example.com
  [receive_html] => 1
  [button_4] => Subscribe
    . . .
```

That all looks fine, but it doesn't connect to Acajoom.

To do that we'll enable and configure the cURL plugin on this form.

> We could just set the **OnSubmit URL** to 'index.php?option=com_acajoom' to send the information to Acajoom – that would work (provided that we added the hidden inputs). But in that case, we could just stay with the Acajoom module.

Creating Common Forms

3. Configuring the **cURL** plugin:

    Check the box next to the form name and click the **cURL** link in the left hand column of the Forms Manager.

    When the dialogue opens, click the **cURL Params**, enter the URL we want to submit to (from the `<form . . . >` tag of the Acajoom form), and set **Flow Control** to **After Email**.

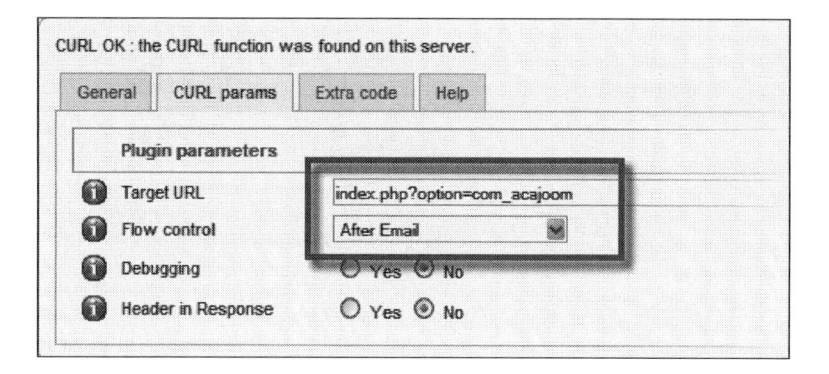

    > We set the Flow Control simply because ChronoForms does not execute "Before Email" plugins if "Send Emails" is not enabled on the Form **General** tab. It's easier to remove one possible cause of unexpected behavior.

    Now click the **General** tab and we'll enter the input field values. We'll need to pick up the values of the hidden fields here and enter them in the bottom textarea using the `name=value` format. Here they are:

    ```
    sub_list_id[1]=17
    acc_level[1]=0
    act=subscribe
    redirectlink=""
    listname=1
    passwordA=PaTcQBUT1lokM
    fromSubscribe=1
    ```

We can ignore `redirectlink`, as we'll handle that in ChronoForms. In your case the password may well be different (it should be) so make sure you enter the correct values.

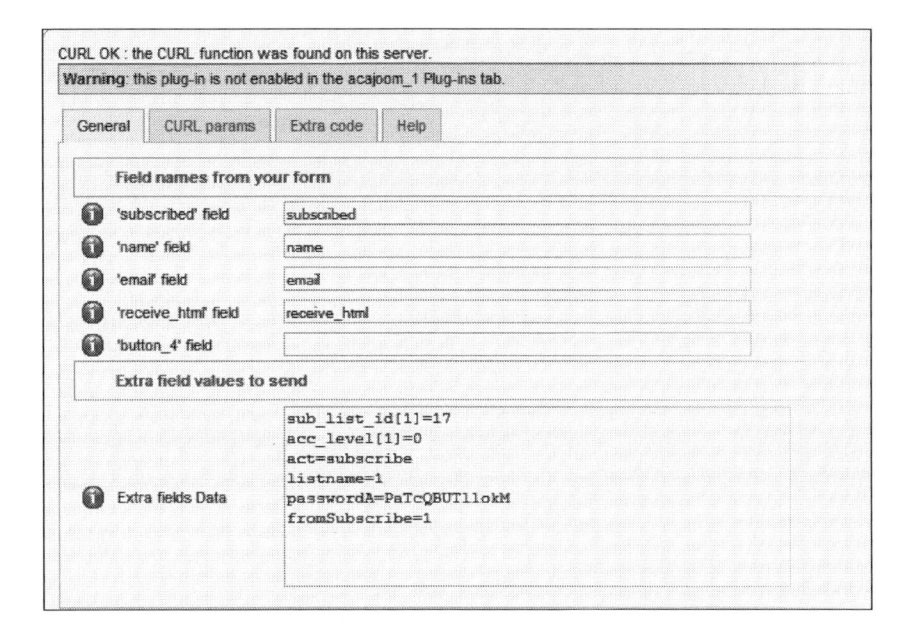

```
CURL OK : the CURL function was found on this server.
Warning: this plug-in is not enabled in the acajoom_1 Plug-ins tab.

General    CURL params    Extra code    Help

    Field names from your form
    'subscribed' field      subscribed
    'name' field            name
    'email' field           email
    'receive_html' field    receive_html
    'button_4' field        

    Extra field values to send

    Extra fields Data      sub_list_id[1]=17
                           acc_level[1]=0
                           act=subscribe
                           listname=1
                           passwordA=PaTcQBUT1lokM
                           fromSubscribe=1
```

All of this is quite straightforward; the top block are the inputs from our form. In this case we chose the names to be the same, though they don't need to be. Also notice that for the **subscribed** entry at the top, which is an array result, we just use the name of the array.

> Earlier versions of the cURL plugin could not handle arrays correctly. If you have problems you may need to upgrade to a later version.

In the bottom box are the fixed entries that have the same value each time the form is submitted. Here we've specified the array keys as well as the values; for example, `acc_level[1]=0`.

Notice that there is a yellow warning bar above the configuration dialogue, which tells us that the plugin isn't enabled.

4. Enabling the cURL plugin:

   Save the plugin configuration and open the Form Editor again. Click the **Plugins** tab and then click the **cURL** plugin bar so that it changes from red to green.

5. Testing the form:

   Save or Apply the form and refresh it in a browser view.

   Complete the form with some test data and submit it.

Creating Common Forms

6. Now go to the Acajoom administration page and check if the subscription has been successful.

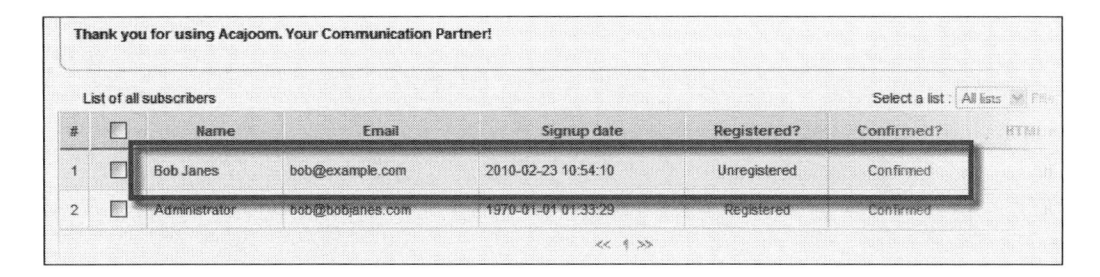

There's more...

The ideas in this recipe can be extended to connect a form to many other Joomla! components.

Creating a form to publish a Joomla! article

At the core of Joomla! are the articles in the "Content" component. This form lets you create an article directly from the user's input.

Getting ready

Go to the ChronoEngine.com Downloads area, navigate to **ChronoForms | ChronoForms Applications**, and download the `submitcontent.cfbak` file.

How to do it...

1. Restore the form into your Forms Manager.
2. Save and publish it if you need to. View the form in your browser and enter some test data.
3. Open the Article manager in the Site Administration area and check that the article is there.

See also

> There's a much longer and more detailed version of this recipe in *Chapter 6, Showing your Form in your Site*, in the *Using a form to create a Joomla! Article* and a more advanced version using a multi-page form in the recipe *Building a complex multi-page form* in *Chapter 12, Adding Advanced Features*.

- Chapter 8, *Uploading Files from your Forms*, the *Displaying images in e-mails and articles* section may also be useful.

Creating a "Contact us" form

Joomla! has a "Contacts" component, which includes a Contact form that looks like the image below. This functions perfectly well and is quite flexible but sometimes you want a different layout or different functionality. In this recipe we'll create a "Contact us" form, like the Joomla! one, which works inside ChronoForms. That leaves you free to add in any other ChronoForms features that you need.

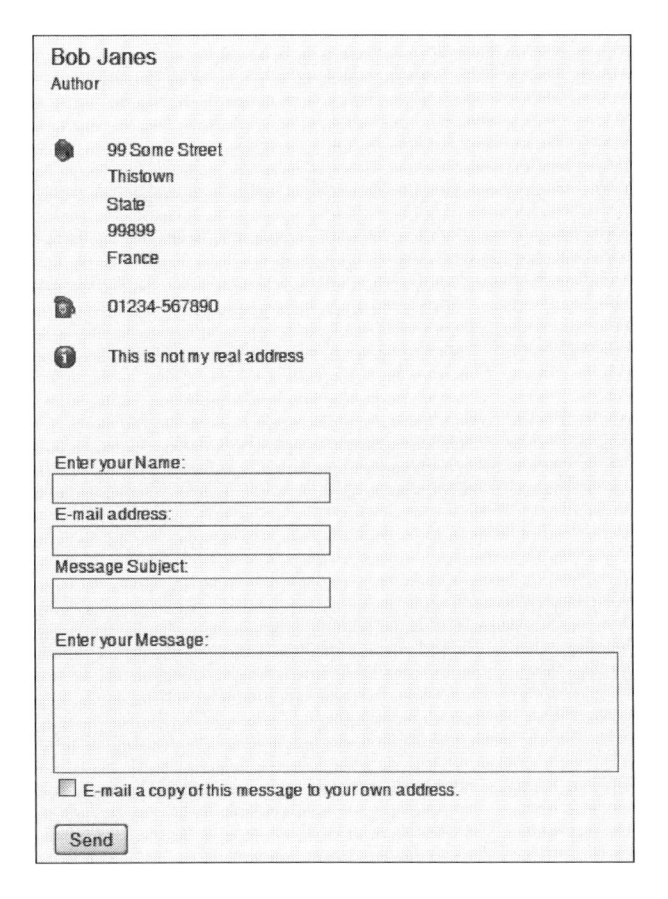

Bob Janes
Author

99 Some Street
Thistown
State
99899
France

01234-567890

This is not my real address

Enter your Name:

E-mail address:

Message Subject:

Enter your Message:

☐ E-mail a copy of this message to your own address.

Send

Getting ready

Nothing special is needed.

Creating Common Forms

How to do it...

1. Open the ChronoForms Form Wizard and create a new form, like the "form" part of the Joomla! contact form shown above: drag in three **TextBoxes**, a **TextArea**, a **CheckBox**, and a **Button**.

   Make all four text elements **required** and check **validate-email** for the e-mail address box. Add the labels that you want for your form.

   For clarity, also change the names of the inputs to "name", "email", "subject", and "message".

   > We suggest that you later edit the IDs of the inputs to match; you have to do this in the Form Editor though.

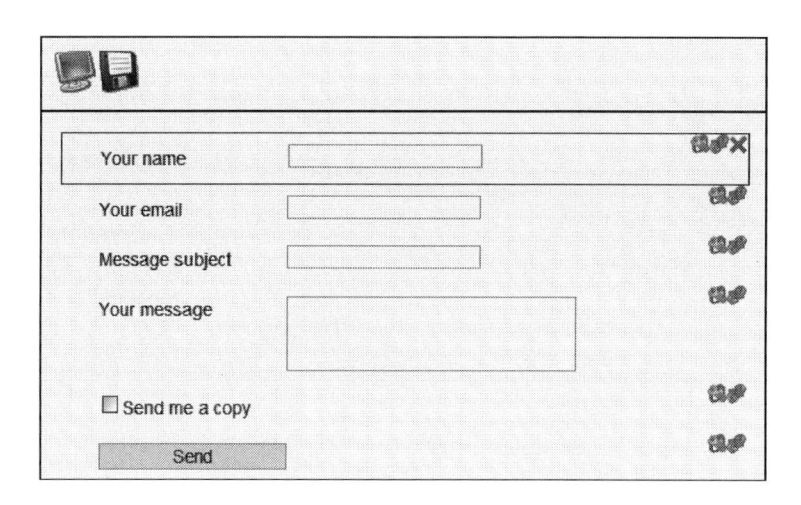

   Notice that for the CheckBox we have checked the **Hide Label** option in the Properties box.

2. Go on to **Step 2** and create the Email Setup. We need rather more inputs here than usual: **To**, **Dynamic Subject**, **From Name** and **From Email** are the basic set, and we'll also add **Dynamic CC** (to send a copy back to the submitter), **Dynamic ReplyTo Email**, and **Dynamic ReplyTo Name**.

   > If your site uses **PHP Mail Function** as the mailer, then CC & BCC are not supported, you can use a '**Dynamic To**' element instead (or a second Email Setup if you prefer).

Add the input names to the "dynamic" element boxes and your site details into the **To**, **From Name**, and **From Email** boxes. The Dynamic versions of the inputs take "input names" from the form as values whereas the "static" equivalents take fixed string values.

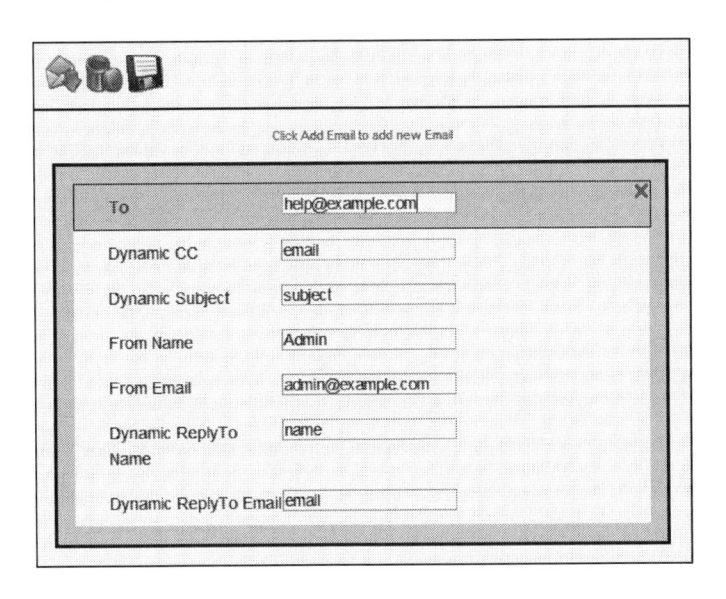

3. We'll let ChronoForms create the e-mail template, so skip that step and add a brief message in Step 4: After form submission.
4. Save the form and give it a name. In the Form Manager publish the form and view it in a browser window.

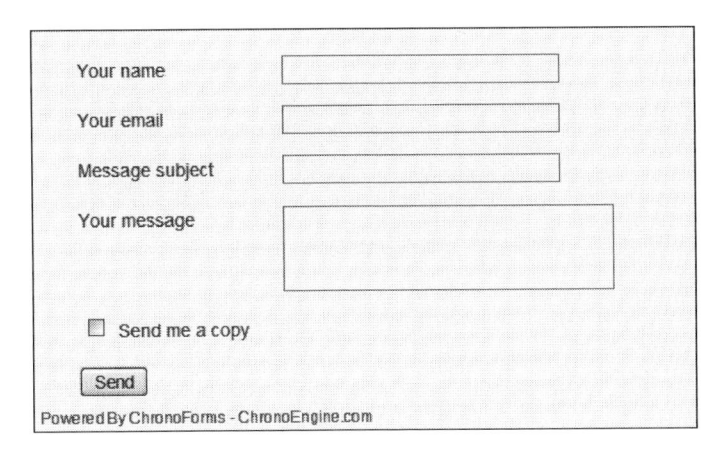

So, we have our basic form setup here.

Creating Common Forms

5. Go to the Form Editor, and set **Email the results?** to **Yes** on the **General** tab.

   While you are there, turn **Debug** on; save or apply the form, view it in your browser, submit some data, and see how it looks.

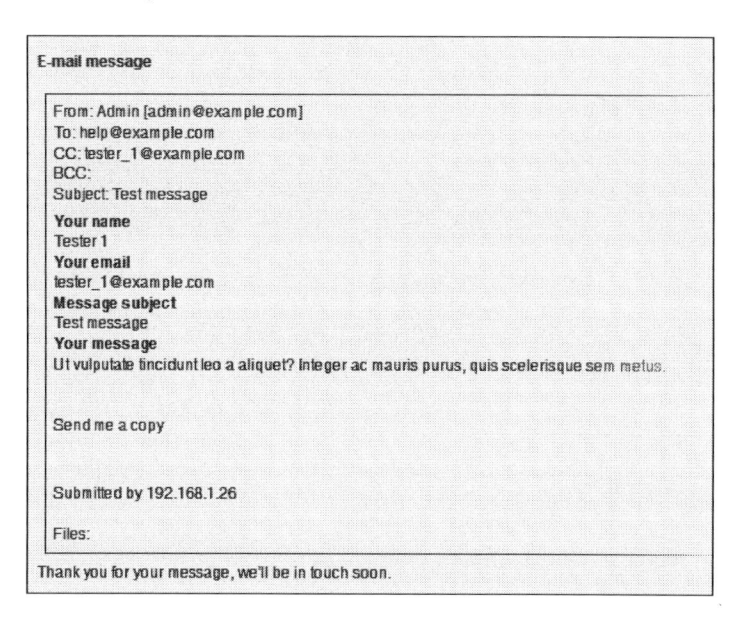

   ```
   E-mail message

   From: Admin [admin@example.com]
   To: help@example.com
   CC: tester_1@example.com
   BCC:
   Subject: Test message

   Your name
   Tester 1
   Your email
   tester_1@example.com
   Message subject
   Test message
   Your message
   Ut vulputate tincidunt leo a aliquet? Integer ac mauris purus, quis scelerisque sem metus.


   Send me a copy


   Submitted by 192.168.1.26

   Files:

   Thank you for your message, we'll be in touch soon.
   ```

   That looks as though it is working fine.

6. There is one thing left to do though, we have to turn off the **Copy to the User** if they don't check the box.

   For this we need a little PHP in the **OnSubmit Before sending email** box. You'll find the box on the **Form Code** tab in the Form Editor. Here's the code:

   ```php
   <?php
   $MyForm =& CFChronoForm::getInstance();
   $MyFormEmails =& CFEMails::getInstance($MyForm->formrow->id);
   $copy =& JRequest::getBool('check0', false, 'post');
   if ( !$copy ) {
     $MyFormEmails->setEmailData(1, 'dcc', '');
   }
   ?>
   ```

   Taking this step by step:

   First we get the Form Object.

   ```
   $MyForm =& CFChronoForm::getInstance();
   ```

   Then we use the Form ID to get the related Email object.

   ```
   $MyFormEmails =& CFEMails::getInstance($MyForm->formrow->id);
   ```

Next we look up the submitted value for the CheckBox using the `getBool()` method, to give us a true/false result with a default value of 'false'. This will work because a CheckBox only returns a value if it is checked, so we are effectively checking for its presence or absence rather than for any specific value:

```
$copy =& JRequest::getBool('check0', false, 'post');
```

Lastly, if `$copy` is 'false' we clear the setting for '`dcc`' ('Dynamic CC') in the e-mail setup:

```
if ( !$copy ) {
   $MyFormEmails->setEmailData(1, 'dcc', '');
}
```

Now add the code to the **OnSubmit Before** box and test with the checkbox ticked and not ticked. If you look at the "dummy e-mail" in the debug output you can see that the CC entry changes.

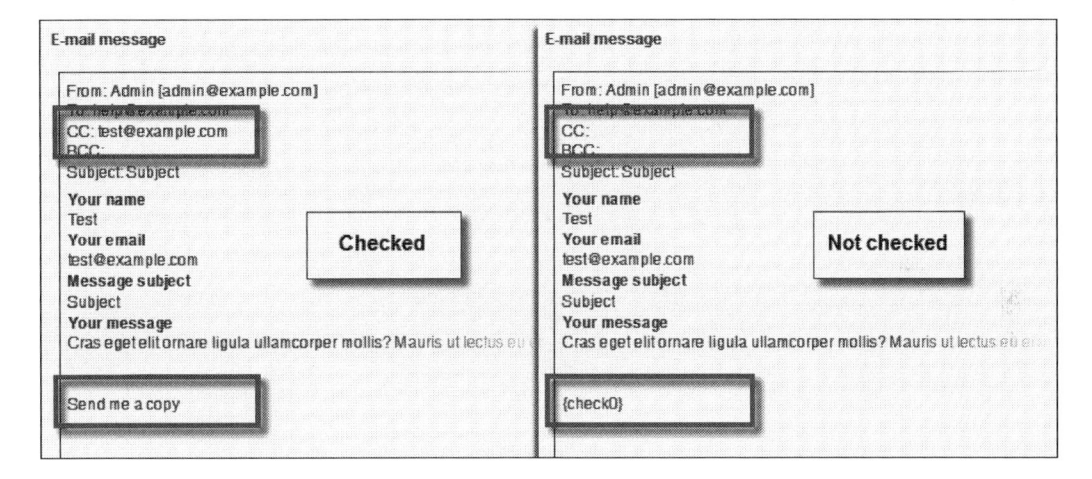

You can see here the change in the **CC** address, and in the body of the e-mail where the rather untidy **{check0}** is shown if the box is not checked. We can get rid of this by editing the Email template as the **{check0}** entry doesn't need to be included.

7. Lastly, let's clean up the Email template. ChronoForms does a fair job of creating a "replica" of the form layout in the e-mail. But this doesn't always make good sense.

   We'll make some changes by editing the template. (You can do this in the Form Editor, or the Wizard Edit, but note that you will lose any changes to the Form HTML if you use the Wizard Edit.)

Creating Common Forms

Here's an alternative version:

```
You have received a new website contact message from {name}
({email})

{subject}
{message}
```

> The "horizontal rule" needs to be added from the editor icon.

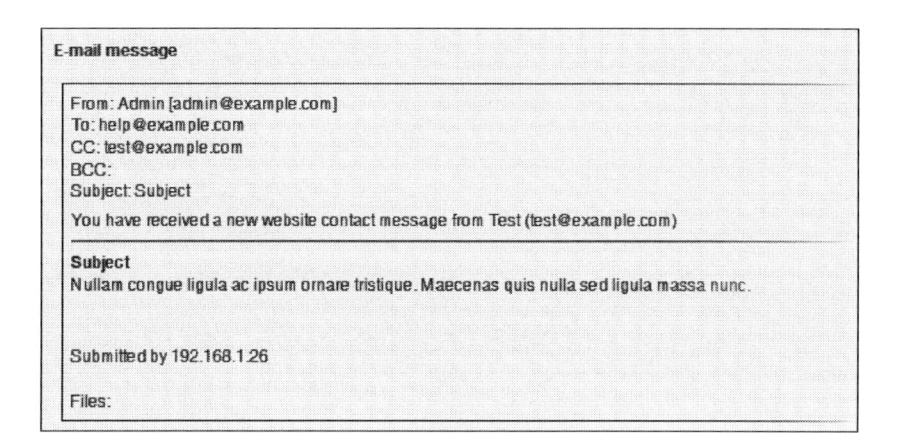

E-mail message

From: Admin [admin@example.com]
To: help@example.com
CC: test@example.com
BCC:
Subject: Subject

You have received a new website contact message from Test (test@example.com)

Subject
Nullam congue ligula ac ipsum ornare tristique. Maecenas quis nulla sed ligula massa nunc.

Submitted by 192.168.1.26

Files:

How it works...

There's one small item to pick up and look at here. When we created the **Email Setup** we added **Dynamic ReplyTo Name** and **Dynamic ReplyTo Email** elements and entered the user's name and e-mail in the related boxes. But why?

You are probably going to want to reply to a Contact email like this and that leads to the obvious solution of putting the user's name and e-mail in the **From Name** and **From Email** fields so that the email appears to come from them.

This would work if it were not for the increasingly tight spam checks that ISPs and e-mail systems apply to mails that they handle. One common check is to require that the domain of the "From Email" matches the site domain. (Sometimes they go further and only allow "registered" e-mails). If they do not match then the e-mail may be marked as potential spam, returned to the "sender", marked "relaying not allowed", or just quietly dropped into the scrap bin.

Chapter 10

The result is that ChronoForms shows the e-mail as sent but it never arrives. Not good.

Using the site address as the From Email gets round this, and adding the user Email as the ReplyTo Email will include this too. And when you click "Reply", this is (probably) the e-mail address that will be shown (probably because different e-mail readers have different behaviors, but the majority work fine).

There's more...

The first part of the Joomla! Contact Form we looked at earlier also shows some selected information about specified contact individuals. If you like, you can add this information to your contact form by borrowing a little code from Joomla!.

Here we'll create some very simple code to show a single contact. You could do more complex coding to show more contacts with categories, if you wish.

In the **Site Admin Contacts Manager** screen, you'll see a list of all the contact entries. In the right hand column is the **Contact ID**. Make a note of the ID you want to use (here we are using 1).

Here's the code that we'll add at the beginning of the Form HTML:

```
<?php
if ( !$mainframe->isSite() ) { return; }
// set the id we want
$id = 1;
// build the database query
$db = &JFactory::getDBO();
$query = "
  SELECT *
    FROM `#__contact_details`
    WHERE `id` = $id ;
";
$db->setQuery($query);
// load the results for our contact
$contact = $db->loadObject();
?>
```

This gets the contact details into the `$contact` object; then we just need to display them. Here we've borrowed the ChronoForms HTML to make the layout match and we've inserted the labels and values from the `$contact` object; just a couple here but you can add more and change the layout and styling to meet your needs.

```
<div class="form_item">
  <div class="form_element cf_textbox">
    <label style="width: 150px;"
```

```
          class="cf_label">Name</label>
      <?php echo $contact->name; ?>
   </div>
   <div class="form_element cf_textbox">
      <label style="width: 150px;"
          class="cf_label">Phone</label>
      <?php echo $contact->telephone; ?>
   </div>
   <div class="cfclear"> </div>
</div>
```

Creating an image or document upload form

We often want to allow users to upload files – usually documents or images. *Chapter 8, Uploading Files from your Forms* deals with this in detail so we'll just set out the bare bones in this recipe.

Getting ready

Nothing special is required, but you'll need to have a note of the file extensions; for example, `.doc`, `.jpg`, `.pdf`, `.gif`, and so on that you want to allow; and the maximum and minimum file sizes that you will allow.

Chapter 10

How to do it...

1. Create a new file with the Form Wizard and drag in a **FileUpload** element and a **Button**. Save the form giving it a suitable name.

2. In the **Properties** box, add the list of file types separated by "|"; for example, `jpg|png` or `doc|pdf|xls` and enter the maximum and minimum file sizes (in KB). Change the label text for the inputs if you wish.

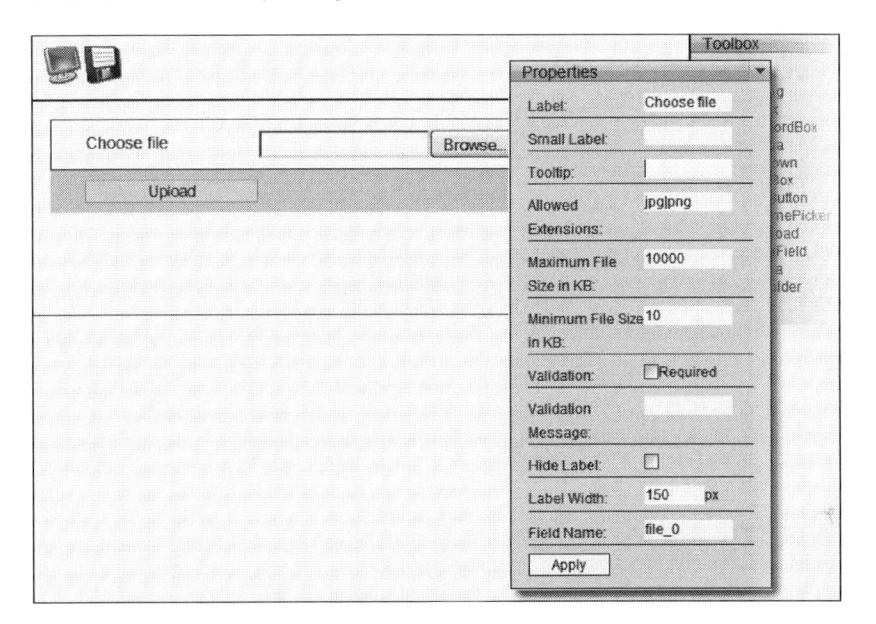

3. Save the form giving it a suitable name, and publish it in the Forms Manager. Click the link to view the form in a browser window.

273

Creating Common Forms

4. Now use your site file browser to look in the `components/com_chronocontact/uploads/` folder. You should find in there a new folder named after your form; and inside that folder your uploaded file.

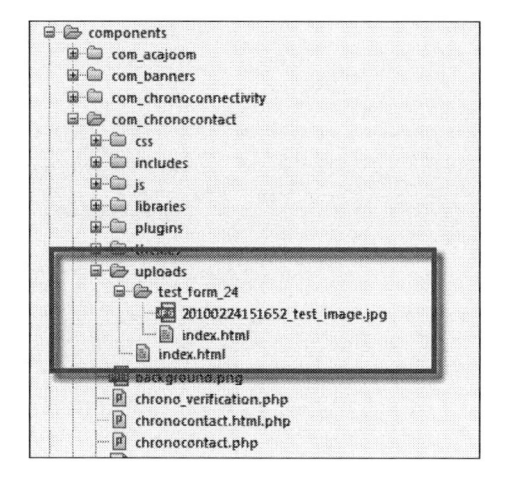

```
components
  com_acajoom
  com_banners
  com_chronoconnectivity
  com_chronocontact
    css
    includes
    js
    libraries
    plugins
    uploads
      test_form_24
        20100224151652_test_image.jpg
        index.html
      index.html
    background.png
    chrono_verification.php
    chronocontact.html.php
    chronocontact.php
```

> Notice that ChronoForms has added a prefix to the file name to avoid problems with multiple uploads, with the same name blocking or over-writing each other.

There's more...

You can change more or less all of the file upload settings, add custom error messages, change the file name or upload folder, and more in the **Form Editor | File Uploads** tab.

Adding a file upload to an existing form

If you have a form where the Form HTML hasn't been edited then you may still be able to use the Wizard Edit to add an extra element. If the Form HTML has been changed, then doing this will wipe out the changes; so it's generally not a good idea.

Instead, create a new, temporary form with the file upload settings that you want. Save it, then open both the forms in the Form Editor (use two browser windows) and copy and paste over the Form HTML and the File Upload settings.

Save the amended form and delete the temporary form.

You can do this with any form element but the File Upload is the most complex to set up by hand, and this copy and paste approach is especially useful.

See also

- Chapter 8, *Uploading Files from your Forms* and the rest of that chapter for more options.

Creating a multi-page form

Some forms get very big and it can be overwhelming for the user. There are two main techniques for "breaking up" a big form into bite-sized chunks.

The first is to use panes which look like the tabs in the ChronoForms Forms Manager. These use the standard Joomla! "panes and sliders" code and can fairly easily be added to a ChronoForm. However, there are some difficulties in validating entries on separate tabs—it can be done with server-side validation or with a custom LiveValidation, but those are beyond our ability to address here.

The second is to break the form up into separate sub-forms so that after the user submits one page they are shown the next one. This allows you to validate each step, and to "adjust" the following pages using information from the earlier steps.

You can do this using some quite complex PHP in a single form, or you can use the ChronoForms Multi-page plugin which provides a simple way to link several forms together into a sequence.

Getting ready

We're going to create a two-page form and so we need two simple forms, one for each page. Use the wizard edit to create a form with a **Header**, a **TextBox**, and a **Button**. Change the Header to read "Step 1" and the TextBox label and name to "product". Save the form as "step_1".

In the Form Manager, check the box by the name and click the **Copy form** icon in the toolbar. Open the new copy in the Form Wizard and edit the elements. Change the header to "Step 2" and the TextBox to "Your name" and "name". Save the form as "step_2".

There is nothing special about these forms; you can link any forms into a Multi-Page form, though it's probably better not to duplicate input names between them as the later ones will over-write the earlier.

How to do it...

1. We'll call these two forms the "child forms"; to link them together we need to create a "mother form".

   Click the "New" icon in the Toolbar; put "mother_form" in the **Form Name** box and save the form - nothing else, just the form name.

Creating Common Forms

2. Check the box by the **mother_form** name and click the **Multi Page** plug-in link in the left hand column.

   In the Configuration dialog set the **Number of Steps** drop-down to 2 and put the two child form names in the next box as `step_1, step_2`.

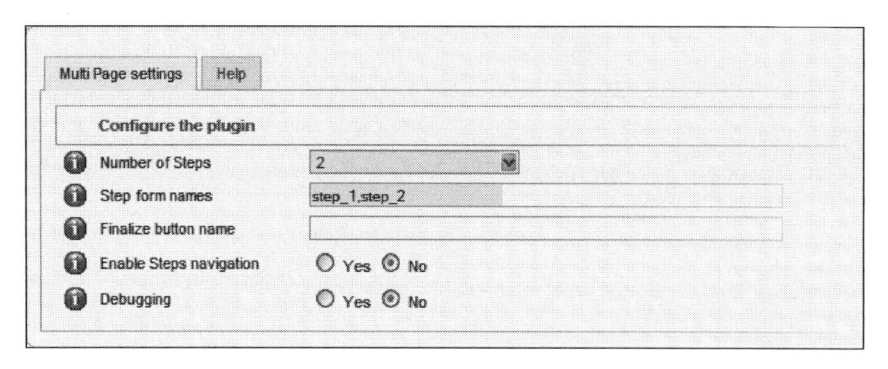

3. Save the plug-in configuration; open the mother form in the Form Editor and enable the plugin on the **Plug-ins** tab, save the form, publish it, and click the link to view the form in the browser.

   Notice that although we clicked the link for the Mother form, what shows up is the first Child form. Put something in the **Product** box and submit the form.

   . . . and there is the second child form.

4. If we just submit the second step we'll get a blank 'Thank you' page showing up. So before doing that, open the Mother form in the Form Editor and turn **Debug** on in the **General** tab, then open the Multi-page plug-in configuration and set **Debugging** to **Yes** there too.

   Now, type something into the **Your name** box and submit Step 2.

   You'll see some debugging information from the Plug-in at the top of the page, and the 'usual' ChronoForms debugging info further down.

   Notice that the ChronoForms debugging information in the blue box only includes the input data from Step 2. But if you look at the top of the page the Multi-page plug-in debugging information has the inputs from both steps:

   ```
   Posted: Array (
     [product] => teddy bear
     [button_2] => Submit
     [c79b57e8cb159e8386f0652c415da2b6] => 1
     [1cf1] => b022778a7806d2fe1109a7a04eec0f59
     [chronoformname] => mother_form
     [name] => Bob Janes
     [cfformstep] => 1 )
   ```

   ChronoForms accumulates the inputs in the user session so that it is all available at the end of the Multi-page process.

5. We can see this fairly easily by setting up a test e-mail. In the Mother form, create a simple Email Setup, enable it, and enable e-mails in the **General** tab. In the Email template put these two lines:

   ```
   Step 1 : {product}
   Step 2 : {name}
   ```

   > ChronoForms will find no Form HTML in the Mother form, so the default template it creates will be empty.

6. Submit the form sequence again and check the dummy e-mail in the final debug report:

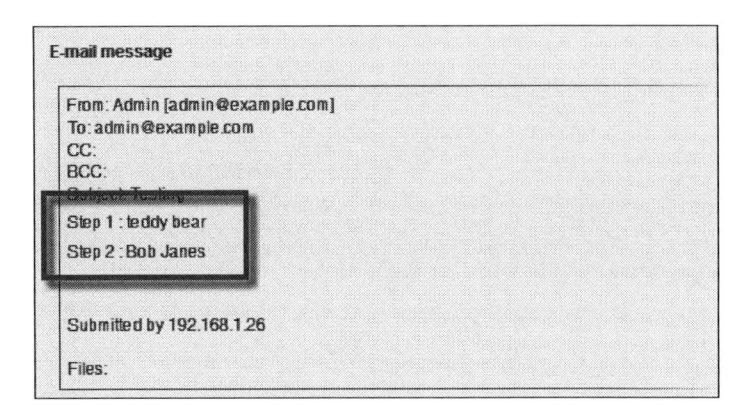

```
E-mail message

From: Admin [admin@example.com]
To: admin@example.com
CC:
BCC:
Subject: Testing
Step 1 : teddy bear
Step 2 : Bob Janes


Submitted by 192.168.1.26

Files:
```

There are both inputs—from Step 1 and from Step 2—both included as we would like.

7. The same is true of the DB Connection. Make a connection on the Mother form, add the columns from both steps to the table and both will be saved.

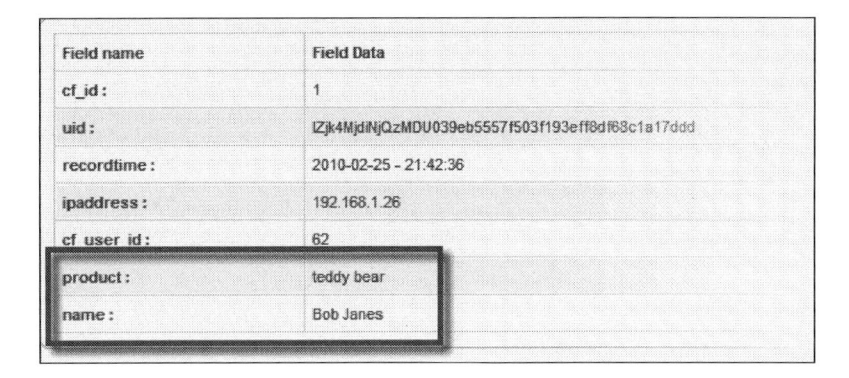

Field name	Field Data
cf_id :	1
uid :	IZjk4MjdiNjQzMDU039eb5557f503f193eff8df63c1a17ddd
recordtime :	2010-02-25 - 21:42:36
ipaddress :	192.168.1.26
cf_user_id :	62
product :	teddy bear
name :	Bob Janes

8. So, we have a working Multi-page form. This is a simple example, but it demonstrates all the key features that you might need in a more complex form.

> As there are several forms involved you need to keep a clear head when working with multi-page forms. Mainly, if it affects the display of the step forms, or the results of a single step, then add it into the Child forms; if it relates to the results as a whole, then add it to the Mother form.
>
> It also helps to set out, as we did here, with very simple forms to get the flow of the forms working correctly before going on to add many more inputs.

How it works...

The Mother Form acts as a 'wrapper' around the Child forms; they still do their own stuff, but the overall control is with the Mother form. Once the Child Form is complete, control is passed back to the Mother form which saves the data and the form step in the User session data and calls the next form step, or, if it was the last step, ends by running its own e-mail, DB Connection, and Redirect settings.

There's more...

It's often helpful to be able to refer to the results from previous pages; either to display as a reminder, to use them in calculations, or to control the form inputs that are displayed.

ChronoForms stores the "cumulated" results in the user session, so we can get them back from there with a few lines of PHP at the beginning of the Form HTML:

```php
<?php
if ( !$mainframe->isSite() ) { return; }
$formname =&
   JRequest::getString('chronoformname', '', 'post');
$session =& JFactory::getSession();
$posted = $session->get('chrono_formpages_data_'.$formname,
   array(), md5('chrono'));
?>
```

This snippet gets the current form name from the result array, accesses the session, then uses the form name to extract the chunk of data that ChronoForms has saved there into a `$posted` array.

Once that is done, you can access previous results by using the array. For example:

```
<div>You entered <b><?php echo $posted['product']; ?></b></div>
```

Step 2
You entered teddy bear
Your name
Submit
Powered By ChronoForms - ChronoEngine.com

See also

- The recipe *Building a complex multi-page form* in *Chapter 12, Adding Advanced Features* has a longer example of a multi-page form used to construct a Joomla! article.

11
Using Form Plug-ins

In this chapter, we will cover:

- Controlling form access by user group, day, and/or time with the WatchMan plug-in
- Creating multi-lingual forms with the Multi-Language plug-in
- Showing and editing saved information with the Profile plug-in
- Registering users with the Joomla! Registration plug-in
- Creating a PayPal purchase form with the ReDirect plug-in

Introduction

As ChronoForms has developed, there have been an astonishing variety of applications that it has been used for and we continue to be surprised when we see yet another one. However, amongst the variety, there have been some common threads, some tasks that users often want to do. Some of these have been built in to the core of ChronoForms—sending e-mails, saving to the database, validation, and so on.

Others that were used less frequently have been packaged as **ChronoForms Plugins**, separate code packages that can be enabled for some forms and ignored for others.

> Calling them plug-ins is accurate but unhelpful as they get confused with the Joomla! plug-ins, which work in a similar way with the whole of Joomla!. "ChronoForms plug-ins" are installed with ChronoForms and are only useful with ChronoForms.

The ChronoForms plug-ins come as a part of the ChronoForms package when you download and install it. Each plug-in is a separate file in the ChronoForms `plugins` folder (and there are also some plug-in helper files that live in the ChronoForms `administration/helpers` folder).

Using Form Plug-ins

ChronoForms plug-ins are developed separately from ChronoForms itself and updated versions may be released or posted in the ChronoForms forums from time to time. If you need to upgrade a plug-in or a helper, you just need to upload the new version to replace the old one.

You'll see the list of currently-installed ChronoForms plug-ins in the left hand column of the ChronoForms Forms Manager. At the time of writing, there are 14 of them:

- **Authorize.NET** : Used for connecting to Authorize.net for payments
- **cURL** : Used for passing data to other sites or applications (introduced in *Chapter 7, Adding Features to your Form*)
- **CB registration**: Used to register users in Joomla! and Community Builder (similar to the Joomla! Registration plug-in)
- **Confirmation page**: Used to show form data to allow the user to confirm it is correct
- **E-mail verification**: Used to send an e-mail to a user to confirm their e-mail address
- **Image resize and thumbnail**: Used to resize and copy an uploaded image (introduced in *Chapter 8, Uploading Files from your Forms*)
- **Joomla! registration**: Used to register users in Joomla!
- **Multi language**: Used to translate forms in several languages
- **Multi page**: Used to construct multi-page forms (introduced in *Chapter 10, Creating Common Forms*)
- **PayPal API**: Used for connecting to PayPal for payments using the PayPal API
- **Profile page**: Used to display a single database record to view or edit
- **ReCaptcha verification**: Used to include a ReCaptcha anti-spam element in a form (introduced in *Chapter 5, Form Validation and Security*)
- **ReDirect**: Used for transferring the user with some data to another site
- **Watchman**: Used to control form access

In this chapter, we'll look at a selection of these plug-ins that haven't been introduced earlier in this book and see how to use them with your forms.

> The Authorize.net and PayPal API plug-ins included with ChronoForms are development versions only. They are fully functional but randomize the amount of the payment so should not be used, except for development. Versions without the randomizing feature are available for a small payment.
>
> Note that the ReDirect plug-in can be used to make payments through a standard PayPal account.

Controlling form access by user group, day, and/or time with the Watchman plug-in

The **Watchman plugin** was born from a user request for a form that was only "open" in office hours when there was someone around to reply. Hence the name "Watchman" for a gate-keeper of sorts. The code that was written for that user later formed a part of the plug-in.

Along with dates and times, the current version of the plug-in also lets you control access by user group so that you can, for example, limit a form to just Registered Users, or just Super Administrators.

> There is a development version that also allows you to block IP addresses, or address blocks, if you wish to. This may be released by the time you read this.

Getting ready

The Watchman plug-in will work with any form and has no special requirements.

How to do it...

1. In the Forms Manager, check the box by your form **Name**, then click the name of the plug-in in the left hand column, **Watchman** in this case, down at the bottom of the list.

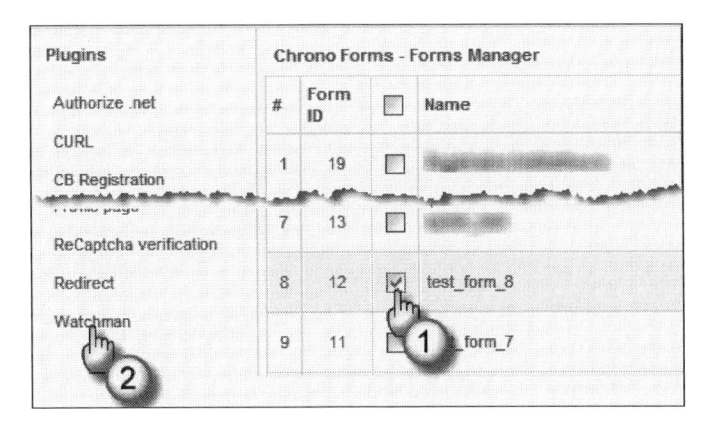

Using Form Plug-ins

2. The Watchman plug-in configuration dialog will then open up. All of the plug-in dialogs have a similar structure. There are several tabs with the essential settings and, in the more recent plug-ins, a **Help** tab with some notes about the main features of the plug-in.

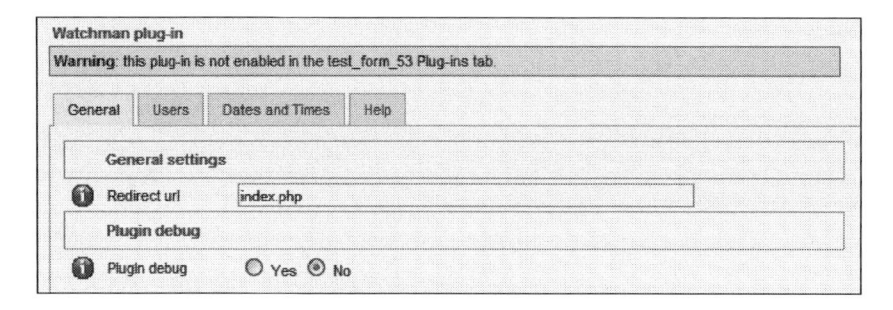

> Note that this image shows a development version of the plug-in dialogue. The release version may be slightly different.

The first thing to notice here is the **Warning** at the top of the dialogue. It's not enough just to configure the plug-in; you also have to enable it on the **Plugins** tab in the Form Editor. This may be a little inconvenient to start with, but it does mean that you can keep the configuration settings while you turn a plug-in on and off for testing.

3. On the plug-in **General** tab, there are just two settings. The bottom one turns the plug-in Debug messages on and off. The top one sets the redirection page for the plug-in—this is the page that a user will be sent to if the Form is turned "Off" by the plug-in settings. By default this is the site home page, but you can enter any other valid URL in the box.

4. The next two tabs, **Users** and **Dates and Times**, configure the plug-in to limit access in either one or both of these ways. Most often you'll use one or the other but there is nothing to stop you limiting access to, for example, only the "Editor" group on Thursday afternoons from 2-4 pm.

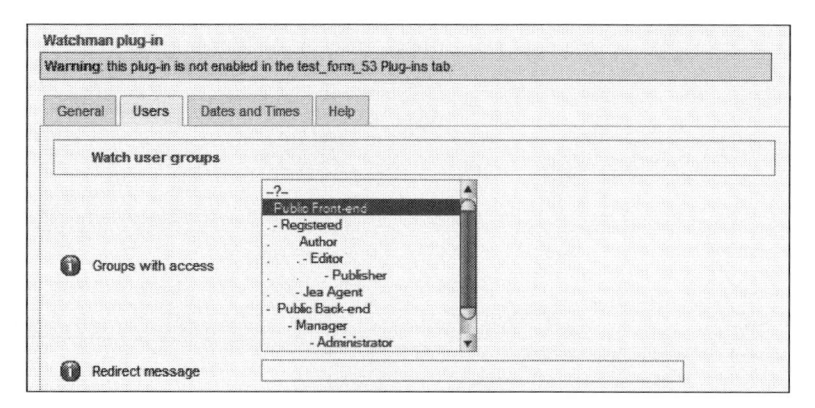

5. The **Users** tab shows the familiar Joomla! User Groups multi-select box. You can select one or more of these groups to give them access to the form.

   The lower **Redirect message** box allows you to enter a message that will be shown if the user is redirected away from the form because they don't have access. If you leave the box empty, then there will be a "silent" redirection with no message.

   > Note that the messages are displayed as Joomla! System Messages (the ones that show up in a blue bar in the default Joomla! templates). Not all templates display these correctly, if they don't display, you may need to add the code `<jdoc:include type="message" />` to your template `index.php` file.

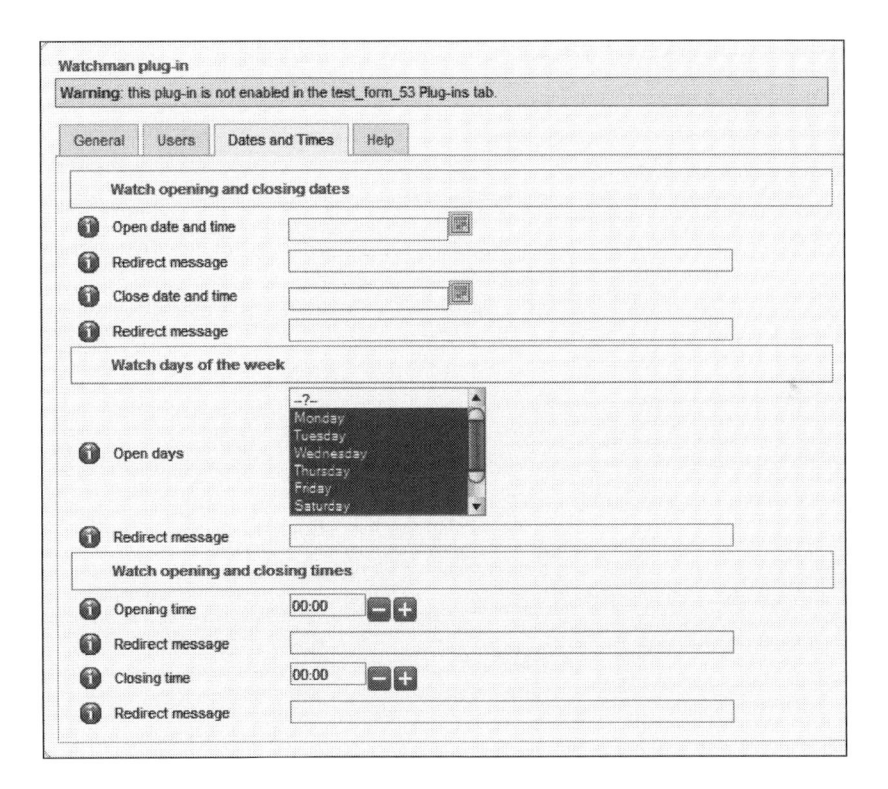

6. The **Dates and Times** tab looks a little more complex but is essentially similar.

   The top block lets you chose an **Open Date and Time**. This is equivalent to the Joomla! article "publish" and "unpublish" settings and is useful if you are, say, running an event and want the form open for bookings from noon on September 1st until 4pm on September 16th.

   There are separate redirect messages for the two times so that you can tell users that they are "too early" or "too late".

Using Form Plug-ins

The second block lets you choose days of the week, so that you could have a form that is only open on working days. The bottom block lets you select the opening and closing times that will apply every day.

As you can see, these two work together to solve the original problem of a form that is only available in office hours.

> Notice that the standard Joomla! calendar used for the top block has the time selector enabled. This can be useful for forms where you need to set precise times. (The Aeron calendar that ChronoForms uses does not include a time-picker.)
>
> The Time-spinner used in the bottom box is also useful if you need to select times. The code is included in the ChronoForms installation package and the spinner can be configured fairly easily. (This one is configured to work in five-minute "clicks".)

7. When you have completed the configuration, click on the **Save** icon in the toolbar to save the plug-in setup.

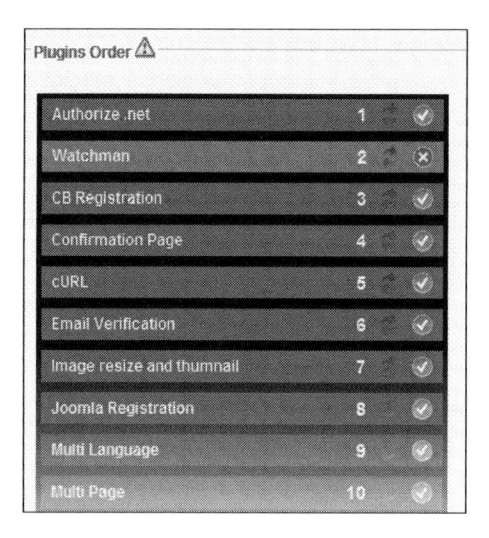

Plugins Order	
Authorize .net	1
Watchman	2
CB Registration	3
Confirmation Page	4
cURL	5
Email Verification	6
Image resize and thumnail	7
Joomla Registration	8
Multi Language	9
Multi Page	10

8. Lastly, remember to enable the plug-in in the **Form Editor | Plugins** tab (green bars are enabled and red bars are disabled).

You can also use your mouse to drag and drop the plug-in bars into a different order; here the Watchman has been moved from the bottom of the list to near the top. With only one plug-in enabled this makes no difference; if you have more than one, then the order they run in can be critical.

> If you have several plug-ins enabled, make sure that Watchman is the first to run as it needs to stop rest of the form loading.

How it works...

The plug-ins are more or less literally "plugged in" to the ChronoForms work-flow, either when the form is loaded, or when it is submitted, or on both occasions. The Watchman does its work when the form is loaded, so is only called then and needs to be the first plug-in loaded if there is more than one enabled.

On the other hand, the ReDirect plug-in is only needed after the form is submitted and is typically the last plug-in to be run.

See also

- The recipe *Limiting form access to registered users* in Chapter 5, *Form Validation and Security* shows another way of restricting form users, if that is all that you need
- The Source code for the MooTools based Timespinner is available from http://j.a.l.free.fr/mootools/timespinner/

Creating multi-lingual forms with the Multi-Language plug-in

For better or worse, ChronoForms doesn't have **JoomFish** support built in. Perhaps a future version will. So, for the moment the **Multi-Language plugin** lets us do almost everything that we need to create multi-lingual forms.

Getting ready

The best way to use this plug-in, as with most of the other plug-ins, is to get your form working just as you want it in a single language, then come back and configure the plug-in.

We will see it working here with a simple newsletter subscription form but the same principals will work with more complex forms.

> There are some pitfalls to avoid with this plug-in; we'll point out most of them on the way through the tutorial. If you have problems, then most likely you are translating something that you didn't intend to. Take a careful look at the page source in your browser to see exactly what is happening.

Using Form Plug-ins

Here's the form that we'll be working with:

And here's the Form HTML that creates it. We'll need to look at this from time to time, so it's convenient to have it available. The text snippets that need to be translated are highlighted:

```
<div class="form_item">
  <div class="form_element cf_heading">
    <h2 class="cf_text">Subscribe to our newsletter</h2>
  </div>
  <div class="cfclear"> </div>
</div>

<div class="form_item">
  <div class="form_element cf_text"><span
    class="cf_text">Please enter your name and email address
    in the boxes below.</span> </div>
  <div class="cfclear"> </div>
</div>

<div class="form_item">
  <div class="form_element cf_textbox">
    <label class="cf_label" style="width: 150px;">Name</label>
    <input class="cf_inputbox" maxlength="150" size="30"
      title="" id="text_0" name="name" type="text" />
  </div>
  <div class="cfclear"> </div>
</div>

<div class="form_item">
  <div class="form_element cf_textbox">
    <label class="cf_label"
      style="width: 150px;">Email</label>
    <input class="cf_inputbox" maxlength="150" size="30"
      title="" id="text_1" name="email" type="text" />
```

```
    </div>
    <div class="cfclear"> </div>
</div>

<div class="form_item">
    <div class="form_element cf_button">
      <input value="Submit" name="button_2" type="submit" />
    </div>
    <div class="cfclear"> </div>
</div>
```

How to do it...

1. Just as in the last recipe, check the box by the Form Name in the Form Editor and click the Multi Language plug-in link in the left-hand column.

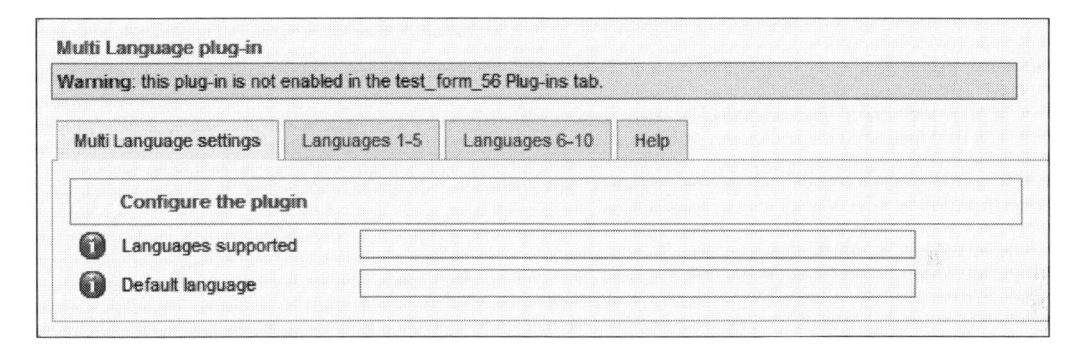

As you see, the first tab is very simple (the others are too!); it just asks you to say which languages you want to support.

Enter the list of language tags in the **Languages supported** box, and then identify one of these as the **Default language** in the second box. The default language translations are the ones that will be used if any translations are missing from one of the other boxes so it's usually best to set this to the site default language.

You enter the languages as Language tags in the form en-GB, fr-FR, or pt-BR.

> These widely used tags typically have two parts—the first two letters identify the language from the ISO 639-1 language code list (for example, en = English, fr = French); and the second two letters identify the country from the ISO 3166-1 alpha-2 code list (for example, GB = Great Britain, BR = Brazil).

For our purposes we'll use these three tags and designate en-GB as the Default language. Enter the language tags as a comma separated list: en-GB, fr-FR, pt-BR.

Using Form Plug-ins

2. If you click on the **Languages 1-5** tab now, you'll see five empty text areas where we are going to enter our translations. These relate to the languages in the same sequence as we've put them in the **Languages supported** box, but that's not obvious. Save the plug-in configuration, then open it again, and click on the **Languages 1-5** tab again.

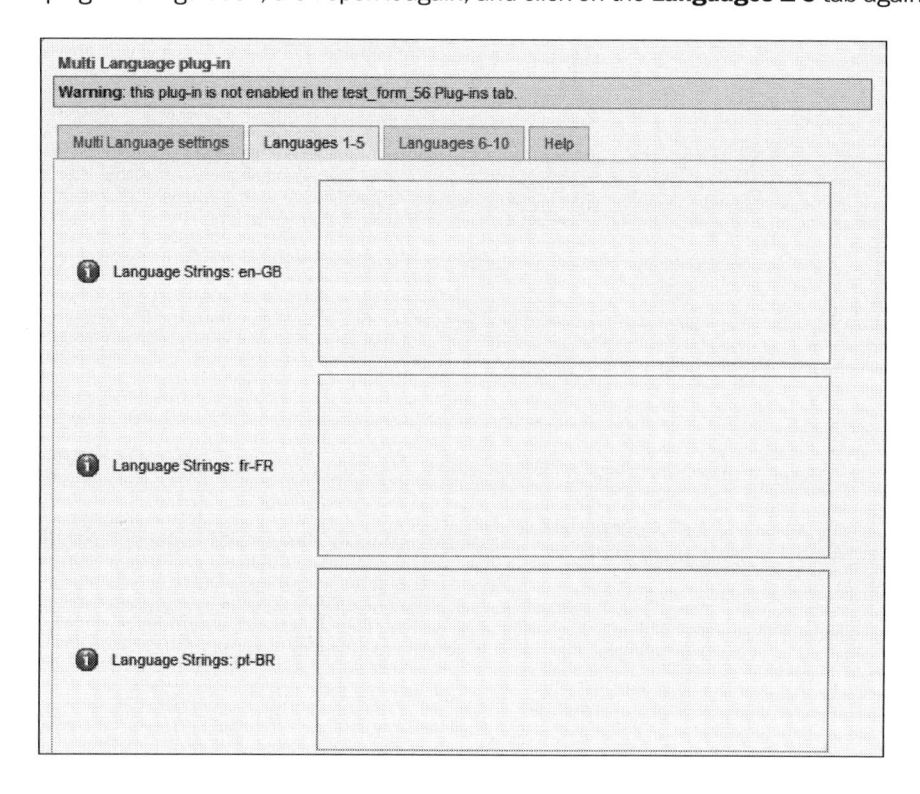

Now you can see that the labels of the first three boxes show the language tags.

3. The first string that we need to translate is **Subscribe to our newsletter** so we'll paste that into our **en-GB** box.

   The syntax here is very simple, we add an "=" and follow it with the translation (in this case the translated language is still English so we can repeat the same text):

   ```
   Subscribe to our newsletter=Subscribe to our newsletter
   ```

   In the **fr-FR** box and **pt-BR** boxes we can use "real" translations:

   ```
   Subscribe to our newsletter=Abonnez-vous à notre newsletter
   Subscribe to our newsletter=Inscrever-se na nossa newsletter
   ```

   > The translations in this recipe all come courtesy of Google Translations, apologies if they are not perfect.

4. Save the plug-in configuration; enable the plug-in on the Form **Plugins** tab and save or apply the form.

> Note: For the next step to work correctly you will probably need the appropriate language packs installed to enable language switching. JoomFish has also been installed here to allow us to use the Language Switcher module.

5. View the form in your browser and switch between the languages. You will see that the header text changes as you switch.

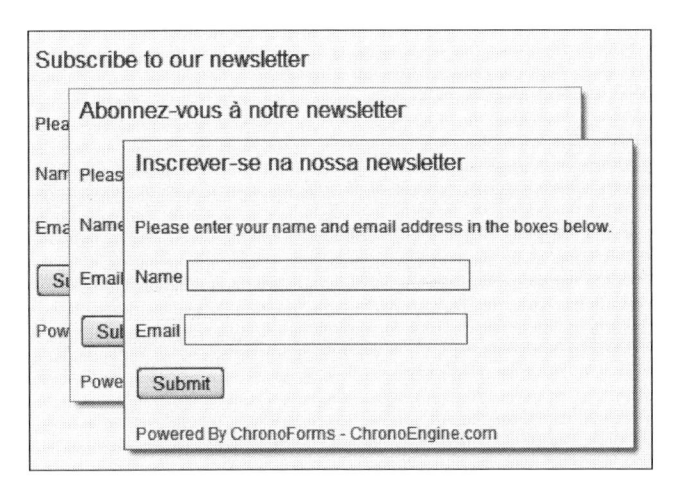

6. All we need to do now is to repeat the same process for the other text snippets.

   In most cases this will work correctly but, as we said earlier, there are a few pitfalls. The Multi-Language plug-in works using a very simple search-and-replace process. As long as we keep that in mind, all will be well.

7. The next text snippet is **Please enter your name and email address in the boxes below**. We could put all of this in the translation boxes just as we did before but it gets a bit cumbersome with long lines. We'll try something a little different.

   Open the Form HTML in the Form Editor and replace this text with `SNIPPET_1` so the line becomes:

   ```
   <div class="form_element cf_text"><span
     class="cf_text">SNIPPET_1</span> </div>
   ```

291

8. Save the form and reopen the plug-in configuration. This time, we'll use `SNIPPET_1` as the basis for our translations so they become:

   ```
   SNIPPET_1=Please enter your name and email address in the boxes below.
   SNIPPET_1=S'il vous plaît entrer votre nom et votre adresse email dans le champs ci-dessous.
   SNIPPET_1=Por favor, digite seu nome e endereço de e-mail nos campos abaixo.
   ```

9. Test the form again and you will find that the text snippet translates nicely.

   This technique is useful and you should probably use it quite often. It keeps the text lines shorter and it removes some pitfalls.

> **Pitfall 1:** Translating text with "=" in it. The plug-in takes the first "=" it finds as marking the dividing line between the source and the translations. So, for example, using `one + one = two=un + un = deux` will end up translating `one = one` as `two=un + un = deux`, which is not ideal.
>
> **Pitfall 2:** Long text. The translator will quite happily handle quite long text snippets but they must all—source and translation—be on one line in the text area. Any line-breaks mean that the text after the line-break will be treated as a new snippet and this may stop the translation working correctly.

10. The next snippet is nice and short: "name" which should be easy. But take a look at the Form HTML again—"name" occurs several times and we only want to translate this single occurrence. If we ended up replacing `name='name'` with `nom='nom'` we would run into all kinds of problems. So again it's prudent to replace the source in the Form HTML with, say, `SNIPPET_2` to remove the ambiguity.

    The `Email` and `Submit` snippets are also used in input attributes so the same approach would be prudent here.

> **Pitfall 3**: Mistaken translations, those cases where we translate something that we didn't intend to translate. These can be difficult to track down after they occur so it's safer to be careful in the beginning.
>
> **Note**: The plug-in is case sensitive so it should distinguish between "Name" and "name", but it's better to be safe.
>
> **Pitfall 4**: Double translations. This is a little harder to explain but if we have say, "Password" followed by "Repeat Password" then the plug-in will translate "Password" everywhere. So, by the time it comes to look for "Repeat Password" the text will be "Repeat Mot de Passe" and the translation will fail.

> This may sound like a long list of pitfalls but, with a little care, they are easy to avoid and all will be well.

11. Here's the final form of this translation:

Language Strings: en-GB
```
Subscribe to our newsletter=Subscribe to our
newsletter
SNIPPET_1=Please enter your name and email address
in the boxes below.
SNIPPET_2=Name
SNIPPET_3=Email
SNIPPET_4=Submit
```

Language Strings: fr-FR
```
Subscribe to our newsletter=Abonnez-vous à notre
newsletter
SNIPPET_1=S'il vous plaît entrer votre nom et
votre adresse email dans le champs ci-dessous.
SNIPPET_2=Nom
SNIPPET_3=Email
SNIPPET_4=Soumettre
```

Language Strings: pt-BR
```
Subscribe to our newsletter=Inscrever-se na nossa
newsletter
SNIPPET_1=Por favor, digite seu nome e endereço de
e-mail nos campos abaixo.
SNIPPET_2=Nome
SNIPPET_3=Email
SNIPPET_4=Submeter
```

12. And the resulting form in the Portuguese version:

Inscrever-se na nossa newsletter

Por favor, digite seu nome e endereço de e-mail nos campos abaixo.

Nome

Email

[Submeter]

Powered By ChronoForms - ChronoEngine.com

Using Form Plug-ins

How it works...

The plug-in works through a very simple search and replace applied to the contents of the Form HTML box, provided that you remember that this is what it is doing it can be a very effective translation tool.

There's more...

Here are some more suggestions to help you get the best out of this plug-in.

Translating form error messages

The plug-in will also work in exactly the same way to translate any of the form error messages that you can set up in the Form Editor or that will be visible when the Form is loaded or reloaded. These include the anti-spam error message, file uploade Error messages, server-side validation error messages, and validation messages included in the input "title" attributes.

With ingenuity it may well be possible to extend this list.

Translating form images

If you have customized images containing text in your form—a "submit" image for example—then it's possible to translate the image name in using the plug-in:

```
<img src='some_path/submit_img_en.jpg' />
```

Can be translated with:

```
submit_img_en.jpg= submit_img_fr.jpg

submit_img_en.jpg= submit_img_pt.jpg
```

This can be done, provided that the corresponding images exist in the same folder.

Translating more complicated code

The plug-in works, as we have described, by using search and replace on the Form HTML. Sometimes, this is not enough to handle more complex forms.

These can usually be managed using a PHP switch statement to change the code depending on the language in use. We want to switch depending on the current language, so this is the basic structure:

```
<?php
$lang =& JFactory::getLanguage();
$cf_tag =& $lang->getTag();
switch ( $cf_tag ) {
  case 'en-GB':
```

```
      default:
        // use English
        break;
      case 'fr-FR':
        // use French
        break;
      case 'pt-BR':
        // use Brazilian Portuguese
        break;
    }
    ?>
```

In practice, of course, we'd replace each of those `// use English`, `// use French`, and `// Use Brazilian Portuguese` comments with a block of code suitable for that particular language. There are several ways we might do that depending on the form we are working with.

Including HTML

The most basic of these is simply to replace the comment with the whole of our Form HTML in each of the languages. For example:

```
    . . .
      case 'fr-FR':
        // use French
    <?
    <div class="form_item">
      <div class="form_element cf_heading">
        <h2 class="cf_text">Abonnez-vous à notre newsletter </h2>
      </div>
      <div class="cfclear"> </div>
    </div>
    . . .
    <?php
        break;
    . . .
```

This will work perfectly well and can be really useful for short blocks of code. For longer blocks it makes for difficult reading, but you can get round that with the next approach.

Including files

We can use the PHP `include()` statement to import a whole external file in as we need it. In this case we could have three external files, one with the form in each language. Our code then becomes:

```
. . .
   case 'fr-FR':
      // use French
      include('some_path/file_name_fr-FR.php');
      break;
. . .
```

This makes for neater code and is useful if there are structural differences between the forms—if, for example, we need to request different information in each language. If the forms are more or less the same though, having multiple forms still leaves us with the problem that we need to update all three (or more) forms if the form is changed.

The third approach takes us back closer to the way the Multi-Language plug-in works.

Including variables

We can also use the PHP `include()` statement to import just the parts of our form that change between the languages. These can be single words, blocks of text, or whole chunks of the form.

The basic structure is exactly the same as in the previous approach but the content of the included file is very different. We might have:

```
<?php
define('CF_EMAIL', 'Email');
define('CF_NAME', 'Nom');
. . .
$intro_text = 'S&srquo;il vous pla&icirc;t entrer votre nom et votre
adresse email dans le champs ci-dessous.';
. . .
$send_image = 'submit_img_fr.jpg'
. . .
```

And then we write our form HTML just once, but building in these variable names at the appropriate places. Using this approach with the PHP `sprintf()` function can give extensive control over the form language and layout.

Translating e-mail templates and thank you pages

The Multi-language plug-in only translates strings found when the Form is loaded. It does not affect anything that happens after the form is submitted. Although theoretically you could pass translation strings in hidden fields in the form, it is not very practical.

You can however use the techniques we described for handling more complicated code in both the **OnSubmit** boxes and the **Email Template** box. (Note that you need to set **Use Template Editor** to **No** in the **Email Setup | Properties** box to add PHP to an Email Template.)

Showing and editing saved information with the Profile plug-in

ChronoForms is an excellent component for creating forms and e-mailing or saving the information submitted by the user. If the data is saved, then one of the frequent tasks that we have to do with that data is to either take a look at it, or to edit it.

ChronoForms has a simple data viewer in the Admin area but it's not available in the Front-end for users to access and it doesn't allow data editing.

The **Profile Plugin** is the answer to this when working with a single record. The plug-in allows us to connect to a database table, extract a single record and display it, either for viewing or as an editable form.

(There's also ChronoForms, sister product **ChronoConnectivity** that is designed to work with lists of many records.)

Getting ready

The Profile plug-in will work with any data that is stored in a database table (provided that the table has a Primary Key column so that you can uniquely identify a record).

> Note: This means that you can use it with any Joomla! database table. We do not recommend that you use it to edit any of the core Joomla! tables unless you know exactly what you are doing. There are relationships between tables that need to be carefully managed, and using the Profile plug-in may break these and damage your site.

We'll work with a few records saved from one of our newsletter sign-up forms. The form needs to have a working **DB Connection**.

How to do it...

1. We need to create a new form to work with the Profile plug-in. We could do this from scratch but the easy way is to use the ChronoForms **Copy** icon to copy the newsletter sign-up form. When the form is created, open it in the editor and rename it, then go to the **Form Code** box on the Form HTML tab.

2. What we need to do here is to replace the old form inputs with {name} tags; these will be "place-holders" for the data to be displayed. And, for the moment, remove the submit button block from the end:

```
<div class="form_item">
  <div class="form_element cf_heading">
    <h2 class="cf_text">Subscribe to our newsletter</h2>
  </div>
  <div class="cfclear"> </div>
</div>
<div class="form_item">
  <div class="form_element cf_textbox">
    <label class="cf_label" style="width: 150px;">Name</label>
    {name}
  </div>
  <div class="cfclear"> </div>
</div>

<div class="form_item">
  <div class="form_element cf_textbox">
    <label class="cf_label"
      style="width: 150px;">Email</label>
    {email}
  </div>
  <div class="cfclear"> </div>
</div>
```

> The {name} tags we use need to match up with the column names in the database table that the data will be taken from. If the table was created from this form using the ChronoForms "Create Table", then they will probably match the names of the form inputs. However, this may not always be the case.
>
> If you get unexpected results (or no results) then double-check that the place-holder names used here exactly match the column names in the database table.

3. Save the modified form. Then, as in the earlier recipes, check the box by the Form Name in the Forms Manager and then click the **Profile page plug-in** link in the left-hand column. This will open up the Plug-in configuration dialogue:

Chapter 11

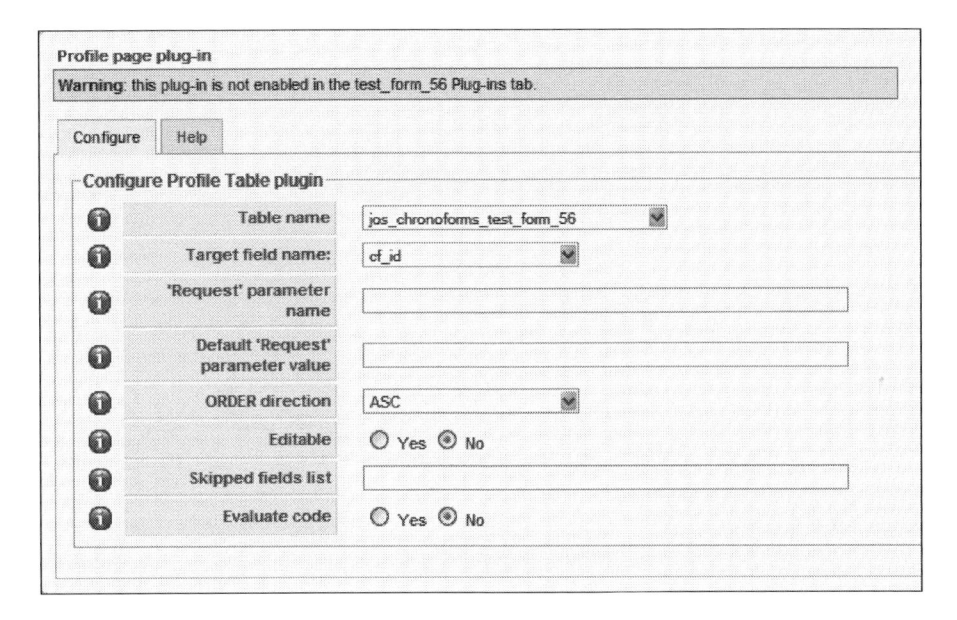

Profile page plug-in
Warning: this plug-in is not enabled in the test_form_56 Plug-ins tab.

Configure | Help

Configure Profile Table plugin

ⓘ	Table name	jos_chronoforms_test_form_56
ⓘ	Target field name:	cf_id
ⓘ	'Request' parameter name	
ⓘ	Default 'Request' parameter value	
ⓘ	ORDER direction	ASC
ⓘ	Editable	○ Yes ● No
ⓘ	Skipped fields list	
ⓘ	Evaluate code	○ Yes ● No

There's only one configuration tab for this plug-in and the settings are fairly straightforward.

The first two boxes are already completed in the image—**Table name** is a drop-down select list of all the tables in the Joomla! database and we need to select the table linked to our form—tables created by ChronoForms are typically named `jos_chronoforms_form_name`.

The second box is called the **Target Field Name**. When you first open the dialogue there is no box there, but a drop-down menu appears when you choose a table name. The drop-down shows the column names from the selected table. You need to choose one that uniquely identifies the record in the table. We will stay with the first option `cf_id` which is the default record identifier (and the Primary Key) for a table created by ChronoForms.

Those two entries tell us how to select a record from a table. Now we need to identify which record – that is, what value for `cf_id` ChronoForms should use to pull the data from the table for us.

We typically pass that information by adding it to a link from another page, or from another form. Either way we'll pass a parameter `name=value` pair. What the next box needs is the '`name`' we'll be using so that ChronoForms can find the corresponding value.

In this case we'll use the same name as the database column `cf_id` – though we could equally have used `subscriber`, `xspeft` or any other convenient string.

4. That's all we need right now so save the configuration; then open the Form in the Form Editor and enable the plug-in in the **Plug-ins** tab.

299

5. If you now view the form in your browser it will look a little bare:

> **Subscribe to our newsletter**
>
> Name
>
> Email
>
> Powered By ChronoForms - ChronoEngine.com

The labels are there but there are no form inputs and no values.

6. But if we now add the `name=value` parameter pair to the end of the URL in the browser and load that, we see something different. We specified `cf_id` as the parameter name earlier so try adding `&cf_id=1` so that the end of the URL looks something like this:

   `?option=com_chronocontact&chronoformname=test_form_56&cf_id=1`

   In your case the value of `chronoformname` may be different. (And you need to find a valid value for `cf_id` that matches an existing record in the database table.) Viewing this URL shows me the results for the record with `cf_id = 1` from the table:

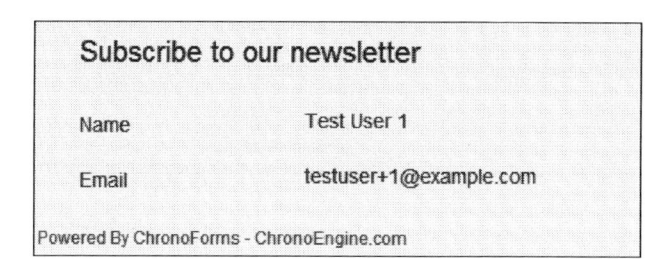

> **Subscribe to our newsletter**
>
> Name   Test User 1
>
> Email   testuser+1@example.com
>
> Powered By ChronoForms - ChronoEngine.com

7. In this example we copied the form layout, but in practice we could put any text here and use the `{input_name}` tags to insert information wherever we wanted it to display. This is of course similar to the way in which we can lay out an Email template.

How it works...

Behind the scenes, ChronoForms is really just doing a search and replace on the `{input_name}` tags.

In the editable version described below, no tags are used and there is a more complex search and replace to find input names and add the values taken from the database to them.

There's more...

This is fine if you want to view the data, but what if you want to edit it as well?

In that case, go back to the plug-in configuration and check the **Editable** radio button. We also need to put the inputs and the submit button back into the Form HTML (or go back to the original Form and make a new copy). And if we want to update the existing record rather than add a new one, we need to add a hidden input to track the record id:

```html
<div class="form_item">
  <div class="form_element cf_textbox">
    <label class="cf_label" style="width: 150px;">Name</label>
    <input class="cf_inputbox" maxlength="150" size="30"
      title="" id="text_0" name="name" type="text" />
  </div>
  <div class="cfclear"> </div>
</div>

<div class="form_item">
  <div class="form_element cf_textbox">
    <label class="cf_label"
      style="width: 150px;">Email</label>
    <input class="cf_inputbox" maxlength="150" size="30"
      title="" id="text_1" name="email" type="text" />
  </div>
  <div class="cfclear"> </div>
</div>
// insert submit button code here
<input type="hidden" name="cf_id" />
```

Now when we load the file we see the form with the data for the selected record pre-loaded.

If we edit this and then submit the form, then the updated information will be saved to the database.

Using Form Plug-ins

This "editing" application of the plug-in is very useful, not only to let users update records but also for supervisor updating or approval of records. With a little planning you can create forms that allow some parts of the data to be updated by different users or user groups.

> ChronoForms uses the **Joomla! JTable class** to save data through a DB Connection. If a primary key for an existing record is included in the data submitted then that record will be updated with the values of any other data submitted (data in columns that aren't matched are left unchanged); otherwise a new record is created.

See also

- ChronoConnectivity, available from chronoengine.com, is a Joomla! component that works alongside ChronoForms and helps build a table or list of many results taken from a database table.

Registering users with the Joomla! Registration plug-in

In this recipe we'll start out by copying the standard Joomla! Registration process using a ChronoForm and the ChronoForms **Joomla! Registration plugin**.

Getting ready

We'll start off with a standard Joomla! Registration. The default Joomla! registration form looks like this:

We could use the techniques from *Chapter 10, Creating Common Forms* to copy the HTML from this form, but instead we'll use the ChronoForms Wizard to create a new version.

Add these five text inputs with the names and IDs `name`, `username`, `email`, `password` and `password_2` and then add the submit button. Use **PasswordBox** elements for the two password elements; they conceal the entries with asterisks. Make all the elements **Required** and check **E-mail Validation** for the e-mail element.

Save the form with a suitable name like `registration_1`. Publish it and click the link to open it in a browser window to check that it looks fine.

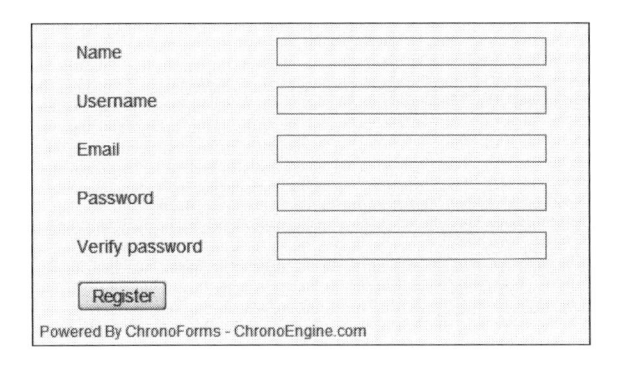

If you like you can add asterisks and extra text elements by editing the Form HTML in the Form Editor.

How to do it...

1. From the Forms Manager, check the box beside the form name then click the Joomla! Registration plug-in link in the left hand column.

   The plug-in configuration will open with four tabs: **Field names**, **Configuration**, **Extra code**, and **Help**. Stay with the **Field names** tab for the moment.

   The tab has boxes for the five fields that are required for Joomla! registration—these correspond exactly with the five inputs in our form, so we just need to add the input names to complete the tab:

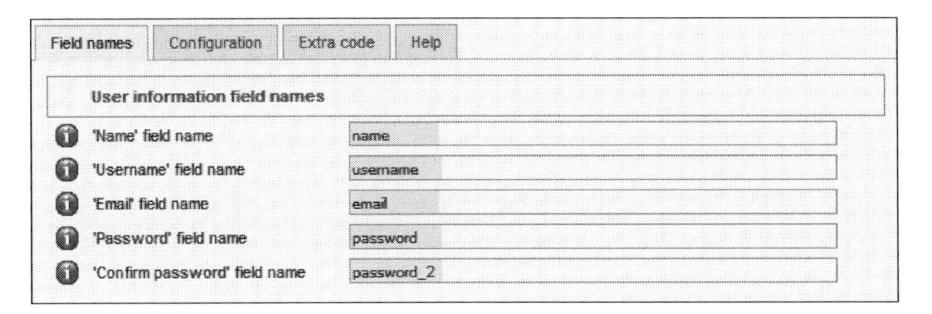

Using Form Plug-ins

2. Save the configuration—by all means check out the other tabs, but don't change any other settings—then open the Form Editor and enable the plug-in on the **Plug-ins** tab.
3. Save the form, refresh it in the browser window, and then do a test submission.

   If you complete the form correctly you should see the standard Joomla! message: **Your account has been created and an activation link has been sent to the e-mail address you entered. Note that you must activate the account by clicking on the activation link when you get the e-mail before you can login.**
4. In Site Admin go to the **User Manager** and check if the new user has been created:

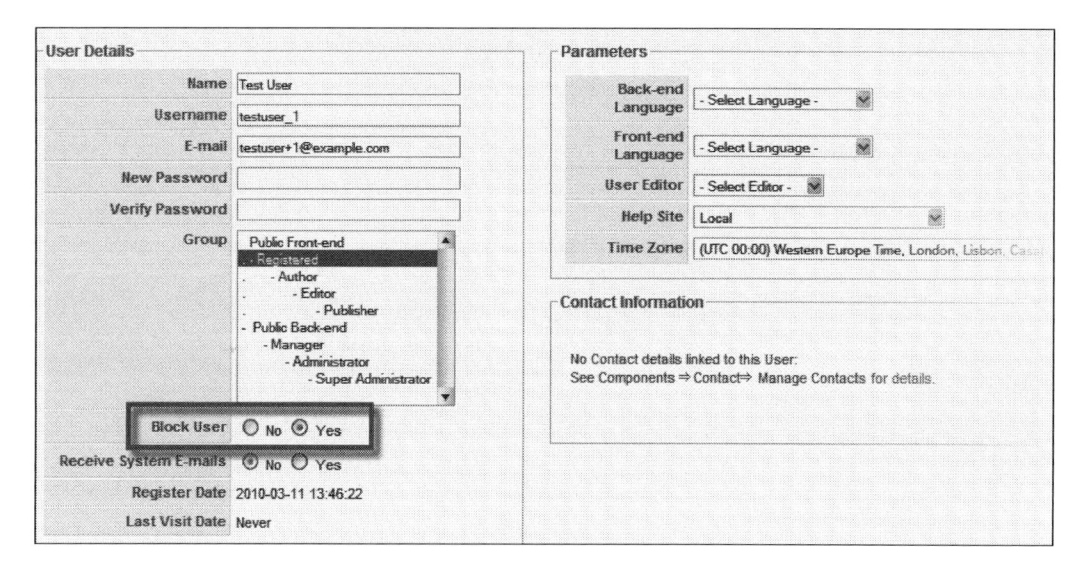

There are all the entries that we would expect. Note that the user is shown as **Blocked** until their e-mail is verified by clicking the link in the e-mail. Also the password entries are not shown; these fields are only used for creating or changing passwords.

> Joomla! doesn't actually store the users password at all, instead a 'hash' created from the password is saved. When the password is used to log in, the password input is 'hashed' in the same way and the two hashes are compared. This means that you can't find a user's password by digging into the database (though the hashes for common passwords can sometimes be looked up).

5. There is one step left—we need to connect our new form to Joomla!. We want to redirect users from the default Joomla! registration from to our new one. The easiest way to do this is to hack the Joomla! core code which means that you may need to re-do the hack if a Joomla! upgrade stops the hack working.

Open the file `components\com_user\views\register\tmpl\default.php` in a text editor and add one extra line near the beginning. The effect of this is to redirect the user to your new registration form.

```
<?php // no direct access
defined('_JEXEC') or die('Restricted access');
$mainframe->redirect( JURI::base()
.'index.php?option=com_chronocontact&chronoformname=register_1');
?>
```

6. That is all that needs to be done to create a ChronoForm to replace the default Joomla! User registration form. You can now change the layout or styling and place this form in a module or inside an article as you can with any ChronoForm.

How it works...

The guts of this are hidden away inside the plug-in code. In essence, the plug-in wraps some ChronoForms code around the standard Joomla! user registration code. This way Joomla! 'does the registration' using the information provided by ChronoForms.

There's more...

Usually the reason for creating a new registration form is not just for the look but so that you can change the registration process in some way. We'll look at some of these here.

There are two sets of settings that affect how the registration process works. One is the Joomla! Registration plug-in **Configuration** tab settings:

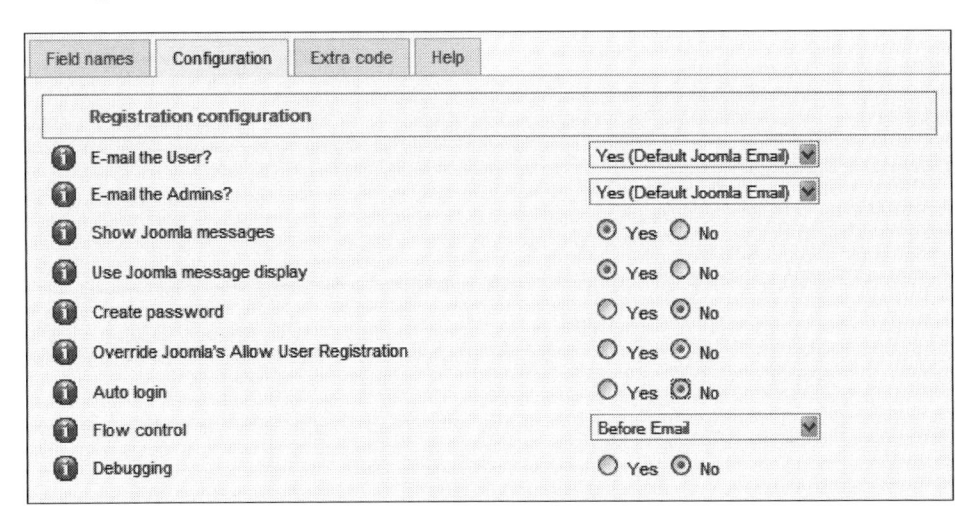

Registration configuration	
E-mail the User?	Yes (Default Joomla Email)
E-mail the Admins?	Yes (Default Joomla Email)
Show Joomla messages	● Yes ○ No
Use Joomla message display	● Yes ○ No
Create password	○ Yes ● No
Override Joomla's Allow User Registration	○ Yes ● No
Auto login	○ Yes ● No
Flow control	Before Email
Debugging	○ Yes ● No

Using Form Plug-ins

The other is the User Settings on the **Site | Global Configuration | System** tab:

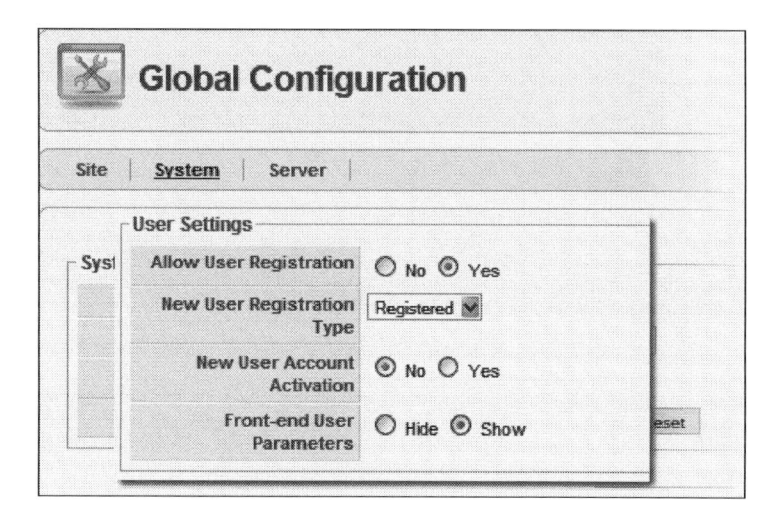

In setting up your registration process, you may need to change settings on either or both of these.

Sending custom e-mails

By default the registration process sends out an e-mail to the user and another to Site Administrators (actually it goes to any user with **Receive System Emails** set to **Yes** in their User Profile). The text for these emails is set in the site language files, for example:

```
SEND_MSG_ACTIVATE=Hello %s,\n\nThank you for registering at %s. Your
account is created and must be activated before you can use it.\nTo
activate the account click on the following link or copy-paste it in
your browser:\n%s\n\nAfter activation you may login to %s using the
following username and password:\n\nUsername: %s\nPassword: %s
```

The ChronoForms Joomla! Registration plug-in allows you to create custom e-mails to replace these system messages.

You need to create an E-mail Setup for the Registration Form – remembering to include {vlink} if you want the validation link to appear. In the Plug-in Configuration tab you can use the **E-mail the User** and **E-mail the Admins** drop-downs to select the E-mail Setups to use; or leave the default settings to use the Joomla! messages.

Displaying custom messages

The next two inputs on the Plug-in Configuration control the display of the success messages. If you want to suppress the standard Joomla! messages then set **Show Joomla! Messages** to **No** and add your own message in the form "Thank You" page.

> The **Use Joomla! message display** input (found in some versions of the plug-in) does not do anything at present. There used to be an option to have messages displayed as Joomla! System Messages but many templates don't include the code to do this so ChronoForms uses its own message display for greater reliability.

Creating a "silent" registration

While the standard registration process is fairly simple sometimes it is still too much to ask users for. It's possible to create a 'silent' registration where we have only the minimum input from the user—an e-mail address.

Let's suppose that we have a newsletter sign-up form with just a single `email` field.

In the Joomla! Registration plug-in configuration we need to do a couple of things.

First we'll go to the **Extra Code** tab and use the **Extra Code Before Registration** box to copy the e-mail into both the name and username fields.

```
<?php
$email = JRequest::getString('email', '', 'post');
JRequest::setVar('name', $email);
JRequest::setVar('username', $email);
?>
```

Next, go to the **Configuration** tab and set **Create Password** to **Yes**. ChronoForms will now create a random password for you and include that in the validation e-mail to the user.

Check that the **Field Names** tab has `name`, `username`, and `email` in the top three boxes (the password fields will be ignored).

Using Form Plug-ins

Save the plug-in Configuration and enable the plug-in in the Form Plug-ins tab. Test the form and you will find that it creates a new user with both the '**Name**' and '**Username**' set to the e-mail address.

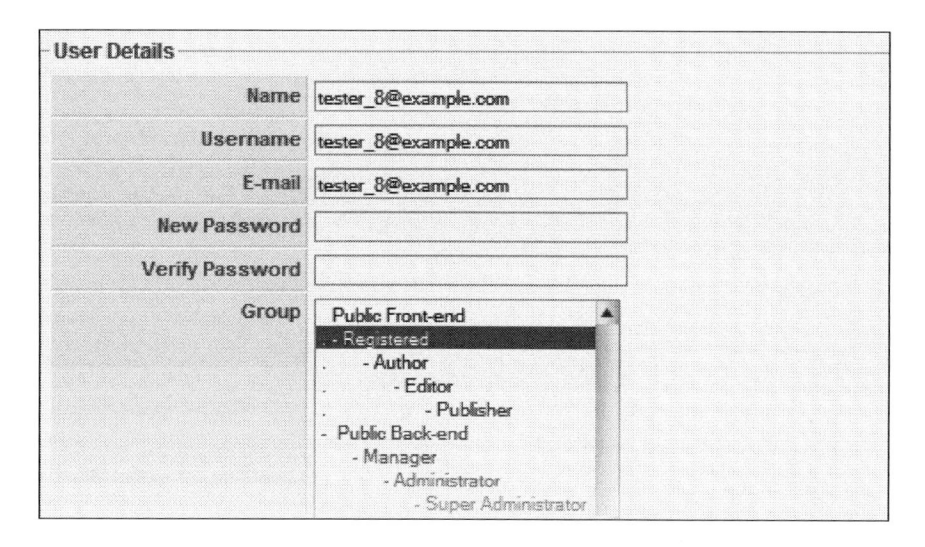

Creating a "Name" from other field inputs

The Joomla! **Name** field only takes a single input, but we very often prefer to collect a user's "first name" and "last name" as separate entries.

We can extend the ideas from the "silent" registration to handle this quite easily.

If we have a form with `first_name` and `last_name` inputs then we can add code to the Joomla! Registration plug-in **Before** box to join them into a single 'name' for the registration.

The code we need is:

```
<?php
$first_name = JRequest::getString('first_name', '', 'post');
$last_name = JRequest::getString('last_name', '', 'post');
$name = $first_name.' '.$last_name;
JRequest::setVar('name', $name);
?>
```

This joins together the two parts of the name and puts them into the name field in the `$_POST` array.

Check that the Field Names tab has `name`, `username` and `email` in the top three boxes; save and enable the plug-in, and test the form.

Creating a Username from other fields

A Joomla! username has to be unique so we can't assume that the same process will work. There may already be a "John Smith" registered.

Let's do something a little more complicated. We'll remove any special characters from the names by using `getCmd()` and then add a short random string to the end of the user name to make sure that it is unique.

Note that this is in addition to the code in the previous section to build a name.

```
.  .  .
$first_name = JRequest::getCmd('first_name', '', 'post');
$last_name = JRequest::getCmd('last_name', '', 'post');
$username = $last_name.$first_name;
// add a random integer between 100 and 999
$username .= mt_rand(100, 999);
JRequest::setVar('username', $username);
?>
```

Check that the Field Names tab has `name`, `username`, and `email` in the top three boxes; save and enable the plug-in, and test the form.

Using these two code snippets together we have this as our registered user:

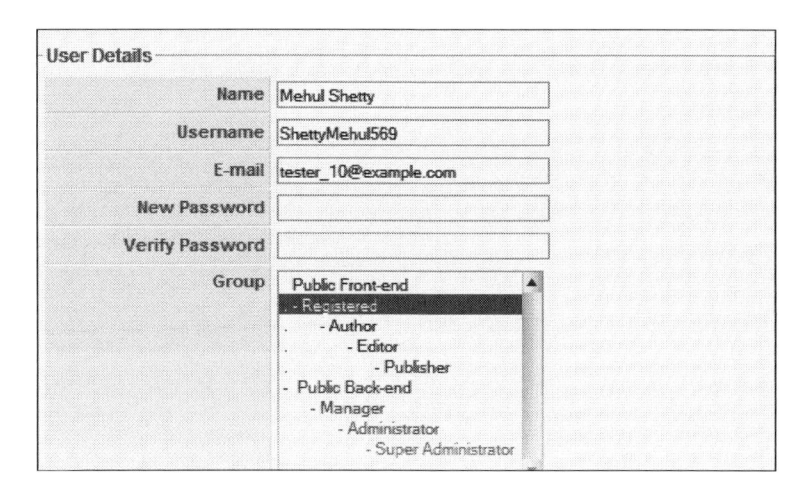

Allowing secret registration

You may want to have your site appear as though it is still private with no registration allowed but yet allow registration in certain circumstances.

To do this you can set **Allow User Registration** to **Off** in the Site Global Configuration but set **Override Joomla!'s Allow User Registration** to **Yes** in the Joomla! Registration plug-in.

Presumably you would link this to some validation of the form entries to check that the submitter is qualified to register.

Logging in new members automatically

You can use the **Auto login** setting in the Joomla! Registration plug-in configuration to automatically log newly registered members into the site.

For this to work the Site Global Configuration must have **New User Account Activation** set to **No** which means that there will be no verification e-mail sent and thus some extra security risks that you will need to manage.

Saving extra data

In the previous examples, our form collected data for the user's first and last names but this was not saved except in the joined together version in the `username` field.

We often want to collect extra information about users that is not in the standard User Registration. It's tempting to hack the `jos_users` table and add a few extra columns but this is not advised as hacking the core code often causes future problems that can be hard to diagnose and solve.

It's better to create a separate table for the additional data and to link that to the Joomla! User data through the user ID.

We'll test this with the form including the `first_name` and `last_name` inputs.

In the Forms Manager use the Create Table icon to create a new table with these two fields in it. (We don't need the e-mail field, as this value will be saved in the User information).

Open the Form Editor and enable the DB Connection to the new table, then Apply or Save the form and test by submitting a new entry.

Check in the site User Manager that the new user is registered and note the User ID in the far right-hand column. Go to the ChronoForms Forms Manager and click the entry in the Tables Connected column to open the data viewer and open the new record.

You will see there that the `first_name` and `last_name` have been saved and that the `cf_user_id` entry matches the new `UserID`.

Field name	Field Data
cf_id:	1
uid:	INTRiMzUyMTE2MDY5e21176a2240ce62ad9c0e76e3ca7ea3f
recordtime:	2010-03-12 - 16:37:37
ipaddress:	192.168.1.26
cf_user_id:	**76**
first_name:	**Usha**
last_name:	**Iyer**

Changing user parameters

As well as the familiar user attributes that we've been working with, there are another group of user parameters that you can see in the Site User Editor. You can, if you need to, set these on registration (or at other times). The technique is to use the Joomla! User Object to get or set the parameters.

Let's set the time zone for a new user (presumably based on some information from the form). We will need to do this after Registration when there is a user object to update; so this code goes in the **Extra after Registration code** box. Here's the code that would go set the user time zone to UTC-10 (Hawaii).

```php
<?php
$user =& JFactory::getUser();
$user->setParam('timezone', -10);
$user->save();
?>
```

You can also set the user language with the `language` parameter (and one or two others that may be less useful).

This same technique can be used to create and manage new parameters too. Let's say that you want to track the gender of your users and have asked this question in your form in an input named `gender` with values of `male` or `female`:

```php
<?php
$gender = JRequest::getString('gender', '', 'post');
$user =& JFactory::getUser();
$user->setParam('gender', $gender);
$user->save();
?>
```

Using Form Plug-ins

This new parameter will not show up in the User Editor, or in the User Edit Account form; but you can refer to it by accessing the Joomla! User Object in the same way as you would to get the username or user e-mail.

Creating a PayPal purchase form with the ReDirect plug-in

So you want the user to pay you! There are of course many ways to do this, but we're going to work with **PayPal** here as it is very commonly used. A similar approach will often work with other payment gateways.

> ChronoForms has two payment gateway plug-ins included in the package (for Authorise.net and for the PayPal WebPayments Pro API). Both of these work for testing purposes, except that they randomise the amounts unless you pay a small license fee.

Getting ready

Nothing special is required for the recipe, though it won't be of much use unless you have an active PayPal account. The basic account will work with this recipe; you don't need the advanced API that the ChronoForms PayPal plug-in requires.

How to do it...

1. Any purchase form will do, we're going to be working in the back end for most of the time.

2. We'll start by looking at the code for a PayPal **Buy Now** button. Here's the code from an example at `https://www.paypal.com/cgi-bin/webscr?cmd=_pdn_xclick_techview_outside` (as usual we've added some line breaks and spacing for clarity):

```
<form name="_xclick" method="post"
  action="https://www.paypal.com/cgi-bin/webscr" >
<input type="hidden" name="cmd" value="_xclick">
<input type="hidden" name="business"
  value="me@mybusiness.com">
<input type="hidden" name="currency_code" value="USD">
<input type="hidden" name="item_name" value="Teddy Bear">
<input type="hidden" name="amount" value="12.99">
<input type="image"
  src="http://www.paypal.com/en_US/i/btn/btn_buynow_LG.gif"
```

```
    border="0" name="submit"
    alt="Make payments with PayPal -
        it's fast, free and secure!">
</form>
```

Notice that this is form HTML; we could strip off the `<form . . . >` and `</form>` tags and put this into a ChronoForm. Indeed, if we then put the action URL from this form—`https://www.paypal.com/cgi-bin/webscr`—into the Submit URL box in our ChronoForm it would work exactly as this form does.

However, in that case ChronoForms would never see the submitted data and would not be able to save it, send e-mails, or anything else.

So we want a way to let ChronoForms do its work and then submit the information and transfer the user to PayPal to make the payment.

3. We are going to use the ChronoForms' **ReDirect Plugin** shortly, but to get the basic idea we'll start out using the **ReDirect URL** box to set a fixed ReDirect URL.

   First let's look a bit more at the data we need to pass to PayPal by pulling the key fields out of the previous form HTML:

   ```
   action="https://www.paypal.com/cgi-bin/webscr"
   name="cmd" value="_xclick"
   name="business" value="me@mybusiness.com"
   name="currency_code" value="USD"
   name="item_name" value="Teddy Bear"
   name="amount" value="12.99"
   ```

   That's all there is (there are many other values that could be there but we'll stay with the minimum required fields for the moment).

   This form is only going to be used to sell teddy bears at $12.99 so nothing will change between one submission and the next. In this case we can therefore build a fixed URL and put that into the ReDirect URL box.

   The query string for a URL starts with `?` and is followed by a series of `name=value` pairs separated by `&`; for example, `?name1=value1&name2=value2 . . .`

   Turning our fixed fields into a query string we get:

   ```
   ?cmd=_xclick&businessme@mybusiness.com&currency_code=USD
   &item_name=Teddy+Bear&amount=12.99
   ```

   > Notice that as spaces aren't allowed in URLs we've replaced the space in teddy bear with a + sign.

Using Form Plug-ins

4. Now add the PayPal URL on the front to complete the URL and copy and paste it into the ReDirect URL box on the form General tab (all on one line with no line-breaks or spaces):

   ```
   https://www.paypal.com/cgi-bin/
   webscr?cmd=_xclick&business=me@mybusiness.com&currency_code=USD
   &item_name=Teddy+Bear&amount=12.99
   ```

5. Save the form and submit it, and all being well, you will be transferred to PayPal to buy your teddy bear.

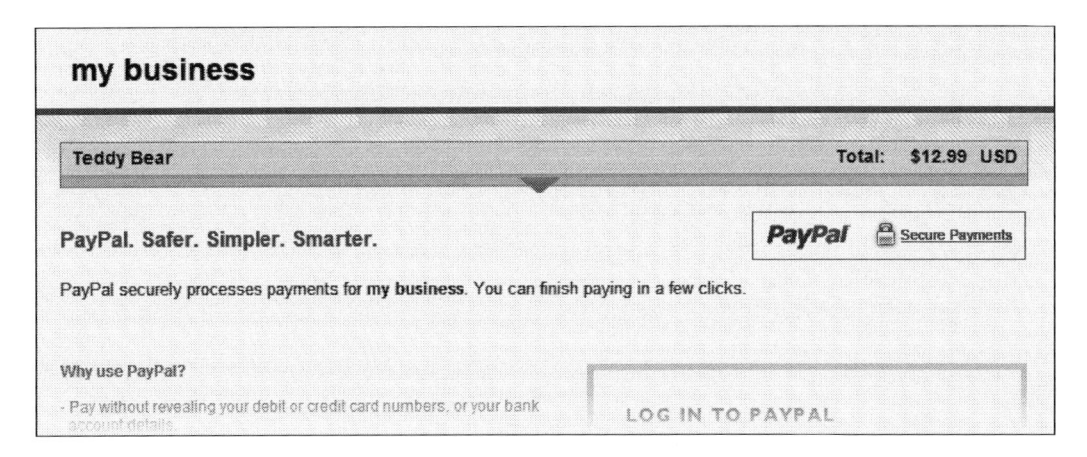

my business

| Teddy Bear | Total: $12.99 USD |

PayPal. Safer. Simpler. Smarter.

PayPal securely processes payments for **my business**. You can finish paying in a few clicks.

Why use PayPal?
- Pay without revealing your debit or credit card numbers, or your bank account details.

LOG IN TO PAYPAL

> This works perfectly well as a demonstration but, to use it in a real form, remember to replace `me@mybusiness.com` with your PayPal account ID.

> Note: PayPal use `me@mybusiness.com` in their code example but it appears to be a real PayPal account so be very careful in testing if you leave the code unchanged.

This is all very well but it's not easy to maintain and you can't include any variable values.

6. So the next step is to remove our ReDirect URL and use the ReDirect plug-in instead.

   The ReDirect plug-in works like the ReDirect URL but it builds the URL after the form is submitted, so it's entirely possible to include values that are taken from the form inputs, looked up in a database table or calculated.

   For this recipe, we'll stay with our teddy bears but we'll offer a 20% discount to registered (and signed-in) members.

7. We need to make one change to the Form HTML to make this work more easily. If you don't already have an `amount` input, then add a hidden input at the end of the HTML:

    `<input type='hidden' name='amount' value='' />`

    The only purpose of this is to act as a "placeholder" so that ChronoForms will find the field when it scans the Form HTML to set up the plug-in.

8. Now remove any entry from the **ReDirect URL** box on the **General** tab, save the form, check the box by the name and click the **ReDirect** plug-in link in the left-hand column.

    When the configuration dialog opens, click the **URL parameters** tab.

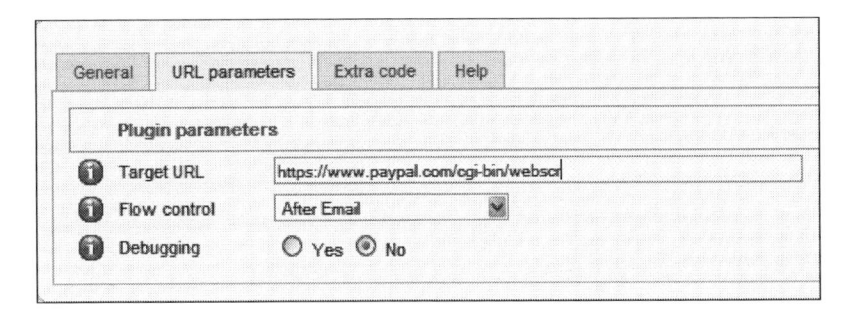

9. Copy and paste the PayPal root URL into the Target URL box and set **Flow Control** to **After Email**; leave **Debugging** as **No** for the moment. (Turning Debugging on here and in the Form **Editor | General** tab will show more debug messages before the redirect takes place and can be invaluable in seeing exactly what is being passed to PayPal.)

10. Now click the **General** tab in the dialogue:

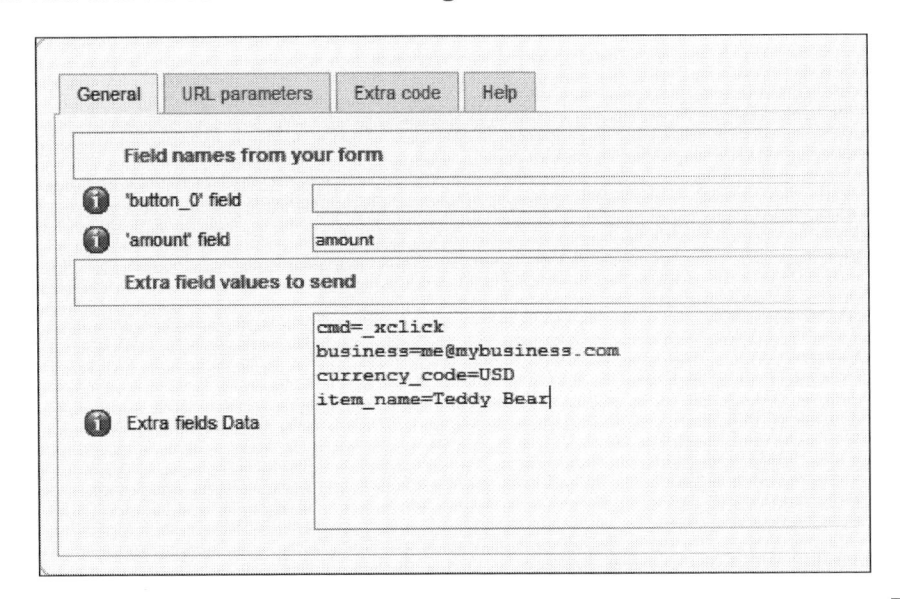

Using Form Plug-ins

The field names in the top section are taken from the Form HTML so you may see a different set there. The **'button_0'** field is a submit button so we can ignore that. The **'amount'** field is the empty hidden field that we just added so it has no value yet. Here we'll just enter **amount** in the box to tell the plug-in that this field is to be passed to PayPal as "amount".

> Here the names of the form input and the PayPal parameter are the same. They don't need to be - we could have had `text_77` and `amount`. That said, using consistent naming makes debugging complex forms much easier.

In the bottom box we have the four remaining fixed value parameters. These entries are very much the same as those we added to the URL query string – except that we can leave the space in `'Teddy Bear'` and let ChronoForms fill it in for us.

11. Lastly, go to the **Extra Code** tab, where there is a box for extra PHP (or HTML). that will be executed before the redirection to PayPal. We will add the code to calculate the amount in here.

```php
<?php
// set the price & discount rate
$price = 12.99;
$user_discount = 0.20;
// get the User object
$user =& JFactory::getUser();
// Check if this is a logged in user
if ( $user->id ) {
  // if it is then apply the discount
  $price = $price*(1 - $user_discount);
  $price = round($price, 2);
}
// set the price in the 'amount' field
JRequest::setVar('amount', $price);
?>
```

12. Save the plug-in configuration, open the Form Editor again, and enable the plug-in on the **Plug-ins** tab (a green bar shows the plug-in is enabled, red is disabled).

13. Go back to the browser view of the form, make sure that you are not logged in to the front-end of the site and submit the form. You should be redirected to PayPal in exactly the same way as with the plain ReDirect URL.

14. Now log in to the front-end, refresh the form page if necessary and re-submit the form. You will be redirected to PayPal again, but this time you'll be charged the special "user price" for your teddy bear.

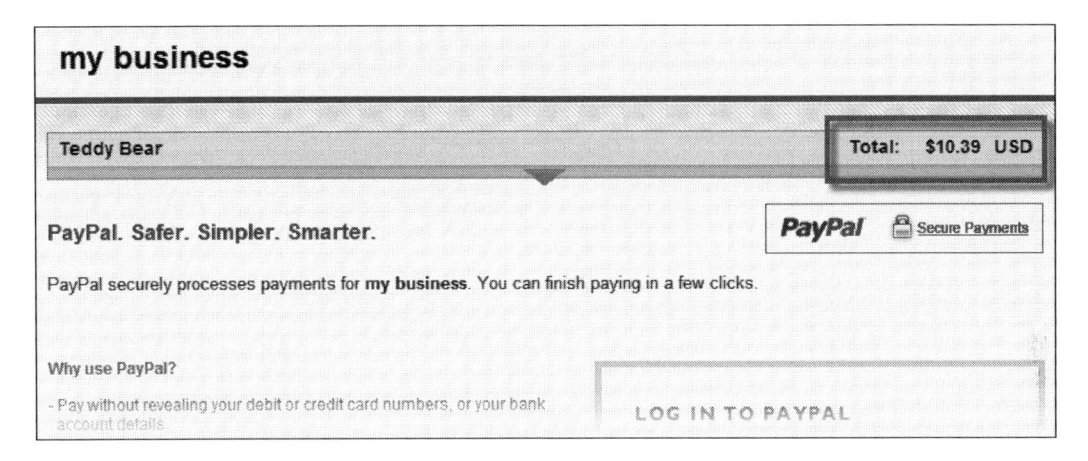

See also

- *Chapter4, Saving Form Data in the Database.*
- **PayPal** : HTML variables for Website Payments Standard

12
Adding Advanced Features

In this chapter, we will cover:

- Using PHP to create "select" drop-downs
- Using Ajax to look up e-mail addresses
- Get information from a DB table to include in your form
- Show a form in a smoothbox
- Track source pages using hidden form fields
- Controlling e-mails from form inputs
- Building a complex multi-page form
- Troubleshooting problems with forms

Introduction

Once you have a basic form working, you can be certain that you (or your client) will see ways that it can be improved with just a little extra something here or there.

This chapter gives you recipes for some typical advanced form features—we encourage you to adopt and adapt to the ideas here to meet your particular needs.

Using PHP to create "select" dropdowns

One frequent request is to create a select drop-down from a set of records in a database table. The example here lists all the published articles in section 1.

Adding Advanced Features

Getting ready

You'll need to know the MySQL query to extract the records you need from the database table. This requires some Joomla! knowledge and some MySQL know-how.

Joomla! keeps its articles in the `jos_content` database table and the two-table columns that we want are the article title and the article id. A quick check in the database tells us that the columns are appropriately called `title` and `id`. We can also see that the section id column is called `sectionid` (with no spaces); the column that tells us if the article is published or not is called `state` and takes the values `1` for published and `0` for not published.

How to do it . . .

We are going to use some PHP to look up the information about the articles in the database table and then output the results it finds as a series of options for our drop-down box.

You'll recall that normal HTML code for a drop-down box looks something like this:

```
<select . . .>
  <option value='option_value_1'>Option 1 text</option>
  <option value='option_value_2'>Option 2 text</option>
  . . .
</select>
```

This is simplified a little so that we can see the main parts that concern us here—the options. Each option uses the same code with two variables—a value attribute and a text description. The value will be returned when the form is submitted; the text description is shown when the form is displayed on your site.

In simple forms, the value and the description text are often the same. This can be useful if all you are doing with the results is to display them on a web page or in an e-mail. If you are going to use them for anything more complicated than that, it can be much more useful to use a simplified, coded form in the value.

For our list of articles, it will be helpful if our form returns the ID of the article rather than its title. Hence, we need to set the options to be something like this:

```
<option value='99'>Article title</option>
```

Having the article ID will let us look up the article in the database and extract any other information that we might need, or to update the record to change the corresponding record.

Here's the code that we'll use. The beginning and ending HTML lines are exactly the same as the standard drop-down code that ChronoForms generates but the "option" lines are replaced by the section inside the `<?php . . . ?>` tags.

The PHP snippet looks up the article IDs and titles from the `jos_content` table, then loops through the results writing an `<option>` tag for each one:

```
<div class="form_item">
  <div class="form_element cf_dropdown">
    <label class="cf_label" style="width: 150px;">
      Articles</label>
    <select class="cf_inputbox validate-selection"
        id="articles" size="1" name="articles">
    <option value=''>--?--</option>
<?php
if (!$mainframe->isSite() ) {return;}
$db =& JFactory::getDBO();
$query = "
  SELECT `id`, `title`
    FROM `#__content`
   WHERE `sectionid` = 1
     AND `state` = 1 ;
";
$db->setQuery($query);
$options = $db->loadAssocList();
foreach ( $options as $o ) {
  echo "<option value='".$o[id]."'>".$o[title]."</option>";
}
?>
    </select>
  </div>
  <div class="cfclear"> </div>
</div>
```

The resulting HTML will be a standard select drop-down that displays the list of titles and returns the article ID when the form is submitted. Here's what the form input looks like:

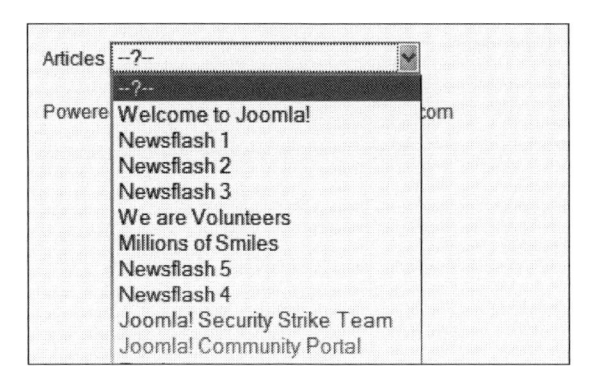

```
Articles  --?--
          --?--
  Powere  Welcome to Joomla!              com
          Newsflash 1
          Newsflash 2
          Newsflash 3
          We are Volunteers
          Millions of Smiles
          Newsflash 5
          Newsflash 4
          Joomla! Security Strike Team
          Joomla! Community Portal
```

Adding Advanced Features

A few of the options from the page source are shown:

```
<option value='1'>Welcome to Joomla!</option>
<option value='2'>Newsflash 1</option>
<option value='3'>Newsflash 2</option>
. . .
```

How it works...

We are loading the values of the `id` and `title` columns from the database record and then using a PHP for each loop to go through the results and add each `id` and `title` pair into an `<option>` tag.

There's more...

There are many occasions when we want to add select drop-downs into forms with long lists of options. Date and time selectors, country and language lists, and many others are frequently used.

We looked here to get the information from a database table which is simple and straightforward when the data is in a table or when the data can conveniently be stored in a table. It is the preferred solution for data such as article titles that can change from day to day.

There are a couple of other solutions that can also be useful:

- Creating numeric options lists directly from PHP
- Using arrays to manage option lists that change infrequently

Creating numeric options lists

Let's imagine that we need to create a set of six numeric drop-downs to select: day, month, year, hour, minute, and second. We could clearly do these with manually-created option lists but it soon gets boring creating sixty similar options.

There is a PHP method `range()` that lets us use a similar approach to the one in the recipe. For a range of zero to 60, we can use `range(0, 60)`. Now, the PHP part of our code becomes:

```
<div class="form_item">
  <div class="form_element cf_dropdown">
    <label class="cf_label" style="width: 150px;">
      Minutes</label>
    <select class="cf_inputbox validate-selection"
        id="minutes" size="1" name="minutes">
      <option value=''>--?--</option>
<?php
```

```
if (!$mainframe->isSite() ) {return;}
foreach ( range(0, 60) as $v ) {
  echo "<option value='$v'>$v</option>";
}
?>
    </select>
  </div>
  <div class="cfclear"> </div>
</div>
```

This is slightly simpler than the database `foreach` code, as we don't need the quotes round the array values.

This will work very nicely and we could repeat something very similar for each of the other five drop-downs. However, when we think about it, they will all be very similar and that's usually a sign that we can use more PHP to do some of the work for us.

Indeed we can create our own little PHP function to output blocks of HTML for us.

Looking at this example, there are four things that will change between the blocks—the label text, the name and id, and the range start and the range end. We can set these as variables in a PHP function:

```
<?php
if ( !$mainframe->isSite() ) {return;}
function createRangeSelect($label, $name, $start, $end) {
?>
<div class="form_item">
  <div class="form_element cf_dropdown">
    <label class="cf_label" style="width: 150px;">
      <?php echo $label; ?></label>
    <select class="cf_inputbox validate-selection"
        id="<?php echo $name; ?>" size="1"
        name="<?php echo $name; ?>">
      <option value=''>--?--</option>
<?php
  foreach ( range($start, $end) as $v ) {
    echo "<option value='$v'>$v</option>";
  }
?>
    </select>
  </div>
  <div class="cfclear"> </div>
</div>
<?php
}
?>
```

Adding Advanced Features

Notice that this is very similar to the previous code example. We've added the `function . . .` line at the start, the `}` at the end, and replaced the values with variable names.

> It's important to get the placement of the `<?php . . . ?>` tags right. Code inside the tags will be treated as PHP, outside them as HTML.

All that remains now is to call the function to generate our drop-downs:

```php
<?php
if (!$mainframe->isSite() ) {return;}
createRangeSelect('Day', 'day', 0, 31);
createRangeSelect('Month', 'month', 1, 12);
createRangeSelect('Year', 'year', 2000, 2020);
createRangeSelect('Hour', 'hour', 0, 24);
createRangeSelect('Minute', 'minute', 0, 60);
createRangeSelect('Second', 'second', 0, 60);
function createRangeSelect($label, $name, $start, $end) {
. . .
```

The result tells us that we have more work to do on the layout, but the form elements work perfectly well.

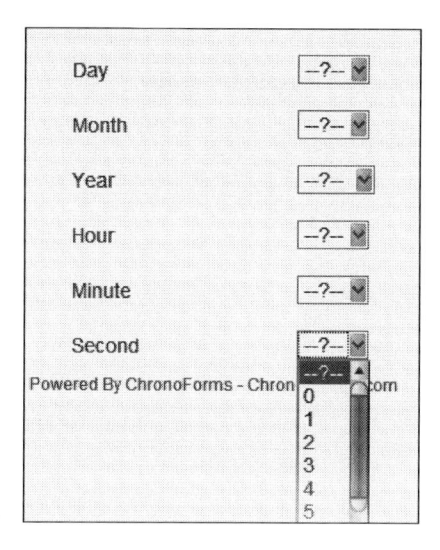

Creating a drop-down from an array

In the previous example, we used the PHP `range()` method to generate our options. This works well for numbers but not for text. Imagine that we have to manage a country list. These do change, but not frequently. So they are good candidates for keeping in an array in the Form HTML.

It's not too difficult to find pre-created PHP arrays of countries with a little Google research and it's probably easier to use one of these and correct it for your needs than to start from scratch.

> As we mentioned with the Article list, it's generally simpler and more flexible to use a list with standard IDs (we've used two-letter codes below). With countries, this can remove many problems with special characters and translations.

Here are the first few lines of a country list:

```
$countries = array(
  'AF'=>'Afghanistan',
  'AL'=>'Albania',
  'DZ'=>'Algeria',
  'AS'=>'American Samoa',
  . . .
);
```

Once we have this, it's easy to modify our `foreach . . .` loop to use it:

```
foreach ( $countries as $k => $v ) {
  echo "<option value='$k'>$v</option>";
}
```

> If you are going to use the country list in more than one form, then it may be worthwhile keeping it in a separate file that is included in the Form HTML. That way, any changes you make will be updated immediately in all of your forms.

Using Ajax to look up e-mail addresses

We mentioned in a much earlier recipe that we would come back to an Ajax example later. There's a reason for that—it's not very difficult to add Ajax functionality to ChronoForms, but it's not the easiest task in the world either.

We'll walk through a fairly simple example here which will provide you with the basic experience to build more complex applications. You will need some knowledge of JavaScript to follow through this recipe.

Normally, the only communication between the ChronoForms client (the user in their browser) and the server (the website host) is when a page is loaded or a form is submitted. Form HTML is sent to the client and a `$_POST` array of results is returned. Ajax is a technique, or a group of techniques, that enables communication while the user is browsing the page without them having to submit the form.

Adding Advanced Features

As usual, at the browser end the Ajax communication is driven by JavaScript and at the server end we'll be responding using PHP. Put simply, the browser asks a question, the server replies, then the browser shows the reply to the user.

For the browser JavaScript and the server PHP to communicate, there needs to be an agreed set of rules about how the information will be packaged. We'll be using the **JSON** (www.json.org) format.

The task we will work on will use our familiar newsletter form. We'll check to see if the user's e-mail is already listed in our user database. This is slightly artificial but the same code can easily be adapted to work with the other database tables and use more complex checks.

Getting ready

We'll need a form with an e-mail text input. The input `id` needs to be `email` for the following code to work:

```
<div class="form_item">
  <div class="form_element cf_textbox">
    <label class="cf_label"
      style="width: 150px;">Email</label>
    <input class="cf_inputbox" maxlength="150" size="30"
      title="" id="email" name="email" type="text" />
  </div>
  <div class="cfclear"> </div>
</div>
```

The form we use will also have a name text input and a submit button, but they are to make it look like a real form and aren't used in the Ajax coding.

How to do it . . .

We'll follow the action and start with the user action in the browser. We need to start our check when the user makes an entry in the e-mail input. So, we'll link our JavaScript to the `blur` event in that input. Here's the core of the code that goes in the Form JavaScript box:

```
// set the url to send the request to
var url = 'index.php?option=com_chronocontact
  &chronoformname=form_name&task=extra&format=raw';
// define 'email'
var email = $('email');
// set the Ajax call to run
// when the email field loses focus
email.addEvent('blur', function() {
  // Send the JSON request
  var jSonRequest = new Json.Remote(url, {
    . . .
  }).send({'email': email.value});
});
```

> Note that the long line starting with `var url = . . . &format=raw';` is all one line and should not have any breaks in it. You also need to replace `'form_name'` with the name of your form in this URL.

There really isn't too much to this. We are using the MooTools JSON functions and they make sending the code very simple.

The next step is to look at what happens back on the server.

The URL we used in the JavaScript includes the `task=extra` parameter. When ChronoForms sees this, it will ignore the normal Form Code and instead run the code from the **Extra Code** boxes at the bottom of the **Form Code** tab.

> By default, ChronoForms will execute the code from **Extra code 1**. If you need to access one of the other boxes, then use for example, `task=extra&extraid=3` to run the code from Extra Code box 3.

Now, we are working back on the server. So, we need to use PHP to unpack the Ajax message, check the database, and send a message back:

```php
<?php
// clean up the JSON message
$json = stripslashes($_POST['json']);
$json = json_decode($json);
$email = strtolower(trim($json->email));
// check that the email field isn't empty
$response = false;
if ( $email ) {
  // Check the database
  $db =& JFactory::getDBO();
  $query = "
    SELECT COUNT(*)
      FROM `#__users`
      WHERE LOWER(`email`) = ".$db->quote($email).";
  ";
  $db->setQuery($query);
  $response = (bool) !$db->loadResult();
}
$response = array('email_ok' => $response );
//send the reply
echo json_encode($response);
// stop the from running
$MyForm->stopRunning = true;
die;
?>
```

Adding Advanced Features

This code has three main parts:

1. To start with, we "unwrap" the JSON message.
2. Then, we check if it isn't empty and run the database query.
3. Lastly, we package up the reply and tidy up at the end to stop any more form processing from this request.

The result we send will be `array('email_ok' => $response)` where `$response` will be either `true` or `false`. This is probably the simplest JSON message possible, but is enough for our purpose.

> Note that here, `true` means that this e-mail is not listed and is OK to use.

The third step is to go back to the form JavaScript and decide how we are going to respond to the JSON reply. Again, we'll keep it simple and just change the background color of the box—red if the e-mail is already in use (or isn't a valid e-mail) or green if the entry isn't in use and is OK to submit.

Here's the code snippet to do this using the `onComplete` parameter of the MooTools JSON function:

```
onComplete: function(r) {
  // check the result and set the background color
  if ( r.email_ok ) {
    email.setStyle('background-color', 'green');
  } else {
    email.setStyle('background-color', 'red');
  }
}
```

Instead of (or as well as) changing the background color, we could make other CSS changes, display a message, show a pop-up alert, or almost anything else.

Lastly let's put the two parts of the client-side JavaScript together with a little more code to make it run smoothly and to check that there is a valid e-mail before sending the JSON request.

```
window.addEvent('domready', function() {
  // set the url to send the request to
  var url = 'index.php?option=com_chronocontact
    &chronoformname=form_name&task=extra&format=raw';
  var email = $('email');
  email.addEvent('blur', function() {
    // clear any background color from the input
    email.setStyle('background-color', 'white');
```

```
      // check that the email address is valid
      regex = /^([^@\s]+)@((?:[-a-z0-9]+\.)+[a-z]{2,})$/i;
      var value = email.value.trim();
      if ( value.length > 6 && regex.test(value) ) {
        // if all is well send the JSON request
        var jSonRequest = new Json.Remote(url, {
          onComplete: function(r) {
            // check the result and set the background color
            if ( r.email_ok ) {
              email.setStyle('background-color', 'green');
            } else {
              email.setStyle('background-color', 'red');
            }
          }
        }).send({'email': email.value});
      } else {
        // if this isn't a valid email set background color red
        email.setStyle('background-color', 'red');
      }
    });
  });
```

> Note that the long line starting with `var url = . . . &format=raw';` is all one line and should not have any breaks in it. You also need to replace `form_name` with the name of your form in this URL.

Make sure both the code blocks are in place in the **Form JavaScript** box and in the **Extra Code 1 box**, save, and publish your form. Then, test it to make sure that the code is working OK. The Ajax may take a second or two to respond but once you move out of the e-mail, input by tabbing on to another input or clicking somewhere else; the background colour should go red or green.

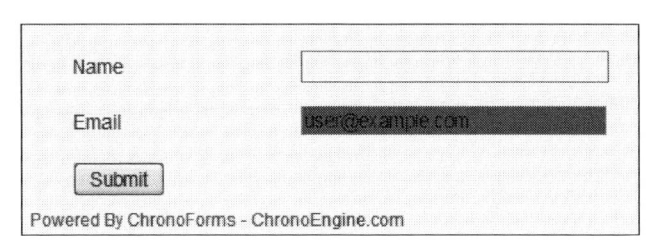

Adding Advanced Features

How it works...

As far as the Ajax and JSON parts of this are concerned, all we can say here is that it works. You'll need to dig into the MooTools, Ajax, or JSON documents to find out more.

From the point of view of ChronoForms, the "clever" bit is the ability to interpret the URL that the Ajax message uses. We ignored most of it at the time but the JavaScript included this long URL (with the query string broken up into separate parameters):

```
index.php
?option=com_chronocontact
&chronoformname=form_name
&task=extra
&format=raw
```

The `option` parameter is the standard Joomla! way to identify which extension to pass the URL to.

The `chronoformname` parameter tells ChronoForms which form to pass the URL to.

The `task=extra` parameter tells ChronoForms that this URL is a little out of the ordinary (you may have noticed that forms usually have `&task=send` in the onSubmit URL). When ChronoForms sees this, it will pass the URL to the **Extra Code** box for processing and bypass the usual OnSubmit processing.

Lastly, the `format=raw` parameter tells Joomla! to show the resulting code without any extra formatting and without adding the template code. This means that all that is sent back is just the JSON message. Without it we'd have to dig the message out from loads of surrounding HTML we don't need.

Getting information from a DB table to include in your form

ChonoForms' DB Connection provides a useful tool for saving to the database but is more limited when it comes to getting data back again and using it to control forms or to display for editing. The Profile plug-in lets you recover a single record, and ChronoForms' sister product, **ChronoConnectivity**, is intended to help you display longer lists of results.

In this recipe, we'll look at getting information from one or more database tables for use in our Form HTML. Very similar code can be used to get information for use in other parts of a ChronoForms form, for example into an e-mail template.

Getting ready

There isn't any obvious preparation for this recipe. What we'll do is look at each of the common types of form input in turn and see how to display the extracted information in the Form HTML.

How to do it...

1. Getting the information from the database

    We've seen several examples of this in this book already, most recently in the drop-down recipe at the start of this chapter. The code we used there was as follows:

    ```
    $db =& JFactory::getDBO();
    $query = "
       SELECT `id`, `title`
         FROM `#__content`
         WHERE `sectionid` = 1
           AND `state` = 1 ;
    ";
    $db->setQuery($query);
    $options = $db->loadAssocList();
    ```

    The first line of this calls the Joomla! database object to give us a connection to the database that Joomla! is using.

    > See the *There's more...* section below if you need to connect to another database.

    The next set of lines define a `$query` variable that is the MySQL instruction that will be used to extract the data from the database. This is a simple example of getting two columns from the Joomla! `jos_content` table. To get all the columns, we can change one line to read `SELECT *`.

    > Much more complex queries are possible but they are beyond our scope here. See the Joomla! documents and the MySQL manual for more info.

    The last two lines set the query and then execute it, getting our results back into a `$options` array in this case. There are several different methods that you can use to execute the query depending on the form in which you want the results. There's a helpful page on the Joomla! docs that tells you what choices you have (see the *See also* section below).

Adding Advanced Features

You can find some more examples of Joomla! database queries here and many more in the ChronoForms forums.

The example above extracted several records from the table to create a set of options. In the rest of this recipe, we'll assume that we've extracted a single record into a `$cf_data` object so that we can address column values as `$cf_data->column_name`.

2. Adding a value to text or hidden inputs

   This is probably the most common and the easiest value to restore.

   ```
   <input type='text' . . .
     value='<?php echo $cf_data->column_name; ?>' />
   <input type='hidden' . . .
     value='<?php echo $cf_data->column_name; ?>' />
   ```

3. Adding a value to a textarea

   Very similar to the text input but the value goes between the tags:

   ```
   <textarea . . . ><?php echo $cf_data->column_name; ?></textarea>
   ```

4. Adding a value to radio buttons

   The remaining form elements are more complicated because they don't take simple text values but instead need to be marked as checked or unchecked.

   ```
   <?php
   $c1 = $c2 = '';
   if ( $cf_data->column_name == 'xxx' ) {
     $c1 = "checked='checked'";
   } elseif ( $cf_data->column_name == 'yyy' ) {
     $c2 = "checked='checked'";
   }
   ?>
   <input type='radio' value='xxx' . . . <?php echo $c1; ?> />
   <input type='radio' value='yyy' . . . <?php echo $c2; ?> />
   ```

   Here we check to see if the result matches the value of the radio input and if it does then we set `$c1` or `$c2` to show the corresponding input as selected.

5. Adding a value to checkbox groups

   Checkbox groups can have many buttons and all or none of them can be checked so it's easier to use a loop to check them than a series of if statements. The result has also probably been stored in the database table as a comma separated string like `aaa,ccc,eee` that we will need to unpack.

   ```
   <?php
   // unpack the results into an array
   $result_array = explode(',', $cf_data->column_name);
   // create an array matching the check-boxes
   $checkbox_array = array('1' => 'aaa', . . . '6' => 'fff');
   ```

```
foreach ( $checkbox_array as $k => $v ) {
  if ( in_array($v, $result_array) {
    $c[$k] = "checked='checked'";
  } else {
    $c[$k] = "";
  }
}
?>
<input type='checkbox' value='aaa' . . .
  <?php echo $c[1]; ?> />
<input type='checkbox' value='bbb' . . .
  <?php echo $c[2]; ?> />
. . .
<input type='checkbox' value='fff' . . .
  <?php echo $c[6]; ?> />
```

Although this is more complicated, it is following essentially the same method as we used for the radio buttons above. The big difference is that we are using an array to tell us what checkboxes there are that might be checked. We need to do this to let us create all of the checkboxes correctly.

6. Adding a value to a select drop-down

    The code for a select drop-down is very similar. Rather than repeating it with just the minor changes, we'll go back and modify the code from the first recipe in this chapter to create the options using PHP and set one value as selected.

    > To use the code with a multi-select drop-down requires some small changes to be more like the checkbox code above.

    Let's start with the code for creating the drop-down options from a country array:

    ```
    foreach ( $countries as $k => $v ) {
      echo "<option value='$k'>$v</option>";
    }
    ```

    Here's how we adjust this to set a particular value. Let's assume that we have the saved value as $country:

    ```
    foreach ( $countries as $k => $v ) {
      $s = '';
      if ( $country == $k ) {
        $s = "selected='selected'";
      }
      echo "<option value='$k' $s >$v</option>";
    }
    ```

    That's it!

Adding Advanced Features

How it works...

Each of these methods uses a combination of PHP, MySQL, and HTML to add customised values to your forms. This combination of server-side code, database, and browser code is very powerful and forms the core of any CMS. These simple examples can be extended to make very sophisticated applications based around ChronoForms.

The critical steps that are at work here are: using PHP, as the web page is being built to pull specific information from the database, and then using that information to customise parts of the HTML displayed to the user in the browser.

See also

- There's a Joomla! docs article "How to use the database classes in your script" that is a useful reference to some of the Joomla! database methods http://docs.joomla.org/How_to_use_the_database_classes_in_your_script

Show a form in a light-box

There are many kinds of pop-up boxes or light-boxes available to use with Joomla!. In this recipe, we'll use the standard Joomla! light-box (called **Squeezebox**) to show a form in a pop-up box. This approach should be easily adaptable to other similar boxes.

Thanks to Vicki Payne for working out how to do this and posting her results in the ChronoForms forum. We'll use an improved version of her approach here.

Getting ready

Any form will pretty much do, provided that is it small enough to sit comfortably inside the Squeezebox. Here, we'll use our familiar newsletter signup form.

You'll also need the ChronoForms Module if it isn't already installed.

How to do it...

1. First off create a new form; we'll need two forms to make this work smoothly.

    We're going to use this second form to create a module with a link to launch the Squeezebox. In the Form HTML put the following code:

    ```
    <?php
    JHTML::_('behavior.modal');
    ?>
    <a class="modal"
    ```

```
href="index.php?option=com_chronocontact&amp;
chronoformname=form_name&amp;tmpl=component"
rel="{handler: 'iframe', size: {x: 400, y: 200}}"
>Subscribe to our newsletter</a>
```

Make sure that you have the correct value for `form_name` (the form that will appear in the Squeezebox) and that the `href='...'` code is all in one unbroken line. Set the `x` & `y` values to the size of the box that suits your form.

2. Save the form and go to the **Admin | Extensions | Module Manager**. Create a new module of type **ChronoForms**, add the name of this form, enable the module, and save it.

3. Browse to a page where the module is displayed and you will see a link in the module. Click the link and your form will open in a Squeezebox.

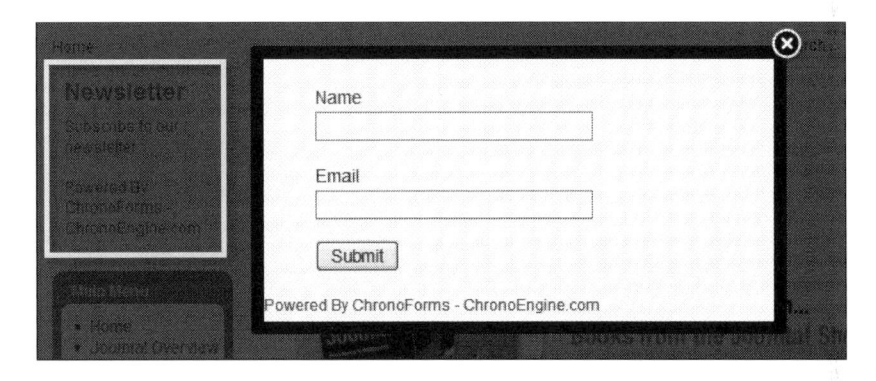

You can see the form open in the Squeezebox and, on the left in the background, the module with the link that opens the form.

This looks neat and works well, but with one exception. After you submit the form, the "Thank You" page shows up inside the Squeezebox with the complete Joomla! template.

We avoided this with the form by adding `tmpl=component` to the URL link. To fix it for the Thank You page, we need to do the same thing for the OnSubmit URL for the form. If we look at the page source, we can see that the OnSubmit URL is `http://example.com/index.php?option=com_chronocontact&amp;task=send&chronoformname=form_name`.

This is hard-coded in ChronoForms and we can't change it directly through the form settings. But we can over-write it using the Submit URL box on the **Form Editor | General** tab.

4. So, we can put this into the **Submit URL** box at `http://example.com/index.php?option=com_chronocontact&amp;task=send&amp;chronoformname=form_name&amp;tmpl=component`.

Adding Advanced Features

[💡 Note: We've corrected a little ChronoForms bug in this version by replacing `&chronoformname=` with `&amp;chronoformname=`.]

5. Then, put a "Thank You" message into the **Form Code | On Submit after** box:

   ```
   <div style='text-align:center; padding:12px;' >
   <h3>Thanks for subscribing</h3>
   </div>
   ```

6. Try submitting the form again and we will have a nice, clear message:

How it works...

Here we are using the second ChronoForm not as a form, but as a way of adding some PHP into the page using a module. To trigger the Squeezebox, we need to give Joomla! the instruction to load the code:

```
JHTML::_('behavior.modal');
```

Some Joomla! templates may already include this instruction, in which case you could use a standard module to create the link. However, it's perfectly safe if the instruction is given twice, in the template and again in the module.

We can't do this in the form itself as it isn't loaded when the page with the link is loaded. Most of the Joomla! elements—articles, modules, and so on won't allow PHP codes like this (though there are other specialist extensions like **Jumi** that do support this).

This is one of those occasions when we can use ChronoForms capabilities in a slightly unorthodox way to get the result we want.

There's more...

Keeping our options open
Putting the URL in the Submit URL box works well, but has one drawback. If we try to use the form without the Squeezebox, the "Thank You" page will still display without the template and users will see a blank screen mainly.

To get round this, we need to check if the form is being called normally or modally. The easiest difference to spot is the `tmpl=component` in the URL. We can add a few lines of PHP to the Form HTML to detect this and set a hidden input value:

```
<?php
if ( !$mainframe->isSite() ) { return; }
$modal = JRequest::getString('tmpl', 'false', 'get');
?>
<input type='hidden' id='modal' name='modal'
  value='<?php echo $modal; ?>' />
```

Then, we can use some JavaScript in the **Form JavaScript** box to read this and change the Form Action URL when the form is loaded:

```
window.addEvent('domready', function() {
  var modal = $('modal').value;
  if ( modal == 'component' ) {
    var url = $('ChronoContact_form_name');
    var action = url.getProperty('action');
    url.setProperty('action', action+'&amp;tmpl=component');
  }
});
```

This script snippet checks to see if the `modal` hidden input is set to `component`. If it is, then it gets the form action URL and adds `&amp;tmpl=component` to the end.

Now we can use the same form either normally or modally in the Squeezebox.

Adding PHP to the page
We added the required PHP to the page using the ChronoForms module. This is OK if we want to show the link in a module (or in an article using the ChronoForms plug-in/Mambot). However, if we don't want to use do this, how can we add the PHP?

It's possible to simply add the line to the template `index.php` page but this will load it on every page whether we need it or not.

Adding Advanced Features

Another approach is to add it into a hidden module. That is a module that doesn't display anything. You can tuck this away in the template footer or debug locations, and it will still load the PHP that we need.

If you have a licensed copy of ChronoForms then the code we put in the module above—without the link—will work OK. Otherwise you'll need to use Jumi or some other extension that will permit PHP.

> Note: The unlicensed copy of ChronoForms shows the tag line at the bottom of the form and so it won't be "invisible" on your page.

Tracking site information

Sometimes, we want to track where users have come from, or capture other information about them as they move around the site. This may be to customise what we show them, or to build up our knowledge of how the site is used in some way.

We've seen some parts of this earlier in the book and in this recipe, we'll revisit some of that content.

Getting ready

Nothing special is required; these techniques will work with any form.

The recipe below looks at several different ways that you might want to track your user. Pick out the one (or maybe two) that will be most useful to you.

How to do it...

1. If you need to track the user

   Fortunately, Joomla! makes this very easy for us as Joomla! does the basic tracking. When you visit a Joomla! Site, a "session" is created that contains some personal identifiers. This follows you as you browse the site until the current visit ends.

   Among the information saved in the session is the Joomla! User ID, which in turn, lets us access the Joomla! User Object. Now, if the user is a guest, the User ID will be 0 so this information is of limited use. If they have signed in, then the User ID will be their Joomla! User ID.

   You can access the Joomla! User Object with this PHP

   ```
   $user =& JFactory::getUser();
   ```

   The user information is then available as, for example `$user->name`, `$user->email`.

2. If you need to track the article the user was reading

   We saw how to identify an article in Chapter 6 using this code in the form HTML:

   ```
   <?php
   $article_id =& JRequest::getInt('id', '', 'get');
   ?>
   <input type='hidden' name='article_id'
     value='<?php echo $article_id; ?>' />
   ```

   When the form is submitted, we can access this value and use it. We might, for instance, want to get the article title and we can look this up in the `jos_content` database table:

   ```
   <?php
   $article_id = JRequest::getInt('article_id', '', 'post');
   if ( $article_id ) {
     $db =& JFactory::getDBO();
     $query = "
       SELECT `title`
         FROM `#__content`
         WHERE `id` = '$article_id';
   ";
   $db->setQuery($query);
   $article_title = $db->loadResult();
   ```

3. If you need to track the menu that the page was called from

   If you need to know the menu item of the page, perhaps to match the content or formatting of a form to a section of your site, then you can get the menu ItemID in exactly the same way as the article id in the last section using `ItemID` instead of `id`.

4. Using a hidden menu to track a user

   Sometimes, you want to control the template or module display of a form without having the form attached to a menu item. You can do this by using a "hidden" menu.

   In **Site Admin | Menu Manager**, create a new menu named **hidden**.

   Click the **Menu Items** link for the new menu and create a new ChronoForms menu link. Make sure your link is published, and **Display in** is set for your new hidden menu.

   Now go to **Site Admin | Module Manager** and create a new module with type **Menu**. In **Details**, set up the **Position** as **hidden**; it's probably not in the drop-down list, but you can type it in. This will leave **Order** empty, but that's OK. In the **Parameters | Menu Name** drop-down, select your dummy menu.

   Now your form has a valid menu link (it won't be rendered by your template, but that does not matter). Make sure your link to the form uses this new URL.

Adding Advanced Features

Controlling e-mails from form inputs

Back in *Chapter 2, E-mailing Form Results,* we saw how to send e-mails to different people depending on what is in the form. It is also possible to turn e-mails on or off or to send different e-mails depending on what is in the form.

Here, we'll look at an example where there are three different e-mails and which ones are sent is controlled by three checkboxes in the form.

Getting ready

Nothing special is required except that your form has the appropriate check-boxes and that there are three Email Setups.

How to do it...

1. Here's the HTML for the checkboxes:

```
<div class="form_item">
  <div class="form_element cf_checkbox">
    <label class="cf_label" style="width: 150px;">
      Click Me to Edit</label>
    <div class="float_left">
      <input value="1" title="" class="radio" id="check00"
        name="check0[]" type="checkbox" />
      <label for="check00" class="check_label"
        >e-mail 1</label><br />
      <input value="2" title="" class="radio" id="check01"
        name="check0[]" type="checkbox" />
      <label for="check01" class="check_label"
        >e-mail 2</label><br />
      <input value="3" title="" class="radio" id="check02"
        name="check0[]" type="checkbox" />
      <label for="check02" class="check_label"
        >e-mail 3</label><br />
    </div>
  </div>
  <div class="cfclear"> </div>
</div>
```

As you can see, the three checkboxes are in the check0 array and have values 1, 2, and 3 respectively. We also have the three Email Setups that ChronoForms will automatically have numbered 1, 2, and 3 starting from the first Setup. All of the Email Setups should be disabled. That is set to **Enabled=No** in the **Email Setup | Properties** box.

2. In the form OnSubmit Before box, we use this code to enable the e-mails that we want to send. ChronoForms keeps the e-mail settings in the `CFEMails` object. So, we start by accessing that, then look through the `check0` array deciding if we turn the e-mails on or not.

```
<?php
$MyFormEmails =& CFEMails::getInstance($MyForm->formrow->id);
$check0 = JRequest::getString('check0', '', 'post');
if ( $check0 ) {
  $check0 = explode(', ', $check0);
  foreach ($check0 as $v ) {
    $MyFormEmails->setEmailData($v, 'enabled', true);
  }
}
?>
```

You can see that the last line of code is setting `enabled= true` for one of the e-mails.

There's more...

Disabling e-mails

You could turn e-mails off too by using:

```
$MyFormEmails->setEmailData('email_id, 'enabled', false);
```

Here, `email_id` is the ID of a particular Email Setup.

Changing the attached files

Like the e-mails above, ChronoForms keeps the file attachments in the `CFUploads` object for the form. Once we have access to that, we can add files paths to the `$MyUploads->attachments` array to have them attached to the e-mail.

This time, the values of our checkboxes identify the files that we want to attach: `file_1`, `file_2`, and so on. Then, we can loop through the `check0` array, making sure that the files exist before marking them to be attached.

Here's the kind of code that we would use in the **OnSubmit Before Email** box. The exact code to use will depend on where your files are and the way your form is set up.

```
<?php
$MyUploads =& CFUploads::getInstance($MyForm->formrow->id);
// set the path to the files folder
$path = DS.'path_to'.DS.'files'.DS.'folder'.DS;
// load the Joomla! file libraries
```

Adding Advanced Features

```
jimport('joomla.filesystem.file');
// get the form results for the checkboxes
$check0 = JRequest::get('check0', array());
foreach ( $check0 as $file ) {
  // check if the file exists
  if ( JFile::exists($path.$file) {
    // add the file to the attachments
    $MyUploads->attachments[] = $path.$file;
  }
}
?>
```

> Note: Because ChronoForms only keeps one `CFUploads` object for the form, you can't easily combine this with the code in the recipe and have different files attached to different e-mails. That is possible but not with the ChronoForms built-in e-mail sender; instead you'd need to hand-code the sending.

See also

- Refer *Chapter 2, E-mailing Form Results* for basic information on Email Setups.

Building a complex multi-page form

We've looked at all kinds of recipes through this book so far, mostly using simple forms to keep the recipes short and clear. For this last but one recipe, we'll step through the creation of a ChronoForms-based application. We won't go into all the details; most of those are covered elsewhere. We will instead focus on the user workflow.

The brief here is to create a form application that allows users to create mini websites using a Joomla! article with page breaks, so that it appears as five pages. Page 1 is an introduction that identifies three key issues, pages 2-4 look at each issue in more detail, and page 5 looks at products and/or services that might help with the issues.

Getting ready

We'll start from scratch with just ChronoForms.

How to do it...

1. Setting up the form

   We're going to use a separate form for each of the steps linked together by a mother form and the Multi-Page plug-in.

   The forms themselves are fairly straightforward as all of them are created with the ChronoForms Wizard (steps 2-4 are identical, apart from the form and input names).

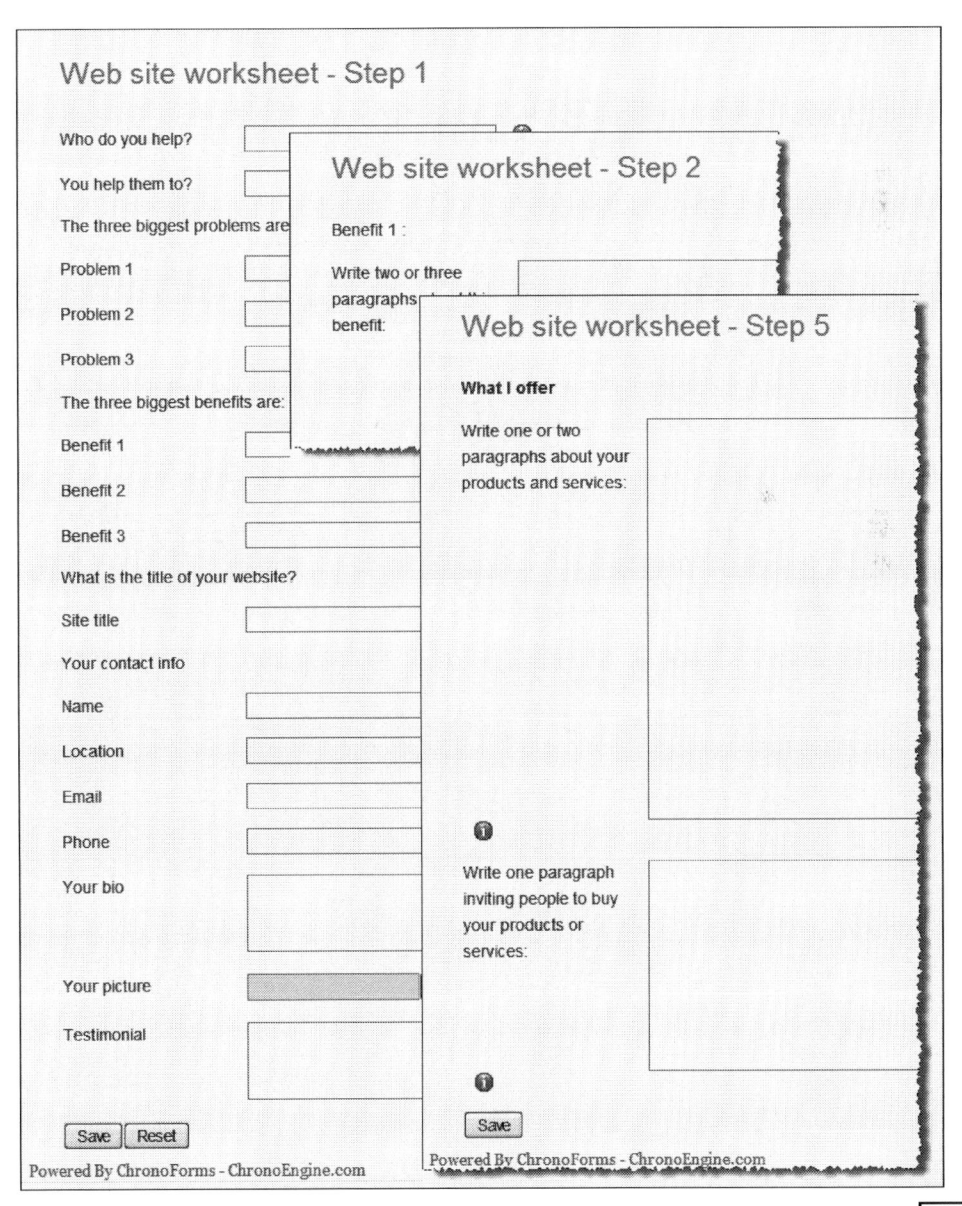

Web site worksheet - Step 1

- Who do you help?
- You help them to?
- The three biggest problems are:
  - Problem 1
  - Problem 2
  - Problem 3
- The three biggest benefits are:
  - Benefit 1
  - Benefit 2
  - Benefit 3
- What is the title of your website?
- Site title
- Your contact info
  - Name
  - Location
  - Email
  - Phone
  - Your bio
  - Your picture
  - Testimonial

[Save] [Reset]

Powered By ChronoForms - ChronoEngine.com

Web site worksheet - Step 2

- Benefit 1 :
- Write two or three paragraphs about the benefit:

Web site worksheet - Step 5

- **What I offer**
- Write one or two paragraphs about your products and services:
- Write one paragraph inviting people to buy your products or services:

[Save]

Powered By ChronoForms - ChronoEngine.com

Adding Advanced Features

These five child forms are named `web_1`, `web_2`, `web_3`, `web_4`, and `web_5`. The sixth form, the mother form named `web_creator`, has no Form HTML but is used to tie these forms together using the Multi-Page plug-in configured on the Mother Form (and only on the Mother Form).

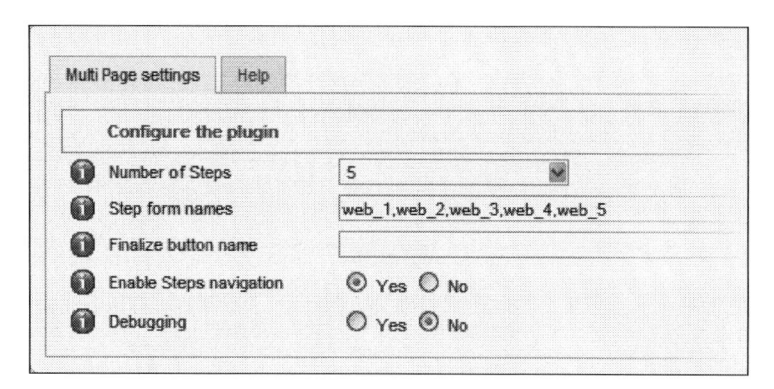

Multi Page settings	Help
Configure the plugin	
Number of Steps	5
Step form names	web_1,web_2,web_3,web_4,web_5
Finalize button name	
Enable Steps navigation	● Yes ○ No
Debugging	○ Yes ● No

2. Now, we have our forms created and linked together. Next, we need a database table to store the results. They are ultimately going to end up in articles but we also want to store the raw data as well. So, we'll create a single table for that. The easy way is to temporarily copy the Form HTML from all of the steps into one form, to use the ChronoForms **Create Table** icon taking care to remove any duplicates, and to set appropriate column types.

   Once that is done, we can start to follow the work flow process through the form steps.

3. Step 1 will need to save its data to our new table. So, we setup a **DB Connection** and we'll need to configure the file upload on the **File Uploads** tab. That's completely straightforward.

4. Step 2 is a little different because we want to use the data from one of the inputs from step 1 and display it as a part of the page title. So at the start of the Form HTML, we'll get the information that ChronoForms has stored in the User session (this is saved there by the Multi-Page plug-in). Here's the code we need (note that `web_creator`, the name of the mother form, is used to identify the form data we need):

```
<?php
if ( !$mainframe->isSite() ) { return; }
$session =& JFactory::getSession();
$posted = $session->get('chrono_formpages_data_web_creator',
array(),
   md5('chrono'));
?>
```

This puts all of the results so far into the $posted array. We then access this to show the form header as a reminder to the user:

```
<div class="form_item">
  <div class="form_element cf_text">
    <span class="cf_text">Benefit 1 :
      <strong><?php echo $posted['benefit_1']; ?></strong></span>
  </div>
  <div class="cfclear"> </div>
</div>
```

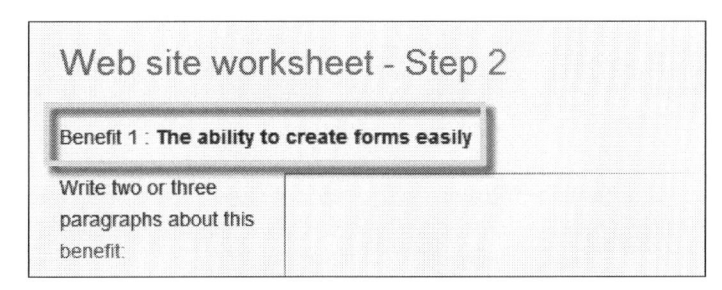

Web site worksheet - Step 2

Benefit 1 : **The ability to create forms easily**

Write two or three paragraphs about this benefit:

Now that we have saved the data to the database table, we also need to track the record using the value of the cf_id column. ChronoForms has saved this for us, so we just need a second PHP snippet in our **Form HTML** to put the value into a hidden input.

```
<?php
$MyForm =& CFChronoForm::getInstance();
$data = $MyForm->tablerow['jos_chronoforms_web_1'];
?>
<input type='hidden' name='cf_id'
  value='<?php echo $data->cf_id; ?>' />
```

> Note that you need to insert the correct name for the database table that you are using.

Now, when the step 2 form is submitted, the information will be added to the same record in the table.

Adding Advanced Features

5. Step 3, step 4, and step 5 are functionally identical to step 2; only the input names are different. So we don't need to spend time on them here. Just remember that the value of `cf_id` needs to be carried forward each time in a hidden field, though now it will be in the `$posted` array so we can use that to set it, just like the header.

6. The last step is to assemble the data we have gathered into our Joomla! article. To do this, we'll go back to the mother form.

    While designing multi-page forms, it's important to think of the mother form as wrapping the child-forms. So, you start out by calling the mother form, each of the child forms then runs them (with its database saves, e-mails, and so on, if any are set), and then finally the back-end of the mother form runs. It's that final wrapping-up process that we'll use now.

    On the final step, we start by cleaning up the replies a little and then we re-assemble them all into one long text string that will become the main body of our Joomla! Article. We'll do this in the **OnSubmit Before Email** box of the mother form.

    Remember that **Send Emails** needs to be set to **Yes** in the mother form **General** tab for this code to be run even though we may not be sending any e-mails.

```php
<?php
if ( ! $mainframe->isSite() ) { return; }
$order    = array("\r\n", "\n", "\r");
foreach ( $posted as $k => $v ) {
   $posted[$k] = str_replace($order, '<br />', $v);
}
$_POST['fulltext'] = "<h2>".$posted['site_title']."</h2>
<h3>I help ".$posted['who']." to ".$posted['what'].".</h3> <h3>The
three biggest problems in this market are:</h3>
<ul><li>".$posted['problem_1']." </li>
<li>".$posted['problem_2']." </li>
<li>".$posted['problem_3']." </li></ul>

<h3>The three biggest benefits I offer are:</h3>
<ul><li>".$posted['benefit_1']."</li>
<li>".$posted['benefit_2']."</li>
<li>".$posted['benefit_3']."</li></ul>
<h3>About me:</h3>
<ul><li>".$posted['ci_name']."</li>
<li>".$posted['ci_location']."</li>
<li>".$posted['ci_email']."</li>
<li>".$posted['ci_phone']." </li></ul>
<p>".$posted['bio']."</p>
<h3>What other people say:</h3>
```

```php
<p>".$posted['testimonial']."</p>
<p>// picture to be added </p>
<hr title='Benefit 1' alt='Benefit 1'
  class='system-pagebreak' />
<h2>".$posted['benefit_1']."</h2>
<p>".$posted['benefit_exp_1']."</p>
<hr title='Benefit 2' alt='Benefit 2'
  class='system-pagebreak' />
<h2>".$posted['benefit_2']."</h2>
<p>".$posted['benefit_exp_2']."</p>
<hr title='Benefit 3' alt='Benefit 3'
  class='system-pagebreak' />
<h2>".$posted['benefit_3']."</h2>
<p>".$posted['benefit_exp_3']."</p>
<hr title='Products and Services' alt='Products and Services'
  class='system-pagebreak' />
<h2>My Products and Services</h2>
<p>".$posted['prod_serv']."</p>
<p>".$posted['invitation']."</p>
";
?>
```

> Note that we use lines like `<hr title='Products and Services' alt='Products and Services' class='system-pagebreak' />` to break the article into pages.

Next, we add the additional values that we need to create a valid article entry:

```php
$_POST['sectionid'] = '5';
$_POST['catid'] = '34';
$_POST['id'] = '';
$_POST['state'] = '1';
$_POST['created'] = date("Y-m-d H:i:s");
$_POST['title'] =
  JRequest::getString('site_title', 'My website', 'post');
$user =& JFactory::getUser();
if ( $user->id ) {
  $_POST['created_by'] = $user->id;
}
$_POST['created_by_alias'] =
  JRequest::getString('ci_name', 'Me', 'post');
?>
```

Adding Advanced Features

These identify the Section, Category, Created date, the User ID, and so on.

7. Now, we want to save this information to the Joomla! `jos_content` table and possibly, we may also want to update our own raw data table at the same time. ChronoForms' ability to support multiple DB Connections makes this simple—we just select both tables in the **DB Connection** select box for the mother form.

8. Lastly, we want to show a "Thank You" message to the user so that we can add that in the Mother Form **On Submit After Email** box:

    ```
    <div style='border:1px solid silver; padding:6px;'>
    <h3>Next . . .</h3>
    <p>In a moment click on the 'Sites' menu item above. You will see a list of mini-sites including the one you have just created. Click on the title of your site to see it.</p>
    <p>At the top is a contents list that will let you see the individual pages, or click the 'All pages' link to see all the content on a single page.</p>
    <p>You can use the small icons at the top right of the page to (a) create a pdf version (b) print out or (c) mail a link to a friend.</p>
    <p>Enjoy!<br />
    Bob</p>
    </div>
    ```

9. That's it! Of course, there are many tweaks and improvements that we could make but we have a functioning multi-page form creating quite a complex Joomla! article.

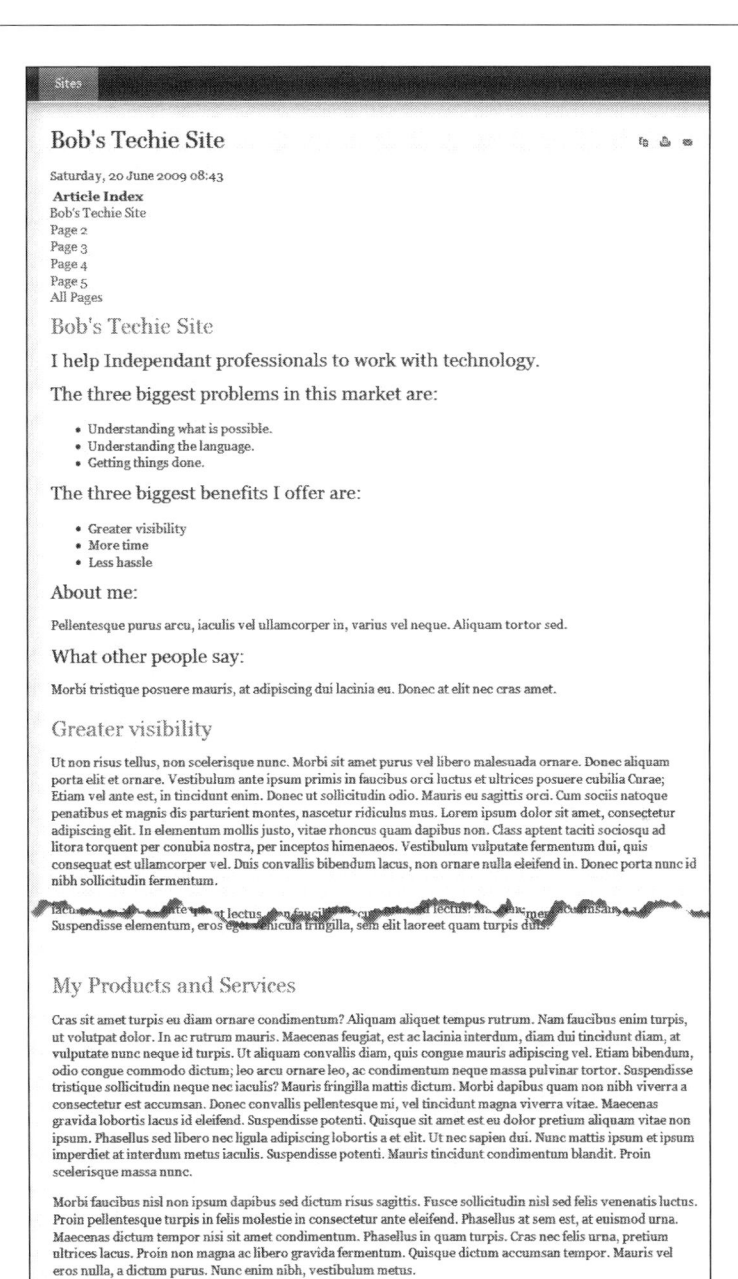

See also

▶ This example draws on many of the other recipes in this book and we have not repeated all of the details here. Check out the earlier recipes if you have any queries.

Adding Advanced Features

Troubleshooting problems with forms

So we are almost at the end; the last recipe in the book is about things to do when things go wrong. As we've seen, ChronoForms is a complex and flexible extension that offers many ways to get things done with Joomla!, and almost as many ways for them to fail.

We'll look here at a few techniques that can help sort out problems when they arise. You have, of course, already taken a big step by getting this book.

Troubleshooting is as much an art as a science. A logical approach will help, and so will experience with Joomla! and with website coding. While the recipe here has a sequence of steps, it should be viewed as a list of suggestions for you to try rather than a rigid procedure to work through.

How to do it...

1. Removing Submit URLs

    If there is an entry in the **Submit URL** box on the **Form Editor | General** tab, then Joomla! will submit the form to that address. ChronoForms will never see it and therefore can't send e-mails, save data, or do anything else.

    So remove anything from that box unless you know *exactly* what you are doing.

2. Using form Debug

    On the **Form Editor | General** tab, there is a **Debug** setting that you can set to **ON** or **OFF**. To debug your form, turn it to **ON**. Then, when you submit your form, ChronoForms will show several things:

    - First, if you have an Email Setup, there will be a dummy e-mail.
    - Then, there are a series of debug messages in a blue box that show step-by-step what ChronoForms is doing.
    - The last debug message will show the value of any **ReDirect URL** you have set. **Automatic ReDirection** is stopped so that the deBug messages display. There's a link that you can click to continue with the redirection if you need to.

    Check these messages carefully; there is a lot of useful information there.

3. Checking the submitted values

    The data from your form is submitted in the `$_POST` array a series of "key" and "value" pairs.

    One of the blue debug messages (normally #5) shows the `$_POST` array. Look carefully at the results in the array and see if they are what you are expecting. Sometimes, results have a different format or an input is misnamed.

> Checkboxes often cause problems. If they are not checked, they will not appear in the `$_POST` array. If they are checked, then the value will be shown. If they don't appear, it's probably because no value attribute has been set in the input tag.

4. Checking e-mail results

    Look at the dummy e-mail; there should be valid entries for both the **From** and **To** e-mail addresses. You should also be able to see the results from some or all of the form inputs in the body of the e-mail: Are these what you expect?

    > Refer the recipe *Geting your e-mails delivered safely* in Chapter 2.

5. Checking the ReDirect URL

    If you have a `ReDirect URL` set, then it will be shown in the last debug message (it's linked so that you can click to complete the redirection if you need to). Check that the link is exactly what you need; it's easy to miss out critical separators or include a little typo.

6. Checking that the plug-ins are working

    The debug support isn't quite so good here, but many of the plug-ins have their own debug switches You should turn them on to get some useful (though sometimes cryptic) information displayed.

7. Checking problems with File Uploads

    Please see *Chapter 8, Uploading Files from your Forms*.

8. Checking the DB Connection

    The Debug report doesn't help with the DB Connections. So, you need to look at the database table itself. You can do this with the ChronoForms **Table Manager** or **Data Viewer**; these are simple but effective tools. If they don't give you what you need, then use a better database tools. PHPMyAdmin is almost always available if you have access; or the EasySQL Joomla! extension will run from the Site Admin area.

    The most common database problems are:

    - The columns you need don't exist in the table
    - There is a dash, space, or other special character in one of the form input names or table column names that breaks the ChronoForms database code
    - The query is incorrectly quoted—you need backticks ` `` ` for table and column names and single quotes `' '` for text strings (or better use the Joomla! `$db->quote()` and `$db->nameQuote()` methods)

Adding Advanced Features

If the database error remains elusive, then set Site **Debug** to **On** in the **Site | Global Configuration | System** tab. Then, all the MySQL queries are sent as output to the template debug module, which is usually at the bottom of the page.

Browse through the list until you find the query that relates to your form and check it carefully. Copying and pasting it into PHPMyAdmin may give you more useful error reports.

9. Checking problems with form layout

    The default ChronoForms HTML and CSS is reasonably good but it won't necessarily work with all templates.

    Here, a good website debugging tool is invaluable. **FireBug** in FireFox is excellent; there are tools now being included in or developed for Chrome and probably Safari. IE is more difficult but **DeBugBar** or **FireBug Lite** can help.

10. Checking problems with form JavaScript

    Quite a lot of ChronoForms functionality is driven by JavaScript—validation, calendars, republishing, tooltips, and so on. If any of these don't work, then it's most likely that there is a JavaScript problem.

    In the first place, use FireBug in Firefox to check for JavaScript errors. The console error reports are invaluable.

    Add `&tmpl=component` to the end of the form URL and see if the errors go away. If they do, there is probably a conflict with a script in the template.

    Look at the script list in the page head, or in FireBug. If you see **jQuery**, or **ProtoType**, or more than one version of **MooTools**, then there is probably a conflict between the libraries. jQuery can be put into "no conflict" mode very easily. For the other libraries, you may need to disable them step-by-step to pin down the exact problem.

    Debugging JavaScript in IE is more difficult and IE can show errors with scripts that run smoothly in other browsers. Again DeBugBar can be useful, and its sister product, **IETester** will emulate different IE versions.

11. Checking problems with PHP

    When you start adding PHP to your forms, another category of errors becomes possible.

    If you see a completely blank page, then most likely there is a PHP Fatal Error. Try temporarily setting **Error Reporting** to **Maximum** in the **Site | Global Configuration | Server** tab and you should see the error report which will usually give you a clue to the file that is causing the error and often the type of error. Here's an example:

    ```
    Parse error: parse error in D:\path\components\com_
    chronocontact\chronocontact.html.php(183) : eval()'d code
    on line 2
    ```

The (183) is a reference to the line number in the file, but the part that reads `eval()'d code on line 2` tells us that this problem is in the code from one of the Form Code boxes; here it is in line 2 of the Form HTML box.

If you are not getting the results that you expect from your PHP, then add temporary lines to output the results from intermediate steps so that you can track exactly what is happening.

Code like this

```
echo '<div>$some_var: '.print_r($some_var, true). '</div>';
```

This will print out the value of `$some_var`.

Occasionally, the code you are working on cannot write directly to the browser. In that case, the Joomla! system message code will display on the next page shown (provided that the template supports Joomla! system messages):

```
Global $mainframe;
$mainframe->enqueuemessage('$some_var:
  '.print_r($some_var, true));
```

12. Checking the ChronoForms forums

    It's unlikely (though not impossible) that you are the first person to have this problem. Please search the ChronoForms forums on likely key words; if you don't find an answer, then post your query in the forums giving us as much information as you can.

    See you there . . .

See also

- For problems with File Uploads please see the *Trouble-shooting problems with files* section in *Chapter 8, Uploading Files from your Forms*
- For advice on e-mail problems, check the recipe *Get your e-mails delivered safely* in *Chapter 2, E-mailing Form Results*
- Get FireBug for FireFox from `http://getfirebug.com/` where you will also find some documentation
- DeBug Bar and IETester for Internet Explorer development are available at `http://www.debugbar.com/`
- There are notes on using jQuery with other libraries at `http://docs.jquery.com/Using_jQuery_with_Other_Libraries`

Index

Symbols

$doc =& JFactory::getDocument() 230
$_POST Array 51
$posted array 279
$row->store() 87
.cfxbak file 36

A

Acajoom 257-264
Action URL 171
addEvent() 163
addScriptDeclaration() method 230
Ajax
  using, for e-mail addresses lookup 325-329
Akeeba Backup
  URL 94
API (Application Programming Interface) 166

B

Backup Form icon 34, 36
barcode, adding to form e-mail
  about 178
  OnSubmit Before code, using 183
  starting with 179
  steps 179-183
  working 183
browser specific CSS files
  loading, into page head 233, 234

C

Cancel icon 35
cf_botlabel class 68
checkbox groups 89
ChronoConnectivity 297, 330
ChronoEngine web site
  URL 8
chronoformname parameter 330
ChronoForms
  about 7
  CSV file download 98
  data exporting, to CSV file 97, 98
  data exporting, to Excel 97, 98
  DB Connection, actions 85, 86
  default style, using 63
  downloading 7
  Excel download 98
  existing form, moving to 222-225
  existing form, working 225
  field, adding 75, 76
  Forms Manager 18
  installing 7
  plug-ins 281
ChronoForms default style
  using 64
  using, steps 64-66
ChronoForms Form Manager
  Confirmation Page plug-in, setting up 118-120
  working 121
ChronoForms installations
  components 10
  Forms Manager 11
  Joomla! Extension Manager 9
  requirements 8
  starting with 9
  steps 8-10, 12
ChronoForms module
  about 10
  display, controlling 141-144

form, displaying on selected pages 138-141
working 141
ChronoForms Plugin/Mambot 10
ChronoForms Plugins
  about 281
  Authorize .NET 282
  CB registration 282
  Confirmation page 282
  cURL 282
  debugging 137
  E-mail verification 282
  form, including in article 134-136
  Image resize and thumbnail 282
  Joomla! registration 282
  multi language 282
  Multi page 282
  PayPal API 282
  Profile page 282
  ReCaptcha verification 282
  ReDirect 282
  Watchman 282
  working 137
ChronoForms theme
  default 67
  style switching, Transform Form used 67
  theme 1 67
  working 68
ChronoForms Uploads Object 59
class
  cf_botlabel 68
  validate-one-required class 158
client-side validation 108
complex multi-page form
  about 342
  building, steps 343-348
complicated code, translating
  about 294
  files, including 296
  HTML, including 295
  variables, including 296
Contact us
  about 265
  creating, steps 266-270
  working 270, 271
conversion tracking script
  adding 173
  adding, steps 173, 174

Create Table
  blue arrows 88
  blue cross, using 88
  key 88
  options, using 88, 89
  tick or cross 88
Cross-site Scripting. *See* **XSS**
CSS
  form, moving 231, 232
cURL plug-in 165

D

DB Connections
  changing 93-95
  columns, reordering 96
  e-mail template, updating 96
  input, removing 96
  updating 93-95
DB table
  information, obtaining 330-333
  working 334
DeBugBar 352
Debug Report 49
Default Separator. *See* **DS**
disk icon 83
document image form. *See* **image upload form**
double drop-down
  creating 187
  creating, steps 188-192
downloading
  ChronoForms 7
Dreamweaver
  form, creating 248-250
drop-downs
  other box, adding 160-163
  whole input, hiding 163, 164
DS 60

E

EasySQL 92
e-mail
  addresses, choosing from list 47-57
  attached files, modifying 341, 342
  controlling, from inputs 340, 341
  delivering safely 41
  disabling 341

files, linking to 205, 206
replying to 38
safe delivery checks 41
standard file, attaching to 58, 59
subject line, creating 60
thank you email, sending 44
uploaded files, attaching to 57
uploaded image, adding to 212-214
e-mail addresses lookup
Ajax, using 325-329
working 330
e-mail, replying to
Forms Manager 38
starting with 38
steps 38-41
e-mail, safe delivery
checking 42-44
working 44
Emails column 23
Email Setup 20
existing form
file upload, adding 274
moving to ChronoForms 222-225
exTplorer Joomla! 194
Extra after Registration code box 311

F

file problems
troubleshooting 215
troubleshooting, steps 216-220
files
e-mailed linked, working 207
image files, copying 208
image files, resizing 208
linking, to e-mails 205, 206
problems, troubleshooting 215
renaming 202
saving to different folder 199-201
files, renaming
steps 202-204
working 204
files, saving to different folder
about 201, 202
starting with 199
steps 200, 201
working 201

file upload field
adding, to form 194-198
working 198, 199
FireFox Lite 352
form
backing up 34, 35
creating, in Dreamweaver 248-250
creating, to link to Acajoom 257-264
creating, to publish Joomla! article 264, 265
creating, Wufoo used 235-242
displaying, ChronoForms module used 137
displaying, light-box 334-336
editing, steps 29
features, adding to 155
file upload field, adding to 194-198
including, ChronoForms plug-in used 134
linking to, Joomla! menus used 144-146
moving, CSS used 231, 232
moving, JavaScript used 225-228
multi-page form, creating 275
problems, troubleshooting 350-353
restoring 35, 36
styling 63
using, to create Joomla! article 147-149
Wizard Edit, editing 29-32
Wizard Edit, working 32
format=raw parameter 330
Form CSS, adding
browser, sniffing 72, 73
conditional CSS 73, 74
requirements 68
steps 69-71
form, editing
steps 31
Form Editor 38
Form link 17
form name
modifying, in ChronoForms 228
Forms Manager 11
Form Wizard
using, for simple Form creation 13-17
working 18

G

getBool() method 116, 269
getCmd() method 116

getFloat() method 116
getInt() method 116
generateIdent() function 182
getString() method 116
getWord() method 116

H

HTML
  adding, steps 77, 78

I

IETester 352
image files
  copying 208, 210-212
  resizing 208, 210-212
images
  adding, to article 215
  displaying, in e-mails 212-214
image upload form
  creating 272
  creating, steps 273, 274
ImageVerification captcha
  adding 121-124
  image non display, debugging 124
  ImageVerification element layout, changing 125
  refresh link, adding to ImageVerification element 125, 126
  server error, debugging 124
  working 124
input type
  built-in checks 106
  Regular Expression, using 105
  specifying 104
  working 105
installations, ChronoForms
  components 10
  Forms Manager 11
  Joomla! Extension Manager 9
  requirements 8
  starting with 9
  steps 8-10, 12
installing
  ChronoForms 7
IP address 25

J

JavaScript
  form, moving 225-228
JavaScript Live validation
  about 102
  Run Validation only On Blur option 103
  Validation Messages type option 103
Joomla!
  ChronoForms 7
  Forms 12
  simple code, creating 271, 272
  simple form, adding 7
Joomla! article
  about 134
  creating, form used 147-149
  publishing, form creating 264, 265
  working 149, 150
Joomla! Documentation site
  URL 9
Joomla! Documentation Wiki 137
Joomla! Extension Manager 9
Joomla! Extensions Defined 137
Joomla! JTable class 302
Joomla! menus
  about 134
  administrator menu item, creating 146
  extra parameters, passing 146
  form, linking from 144, 145
  working 146
Joomla! module 134
Joomla! plug-in 134
Joomla! Registration plug-in
  about 302, 303
  affecting setting 305, 306
  custom e-mails, displaying 307
  custom e-mails, sending 306
  extra data, saving 310
  Joomla! Name field, creating 308, 309
  new members, logging automatically 310
  secret registration, allowing 310
  silent registration, creating 307, 308
  username, creating 309
  user parameters, changing 311, 312
  users, registering 303-305
  viewing 302
  working 305

Joomla! templates 134
JQuery
  using, to fix conflicts 229
JReques::getString() 142
JRequest::getVar() 158
JRequest::getString() 54
JRequest::getVar() 142
JRequest::setVar() 55, 208
Jumi 336

K

key icon, Create Table 88
keys
  reCAPTCHA keys 120

L

language parameter 311
light-box
  form, displaying 334-336
  options, keeping open 337
  PHP, adding to page 337
  working 336
LiveValidation 102

M

maxlength attribute 93
message
  redirecting conditionally 153, 154
  showing, after redirection 152, 153
  showing, before redirection 153
method
  addScriptDeclaration() 230
  getBool() 116, 269
  getCmd() 116
  getFloat() 116
  getInt() 116
  getString() 116
  getWord() 116
  setMetaData() method 153
module, ChronoForms
  about 10
  display, controlling 141-144
  form, displaying on selected pages 138-141
  working 141
MooTools 352

Multi-language plug-in
  complicated code, translating 294
  e-mail templates, translating 296
  form error messages, translating 294
  form images, translating 294
  multi-lingual forms, creating 287-293
  pitfalls 292
  thank you pages, translating 296
  working 294
multi-lingual forms
  creating, Multi-language plug-in used 287-293
multi-page form
  creating 275
  creating, steps 275-278
  working 279
multi-select drop-down 89

N

name=value parameter 300
new form submission
  notifying. email sending 18
  notifying, Wizard Edit used 19-25
newsletter service
  signing up 169
  signing up, steps 170-172
  working 173
newsletter_signup.cfbak file 35
newsletter_signup form 80
noConflict mode 229

O

option parameter 330

P

parameter
  chronoformname 330
  format=raw 330
  language 311
  name=value 300
  option 330
  task=extra 330
PayPal purchase
  creating, ReDirect plug-in used 312
PEAR ExcelWriter 98

PHP
  range() method 322
  select drop-down, creating 320, 321
PHP Mail Function
  using 266
PHP Manual
  error list 219
PHPMyAdmin 92
problems, form
  troubleshooting 350-353
profile plug-in
  about 297
  saved information, editing 297-301
  saved information, showing 297-300
  working 300
Properties box 13

Q

Query Browser 92

R

RadioButton element 48
range() method 322
reCAPTCHA
  adding 126
  adding, steps 126, 127
  getting started 126
  plug-in, configuring 128
  problems 129
  working 128
reCAPTCHA plug-in configuration
  about 128
  reCAPTCHA keys 128
  setup options 128
Redirect message box 285
ReDirect plug-in
  PayPal purchase, creating 312-316
ReDirect URL 152
ReDirect URL box 313
Regex Buddy
  URL 105
registered users
  form access, limiting 129, 130
  user, redirecting 131
  user, redirecting with message 131, 132

required fields, making
  requirements 100
  steps 100, 101
  working 101
Restore Form icon 35

S

saved form results
  EasySQL, using 92
  PHPMyAdmin, using 92
  Query Browser, using 92
  viewing 91, 92
schema 80
sectionid 320
Secure Shell. *See* **SSH**
select drop-down
  adding 322
  creating, from array 324, 325
  creating, PHP used 320, 321
  numeric options lists, creating 322, 324
  working 322
server-side validation
  database, checking 114-116
  error messages, combining 113
  error messages, styling 114
  extra security, adding 108-111
  form data, filtering 116, 117
  several validations, adding 112
  working 112
setMetaData() method 153
SFTP 201
simple Form, creating
  Form Wizard, using 13-17
  requirements 13
simple newsletter signup
  about 252
  creating, steps 252-256
site information
  tracking 338
  tracking, steps 338, 339
SMS message
  sending, on submission 165-168
  working 169
snippets
  loading, into page head 230-233
sprintf() function 296

Squeezebox. *See* light box
SSH 201
SSH FTP. *See* SFTP
standard file
   attaching, to e-mail 58, 59
subject line
   creating 61
   working 61
submitcontent.cfbak file 264

T

table, creating
   form, linking to 80, 84, 85
   results, saving 80
   steps 82, 83
task=extra parameter 330
textarea
   character counter, adding 184-187
   character counter, working 187
TextBox element 29
thank you e-mail
   sending 44-47
Thank You page
   displaying 26
   displaying, steps 26, 28
   information, displaying 28, 29
   working 28
theme, ChronoForms
   default 67
   style switching, Transform Form used 67
   theme 1 67
   working 68
Toolbox 13
Transform Form
   styles, switching to 67

U

uploaded files
   attaching, to e-mail 57
user registration
   Joomla! Registration plug-in, using 302-304
users
   redirecting, to home page 32, 33
   redirecting to Joomla! pages, after submision 151, 152

V

validate-one-required class 158
validated checkbox
   adding 156
   adding, steps 156, 157
   server-side, validating 158, 159
   submit button, locking 159, 160
   working 158
validation error messages
   customizing 107
   working 108
VARCHAR 84

W

Watchman plug-in
   about 283
   form access control, form access used 283-286
   working 287
web form
   The Form backend 222
   The Form CSS 222
   The Form HTML 221
   The Form JavaScript 222
   The Form PHP 222
   The Page HTML 221
Wufoo
   form, creating 235-242
   form, using 244-246
   theme template, modifying 242, 243
   validation, adding to 246-248
   working 242

X

XSS 116

Y

YouTube video
   showing 175
   showing, steps 176-178
   working 178

Thank you for buying
ChronoForms 1.3 for Joomla! Site Cookbook

About Packt Publishing

Packt, pronounced 'packed', published its first book "*Mastering phpMyAdmin for Effective MySQL Management*" in April 2004 and subsequently continued to specialize in publishing highly focused books on specific technologies and solutions.

Our books and publications share the experiences of your fellow IT professionals in adapting and customizing today's systems, applications, and frameworks. Our solution based books give you the knowledge and power to customize the software and technologies you're using to get the job done. Packt books are more specific and less general than the IT books you have seen in the past. Our unique business model allows us to bring you more focused information, giving you more of what you need to know, and less of what you don't.

Packt is a modern, yet unique publishing company, which focuses on producing quality, cutting-edge books for communities of developers, administrators, and newbies alike. For more information, please visit our website: `www.packtpub.com`.

About Packt Open Source

In 2010, Packt launched two new brands, Packt Open Source and Packt Enterprise, in order to continue its focus on specialization. This book is part of the Packt Open Source brand, home to books published on software built around Open Source licences, and offering information to anybody from advanced developers to budding web designers. The Open Source brand also runs Packt's Open Source Royalty Scheme, by which Packt gives a royalty to each Open Source project about whose software a book is sold.

Writing for Packt

We welcome all inquiries from people who are interested in authoring. Book proposals should be sent to author@packtpub.com. If your book idea is still at an early stage and you would like to discuss it first before writing a formal book proposal, contact us; one of our commissioning editors will get in touch with you.

We're not just looking for published authors; if you have strong technical skills but no writing experience, our experienced editors can help you develop a writing career, or simply get some additional reward for your expertise.

[PACKT] open source
community experience distilled
PUBLISHING

Building Websites with Joomla! 1.5

ISBN: 978-1-847195-30-2   Paperback: 384 pages

The best-selling Joomla! tutorial guide updated for the latest 1.5 release

1. Learn Joomla! 1.5 features
2. Install and customize Joomla! 1.5
3. Configure Joomla! administration
4. Create your own Joomla! templates
5. Extend Joomla! with new components, modules, and plug-ins

Joomla! E-Commerce with VirtueMart

ISBN: 978-1-847196-74-3   Paperback: 476 pages

Build feature-rich online stores with Joomla! 1.0/1.5 and VirtueMart 1.1.x

1. Build your own e-commerce web site from scratch by adding features step-by-step to an example e-commerce web site
2. Configure the shop, build product catalogues, configure user registration settings for VirtueMart to take orders from around the world
3. Manage customers, orders, and a variety of currencies to provide the best customer service
4. Handle shipping in all situations and deal with sales tax rules

Please check **www.PacktPub.com** for information on our titles

Joomla! 1.5 Multimedia

ISBN: 978-1-847197-70-2   Paperback: 376 pages

Build media-rich Joomla! web sites by learning to embed and display Multimedia content

1. Build a livelier Joomla! site by adding videos, audios, images and more to your web content
2. Install, configure, and use popular Multimedia Extensions
3. Make your web site collaborate with external resources such as Twitter, YouTube, Google, and Flickr with the help of Joomla! extensions
4. Follow a step-by-step tutorial to create a feature-packed media-rich Joomla! site

Joomla! Web Security

ISBN: 978-1-847194-88-6   Paperback: 264 pages

Secure your Joomla! website from common security threats with this easy-to-use guide

1. Learn how to secure your Joomla! websites
2. Real-world tools to protect against hacks on your site
3. Implement disaster recovery features
4. Set up SSL on your site
5. Covers Joomla! 1.0 as well as 1.5

Please check **www.PacktPub.com** for information on our titles

Made in the USA
Lexington, KY
13 September 2010